THEATRE IN SCOTLAND
A FIELD *of* DREAMS

THEATRE IN SCOTLAND

A FIELD *of* DREAMS

Reviews by Joyce McMillan

Edited by Philip Howard

NICK HERN BOOKS
London
www.nickhernbooks.co.uk

A Nick Hern Book

Theatre in Scotland – A Field of Dreams
first published in Great Britain in 2016
by Nick Hern Books Limited, The Glasshouse,
49a Goldhawk Road, London W12 8QP

Cover image: *The James Plays* by Rona Munro, National
Theatre of Scotland, 2014 (photo by Manuel Harlan)
Author photo: Chris Hill

Designed and typeset by Nick Hern Books
Printed and bound in Great Britain by
Ashford Colour Press, Gosport, Hampshire

A CIP catalogue record for this book is available
from the British Library

ISBN 978 1 84842 292 6

Contents

I first heard the name Joyce McMillan during my early forays to the Edinburgh Festival as an aspiring theatremaker.

Hers was the review we all craved. Hers was the recommendation we took seriously. Hers was the opinion that mattered.

As I got to know Joyce in person and read ever more of her work over the years, I understood why.

Joyce has an unrivalled passion and hunger for theatre – to be surprised by it, challenged by it, moved by it. Her prose when describing something which has done just this is inspiring and affecting.

Her tireless ability to seek out great plays and to place them within the context of her extensive theatrical and political knowledge is extraordinary, and her belief that theatre can bring about change has allowed many of us to continue to aspire to excite her.

Vicky Featherstone
Artistic Director
Royal Court Theatre, London

Foreword   *Philip Howard*

This collection of theatre reviews by Joyce McMillan
traces her journey from self-taught, passionate con-
tributing writer to the short-lived *Sunday Standard*
(1981-1983), to her current life as the chief theatre critic of
The Scotsman. No other critic in Scotland covers as much
ground as she does in her working week, or has done for so
many years. And so the premise of this book is simple:
gather all of the most insightful material from over the past
three decades, add new essays by McMillan herself to
underscore the narrative – and what you have is a history of
modern Scottish theatre, reported from the frontline. The
volume is not a hit parade. While the vast majority of landmark theatre productions in Scotland have been covered, it
was important also to acknowledge McMillan's footfall
across the whole country and celebrate the truly national
portrait that emerges.

McMillan's first reviewing jobs were for BBC Radio Scotland in the 1970s, talking about Edinburgh Festival shows for
Festival View, presented by Neville Garden – and she cred-
its the inspiration of this annual cultural spectacle as a
determining factor in her ambition to write about theatre. In
1978 the great Allen Wright at *The Scotsman* commissioned

her to cover a production of *The Good Person of Szechwan* for him in St Andrews, and she soon became his second-string reviewer. When the *Sunday Standard* was founded in 1981, McMillan set her sights on becoming their principal theatre critic, and, despite the newspaper lasting only two years, it is here that she begins to find her voice, or, as she puts it, 'This is where the dialogue with myself really starts.' There followed ten distinguished years as the *Guardian*'s Scotland theatre critic (1984-1994) and three at *Scotland on Sunday* (1994-1997), where for the first time she was writing a longer weekly column, essay-style, covering all the week's theatre openings, and exploiting her skill in detecting wider cultural resonances and thematic links between the work. After a lightning-quick spell as an arts writer for *The Herald* in 1997, she started in 1998 at *The Scotsman*, and it is in this current incarnation as a critic and political commentator that she has become defined as a leading thinker and writer about Scotland.

She wasn't born to it. There were visits to the theatre as a child – her first memory is of a Kenneth McKellar Christmas show at the Alhambra, Glasgow – but she was never an enthusiastic amateur audience member, or certainly not for very long. A half-completed PhD at the University of Edinburgh on the tragedies of Ben Jonson crystallised for her the indivisibility of theatre and politics, and she talks interestingly about her new passion for theatre at that time stemming from her disenchantment with the direction of British politics, i.e. towards the right, and a conviction that theatre is one place where you might find 'an alternative truth about what it means to be human'. And perhaps it is this wide-angle lens on theatre and parallel enquiry as a political writer which explain her tenacity and longevity. Of course, she's not the only theatre writer to apply herself to political writing – think of Fintan O'Toole, for many years political columnist and chief theatre critic of *The Irish Times*

– but McMillan's career is coinciding with the very period where Scotland is remaking itself more energetically than ever before. The ground is fertile.

It is surely the goal of any critic, certainly in terms of legacy, to contribute in some way to the evolution of the art form itself, Kenneth Tynan in England and America in the 1950s and '60s being the iconic example of this. McMillan has far too long a working life left for it to be possible to make this kind of retrospective analysis, but certain themes do emerge from her critical writing which arguably have tuned with the times, if not influenced them: for example, an obstinate insistence that the director of a classic revival must know very precisely why they are reviving an old play rather than making a new one – her sympathy for directors who also have to run monolithic theatre buildings does not extend to them programming plays just because they feature in compendia of 'the 100 greatest plays'. Predictably, as a leading political commentator, she will despise an unthinkingly or lazily apolitical interpretation of a play, reserving her greatest spleen for the 'Loamshire' play (as Tynan did before her), or self-absorbed new writing that makes no attempt to connect with the public sphere. But then – in a wonderfully contradictory way – she will often surprise us by enthusing about something shamelessly sentimental, entertaining or romantic, as long as it's beautifully executed. Most importantly of all, she has, to my knowledge, an almost unblemished record in never having failed to spot a great new play; and, rare among critics, she has the ability to watch an unsuccessful new play and detect whether it's the playwright or director at fault. This can make for uncomfortable reading. ('Philip Howard's Traverse production seems to fall stillborn on to the stage' on *Grace in America* by Antoine Ó Flatharta, *Scotland on Sunday*, 1 May 1994 – sticks in the mind.)

She isn't shy of skewering some sacred cows: the empty heart of the RSC's *Les Liaisons Dangereuses* (1990); the reactionary flippancy (*Travesties*, 1987) and bourgeois self-satisfaction (*Rough Crossing*, 1996) of Tom Stoppard. And occasionally she deploys a devastating ability to take hold of a superficially successful production – think Bill Bryden's *The Big Picnic* (1994) or the Brian Cox *The Master Builder* (1993) – and then, like a drone or laser, zero in on its fatal flaw. But McMillan is also bold in finding something to commend even in work of mixed success, and stick her neck out to champion unfashionable work which she suspects her colleagues might dismiss. Perhaps this is because she knows it's easier to write a bad review than a good one, intellectually easier to puncture than to validate. And so there are plenty of roses among the barbed wire – and an unswerving commitment to shout praise from the rooftops where it is due, and celebrate the art form in all its mad messy glory (*Macbeth* on the Isle of Inchcolm, 1989).

The book works chronologically rather than thematically, and yet is divided, unevenly, into three parts telling three essential stories of how Scottish theatre has grown in confidence over the decades: the road to 1990, the year of Glasgow's reign as European Capital of Culture, which marked a generational change in how that great city viewed itself and was viewed by the world; the 1990s and early years of the new millennium, which witnessed an extraordinary explosion in self-confidence among both new and older Scottish playwrights, leading to, finally: the birth and hegemony of the National Theatre of Scotland, bringing the role of our theatre culture as close as it has ever got to the heart of the nation. The vast majority of entries in the book are reviews; the rest are feature articles or programme notes. New linking pieces by McMillan range throughout the volume, providing additional context.

Students of theatre criticism may enjoy the underlying portrait of a critic teaching herself to be the best, from the passionate newcomer at the *Sunday Standard* in the early 1980s, trying to find her style but never missing a political beat, through mounting confidence, occasional fierceness of judgement and an increasingly fine writing style, to the older, authoritative and interestingly more mellow critic that we have today. She testifies to the collegiate atmosphere of theatre criticism in Scotland, where being part of that 'public conversation' helps ensure that the genre faces outward – and guards against the lonesomeness of the profession.

Students of theatre literature may, using the index, read the book as a collection of essays on English language playwriting, from the twentieth-century greats (Coward, Osborne, Pinter, etc.) to all the leading Scottish playwrights, from John Byrne and Liz Lochhead to David Greig and David Harrower. And ultimately, it is as a writer about Scotland and about what the art form of theatre can tell us about Scotland that distinguishes McMillan's work: her piece 'Theatre and Nationhood' (1991), written for Tramway's *Theatres and Nations* season which heralded the permanent opening of Glasgow's key Capital of Culture venue from 1990, is a defining essay on Scottishness, written against the backdrop of the dismantlement of the Soviet Union. Sometimes it's in the critique of a theatre production which would not be taken as seriously by the rest of the Scottish theatre community (even if they had seen it), that she writes most flawlessly about the culture of the nation – for example, *Accounts* in Town Yetholm (1991) or *Bright Water* on Easdale Island (2007). The combination of this panoramic view, political acuity, and the ability to marry the head and the heart, has sealed her reputation far beyond Scotland's borders.

Edinburgh
January 2016

Part One

1982–1990: The Road to Glasgow City of Culture

In the first years of the 1980s, Scottish theatre was caught in a strange, subdued place, somewhere between hope and despair. The 1970s had been a time of huge, energetic change in Scotland's theatre culture, as the post-war generation began to claim their place on the nation's stages, and the generous arts funding of the 1960s and 1970s began to bear fruit. It was the decade when Giles Havergal and his co-directors Philip Prowse and Robert David MacDonald came to the Citizens' Theatre in Glasgow, and within a few years made it one of the most famous and spectacular city theatres in Europe. It was the decade when John McGrath launched 7:84 Scotland, with his legendary ceilidh show The Cheviot, the Stag and the Black, Black Oil. *And it was the decade when the Traverse Theatre in Edinburgh – under Chris Parr's directorship – opened its doors to Scottish writers as never before, making space for a whole new generation of groundbreaking playwrights, including John Byrne, Tom McGrath, Donald Campbell, Marcella Evaristi and many others.*

In 1979, though, the process of political change that seemed to match and reflect this cultural shift came to a shuddering halt, as the campaign for Scottish home rule – or devolution within the UK – ended in a failed referendum: a majority of those taking part voted 'yes', but the numbers were not high enough to

3

clear an extra hurdle set by the Westminster Parliament. Scotland berated itself as the 'cowardly lion' of UK politics, and Jim Callaghan's Labour government fell, making way for Margaret Thatcher and her new Conservatives; and in the smaller world of Scottish theatre there was a minor earthquake, as many of the performing stars of the 1970s generation – Bill Paterson, Alex Norton, John Bett, Billy Connolly, Kenny Ireland – left Scotland to build their careers in London.

By 1982 there were signs of recovery, and of a kind of regrouping. Already, the fierce opposition to Margaret Thatcher's government which was to shape Scottish politics for the next twenty years was beginning to generate new ideas about what kind of society Scotland could and should be, if it rejected this new right-wing form of Britishness, and strove again for self-government. As in most stories of European nation-building – think of Ireland or Norway, in the late nineteenth and early twentieth centuries – theatre had a vital role to play, as a place where ideas about the past, the future, the language, the ever-shifting identity of the nation could be tested, developed and enriched.

And by chance – or perhaps for reasons I barely understood at the time – it was around this moment of transition, at the end of the 1970s and the beginning of the 1980s, that I felt myself drawn, perhaps almost driven, to become a theatre critic in Scotland. I had already been reviewing for more than three years, mainly as a second- or third-string critic for The Scotsman, *and an occasional reviewer on BBC Radio Scotland. But in 1981 the management of the* Glasgow Herald *launched a new Sunday paper, the* Sunday Standard; *and with an energy and focus that sometimes surprised me, I began to work my way into the role of the paper's main theatre critic. I was already almost thirty, I had no history of interest in theatre beyond an academic one, and like many people who grew up in the 1960s, I saw theatre as an old-fashioned art form, already half-dead on its feet.*

4

Yet in the late 1970s, I was suddenly gripped by the power of the shared experience of theatre, by the idea of it as a place where ideas could be made flesh, and could be tested against the real reactions of the audience. Perhaps it was a reaction to the repetitiveness, and frequent intellectual rigidity, of the left-wing and feminist politics in which I was vaguely involved. Perhaps it was an unconscious response to the coming of Thatcherism: an insistence that somewhere, even if only in a series of small darkened rooms, a serious collective life would continue through this age of individualism. Or perhaps it was something in Scottish theatre itself, evolving fast and freely after a long age of quiescence and marginalisation. If Scotland's professional theatre tradition had been limited and interrupted by centuries of official Presbyterianism, that very history – or rather the lack of it – meant that it entered the late twentieth century with relatively little baggage, and an exhilarating freedom to reinvent itself, in forms that were both popular and experimental.

So, at the beginning of 1982, I began to set out my stall as the Sunday Standard's *main theatre critic. In the big world beyond theatre, there were three huge arguments in progress. There was one about the future of the British left, after Margaret Thatcher's victory in 1979; in theatre, that was often articulated through my arguments with, and about, John McGrath's 7:84 Company, and its sister company Wildcat Stage Productions. There was an argument about feminism, a fraught coming-to-terms with the huge revolution in consciousness that had taken place during the 1970s. And, of course, there was the argument about Scotland: rousing itself after the failed home-rule referendum of 1979, and once again setting out to redefine and reshape itself. At the time, the Scottish Arts Council was funding around fifteen major professional companies in Scotland, including the building-based ones in Edinburgh, Glasgow, Dundee, Perth and Pitlochry; and, in 1981, it had also decided to fund an initiative by the actor Ewan Hooper to launch a new Scottish Theatre Company, dedicated to creating Scottish-made shows for mainstage theatres, and – in some respects at least – to pursuing a more traditional Scottish repertoire than could be found at the Traverse or the Citizens'. It was through the work of the STC, and my often sceptical reactions to it, that I began to evolve my own ideas about what the word 'Scottish' could and should mean, in the late twentieth century; and about our evolving relationship with the standard repertoire of English-language theatre.*

At the beginning of 1982, though, I was still engaged in an angry young critic's war against the kind of 'dead', conventional theatre that I felt was destroying the art form from within. The early reviews are full of harsh comparisons, for example between a super-conventional The Lady's Not for Burning *at Pitlochry, and the explosive radicalism of Giles* Havergal's *groundbreaking 1982 revival of* Men Should Weep. *And so it was with a kind of vision of the future that I started the year in the* Sunday Standard.

1982

Let All the World Be Our Stage
Sunday Standard, 3 January 1982

I sometimes think it would do Scottish theatre no harm if theatres were knocked flat, and companies consigned to school halls, car parks, and any other space that offered itself. As 1982 begins, almost all the clouds on the theatrical horizon seem to concern bricks and mortar. Dundee Rep have been awaiting completion of their new theatre for so long that the company's harassed director, Robert Robertson, must be wondering whether he should have pitched a tent on the river front and had done with it.

The Traverse Theatre Club [in Edinburgh] seems on the point of beginning the long process of moving to new premises with a larger auditorium – although their present 100-seat premises are rarely full. The threatened implementation of the Stodart Report, which suggested that responsibility for the arts should be transferred from regional to district councils, places a particularly large question mark over the future of those municipally owned theatres which have no resident company to fight for them – the prime example being the King's Theatre in Edinburgh, which now has a vigorous, if ungainly, competitor for funds in the shape of the elephantine Edinburgh Playhouse.

Inside the theatre companies, though, the atmosphere this New Year is far from gloomy. The threat of a standstill in Arts Council funding has been lifted, and, surveying the scene last week, I found it impossible not to admire the combination of optimism, determination and sheer nerve with which directors and administrators continue to plan for the future through continuing crises.

Only three companies – Borderline, the Byre and the Traverse – have been unable to announce plans for 1982, and none seems particularly downcast. The Byre, Scotland's least heavily subsidised theatre in 1981 and 1982, offered a definite opening date for its season – 3 May.

The Royal Lyceum in Edinburgh presents a particularly striking example of skilful navigation in a tight corner this winter – the company has weathered the loss of its major Christmas production, and now finds itself with only two 'dark' weeks between now and the end of April. One of these gaps is likely to be filled by a visiting company, and during the other – the last week in January – the company will be in action at the Eden Court Theatre, Inverness, with its current production of *Absurd Person Singular*. The company's spring season opens on 17 March, and will include productions of Tom Stoppard's *Jumpers*, and of *Piaf*, Pam Gems's wildly successful play about the legendary French singer.

1982 will not be a year of major expansion for Scottish theatre, but it already seems likely to produce another, and possibly even more exciting, trend – a smashing of barriers, a rapid growth of 'sideways' contacts among theatres in Scotland, and between theatres in Scotland and elsewhere. In February, the new Scottish Theatre Company will present a four-week season at the Royal Lyceum in Edinburgh. Cathy Czerkawska's *Heroes and Others*, which deals with the intensely contemporary subject of Poland and the rise of Solidarity, opens there on 4 February, and will be followed by a production of Charles Macklin's *The Man of the World*, starring Iain Cuthbertson. In March, Wildcat will visit the Lyceum with their new production *1982*, directed by Ian Wooldridge of Theatre About Glasgow.

The most interesting prospect for spring, though, is the series of four 'Unity' plays which 7:84 Scotland are to present at the Mitchell Theatre in Glasgow. This is a series of left-wing and broadly 'social realist' plays, dating from the 1930s and 1940s, and depicting Scottish working-class life at that time.

My plea to Scottish theatre companies in 1982 is this: have the confidence to give us the best that world theatre has to offer. Radical, talented companies like 7:84 and Wildcat ought to be cutting their teeth on the best material there is – on production, adaptations and modern versions of Brecht, Shakespeare, Molière, Chekhov. If Shakespeare was not too proud to borrow good, gripping plots wherever he could find one, I can hardly see why Scottish playwrights should not do the same.

The Screens
Citizens', Glasgow
Sunday Standard, 21 March 1982

'Has the revolution reached the whorehouse yet?' says one prostitute to another towards the end of *The Screens*, thereby bringing the cycle of three Genet plays at Glasgow Citizens' Theatre back full-circle to the question with which it began five weeks ago, amid the huge gilded pillars and strategically placed bidets of Madame Irma's Paris brothel in *The Balcony*.

For Jean Genet, it seems, the answer to that question is always 'no'. As he suggests in *The Balcony* – the first and perhaps the most powerful of the plays – the world itself is little more than a great eternal whorehouse; or, as Madame Irma would have it, a 'house of illusions', in which people satisfy their base bodily cravings by acting out vicious and deluded fantasies of power, as generals, bishops, judges, politicians.

Written in 1960 at the height of France's Algerian crisis, *The Screens* brings this corrupt political and military system into conflict with the forces of Arab revolution; but even here, in a turbulent North African village, the winners are neither the deluded imperialists, nor those Arabs who are idealistic or careless enough to die in the revolutionary cause, but the ultimate realists – the whores, the thieves and the pimps who understand the crude price of everything, and set no store by ideas or ideals.

In an attempt to draw a contemporary parallel with the violent nationalism of the Arab terrorists, the cast of *The Screens* deliver their lines in distinctly Irish tones, and the resulting cacophony of silly, distorted Irish-Arab voices – mangling Robert David MacDonald's fine, vigorous translation of the text – is sadly all too typical of director Philip Prowse's general approach in this Genet season.

His designs – all based on the huge, breathtaking mirror image of the theatre auditorium created for *The Balcony*'s 'house of illusions' – have been predictably magnificent, but as a director, he seems unable to communicate to actors the dazzling insight reflected in his sets.

Only in *The Blacks*, the central play of the series, did the company's performance reflect a real sense of the significance of the piece, which concerns the ritual murder of a group of absurd white power figures by a company of negro actors. Elsewhere, they rush at Genet's dense, poetic text boldly but often uncomprehendingly, delivering the lines without the lucid awareness of underlying rhythms and meanings that would give the whole cycle a sense of pace, coherence and shape; and is absolutely essential if the audience's interest is to be caught, held and nurtured through to the end of this vitally important tragedy.

Tomfoolery
Royal Lyceum, Edinburgh

Swan White
Theatre Alba
Sunday Standard, 23 March 1982

Heaven knows, Leslie Lawton's regime at the Royal Lyceum in Edinburgh has never had any pretensions to intellectual respectability. Its aim – solidly backed by the theatre board – has been to turn out slick, professional entertainment, to put bottoms on seats, and to keep on giving the old razzle-dazzle for as long as the Arts Council and local authorities are prepared to finance it.

But last Monday, the august auditorium of the Lyceum witnessed a scene that would surely have astonished any visiting dignitary who happened to be under the impression that this was Edinburgh's prime subsidised theatre.

In the seats, an audience of cheerful punters, including a contingent of ageing Tom Lehrer fans; on the stage, a competent but tired-looking bunch of provincial entertainers, hoofing and warbling their way through a cosy, saccharine version of *Tomfoolery*, an anthology of Lehrer's satirical songs from the fifties and sixties. Told that one of the hoofers – the one with the silver waistcoat, the unbelievably lewd and smutty expression, and (for let no one doubt Mr Lawton's skill as an entertainer) the fearsome ability to manipulate the response of a large section of the audience – was the artistic director of the Lyceum company, the visiting dignitary might well have burst into ribald laughter.

Tom Lehrer was always a fairly respectable kind of dissident, but in their day his songs performed a valuable function in casting a dry, satirical and wickedly intelligent eye over the sacred cows of American society, and they are still well worth hearing – and very funny – today. In this 'Lawtonised' version, however, the sharp, bitter, even angry quality of Lehrer's writing is sugared over with the coy and utterly dated mannerisms of old-style British light entertainment. The mood is more ENSA than *M*A*S*H*, the standard of performance ranges from the routine to the poor, and Mr Lawton demonstrates yet again his complete inability to distinguish between adolescent innuendo and smut – particularly on the subject of homosexuality – and genuine sexual frankness and tolerance.

The audience laughed a great deal, and so did I. But I left the theatre feeling – as I often do, after Mr Lawton's comic performances – that my giggle-buttons had been massaged in a particularly mechanical and unpleasant way.

At the Astoria in Edinburgh, Theatre Alba are rounding off their eight-week season with Strindberg's *Swan White*, a graceful Nordic fairy tale about a sweet young princess, a handsome prince, and a wicked stepmother.

On the whole, Charles Nowosielski's season in this unpromisingly tatty and barn-like venue has been a considerable triumph of enterprise and imagination, and *Swan White* has all the characteristics of his work at its best – a fearless romanticism and lyricism, slow but powerful sense of pace, vivid and symbolic use of visual images and tableaux, of lighting, music, and simple but effective design. The actors involved in this little ensemble are also working together with increasing skill and confidence.

My only reservation about Theatre Alba's work is that their interest in the romantic, the metaphysical, the fey and the supernatural is developing into something of an obsession. Nowosielski has proved himself over the last few years to be one of the most gifted and probably *the* most original young director working in Scotland. What he needs now, although it seems unlikely he'll get it, is the chance to work not with a small band of devotees, but with a strong, confident company of established actors.

The Lady's Not For Burning
Pitlochry Festival Theatre

Men Should Weep
7:84 Scotland
Sunday Standard, 9 May 1982

With a skirl of the pipes and not a few swinging kilts, the exquisite new Festival Theatre at Pitlochry launched its summer season this week; and the gala opening on Friday was graced by an attractive and competent production of *The Lady's Not for Burning*. Thirty-four years after its first performance, Christopher Fry's romantic post-war journey through a mock-medieval neverland of English metaphor and blank verse seems more of a charming curiosity than anything else; it has far too many characters, is unconscionably long, and suffers, in this slightly lethargic production by Brian Shelton, from too reverent an approach to Fry's wild, indulgent cascades of poetic speech.

However, the audience at Pitlochry obviously loved it, for the lyrical simplicity of the story, which deals with suspected witchcraft and the redeeming power of romantic love, for the rich exuberance of the verse, and for Deborah Fairfax's exceptionally intense and beautifully spoken performance as the lovely supposed witch, Jennet.

The 7:84 Company's *Clydebuilt* season of working-class plays from the 1920s, '30s and '40s rolled to a tantalising conclusion this week with a production, by Giles Havergal of Glasgow Citizens' Theatre, of *Men Should Weep*, a particularly powerful drama about a woman struggling to bring up her family in a Glasgow tenement during the depression of the 1930s.

Giles Havergal's production represents a fascinating, if not entirely successful, attempt to marry the straightforward naturalism of Scottish working-class drama with the stylised theatrical approach developed by the Glasgow Citizens' company over the past twelve years.

In true Citizens' style, the actors strut majestically around the stage, changing character at the drop of a hat; they spend much of their time looking meaningfully into the audience, and the rest draped around the grey rubble and ruined walls of Geoff Rose's set, gazing banefully at the action.

The result is an intensely absorbing piece of theatre, which demands total concentration from both actors and audience, and produced some stunning performances from the cast of seven women and two men.

For all its theatrical force and impact, though, Havergal's production seems to me to be marred by some uncharacteristic lapses of insight in relation to the play itself. While the thinking behind the set design is perfectly clear – it anticipates the eventual disintegration and destruction of the whole tenement way of life – in fact it does nothing, symbolically, to illuminate the central theme of the play, which is the economic and physical power of men over women, the emotional and sexual power of women over men, and the more, or less, civilised way in which the two are traded off, under conditions of extreme stress.

On a more practical level, it evokes the ruins of Berlin in 1945 more effectively than the lively squalor of a Glasgow slum in the 1930s, and goes a long way – together with the fierce, non-naturalistic acting style – towards flattening and destroying the precise sense of time, place and closely observed character which is so important in Ena Lamont Stewart's text.

Despite its shortcomings, though, *Men Should Weep* is by far the most interesting and significant production of the *Clyde-built* season. If it had been the first of the four, rather than the last, it might have set the whole project off on an infinitely more challenging course. As it is, it simply whets the appetite for new, sophisticated and exciting theatrical approaches to traditional Scottish material.

The Slab Boys Trilogy
Traverse, Edinburgh
Sunday Standard, 18 July 1982

Arriving at the Traverse Theatre Club last Saturday afternoon to watch the whole of John Byrne's famous *Slab Boys* Trilogy in one day, I had no idea what I was letting myself in for. John Byrne has always claimed that his long-running story of Phil and Spanky, slab-room apprentices at A.F.

Stobo's Paisley carpet factory, their little bespectacled side-kick Hector, and the lovely Lucille Bentley ('every slab boy's dream') would eventually amount to a big, old-fashioned three-act drama, but I couldn't help wondering whether seven solid hours of Byrne's quick-fire, aggressive Paisley wit and frantic slapstick wouldn't seem too much of a good thing.

But by 12.30 a.m., when the exhausted company took the final bows at the end of Byrne's latest play *Still Life*, there were a hundred hot, sweaty and delighted people in the audience who needed no convincing about the stature of Byrne's work. There are plenty of rough edges and minor misjudgements both in the plays and in David Hayman's production, but basically, seen together and whole, the *Slab Boys* Trilogy is a theatrical triumph.

Cuttin' a Rug [the second part] is a less substantial play, but in this superbly staged production there is a good-looking, fast-moving and hilariously funny evocation of the A.F. Stobo Christmas dance, with a sickeningly violent twist in the tail when reality breaks in on Phil and Spanky's drunken night out. And *Still Life*, the final play of the three, makes a hesitant but interesting conclusion to the story, aiming for – if not quite achieving – a completely new mood of realism and calm.

But taken together, these three plays weld into something much greater than the sum of their parts – a strong, memorable moving drama about two fairly ordinary Scottish lads and the extraordinary difficulty they experience in growing up. Scotswomen are fond of saying that their menfolk are 'just big weans'; what Byrne's trilogy does is to examine the sad, funny and in some ways tremendously theatrical roots of that refusal to 'grow up' and 'stop playing games'.

If the plays and production have a fault it is, I think, partly because the actors, the director, and Byrne himself, are obviously so close to the characters in the play. Like Phil at the end of *Still Life* – when we see him groping towards an adult idea of himself as a husband and father – they are just beginning to reach out beyond the clichés of Scottish male comic acting towards something much more real and much more adult – politically, sexually and emotionally. The ideas Byrne is handling are so topical, and so psychologically relevant, that the performances almost visibly grow and develop under the audience's eyes.

Blood and Ice
Traverse, Edinburgh
Sunday Standard, 28 August 1982

Officially, this pre-Festival week on the Fringe has been known as Week Zero, a bleak title which seems, somehow, rather appropriate. To be sure, the Fringe Festival has started: the two huge 'supervenues' at the Assembly Rooms and the Circuit have got their huge operations more or less efficiently underway, and audiences have materialised in respectable numbers. But the weather has been grey and cold and windy, and the real Festival atmosphere has been sadly missed.

Which is not to say, of course, that there have not been some very fine shows on view in Edinburgh this week. The Traverse Theatre Club in the Grassmarket has always been at the very heart of the Fringe; and on Thursday evening the little theatre was packed for the opening of Glasgow poet Liz Lochhead's first full-length play, *Blood and Ice* – a passionate, intense and poetic study of the relationship between Mary Shelley, her husband the poet, and their friend Lord Byron, of the creation of Mary's great novel *Frankenstein*, and of the implications of her story for modern ideas about equal relationships between the sexes, and about the liberation of women.

I dare say there were a few in the audience who were a little disappointed by the occasion, for in this production by Kenny Ireland, *Blood and Ice* certainly looks far from perfect. Some of the scenes seem uncomfortably poised between the horrible and the ridiculous.

But for me, *Blood and Ice* emerges from its weak moments, its moments of bathos and its moments of confusion as a really magnificent debut. Lochhead is not exactly an accomplished playwright and certainly not a tidy one, but she possesses the tremendous, vital dramatic gift of going straight for the jugular.

The question in *Blood and Ice* is the vital and acutely modern one of whether women, bound in blood and pain and love to the business of childbearing, can ever become truly free without becoming frozen monsters of cold reason; and when, at the end of the play, Mary Shelley – struggling to freeze out the painful memories of her drowned husband, her miscarriages, her three dead children – turns to the audience and cries, 'Will the ice save me?', we can see that Lochhead's answer is a sad, and heavily qualified, no.

So the landscape begins to emerge, in these first years of reviews: the brilliance of the Citizens', the link it offered to the wider world of European theatre, the battle against 'dead' theatre wherever I saw it, the emergence of the young poet Liz Lochhead as a serious and powerful playwright. These years also saw the coming of Gerry Mulgrew's Communicado, which married a European repertoire and performance style with a darkly Scottish sensibility in a way that seemed entirely new, and was to reach a climax in 1987 with their acclaimed production of Liz Lochhead's Mary Queen of Scots Got Her Head Chopped Off. *And 1983 marked the first year of Glasgow's Mayfest, which emerged during the 1980s as a hugely influential international festival of popular theatre and music, helping to redefine the city, and becoming an important counterweight, in Scotland, to the mighty Edinburgh International Festival and Fringe.*

In the summer of 1983 the Sunday Standard *ceased publication, and I was approached by Patrick Ensor of* The Guardian *to become their Scottish theatre critic, writing mainly – in those days – for the northern, Manchester-based editions. For me, the job was something of a dream come true; and given the angry, self-interrogating mood of the* Guardian-*reading British left in the 1980s, it demanded a much sharper confrontation with what was right, and wrong, about what passed for radical theatre in Britain. Which is perhaps why my first* Guardian *review of 1984 focused on 7:84 Scotland, and its latest show about the NHS; although by the end of the year, I also had the Scottish Theatre Company firmly in my sights, and was beginning an argument around the STC, and its repertoire, which was to last until the company disbanded three years later.*

1983

Good
Perth Theatre

The Custom of the Country
Citizens', Glasgow
Sunday Standard, 6 March 1983

Every now and again, a new play appears which is so perfect, so timely, so uniquely eloquent in its appeal to audiences, that it soon ceases to seem 'new' at all; it slips quietly into the standard repertoire of the English-speaking stage as if it had always, and inevitably, been there. C.P. Taylor's *Good* – one of the last plays written by this unassumingly brilliant Glasgow-born playwright before his premature death in

1981, and now receiving its first Scottish production at Perth Theatre – is a play of that rare calibre; and despite some severe limitations in the quality of the acting and the detail of the direction, Joan Knight's heartfelt and powerful production at Perth emerges as a wonderful piece of theatre, effective, entertaining, and in the end almost stunning in its emotional impact.

Simply put, *Good* is a well-made lyrical piece about a German intellectual called Halder – an affectionate, thoughtful, slightly ineffectual man, approaching middle life, struggling through the difficult years of the 1930s, and finding himself increasingly entangled in the evil power structures of Hitler's Third Reich.

As a piece of thoroughly modern theatre, it is a play with almost everything. It has music and laughter and a superb central metaphor; it is simply staged, economic and flexible in its theatrical style, refreshingly direct in its approach to the audience; the subjects with which it deals – the moral patterns of human love, the relationship between these private concerns and the larger questions of political morality, and the terrifying inadequacy of private, individual solutions in combating organised evil – could hardly be more important; and they are explored here with a combination, absolutely characteristic of C.P. Taylor, of clear-sighted realism, and almost transfiguring love for the human race – with all its weaknesses and confusions.

For me, Perth Theatre's production of this marvellously humane and thought-provoking play is a theatrical event of quite outstanding significance, and one which will enrich the life of everyone who shares it; for those who are unable to beat a path to the lovely theatre at Perth over the next two weeks, *Good* transfers to Glasgow Theatre Club at the Tron for six days from 22 March.

Down in the Gorbals, the Glasgow Citizens' Company is at it again, resurrecting a sensational sex-and-violence melodrama from the tail-end of the Jacobean period, and serving it up to an astonished audience with posturing, flouncing and shrieking.

This time, the company has hit on a particularly lewd and unpleasant piece – attributed to the playwrights Fletcher and Massinger – called *The Custom of the Country*.

A sweet young couple called Arnoldo and Zenocia, fleeing their native land to preserve her from the nasty local custom which allows the wicked Count to deflower likely looking maidens on their wedding nights, find themselves in a neighbouring country dominated in an equally unpleasant manner by fierce and sexually voracious women. Poor Arnoldo is almost 'raped' by the first lady he meets, and his randy brother Rutilio reduced to exhaustion by the insatiable female clients of the local brothel.

The plot, as you can see, is nonsensical, and most of it passed me by completely; but Robert David MacDonald, who directs, has hit on the clever and witty idea of presenting this land of man-eating matriarchs as a kind of spoof Hollywood, peopled with larger-than-life Mae Wests, Bette Davises and Baby Janes. The result is a hugely entertaining, sustained send-up of all the clichés and mannerisms of American movies in their heyday.

Heaven knows, and I shudder to think, what Robert David MacDonald thinks he might be saying about relationships between men and women, and how they ought to be organised. In that direction, the cynicism both of this production and of the play itself is total and frightening. But as a funny, tasteless and thoroughly outrageous commentary on popular drama – on how it first exaggerates human emotions, then debases them, then ends up poking fun at them – *The Custom of the Country* works tremendously well.

Webster
Citizens', Glasgow
Sunday Standard, 3 April 1983

The production of Robert David MacDonald's new play *Webster*, which opened at the Citizens' Theatre on Thursday, marks the end of an exhausting winter season for the company. Since September, the Citizens' has mounted no fewer than eleven full-scale productions, hacking its way – with its own inimitable combination of flair, inspiration and sheer impertinence – through a huge chunk of the theatrical canon.

The intellectual brilliance which underlies its productions, the visual brilliance of its presentation, and the literary quality of the texts with which it works, still places the Citizens' company in a class of its own among Scottish theatre groups – and indeed among all Britain's regional theatres.

Nevertheless, the company has its artistic problems; and one of the most worrying is a continuing tendency to become absorbed in the examination of its own navel – to function at its best, in other words, when dealing with the distinctly minority-interest subject of theatre itself.

The Citizens' resident man of letters, MacDonald, has produced another backstage drama – this time centred on the enigmatic figure of the Jacobean playwright John Webster, author of those dark, lurid tragedies *The Duchess of Malfi* and *The White Devil*.

MacDonald is interested in examining the curious, haphazard and sometimes dangerous process by which great art can emerge from the most unpromising and banal circumstances. He pictures Webster as a bitter, intelligent, unhappy man, estranged from his wife, blighted by the fact that his only son is a pathetic, brain-damaged idiot, forced to write what he believes to be dreadful plays in order to earn a living, and saddened – as well as inspired – by a desperate, tender, unrequited passion for one of the young actors in the company for which he scribbles.

Out of this almost tragic situation, MacDonald generates a surprisingly entertaining play, full of sharply comic backstage chat, as well as a gentler kind of humour, and some wisdom; I admired the acuteness of his observation, the sensitivity and literacy of the writing, and the particularly fine performances of Ciarán Hinds as Webster, Jane Bertish as his wife, Ron Donachie as a bad-tempered heavyweight actor, and Laurance Rudic as the harassed company manager.

I find MacDonald's painfully honest observations on the art of theatre absorbing and moving, and I'm also excited by the way in which the Citizens' Company seems increasingly willing to open itself to the dangers of exploring real emotion on stage. Whether the man or woman on the Glasgow bus can be expected to give a damn, though – about the art of theatre, the torments of the poet, the jealousies of actors, and the painful absurdities of the creative process – I'm not altogether sure.

Men Should Weep [revival]
7:84 Scotland

The House with Green Shutters
Communicado
Sunday Standard, 17 April 1983

The first time I saw Giles Havergal's production of *Men Should Weep* for the 7:84 Company, I had an urge to leave the auditorium shouting 'I have seen the future, and it works!'

22

Almost a year on from that opening night at the Mitchell Theatre, Glasgow, it seems increasingly clear that this immensely successful and acclaimed production, which is now beginning a two-week run at Glasgow Citizens' Theatre, to be followed by a tour which will visit almost every major theatre in Scotland, marks a vital turning point in the story of Scottish theatre.

As dozens of delighted critics have pointed out, it brings the tradition of gritty, naturalistic drama about Scottish working-class life into a new and thrilling partnership with the bold, flexible and stylish approach which the Citizens' Theatre Company has been developing over the past decade. It also marks the moment when John McGrath's remarkable 7:84 touring company began to come in from the cold, and to think in terms of production which could cope with, and fill, Scotland's greatest theatres.

But perhaps most importantly, *Men Should Weep* is a show which demonstrates the importance of top-class, home-grown touring productions in the future of Scottish theatre. For despite the initial failure of the Scottish Theatre Company to get off the ground, it seems likely that this kind of major production – drawing on many of the finest talents at work in theatre in this country, toured and matured over a long period, and attracting, in time, a very large audience in communities all over Scotland – has a better chance of paying its way. It should also satisfy a sophisticated modern audience more than a hastily produced rep production, which disappears after two or three weeks on the boards.

At the moment, though, the production itself seems in rather fragile condition. The women in the cast – strutting and posing in their dusty black costumes against the fierce, ruinous tenements of Geoff Rose's set – are as fine as ever. But Patrick Hannaway, newly cast as the harassed, unemployed father-of-seven John Morrison, has difficulty in coping with the smooth transitions between the tragic and the comic, the sharply stylised and the gently naturalistic, which this tremendously taxing production demands of its actors.

Meanwhile, out on the road, there seems no shortage of bright young companies willing to continue the tradition of small-scale touring which 7:84 has done so much to develop. In Aberdeen and Edinburgh this week, you can catch up with the Communicado Theatre Company, which is on tour with a powerful, inventive stage version of *The House with Green Shutters*, George Douglas's doleful novel about life in a mean wee Scottish town towards the end of the nineteenth century.

Against the odds, Communicado has succeeded in turning the tale of the dour and horrible Gourlay family into as effective a piece of theatre as you could wish to see, full of colourful, larger-than-life characters, ingeniously staged for a cast of six, and accompanied throughout by superb, jangly original music.

1984

Bedpan Alley
Wildcat
The Guardian, 18 February 1984

It's difficult for anyone who cherishes the idea of a National Health Service to review a show like Wildcat's latest rock cabaret *Bedpan Alley*. Premiered in Scotland last week, due to arrive at London's Shaw Theatre on Tuesday, it's a straightforward piece of pro-NHS propaganda, in the form of a slick, ninety-minute revue.

Surrounded, as usual, by their paraphernalia of keyboards and speakers, whisking in and out of overalls and white coats and mortuary bags, the cast of five move smartly through a series of songs and sketches touching on every aspect of the NHS spending cuts, from the privatisation of laundry contracts, through nurses' wages, to the apparent class bias of death itself.

As usual, the performances range from the passable to the excellent (Elaine C. Smith, David Anderson); the music – composed by Anderson and the whole cast – is strong and unexpectedly varied, featuring a smashing doo-wop sequence for a big-shot consultant and his acolytes, a rumba for two cleaning ladies, and a doom-laden final rallying song against the blandishments of Thatcherite propaganda. 'Agitprop, agitprop,' sing the company fervently. 'Don't give me bullshit, give me truth.'

But the trouble with Wildcat, here as in so many other shows, is that they don't have the application and the intellectual energy to go looking for anything as big, disturbing and complex as the truth. They counter propaganda with more propaganda, selected facts with differently selected facts; and on the level of original thinking, new ideas, and the development of them through a sustained and coherent piece of dramatic writing, *Bedpan Alley* is a lazy and superficial piece of work. It never raises its sights beyond the simple point-scoring that can be achieved in a three-minute sketch, and caricatures its opponents in a way that makes effective confrontation with their ideas impossible.

The Ragged Trousered Philanthropists
7:84 Scotland
The Guardian, 11 May 1984

Heaven knows what a dyed-in-the-wool Tory would have made of it all, but I wouldn't have missed the Mayfest premiere of 7:84 Scotland's *Ragged Trousered Philanthropists* for anything: it was an unforgettable theatrical and political occasion, and small wonder.

Here, after all, was an adaptation of a great socialist classic, opening in front of a packed and overwhelmingly sympathetic audience in a great Labour city, on a day when half the town had apparently been striking and marching in support of the miners.

Inventively and sympathetically directed by David Hayman, and performed with tremendous exuberance by a company of sturdy and familiar Scottish actors, Robert Tressell's straightforward, powerful story about the sufferings of a group of poor tradesmen in Edwardian England was simply carried along on an immense surge of audience response, spontaneous laughter, and political recognition; and when, at the end, the company moved in unison to throw their Mayfest red carnations back into the cheering audience, the whole event seemed like a kind of apotheosis of what Glasgow's people's festival is supposed to be about.

But the problem with occasions like this is that their success belongs at least as much to the audience as to the production, and it's difficult to tell just how well this version of the Stephen Lowe adaptation – now translated into Scots by Archie Hind – would survive a damp night, a small hall, and a sluggish audience.

Lowe's version of the story is certainly clear, imaginative and theatrical enough – he introduces an almost Dickensian element of caricature and nightmare into his portrayal of boss/worker relations – but it's undeniably a little stodgy and static in terms of plot and character development.

But the overwhelming advantage of the Scottish version is that it frees David Hayman's tremendous company – one actress, seven actors – to perform and communicate naturally, in their own Scots voices; and Hayman has brilliantly exploited this freedom, and the theatrical sophistication of Lowe's adaptation, in allowing the company to drop out of character from time to time, to busk and perform their way almost acrobatically through the scene-changes, to make tremendous little comic sketches out of some of the play's tougher theoretical passages.

These episodes not only swing delightfully through some of its duller patches; they also develop a sense of unity and teamwork among the company, which itself acts as a metaphor for the joyful solidarity among workers of which the socialist hero, Owen, dreams, but which his apathetic little bunch of workmen can never quite achieve. In the end, it's that living example of solidarity and combined effort that the audience applauds, as much as Tressell's socialist message; and if the 7:84 company can preserve that precious quality in their performance, they should make an impression on infinitely tougher and much less sympathetic audiences.

Battle Royal
Scottish Theatre Company
The Guardian, 27 September 1984

Let's first say everything nice that there is to say about the Scottish Theatre Company's production of Bruce Daillie's *Battle Royal*, which opened this week at Pitlochry Festival Theatre, before an extensive Scottish tour. The play is a jolly, rollicking comedy set in sixteenth-century Fife, and concerns the habit of the then King of Scots, James V, of passing among his subjects incognito.

The plot revolves around an encounter between the supposed monarch, a rapacious Fife laird called Glendrum, and the laird's three comely unmarried daughters. The first two acts are brisk and neatly structured, and the whole piece, which dates from the early 1960s, is written in a refreshingly crude and vigorous brand of non-academic broad Scots.

The production, directed by Phil McCall with a small cast of seven, radiates a rare quality of confident, buoyant professionalism, and is designed by Helen Wilkinson. It boasts three performances from John Grieve, John Shedden and Juliet Cadzow which are droll, skilful, and theatrically adroit, and I dare say most of those involved would say that *Battle Royal* is simply a harmless piece of fun.

But in this, they deceive themselves. The kind of fun peddled in *Battle Royal* is not harmless; it is reactionary, divisive, and fundamentally damaging to Scottish life. Far from cutting through to the kind of fundamental truth, tragic or comic, that unites human beings, it depends on finding a certain limited audience, old enough not to be offended by the crude sexism on which much of the play's humour depends, and unsophisticated enough not to be disturbed by the stereotypes of Scottish character and manners which it offers.

To see any company indulging in this kind of easy audience exploitation is annoying; to see an organisation called the Scottish Theatre Company doing it – and at such expense of talent, skill and goodwill – is both sad and frustrating.

Commedia
Scottish Theatre Company
The Guardian, 11 October 1984

The Scottish Theatre Company is one of those theatrical organisations that believes the end justifies the means: put on a tripey 'popular' show like our current production of *Battle Royal*, they seem to argue, and it helps to pay for worthwhile projects like this long-awaited Scottish premiere of Marcella Evaristi's *Commedia*, which opened at Edinburgh's King's Theatre on Tuesday before a short Scottish tour. And whatever one may think of the long-term implications of such a policy, it's certainly possible to give an unqualified welcome to the company's intense and highly emotional production of *Commedia*, a quintessential Scottish play by a young Scottish writer, which first appeared in Sheffield in 1982.

Commedia is a big, sweeping domestic drama about the rumpus caused in a Glasgow Italian family when their recently widowed Mamma strikes up a passionate affair with an Italian student twenty-five years her junior. As contemporary drama goes, it has some rare and refreshing qualities. For one thing, it's a rattling good well-crafted yarn, in which the story of the delightful Elena's affair is carefully woven into her developing relationship with her two spoilt grown-up sons and their wives; and the whole action builds to a sensational dramatic climax with the ghastly 1980 bomb incident at Bologna railway station.

For another, it is an uncompromisingly female play, stuffed with painfully acute observations of contemporary women's lives, which, nevertheless, owes nothing to the stark style of committed feminist theatre, and rather seems to draw its inspiration from the epic sweep and lush emotional landscape of popular women's literature, of the romantic novel and the high-class soap opera.

In the end, disappointingly, it also shares some of the limitations of those genres. The characterisation is sketchy and too often stereotyped, and the observation of contemporary sexual behaviour – brilliant and witty though it is – is not matched by the kind of patient investigation into deeper motives which might give the play lasting value. But there is no gainsaying the force with which it speaks to a contemporary audience, the laughs and little cheers of recognition it draws from them, or – despite some surprisingly nervy and superficial direction from the playwright herself, with Michael Boyd – the fierce impact of Anne Kristen's raw and deeply felt performance as Elena. This is a thunderingly clever, observant and moving piece of popular drama, acted – in the end – with real conviction.

The Traverse Theatre had been going through a period of recovery in the early 1980s, following a severe financial crisis. In 1985, though, there was a sudden upsurge in energy, as Jenny Killick arrived at the theatre, first as associate, then as artistic director, bringing with her another director, Stephen Unwin, and a whole generation of brilliant young writers and actors – the actors included Simon Russell Beale, Tilda Swinton and Kate Duchêne, among others. She brought a new wave of European work to the Traverse stage, and found a generation of Scottish-based writers – Chris Hannan, Peter Arnott, Jo Clifford (then John Clifford) – desperate to escape from the world of the naturalistic 'sofa' play, and to write shows with an epic and international sweep; and the voice of theatre in Scotland began to evolve again, in an exciting direction.

As the Traverse looked to a fresh generation of new work, though, there was also an impulse to revisit aspects of Scotland's dramatic and creative past. The young Scottish director Charles Nowosielski, and his company Theatre Alba, began to explore the great Scots-language tradition of folk legends and Border

Ballads, filtering a whole range of neglected songs, poems and stories through an intensely visual, erotic and international theatre aesthetic that transformed perceptions. And in 1985 the Scottish Theatre Company commissioned the great Tom Fleming to direct a production of Scotland's defining piece of classic drama, Ane Satyre of the Thrie Estaitis, *which dates from the 1540s. My view of that production shifted remarkably during its two-year life. But now, at this distance, I wonder whether it was the show that was changing; or myself, the young critic, gradually learning to love a great classic of European drama that I had never encountered before.*

1985

The Flouers o Edinburgh
Perth Theatre
The Guardian, 22 January 1985

Robert McLellan – at seventy-eight, the doyen of Scottish dramatists – is a playwright with many subjects, and only one theme: Scotland's culture, Scotland's language, and the gradual erosion of both through centuries of English domination. His historical drama *Jamie the Saxt* – recently revived by the Scottish Theatre Company – presents a vivid idealised image of Scotland as she might have been in her last decade as an independent kingdom; his later comedy *The Flouers o Edinburgh*, now given a warm, vigorous and handsomely proportioned revival at Perth Theatre, is set in the eighteenth-century aftermath of the Act of Union and the Jacobite Rebellion, and shows Scottish society reeling under the first full impact of 'British' culture and galloping anglicisation.

The plot revolves around the fortunes of a young laird (or squire) called Chairlie (or Charles) Gilchrist, who returns from his Grand Tour with a set of excruciating half-anglicised vowels, and an unshakeable conviction that English is the language of the future; his wooing of a stoutly Scottish lass called Kate, his various contretemps with his crusty old father Lord Stanebyres and Kate's sensible aunt Lady Athelstane, and his frantic attempts to get himself elected to the Westminster parliament, provide ample scope for hilarious linguistic and cultural clashes.

On the whole, the cheap and patronising temptation to play up to the anachronisms in the text – to act as if the old Scots language were comical in itself – is well resisted in Ron Bain's bright and open-minded production at Perth, which features an excellent cast led by the delightful Paul Young – who gives a performance of exemplary wit, integrity and invention as the young Gilchrist – and by Roy Hanlon in the plum role of Lady Athelstane's house-proud servingman, Jock.

In the end, in their best moments, they rise above the traditional clichés of Scots comedy into a genuine and rewarding cultural rapport with their audience; which seems to suggest that, despite the slow linguistic ravages so painstakingly charted by McLellan, the idea of a distinctive Scottish culture is not quite dead yet.

Blithe Spirit
Citizens', Glasgow
The Guardian, 13 February 1985

How Noël Coward ever acquired the reputation of a sly and heartless wit is beyond me; he must have been one of the most disgraceful romantics ever to wield a pen. The theme of his spiritualist comedy *Blithe Spirit* is love, love, love, or at any rate an erotic obsession powerful enough to survive the grave, and last, as the song succinctly puts it, 'Always'; the best joke in the play lies in poor old Condomine's inability to ignore the blandishments and tantrums of his first wife Elvira, even when his heated response to her pouting ghost causes him nothing but social and marital embarrassment.

Its failure to be quite bold enough with this unquenchable fascination between Condomine and the undead Elvira is just part of the profound ordinariness of Giles Havergal's production of *Blithe Spirit*, which brings the Citizens' company back to earth with a bump, after last month's remarkable *Mary Stuart*. Despite an eccentric and pretentious set by Kenny Miller, which surrounds the plush upholstery of the Condomines' drawing room with a clutter of Second World War bomb damage and sandbags, all painted an improbable shade of turquoise, the production emerges as nothing more than run-of-the-mill repertoire Coward.

On one hand, there's Anne Lambton's assured and suitably irresponsible Elvira, and a fine little cameo from Geraldine Hinds as the psychic maid, Edith. On the other, there's Fidelis Morgan's second Mrs Condomine, a little too mannered and emphatic to be entirely effective; Ciarán Hinds' attractive Condomine, nervy and ever so slightly inaudible; and Linda Spurrier who, as an unusually slim and youthful Madame Arcati, makes a generous stab at the beguiling rag-bag of traits that make up that marvellous character without quite scoring a comic bullseye.

The evening moves stylishly enough to a witty conclusion, with searchlights raking the auditorium as the crump of a well-placed bomb blasts Condomine over to 'the other side', and into the arms of his waiting wives. But somewhere – perhaps in this cast's relative inexperience with lightsome and lightweight comedy – there's a bumpy, uneasy feeling, as though the production's comic gears were just failing to mesh.

Dracula
Royal Lyceum, Edinburgh
The Guardian, 18 March 1985

By modern theatrical standards, this new version of Bram Stoker's *Dracula* – adapted for the Royal Lyceum Company by the Scottish poet and playwright Liz Lochhead – is an astonishingly brave and ambitious piece of work. It lasts for three and a half hours, and attempts full-length portraits of no fewer than eight major characters, from the Westermann sisters and their admirers Seward and Harker to Dracula the vampire himself. It delves deep beneath the psychosexual surface of Stoker's story in an attempt to marry his imagery with modern ideas about women's sexuality; its language is a daring and often highly successful mixture of domestic naturalism and high melodrama, pun, alliteration, and pure poetry.

It avoids the spoofs, send-ups and cheap celluloid horrors we've come to associate with *Dracula*, and handles the story with an almost disturbing emotional directness. Its mood emphasises the pure tragedy of Dracula's exile from human happiness, and Stoker's powerful intuition – expressed here through the atmosphere of Seward's horrible Victorian asylum – that the cruelty, bloodthirstiness and arrogance of the vampire underworld reflect human life.

It's hardly surprising, given the scale of the project, that both play and production have substantial faults. Director Hugh Hodgart is much to blame for the inordinate length of the performance, for its indulgent pace and initial lack of narrative drive; the long early arias of the lunatic Renfield, for example, are dangerously overwritten and overplayed, and would have twice the impact at a quarter the length. And faced with a script that demands both melodramatic force and heartfelt emotional realism, Hodgart has not quite succeeded in harnessing them within a consistent performance style.

But John McGlynn's Dracula is a superb, restrained piece of work, strong, sad and sexy. Sean McCarthy takes the right kinds of emotional risks with his great adversary, the histrionic Van Helsing; and Patricia Ross's matronly Mina Westermann comes close to striking exactly the right naturalistic note.

Through the Leaves
Traverse, Edinburgh
The Guardian, 22 April 1985

In the programme note to this British premiere of *Through the Leaves* – a powerful and exquisite two-hander by the Bavarian playwright Franz Xavier Kroetz, which opens the Traverse Theatre Company's enterprising 1985 season – director Jenny Killick suggests that 'the theory of alienation is strong in Kroetz's work... and each form of alienation is focused in the failure to communicate.'

It's true that there is, in this funny and poignant study of an ill-fated love-affair between a fortyish lady butcher and a graceless boor of a slightly younger man, an occasional hint of the style of England's own post-war poet of non-communication, Harold Pinter. There is the grubby, unglamorous setting – in this case the back shop of a Bavarian tripe-butchery, meticulously recreated in the tiny space of the Traverse's downstairs theatre; there are the long silences, and the sad, comical conversations at cross-purposes.

But there, the similarity ends; for Kroetz approaches the problem of alienation in a much more political and combative frame of mind than the cold-eyed Pinter. Not content with simply observing the failure of a relationship, he goes out of his way (through the device of Martha's diary, to which she confesses her romantic and half-baked hopes for the relationship) to show us the real human qualities which are frustrated and crushed by her experiences with a man so locked into tough, insensitive clichés of male behaviour that his rejection of love, and brutalisation of sex, has become an automatic reflex.

It speaks volumes, though, for the subtlety and compassion of Kroetz's writing that while this sympathetic focus on Martha's inner life reveals some pointed feminist truths about the relative roles of men and women in sustaining civilised relationships, the man himself never seems less than human, sad and pitiable; and the actor Ken Stott, playing Otto in the gruff, non-committal accents of the west of Scotland, perfectly captures that sense of perverted and stunted humanity.

It's difficult, in fact, to fault any aspect of Jenny Killick's perfectly paced production, with its combination of powerful, concrete naturalism and understated theatricality, forged through the intensely sympathetic relationship between the audience and Eileen Nicholas's luminous Martha.

But in the end, the evening must belong to Kroetz himself; to the breathtaking economy and ruthless accuracy with which he makes his simple story reach out to encompass the pain of modern living, and to ask us to consider the key question of what it is about our society that makes loving so difficult, and brutality so easy.

In Time o' Strife
Citizens', Glasgow
The Guardian, 10 May 1985

Joe Corrie's *In Time o' Strife* – first performed in Fife in 1927, revived by 7:84 Scotland three years ago, and now revived again to form a dramatic centrepiece of this year's Mayfest – is not one of those working-class plays that presents the case for socialism. It's a biased, affectionate and essentially non-analytic account of life in a Fife pit village towards the bitter end of the 1926 miners' strike; last winter's industrial agony in the coalfields has lent a painful familiarity to the political and moral landscape it describes, but it would take a massively single-minded theatre company – with a ruthless and cavalier attitude to the text – to turn Corrie's ambivalent observations of the aftermath of an industrial dispute into a straightforward piece of socialist polemic.

David Hayman's new version of the play – which plays at the Citizens' Theatre throughout Mayfest – is both enterprising and attractively staged; but it has the uncomfortable look of a production that has set out on that triumphantly socialist road, hesitated, and lost its way. He and his designer Geoff Rose have clearly intended to shape and stylise the play and to clarify its message; the action is set not in a carefully reconstructed cottage kitchen but in a bleak symbolic playing area surrounded by pit tunnels, dominated by high platforms and great, sinister pithead wheels.

But if the aim was to present the play as convincing piece of political rhetoric, then Hayman has apparently failed to involve the whole of his acting company in the enterprise. His well-chosen and exciting ensemble of Scottish actors seem to be pulling in different ideological and stylistic directions: Tom Watson's bravura comic performance as the miner Jock Smith – knowing, cynical, and quite anti-political – might be in a different production from Anne Kristen's warmly heroic portrayal of his wife, Jean. And the result is a production that seems to have lost the warm, explanatory texture of naturalistic theatre, without gaining any thematic force or clarity.

Elizabeth Gordon Quinn
Traverse, Edinburgh
The Guardian, 29 June 1985

Set in a Glasgow tenement during the great women's rent strike of 1915, Chris Hannan's new play *Elizabeth Gordon Quinn*, which opened at the Traverse Theatre this week, is billed as dealing with 'the role of art and personal values at the time of the decay of the British Empire,' and with the state of a family – the remarkable and eccentric Quinns – blessed with 'an imagination they can ill afford'.

In fact, though, imagination as a positive force hardly figures in the play. Instead, there is a witty but ultimately depressing study of imagination as an escape route from reality. Hannan's astonishing heroine, Mrs Quinn – a memorable bravura performance from Eileen Nicholas – is no tenement martyr to artistic truth and freedom, but a monster of working-class false consciousness.

In the early scenes, Hannan's witty script makes an amusing job of satirising Mrs Quinn's pretensions, and exploding the romantic myths of tenement solidarity. Dermot Hayes' bright, unadorned set – a free-standing door there, a dusty window there – is spare and effective. The action cracks along at an impressive pace, and director Steve Unwin has the eccentric Quinns acting in the highly stylised, declaratory manner of characters in an expressionist farce.

But when the plot becomes complicated by the sudden departure of the second Mr Quinn, and the increasing impoverishment and isolation of Mrs Quinn, both writer and director lose their sureness of touch. As the more 'realistic' characters of friends and neighbours gain weight and credibility, the idea that the heroine exists in a psychological world of her own becomes an obstacle to real dialogue, and decisive plot development. Despite an exquisite and impressive performance from Irene Macdougall as a dedicated rent-strike organiser, the play never matures into a wholehearted critique of Mrs Quinn's political inadequacy; nor does the heroine herself emerge as a credible advocate of the individual imagination, against the grim-faced realpolitik of the strike organisers.

Ane Satyre of the Thrie Estaitis
Assembly Hall, Edinburgh
The Guardian, 14 August 1985

Even at its worst, Tom Fleming's Scottish Theatre Company production of *The Thrie Estaitis* – revived at the Assembly Hall after its huge Festival success last year – always gave a useful impression of offering value for money. Here, after all, was a stage full of distinguished and well-known Scottish actors, an impressive yardage of gaudy costumes and banners, a live band, a big male voice choir, and a hefty dose of the old Scots tongue; altogether, a manageable couple of hours of solid yet palatable entertainment, that left behind it an agreeable impression of having seen something both highly prestigious, and undeniably Scottish. What more, in all conscience, could a prudent Edinburgh burgher expect from a theatrical experience, in the hungry 1980s?

The answer, of course, is that he might have expected a sense of purpose and passion, some feeling, on the part of the company, for the powerful structure and lasting significance of Sir David Lyndsay's magnificent, exuberant and wonderfully human parable about the art of good government, both in the state and in the human heart; and last year, success or no, it seemed to many that that sense of shape and meaning, of an important story to tell, was sadly lacking in Tom Fleming's spectacular but empty production.

It's therefore a real delight to report that somehow, in the intervening twelve months, by some massive effort of will or miracle of theatrical chemistry, that vital missing ingredient seems to have been found. It may be something to do with Donald Douglas's remarkably fine performance as Divine Correction, the commanding and Christ-like figure that stands at the play's moral centre; but at any rate, what often looked, last year, like a series of couthy comic turns, a garish and expensive summer pantomime, has suddenly emerged as a thrilling, elegant, muscular and heartfelt account of one of the great plays of European literature.

The production still has its longueurs and little indulgences. The jokey casting of the voluminous Caroline Kaart Raitt as Dame Sensualitie still seems to me a fundamental mistake; the three vices – lovable Scots comics to their fingertips, as played by Walter Carr, John Grieve and Angus Lennie – are not sinister enough.

But on the whole, this new *Thrie Estaitis* offers a powerful momentum, plenty of strong, proud feeling for the play, and a whole clutch of richly enjoyable performances, from Edith Macarthur's completely charming account of the Lady Chastitie, to the delightful, dissolute gambollings of the corrupt Lords Spiritual, led by that grandest old man of the Scottish stage, Andrew Cruickshank himself.

Heartbreak House
Citizens', Glasgow
The Guardian, 2 September 1985

The Glasgow Citizens' new production of *Heartbreak House* – which opened their 1985-86 season this weekend – is a world-class piece of theatre, beautiful, ambitious, intelligent, moving and breathtakingly timely. There is, in fact, a powerful and disturbing sense of inevitability about it, as if the apocalyptic mood of the mid-1980s, and the long moral development of the Citizens' Company as chroniclers of European decadence, had somehow been destined to converge, this autumn, on Shaw's brilliant old evocation – completed in the aftermath of the First World War – of a class of bright, cultivated, liberal and attractive people hopelessly disengaged from the levers of real power, toying with the complexities of sexual politics and cultivating their interest in the arts, while the boors and moneymen in government push the world relentlessly towards some sickening military holocaust.

For this vital production, director-designer Philip Prowse has created an astonishingly beautiful setting, opening out the Citizens' stage into a huge, shimmering, summer-lit space, strewn with wicker tables and chairs, backed by the suggestion of a country-house façade, and shadowed by a great, rippling canopy that suggests both the richness of Virginia creeper and the blood-red of Flanders poppies. On it, he has assembled an outstanding cast of committed Citizens' actors from the last decade and a half, including the company's other two directors, Robert David MacDonald and Giles Havergal (unforgettable as the failed radical Mazzini Dunn), as well as Jane Bertish, Rupert Everett, Jill Spurrier and half a dozen others; and the sheer quality of the result stands as a tremendous tribute to the cumulative value of the company's work over the years.

On the one hand, it makes Shaw's wordy old text seem as if it had been freshly minted last week, so powerfully and intelligently do the cast grasp the contemporary significance of the spiritual situation Shaw describes; on the other, it has a depth, confidence and maturity that seems to indicate years rather than weeks of preparation, as if the company's long experience as anatomists of cultural decline were supplying a unique depth to Shaw's analysis.

But more than that: for the predominant mood of the production – captured in the autumnal beauty of the set – is neither clever nor bitter but elegiac; the Citizens' Company, it seems, are ceasing to be the smart and chattering high priests of decadence, and maturing into sad, sophisticated and highly moral people, who understand the forces of decay, and would like – with playwrights like Shaw and Wilde – to believe in radical alternatives.

1986

Kathie and the Hippopotamus
Traverse, Edinburgh
The Guardian, 4 August 1986

This Traverse premiere of Mario Vargas Llosa's *Kathie and the Hippopotamus* – the first play by this acclaimed Peruvian playwright and novelist to be produced anywhere in Britain – is an event to be welcomed. Vargas Llosa is one of that brilliant new generation of Latin American writers whose work moves effortlessly from the most mundane social realities into all the competing realms of fantasy, memory and interpretation that make up the full human consciousness; and it is high time British audiences had the chance of enjoying the richness of this work.

Kathie and the Hippopotamus is a graceful, intricate and humorous piece of writing about a rich Peruvian banker's wife who, bored witless by her comfortable life, has just been on an extended trip around the world; now, in the attic of her home in Lima, she is having a book about her adventures 'ghosted' for her by a hard-up writer and lecturer called Santiago.

In no time at all – under the influence of the ludicrous and prurient purple passages Santiago weaves round her standard tourist experiences – the pair of them are caught up in a fast-moving, criss-crossing fugue of fantasies about their respective banal lives. Hers involves troops of lovers, a moment of madness in which she shoots her boorish husband, and a strange African encounter with the prodigious sexuality of the male hippo. His are concentrated on a real or imaginary affair with a kittenish student called Adele, and a fatuous identification with the writer and radical hero Victor Hugo.

Bunny Christie has created an elegant and witty set – all plush carpeting, well-placed lamps, and little synthetic images of exotica like palm trees and pyramids; and there are beautifully pitched performances from Alan Barker and Kate Duchêne as Kathie's handsome dimwit of a husband and Santiago's long-suffering wife.

But Janet Amsden and Robert Swann, in the two leading roles, never quite get the measure of this complex play. For one thing, they do not, as yet, seem sure enough of the text to keep Vargas Llosa's delicate interweaving of truth and fiction securely in place. More seriously, they seem unable in the end to grasp that the richness, completeness and humanity of the playwright's vision depends on accepting the equal validity of all the levels of reality he explores.

Here, the actors send up the fantasy as if it was a joke, and play the naturalistic moments as if they represented an unpleasant truth; so the fabric of the play unravels into the spectacle of a pair of unpleasant people indulging in banal and exploitative fantasy. Unless something is done about it, audiences are likely to leave the Traverse with an impression of Vargas Llosa as a writer disgusted by mankind's hypocrisy and cowardice, rather than moved by its plight; and that, I think, is to do the man less than justice.

Oh! What a Lovely War
Brunton, Musselburgh
The Guardian, 3 October 1986

The fundamental question about this best-known of all Joan Littlewood's Theatre Workshop productions – and it's one that Charles Nowosielski's heartfelt but hasty-looking production at the Brunton Theatre hardly resolves – is whether, twenty-three years on, we still really need it.

It's a show that was probably instrumental in creating the critical perspective on the First World War with which we now live; but after two solid decades of Wilfred Owen on the O-level syllabus, of Vera Brittain and Percy Toplis on the telly, of play after play after book of memoirs about horror in the trenches and blinkered idiocy at Allied High Command, its harsh anti-war tone runs the risk of sounding less like a necessary challenge to smug post-war patriotism, and more like the reiteration of a modern orthodoxy. At the Brunton, the programme even comes wrapped in a smart anti-nuclear brochure, produced by a consortium of Scottish local authorities.

For the first half of the evening, it certainly looks as though both the format and the message have become jaded and familiar beyond redemption. This is partly to do with the limitations of the production: Nowosielski's young Scots company of ten actors, singers and musicians struggle to sustain what is, in effect, an evening's music-hall entertainment with barely adequate singing voices, a scanty minimum of musical support, and a chaotic lighting plot which often leaves them groping around in impenetrable shadow.

But somehow, after the interval, the old, terrible fascination of the story begins to work. As the statistics projected on the backcloth become ever more mind-bendingly horrifying (one and a half million men killed in one battle at Verdun, early 1916), and the vacuous music-hall numbers give way to the dark humour of the men's own songs, the ironic force and poignancy of the end-of-the-pier-show format become increasingly obvious.

In the end, the horror of the facts, the searing conviction of the young company, and the chilling continued relevance of the image of a crazed juggernaut of an economic system – that once sacrificed some fifteen million lives in order to create a market for some of its more obscene products – are too insistent to ignore.

Ane Satyre of the Thrie Estaitis
Theatre Royal, Glasgow
The Guardian, 17 November 1986

This weekend, the Scottish Theatre Company's increasingly magnificent production of the great *Satyre of the Thrie Estaitis* opened the proceedings of the International Theatre Meeting in Warsaw, wafted thither by public goodwill messages from Prince Charles and the Lord Provost of Glasgow, and by a creditable chunk of Scottish business sponsorship.

They were cheered on, too, by thunderous roars of approval from a near-capacity Thursday-night audience at Glasgow's Theatre Royal, who were offered a brief glimpse of the latest version of Tom Fleming's production, first seen at the Edinburgh Festival of 1984, before its departure. Never since Ally's ill-fated army left Hampden for Argentina in 1978 can a Scottish team heading abroad have received such a rapturous send-off; and it's pleasant to report that the omens seem a good deal better this time round.

For there is something strange and exciting about this production; now more than two years old, it simply grows stronger and better with every airing. Sir David Lyndsay's satire, first seen in Edinburgh in 1540, is perhaps the only truly great play Scotland has ever produced, a magnificent, rounded, humorous and serious morality pageant about the state of the nation, the abuses of power, and the art of good government under God. Dating from the last century of Scotland's existence as a nation in its own right, it combines a mature and confident grasp of universal political realities with a uniquely brilliant and complete evocation of the character of Scotland itself.

And it's as if the sheer quality of the work has slowly had its effect on what began as a fairly ordinary and aimless-looking company of Scottish actors, welding them into a dazzling ninety-strong performing union (counting choristers, musicians and spear-carriers), passionate about the value of the play's message, and proud of their unique ability to perform it.

This time round, Tom Fleming has had to remake his thrust-stage production for the proscenium arch of Warsaw's Teatr Dramatyczny, losing a little in the great processional entrances (memorable designs for costumes, banners, cloth-of-gold settings by Nadine Bayliss), gaining something in presentation, attack, and intensity of lighting. The production has gained a fine, witty young King Humanitie in James Telfer, and a uniquely sturdy, popular and vehement John the Commonweal in Russell Hunter. And it retains – despite a slight faltering of energy in the opening scenes – its pace, its sweep, its elegance, the profound debt to Scottish pantomime humour in its lighter moments, and the deep central seriousness of Donald Douglas's performance as Divine Correction, the messenger of true religion, come to right the nation's wrongs.

The Shepherd Beguiled
Brunton, Musselburgh
The Guardian, 21 November 1986

In his long quest to bring Scots audiences into closer touch with the powerful, magical folklore of the medieval past, Charles Nowosielski has never unearthed a play more suited to his purposes than Netta Reid's *The Shepherd Beguiled*, which he presents as the final production of his autumn season at the Brunton Theatre in Musselburgh.

Written thirty-odd years ago, in a strong, couthy Perthshire Scots, the play is a haunting account of the torments of one Robert Kirk, minister of Aberfoyle in the 1680s, whose excessive grief at the death of his young wife, Isobel, draws him into dangerous and ultimately fatal dabblings with the supernatural, and in particular with the sinister realm of 'faery', where he believes she is held in thrall.

Ever since Nowosielski's young company first performed this play in 1982, it's been graced by a central performance from Garry Stewart so full of intelligence, poignancy and integrity that it's almost impossible not to be moved by the primal emotions it expresses. And as usual Nowosielski brings to his production a rare quality of emotional fearlessness, some stunning visual and musical imagery (original score for five musicians and ballad singer by Richard Cherns) and an inspired use of the Brunton space. The opening graveyard scene is played in the wide-open spaces of the foyer, and streams of eerily backlit fairies pour down the steep aisles of the auditorium to the rich woodland greens of the set.

Nevertheless, there's something disturbing about this play – and indeed about the whole mystical style of Nowosielski's season. Faced with a story like *The Shepherd Beguiled*, you can dismiss the whole thing as fanciful nonsense, or you can accept it as a kind of moral metaphor, or you can do as Nowosielski sometimes seems to do, and endorse it as a literal truth; in which case it ceases to be meaningful drama, and becomes a mere curiosity.

In 1987 the Scottish Theatre Company faded from the scene; but the 1980s wave of new writing and strong, inventive performance in Scottish theatre was now developing a real critical mass. It was in 1987 that Liz Lochhead, and Gerry Mulgrew's Communicado Theatre, created Mary Queen of Scots Got Her Head Chopped Off, *perhaps the finest and most thrilling Scottish-made play of the decade; in 1987 that Alan Cumming established himself as a terrific new force in Scottish acting. There was massive change afoot, too, in Glasgow, which had been named as European City of Culture for the year 1990 – one of the first cities ever to hold the title – and was beginning a long process of preparation and development, which reached a great staging post with the momentous Glasgow performances [the only ones in the UK] of Peter Brook's* Mahabharata, *early in 1988. And it was perhaps a sign of changing times that Scottish-based artists were becoming ever bolder in their approach to Shakespeare, always the great measure of world theatre. 1988 saw a groundbreaking production of* As You Like It *by the young director Hamish Glen, which used Scots voices to give a whole new dimension to the politics of Shakespeare's great pastoral comedy; in 1989, the great Edinburgh impresario and culture-maker Richard Demarco took audiences to the island of Inchcolm in the Firth of Forth, to witness a rainswept and completely memorable production of* Macbeth.

And meanwhile, across Europe and in South Africa, we were approaching the climactic political year of the post-war era, 1989. Almost every theatre in Scotland was engaged either in presenting South African work, or in an exchange with artists from Eastern Europe, or in both. And the emerging civic politics

48

*of East European dissent was having its impact in Scotland too,
where, early in 1988, all the opposition parties, and a huge range
of organisations from Scottish civil society, set up a Constitutional Convention, to restart the long campaign for a Scottish
Parliament, within the UK.*

1987

Jotters
Crawfurd Theatre, Glasgow
The Guardian, 25 February 1987

Hold on, there's something strange happening here.
According to Wildcat – as radical a theatre company as ever
was – the present government is a callous class-based
conspiracy, not only shockingly indifferent to the needs of
ordinary people in areas like Scotland, but also contemptuous
of the very liberal values – human rights, freedom of speech,
etc. – it purports to defend. And yet this selfsame government,
through the Scottish Arts Council, is paying Wildcat
handsomely – over £100,000 a year – to tour throughout
Scotland and elsewhere, bad-mouthing Thatcherism and all
its works with scarcely a pause for breath.

If I were Wildcat, I would be beginning to wonder just why
this is. It's possible, of course, that the government isn't
quite as intolerant as they suggest; but for myself, I suspect
that the powers-that-be – in deciding whether or not to exert
pressure on this one – have simply come to realise how
deeply ineffective this form of radical theatre is. To threaten
to cut is to get into a nasty public fight; to leave it alone is to
affect the political climate of Scotland scarce a whit.

There are two related reasons why Wildcat find themselves
in this tame-dissident trap, and both were beautifully

demonstrated by the opening of their latest show *Jotters*, which took place in their new home-base at Glasgow's Jordanhill College last weekend. One is that they play largely to people who already agree with them, and their self-selected audience tends not to include people who might feel uncomfortable with a barrage of abuse directed – in this case – at every aspect of government policy on education, as well as at related targets such as the Youth Training Scheme, the Job Restart Scheme, and the deterioration of the Health Service; the performance I attended at Jordanhill, packed with students, lecturers and teachers, was like a kind of union meeting with jokes.

But the other, and more important, reason is that their theatre is not of the persuasive sort anyway. For those of us who agree with most of the points it makes, and have some experience of the education system and of unemployment, *Jotters* is a decent, rousing cabaret entertainment, following the grim educational and employment history of a Glasgow family called Mungo in a series of comic sketches and songs. It has its rough moments (some weak scripting, some signs of under-rehearsal, constant difficulty in hearing the words of songs over over-amplified instruments) and its gems – the Job Restart Song, the *a cappella* playground game, the sacking of a 'surplus to requirements' history teacher by a smarmy headmaster – 'it's all computers and hairdressing noo, you know...'; there's fine acting from David Anderson and fine music from Steve Kettley.

But when it comes to the basic artistic business of changing people, building impossible bridges, presenting a new and original vision of the world, this show is a non-starter; to put it brutally, there was more potent, fundamental dramatic argument against the present economic dispensation in five minutes of the Citizens' recent production of *Death of a Salesman* than there's been in the last half-dozen Wildcat shows; and it's time this talented company hired itself a decent, courageous writer, and set about confronting the basic question of why, given the obvious truth of much of what they say, the point of view they represent remains so impotent in this country.

Mary Queen of Scots Got Her Head Chopped Off
Little Lyceum, Edinburgh
The Guardian, 13 August 1987

Like the official Festival, this year's Fringe seems to be all about Scots and Russians, with a generous sprinkling of Americans and other, more exotic visitors; the English Fringe – as represented by shows like Hull Truck's *Teechers*, playing at the George Square Theatre to large crowds of off-duty educational face-workers, or by the charming *It's a Girl* from the Duke's Playhouse, Lancaster, or even by an oddly laid-back and giggly Jenny Lecoat at the Assembly Rooms – seems in strangely subdued mood. Perhaps, like the Labour Party, English alternative theatre has reached a point where it must rethink its entire politics; at any rate, these soft-centred, well-staged, witty, humanistic and utterly predictable shows look like the last gasp of a Fringe culture that's reached the end of its line.

In Scotland, though, things seem slightly different – rougher, harsher, more colourful and cosmopolitan, shot through with a kind of brash, nothing-to-lose energy. In the official Festival, the energy blisters through the strange, heightened, ritualistically foul-mouthed new-speak of Iain Heggie's *A Wholly Healthy Glasgow*, and shouts from the canvases at the Vigorous Imagination exhibition of new Scottish painting at the Modern Art Gallery. And it's reflected with terrific, show-stopping force in Liz Lochhead's *Mary Queen of Scots Got Her Head Chopped Off*, a ferociously iconoclastic re-examination of Mary Stuart's life and its significance – in sixteenth-century Scots and standard English, fierce poetic monologue, stylised movement and sharp, almost improvised dialogue – that's been one of the brilliant high points of this first Fringe week. Specially commissioned by the young Edinburgh-based touring company Communicado, performed at the Lyceum Studio in the very shadow of Mary's castle, it simply blasts to smithereens the heavy, obscuring deposit of romantic claptrap that has gathered around the story down the centuries, and instead draws the most dramatic and uncomfortable parallels between the sacrifice of Mary in her day, and the myriad sexual, political and religious deformities that still plague the Scottish psyche now.

As a piece of theatre, this *Mary Queen of Scots* is hardly perfect yet. The fierce momentum of Mary's rush to destruction suggests that it would play better as a ninety-minute one-acter than in two halves of a full hour each, and there are moments when it seems to spend too much time retelling Mary's story, and not enough teasing out its meaning; in fact all its most important insights – from Mary's suicidal rush into the arms of Bothwell, through her defeat, imprisonment, execution and enduring significance in the street culture of Scotland – are concentrated into a devastating whirlwind of a ten-minute finale, which left the first-night audience shaken, weak-kneed, and cheering themselves hoarse. But structural hiccups apart, it's difficult to overstate the sheer theatrical invention and bravado Gerry Mulgrew and his company bring to Lochhead's script; from the tattered purplish velvets of the set, through Anne Wood's rich and weird continuo of scraping fiddle-music, to Myra McFadyen's brilliant performance as the archetypal Scottish crow or corbie who narrates the piece, the whole production exudes a fierce, compelling atmosphere of its own, rich and tattered, shabby and sharp, bloody and yet unrepentant, like the history of Scotland itself, or, for that matter, of womankind. In this production, Liz Lochhead's terrific dramatic gifts of richness of language and strength of characterisation find the theatrical home they've been waiting for in the physicality, the visual imagination, the sheer showmanship of Mulgrew's theatre. Even more importantly, the combination has produced, for Scotland, a play that blasts Mary's myths, not out of mindless radicalism, but because it has something more important to say about her and about us, about womanhood, about the nation.

Travesties
Dundee Rep
The Guardian, 18 October 1987

It's interesting to see Tom Stoppard's *Travesties* come perilously close to falling flat on its face, in this new production at Dundee Rep; the atmosphere in the auditorium wavers, throughout, between exasperation, alienation, and outright boredom. Yet this lack of sympathy between stage and audience has very very little to do with any shortcomings in the production, and nothing at all to do with the efforts of Robert Robertson's delightful young company, who throw themselves into Stoppard's glittering tangle of political and philosophical wit with enough verve, energy, intelligence and determination to stop a juggernaut, and win themselves a warm final ovation in the process.

Robert Robertson's idea of pairing productions of *Travesties* and *The Importance of Being Earnest* – using the same cast and set – works startlingly well and very amusingly in exposing the structural links between the plays; and the company that plodded smartly but aimlessly through *Importance* seems to have been goaded by the sheer difficulty and structural ingenuity of Stoppard's text on to a different level of achievement, working flat-out to make his dense rhetorical variations on the idea of revolution and the artist, his clever treatment of the characters and ideas of James Joyce, of Lenin, of Tzara, and of all the intellectual glitterati that converged on Zurich during the First World War, seem interesting and significant to the audience. Peter Forbes's Joyce is brilliant, self-absorbed, superbly Irish, beautifully in tune with Stoppard's satirical use of language and its rhythms; Bridget McCann – faced with the most difficult speech in the play, a ten-minute lecture on the history of Marxism – produces an impressively passionate performance as the Bolshevik librarian, Cecily, buoyed up by the audience's obvious sympathy with her contempt for the politically illiterate Englishman Henry Carr; and the rest of the cast enter into the spirit of the thing with discipline and panache.

The problem is simply that 400 miles north of Oxford and Hampstead – and twenty years on from the age when this critical approach to the sacred cows of revolution would have seemed brilliant and refreshing – the youthful Stoppard's glittering verbal games with the big ideas of the century seem both fundamentally undramatic in conception (hence the boredom) and dangerously quietist in political approach (hence the alienation). This is a play which dismisses Marxism/Leninism as an unpleasant joke, roundly endorses the bourgeois individualist idea of the artist, implicitly advocates a sceptical and reactionary attitude to radical politics, and expects its audience to listen with admiration to ten-minute exhibitions of showy undergraduate wit; small wonder that it cuts no ice in a city like Dundee, which has to live with the human consequences of the smart and cynical New Rightism of which Stoppard, whether he likes it or not, has become a chief scribe. The play contains one decent argument against dialectical materialism, in which Carr says he won't be told that he ended up in the trenches 'because there was a profit in ball-bearings'. But for the most part, the Stoppard of *Travesties* is too much *parti pris*: he allows what should be a passionate debate about how to organise a just society without sacrificing essential freedoms to degenerate into a clever joke at the expense of one side of the argument, and there are places in Britain where that kind of flippancy is hard to admire, and harder to forgive.

No Man's Land
Citizens', Glasgow
The Guardian, 8 November 1987

When Peter Hall first saw the text of Harold Pinter's *No Man's Land* – a few months before his premiere production of it in London in 1975 – he felt, so his diaries tell us, that the play was about 'the real artist harassed by the phoney artist'; as if its central confrontation – between the wealthy middle-aged writer Hirst, and the crumpled, self-aggrandising literary voyeur Spooner, whom he meets on Hampstead Heath and brings home for a drink – were a one-sided affair, with all the virtue, charm and authority resting on Hirst's side. It's perhaps not surprising that this powerful new production at the Citizens' Theatre – featuring Robert David MacDonald as Hirst and Giles Havergal as Spooner – takes a more complex and ambivalent view of Hirst and his worldly success. Peter Hall himself eventually came to feel that the play was about 'opposites – genius against lack of talent, success against failure, drink against sobriety...'; MacDonald and Havergal – with the kind of quiet political rigour that's become a hallmark of their recent work – take the interpretation a stage further, and present the play as a powerful, well-focused reflection on the relationship between haves and have-nots in English society, and on the comical way in which the bland bonhomie of middle-class English discourse – with its pattern of real or imagined contacts at school and Oxford, in the War or in London clubs – can temporarily soften, confuse and conceal irreconcilable differences of status and interest.

The result is a completely fascinating performance, funny, poignant, ultimately sinister and slightly tragic, and full of complex shifts of sympathy between the two characters. If Havergal's poverty-stricken Spooner is bumptious, obsequious, grubby, irritating, and full of the literary equivalent of Walter Mitty fantasies, MacDonald's Hirst is in a complete and dangerous emotional wasteland, literally paralytic with drink, isolated and imprisoned by his wealth, and by the two thuggish hangers-on (Foster and Briggs, played with exaggerated Orton-esque panache by Jonathan Phillips and Patrick Hannaway) it has bought him.

What MacDonald and Havergal give us, in the end, is a meticulous and deeply felt portrait of two men – perhaps even potential friends – whose capacity for real, truthful, affectionate relationships has been damaged beyond repair by the operation of money, or the lack of it, on their lives. Spooner retains the ability to talk, but has lost useful contact with reality; Hirst sees the truth, but cannot break out of his prison to communicate. The language patterns that form a fragile bond between them act – as everywhere in Pinter – like a barrier against reality, an expression of an older and defunct order of things; the little fluttering hand gestures with which the men occasionally reach out to one another are poignant and futile, in the face of the ruthless realism of Foster and Briggs. And in the play's final moments, with Spooner walking away across a darkening stage, and the two heavies standing shoulder to shoulder behind Hirst's chair like guards or warders, I had the most powerful, sudden vision of something lying between them, bleeding messily into the tasteful carpeting of Kathy Strachan's clever, understated set – something like love, or aborted hope, or perhaps an old idea of society as something more than a cold human jungle, where Spooner's poverty is the ultimate unforgivable crime, and success is only bearable if, like Hirst, you keep topping up the drinks, and changing the subject.

The Knicht o the Riddils
Brunton, Musselburgh
The Guardian, 27 November 1987

You would think the Scots language movement might have learned something from the failed Scottish Renaissance of the 1940s, when some of the most talented and fluent Scots-language writers of the century wasted their time concocting mock-medieval Borders comedies that created a deadly, foosty image of the whole idea of Scots language for a generation of schoolchildren. But like many groups marginalised from the mainstream of history, Scots seem doomed to repeat ad infinitum the same cycle of dawning cultural awareness followed by failure and forgetting. David Purves is one of the most effective manipulators and synthesisers of Scots writing today; his language is tough, eclectic, demotic yet scholarly, and a joy to hear. Yet in his new play *The Knicht o the Riddils* – premiered this week at the Brunton Theatre in Musselburgh – he chooses, inexplicably, to squander his skills on a daft medieval fairy story of scant significance, and only intermittent charm.

In itself, *The Knicht o the Riddils* is an attractive enough entertainment, a bold, raunchy, neatly crafted tale about a young Prince of Scotland called Cormac: threatened with poisoning by his ill-tempered stepmother Sheena, he sets off with his loyal stepbrother Alistair – who has no time for his scheming mamma – to the far country of Galloway, to seek the hand of the fair daughter of the Knicht o the Riddils, a gnome-like old curmudgeon who will only give poor Una in marriage to someone who can baffle him with a riddle. Nick Sargent's set and costumes make a gorgeous, fluent, witty pattern of soft storybook colours; many of the performances – particularly Anne Lacey's inimitably graceless Queen Sheena – are delightful; Charles Nowosielski's production moves along with an easy, faultless narrative pace, and his determination to show new Scottish work to his Musselburgh audience is in every way admirable.

But in the end, it's simply a shame to see so much craftsmanship and commitment wasted on an old joke of a story that has no chance of really moving or involving a contemporary audience. Two years ago, Purves wrote a Christmas show for the Traverse based on the story of the princess and the frog; then, the vigour of his language and the robust charm of the old Scottish folktale told for children were impressive enough in themselves. But unless Scots can move on from this medieval dream, and begin to assert itself as a medium capable of carrying serious adult drama about recognisable problems and tensions, the language is a lost cause; and Purves's work will be consigned to that dustbin of cultural history where most twentieth-century Scots-language writing now languishes – completely unmourned, it should be said, by the vast majority of ordinary Scots, who already experience their cultural disinheritance as little more than a dull ache, and spend their time, like everyone else, watching drama like *EastEnders* and *Neighbours*, which has something to say about the way we all live now.

Babes in the Wood
Tron, Glasgow
The Guardian, 13 December 1987

It is night in Kelvinside, a posh part of Glasgow. Up in the nursery – in the dim blue glow of the TV screen – the little dressing-gowned figures of Victor (Forbes Masson, in pink) and Barry (Alan Cumming, in blue) are to be seen grooving and cooing on their bunks to the strains of a video of *South Pacific*, bought that day – along with lots of other Christmas goodies – with the purloined Access card of their daddy, a mad scientist with severe financial problems and, following a recent domestic dispute, no wife. Suddenly, the enraged papa bursts in, and not only smashes the precious video to smithereens ('But *South Pacific* is our *raison d'être*!' wail the twins), but also threatens to chuck out of the house forthwith the Babes' feathered friend Shug, a broken-winged seagull rescued from the lee of the Kibble Palace, Glasgow's famous tropical palm house. The Babes decide to run away into the wilds of the Botanical Gardens, and thus – give or take a hysterical scene or three – begins the big adventure of the Tron's brilliant, naughty, clever and hilarious pantomime for adults, written by the amazing Victor and Barry, *enfants terribles* of the Scottish comedy scene, and very little the worse for that.

There's no point in denying, of course, that wicked send-up pantomimes like this have their problems. For a start, there's the acute moral confusion and tasteless cynicism of it all; in a situation where you're constantly invited to be sceptical about the manners and morals of the heroes, happy endings looks like black farce and plots tend to disintegrate – this one nearly founders completely on a human-sized reincarnation of the seagull, not to mention a nasty militaristic collie dog who's supposed to be a goodie. As for the villains, headed in this case by a crazed geneticist called Dr Vivien Section ('My friends call me Vivi...') who wants to take over the world from a bunker beneath the Botanics, they hardly know what tone to take.

But the characters Victor and Barry have created for themselves in this show – a pair of self-righteous, ecologically minded, middle-class brats, much given to whining about their 'financially insecure background' and the difficulty of getting vegetarian wholefood at school dinners – are just so funny, so well-observed, so brilliantly conceived as a vehicle for satire against the vaguely suspect wishy-washy 'green' politics of the middle-class left in the 1980s (and Glasgow is full, these days, of nice left-wing people with nice big elegant flats), that they carry the whole show effortlessly before them. This is simply the slickest, strongest, best-rehearsed and best-scripted double act on the Scottish pantomime circuit, and its originality and professionalism put many more experienced performers to shame. What's more, it's backed by decent, generous supporting performances from Sandy Neilson as the daddy/villain and Finlay Welsh as the Babes' nanny, a raddled, randy-looking peroxide-blonde Dame; and it's smoothly and humorously directed by Hamish Glen, who somehow manages to manoeuvre his little company successfully through the ethical, musical and dramatic minefields created by Victor and Barry's unstoppably satirical attitude to everything from walking trees to magic pills ('D'you think that's a drug, Barry? Well just say no...') – and that despite some pretty feeble acting further down the cast. So if I were you I would rush to the Tron before tickets sell out completely, and prepare myself to laugh at Vic and Baz until my guts ached; but for heaven's sake, unless you want their infant idealism curdled at birth, leave the kids at home!

1988

The Vortex
Citizens', Glasgow
The Guardian, 24 January 1988

Whatever else he was, Noël Coward was not a conventional thinker. He certainly went in for lavish public endorsements of patriotism, tradition, and sentimental nationalism, as the programme note to this fascinating Citizens' Company revival of *The Vortex* points out. But when it comes to the real stuff of his plays – which are about the conduct of private life in a highly wrought, over-privileged civilisation – he achieves, at his best, a subtle and completely original moral perspective; indeed it's hard not to see something downright revolutionary in the value system of later masterpieces like *Private Lives*, where the attitude taken by Elyot and Amanda – vain, irresponsible, hopelessly aesthetic, reckless in love, bright and defiant in the face of mortality – is seen as a braver, richer and ultimately wiser response to the transience of human existence than the suburban common-sense of rejected spouses Victor and Sybil.

Which is why it is strange, in *The Vortex*, to see the youthful Coward (he was twenty-five in 1924) struggling with a melodramatic style of theatre that demands big gestures, unselfconscious emotion, and, above all, moral simplicity. The play begins confidently enough, with a barrage of conversation as jaggedly sophisticated as even Coward could wish. The scene is the London salon of the heroine Flo Lancaster, where the relentlessly beautiful Flo – her assurance fraying ever so slightly as she approaches her mid-forties – is carrying on as usual with a young Guards officer; and from the moment Maria Aitken sails on to the stage, all brittle defiance and little veiled hats, it becomes apparent that she is offering a comic Coward performance of the very finest quality, full of that lightweight, perfectly timed theatricality that works like a dream in the theatre, but also reflects the reality of the character's social performance, so that even as you laugh you can't help being aware of the frightened, ageing female animal behind the smart public persona.

The trouble with *The Vortex*, though, is that its melodramatic format demands that Coward become heavy-handed with his heroine; it doesn't allow the quiet, tragicomic crumbling of her illusions that Coward might have achieved later in his career. Into the equation stalks Flo's embarrassingly grown-up son, Nicholas, played by Rupert Everett in a strange, twitchy, naturalistic style that's powerful and compelling in itself, but somehow irrelevant both to the play's comedy and to its melodrama. Neurotic, mother-fixated, edgy from snuffing cocaine and tenuously engaged to a sensible type called Bunty, Nicholas propels his mother through a fragmented house-party weekend to a nasty Hamlet-style boudoir confrontation in which he accuses her (oh horror) of having lovers; and it's at this point that Philip Prowse's elegant and deeply amusing production begins to come apart at the seams, Everett seeming to find the whole scenario faintly embarrassing, and Aitken unsure whether to play the scene as just another of Flo's social performances, or to let the real woman come screaming through.

In the end, though, these problems lie at least as much in the play as in the production. It's hardly surprising, given his later record, that Coward found it hard to put much conviction into the fretful Nicky's reactionary demands that Flo stop having lovers and start being a 'proper mother'; the true moral centre of the play lies not with him, but with the more subtle understanding of Flo's wise friend Helen, deftly played by Anne Lambton, and it's perhaps a mark of inexperience that Coward brings the final curtain down without allowing this key figure her final say. Within the limitations of this brave and brittle play, though, Prowse's company create a fascinating, funny and humane piece of theatre, set (by Prowse himself) in a rich black-and-cream dream of 1930s avant-garde decor that carries heavy modern resonances, full of fine supporting performances, and strong enough to cast a powerful, penetrating light on the serious preoccupation with social 'decadence' that went on to underpin Coward's most famous comedies. If the Citizens' go on like this, we shall have to forget the 'talent to amuse' stuff altogether, and begin to recognise Noël Coward as one of the most subtle and significant playwrights of the century; I wonder what the Master would have said to that.

The Mahabharata
Tramway, Glasgow
The Guardian, 18 April 1988

Last week, a few days before the Glasgow opening of Peter Brook's mighty *Mahabharata*, I asked Neil Wallace – Deputy Director of the City's newly formed Festivals Unit, and the 'man with a mission' who has fought and schemed and negotiated tirelessly for almost a year to bring Brook and his company to Glasgow – what it was about this piece of work that he admired, revered, wanted so much. He thought, paused, shook his head. 'I just can't say,' he said. 'I can't disentangle my feelings about the show as a piece of theatre from my feelings about what it represents...'

He was right, and perhaps in more ways than he intended. This event, the *Mahabharata* in Glasgow, is something that simply overflows the bounds of normal theatrical experience. For Glasgow, it represents a magnificent turning point, a key moment in the city's re-emergence from decades of industrial decline to take its place again as one of the great second cities of the world, vigorous, cosmopolitan, handsome even in dilapidation, fizzing with creative energy and civic pride and – most important of all – living proof that the spirit of a city can survive the worst ravages and humiliations of the post-industrial age. To anyone who has watched Glasgow pull itself up by its creative bootstraps these last half-dozen years, and seen the emergence of the unique powerful consensus about the value of the arts in the city's life which makes possible the raising of £350,000 to stage something like the *Mahabharata*, the sheer presence in Glasgow of this most glamorous and remarkable show of the decade is a moving testament to the city's resilience. From the City Council and Strathclyde Region, from the business community, from the public who have already bought almost all the available £140,000-worth of *Mahabharata* tickets, and even from the proverbial man in the street – who seems to feel, without resentment and with pride, that all of this is 'great for Glasgow' – there is what Wallace calls a 'quite remarkable degree of unanimity' that the development of the arts represents a prime investment in the city's future, and, what's more, that Glasgow's artistic life, to develop its full potential, must and should get into dialogue with the richest, most exciting and most subtle work that world theatre has to offer.

And that Peter Brook's *Mahabharata* represents that scale and quality of artistic experience is beyond doubt; indeed it's perhaps the greatest tribute of all to Brook's achievement as a director that the meaning of this work – even without its extraordinary Glasgow dimension – seems to go so far beyond theatre itself. What Brook is doing, in the *Mahabharata*, is taking what is possibly the greatest, wisest and most powerful story ever written – a vast epic of war and peace in India two thousand years ago, fifteen times as long as the Bible, and so subtle and humorous in its perspective that it makes our own great religious epic look like a slim, grim patriarchal episode in a vastly more beautiful and many-layered story – and making it accessible, with courage, with artistry, and with an immense effort of compression, to Western audiences that come to it almost hungrily, so deeply do they seem to need its wisdom and its grace.

At the beginning of the *Mahabharata*, a storyteller called Vyasa appears, together with a little boy. He says he is going to tell the story of the boy's ancestors, which is also 'the poetical history of mankind'; they are joined by Ganesha, a god with an elephant's head, who acts as scribe, and Vyasa proceeds to tell – or perhaps to create – the story of a terrible conflict between two families of cousins, the Pandavas – five fine brothers all married to the same woman, the lovely Draupadi – and the hundred Kauravas, a race of violent, angry malcontents led by the fierce warrior Duryodhana. The story is comic, tragic, magical, erotic, sometimes spectacular, and it ranges through many moods, from a kind of cool, humorous Brechtian distance in telling the story through the commentary of Vyasa and Ganesha, to the most powerful and direct dramatic action, particularly in the third and final play, *The War*, which tells the story of the earth-shaking battle that finally brought the conflict between the cousins to an end, leaving 'eighteen million dead'. This war is given an extra dimension of dread – and a spine-chilling significance for modern audiences – by the existence of a terrible weapon of extermination, which will end the war only by destroying the whole earth; and our intense empathy with the fear of this weapon – the despairing silence in which we finally watch it unleashed – gives a terrific emphasis to the *Mahabharata*'s preoccupation with the source of evil and violence in the world, with questions of how far ends justify means in fighting evil, in the problem of whether passive non-violence or active resistance represents the best response. The poem is also preoccupied with ideas about parenthood and family, about the mysterious, god-given origins of the human being, about the evil that results 'when one prefers one's own children to the children of others'. It asks, again and again, about the meaning of death, whether it is important, whether it is real; and there is a kind of continuous subplot to do with the poet Vyasa, with his role, his moral responsibility, the limits of his power to create the story.

Brook's thirty-strong company of actors and musicians – on their great clay floor at the Old Transport Museum in Pollokshaws, flanked by pools of water and backed by raw brick walls – present all this rich multiplicity of experience with force, with humanity, with a kind of self-conscious simplicity of staging that very rarely tips over into coyness; the look of the production – in earth colours of cream, ochre, deep reds – is often quite stunning, reflecting the basic elements of earth, fire, water that leap and shimmer everywhere in the playing area. It would be wrong to give the impression that this *Mahabharata* represents some kind of continuous triumph of unique theatrical brilliance; it is a very human show, and it has its failings. I can imagine adaptations of the text that might be more ruthless and coherent in finding a single dramatic 'through line' for the play; I can imagine productions that would force a more unified acting style, and achieve a stronger immediate impact. The acting – and particularly the handling of language – is variable in quality; the balance between lightness and serious drama sometimes slips a little too far in the direction of showmanship, just as the production sometimes looks a little over-elaborate, overdressed and over-lit for its ostensibly simple style. The Glasgow audience listened rapt to the deep, reflective moments of the text, but sometimes seemed exasperated by the noisier and more spectacular aspects. As for the space, the *Mahabharata* has to fight every inch of the way against the great, powerful girders of the Transport Museum for the gentle freedom, the room to breathe and grow organically without too much obvious structure, that it enjoyed in the quarries and outdoor spaces where it was born; Glasgow's great new space – and let's hope it becomes a permanent one – seems to demand something more rigid, more real.

But in the end, Brook's great achievement with the *Mahabharata* lies precisely in the self-control with which he and his adaptor Jean-Claude Carrière have shaped it, remade it, presented it, without trying to simplify it, or to impose Western ideas of consistency and coherence on it; they lay it before us in all its rich ambiguity and contradiction, and they do not apologise. What is more, they allow the actors of the company to find their own way – with an extraordinary freedom and integrity – towards the dramatic force of the text, not distorting their own personalities but using them, so that the multiplicity of the text produces a whole world of acting styles, from the fine Shakespearean heroism of Jeffery Kissoon as Karma – the warrior abandoned as a child, doomed to fight for ever against his unknown brothers, the Pandavas – through the fine, filmic naturalism of Andrzej Seweryn as the good king Yudhishthira, the eldest Pandava, to the folksy comedy and melodrama of Miriam Goldschmidt (Kunti) and Tuncel Kurtiz (Shakuri), and the wonderful, Brechtian coolness, mischief and compassion of Bruce Myers as the man-god Krishna, the performance that epitomises the spirit of the whole piece.

A dozen years ago, enchanted by the *Mahabharata* stories they had learned, Brook and Jean-Claude Carrière made a vow, one night in Paris, that they 'would find a way of bringing this material into our world and sharing these stories with an audience in the west.' They have kept their promise, just as the story itself keeps its promise, made in the first moments, that 'when you have heard it, you will be someone else.' So that what is most important about this show is not its inventiveness or its skill, not its beauty, not the quality of the acting and the adaptation, all of which are open to discussion. It is just the fact that it brings back to us – with integrity, with humility, with respect for the strange, unfathomable *dharma*, the underlying order of the piece itself – a priceless and beautiful work of the human imagination that we had lost, and needed to find again.

Great Expectations
Chandler Studio, Glasgow
The Guardian, 17 May 1988

TAG (Theatre About Glasgow) is a small, unassuming theatre company, a theatre-in-education group with a strong commitment to touring in schools, to accessible classics, and to new writing on themes that affect Scottish kids now; even in its native city, it's not the kind of company that gets invited to provide big, centrepiece productions for international festivals. And yet it seems to me that TAG's new version of *Great Expectations* – which played to capacity audiences at the Chandler Studio last week before an extensive tour – is the most rounded, satisfying and successful piece of home-grown Scottish theatre this Mayfest has produced so far. Like the great *Mahabharata*, thundering its way through the final performance at the Old Transport Museum as I write, this deft, tender and intermittently brilliant treatment of Dickens's novel uses a strong and sophisticated range of live-theatre techniques to achieve a relatively simple result – the effective theatrical retelling of a great and gripping story, backed by a passionate feeling for the pity and complexity of human experience.

In technical terms, what this *Great Expectations* does is to pull off, with almost complete success, the kind of combination of dance and drama that many Scottish companies have been striving for this season. Working in close collaboration with writer John Clifford and choreographer Gregory Nash, TAG's director Ian Brown has succeeded in building a company of actors who can move and dance, dancers who can speak and act; and the cross-fertilisation of the two disciplines – helped by Peter Salem's wonderful, jarring live music for keyboard and cello, and most significantly by John Clifford's script, a miracle of intelligent compression that wraps itself elegantly around every essential element of the story in the course of a short evening – has produced a rich, seamless sequence of talk and movement that might have been created to bring to life the peculiar world of caricature and half-nightmare in which Dickens's characters move. At any moment, a prose conversation can surge into a pattern of stylised movement, the characters' lives dissolve into a pattern beyond their control; and in that sense the technique serves as a superb metaphor for the impact of ruthless social forces on individual lives which is one of Dickens's great themes.

Of course, not every writer would yield so successfully to this approach, and not every element of Dickens's story responds to it so well as, say, the surreal scenes in Jaggers's office, or the ball at Richmond where Estella evades Pip. Some of the solo dance sequences seem too long, out of sympathy with the rapid, elliptical rhythm of the text. The opening needs more verbal explanation for those unfamiliar with the story; and towards the end, we need more stillness to let strongly written dialogue speak for itself.

But overall, the technique is stunningly successful; so much so that the production moves easily beyond questions of method, to convince us anew of the terrific relevance and force of Dickens's vision, and to reaffirm his sense of despair (for the original ending of the book was a very bleak one) at the cancer of class- and money-consciousness that blights the social and erotic imagination of his England, and – at an even deeper level – at the tragic way in which that blight of inherited wealth and inherited misery is passed on from generation to generation, touching the expectations of children like Pip and Estella with a dark, inexplicable frost. Among a clutch of fine performances, Alan Cumming is superb as a vain, enthusiastic, vulnerable and ultimately disillusioned Pip, Alistair Galbraith is touchingly strong and clumsy as Joe Gargery the blacksmith, and Forbes Masson magnificently rigid as Jaggers the lawyer. But in the end this is ensemble work of the best kind; and for sheer creative originality matched with true feeling, a passion to communicate, and a decent economy of means, it deserves the biggest red rose in Mayfest's bouquet.

The Conquest of the South Pole
Traverse, Edinburgh
The Guardian, 20 July 1988

It was a few years ago that I first heard the phrase 'the fourth world'; it was bandied about a bit in left-wing circles, and then seemed to slip out of fashion. But the phenomenon it describes has not gone away. It refers to the powerless of the earth wherever they are, to the Third World poor grubbing a living off rubbish dumps in Cairo and Manila, to depressed young mums hanging on on Social Security in Newcastle tower blocks, to people everywhere who work long hours in low-paid jobs because the alternative is no work at all; and it refers to the young unemployed, that unhappy generation born in the 1960s who grew up, all across the developed world, to find the idea of a job-for-life evaporating before their eyes.

What the German writer-director Manfred Karge has done in *The Conquest of the South Pole* – first seen in Germany last year, and now given its British premiere at the Traverse Theatre – is to write a play for and about that fourth world: sharp, funny, tough, searching, and unsentimental, as oblique and fast-moving as a slick video in its range of cultural references, it seems to grasp the whole meaning of that problem of human powerlessness in one rigorous, compassionate political intelligence. It's a play that smells of the future, of new problems, new perceptions, new forms of storytelling, new approaches to language; but its triumph is to be completely new and original, without ever seeming merely bizarre or 'experimental'. The audience responds not with puzzlement, but with gasps of recognition and laughter, as though they had been waiting for just this postmodern combination of the pitiless and the compassionate, the fantastical and the rigorously true; and in Steve Unwin's brilliant production at the Traverse – fierce, vivid, angry and tender by turns, combining real political and emotional subtlety with a terrific voltage of theatrical energy – it emerges as one of the most exhilarating theatre experiences of a demoralised decade, finding the energy to move us on at last into the 1990s, not by turning its back on the pain and anger of the '80s, but by using it and moving beyond it.

Set in some bleak German backwater called Herne, the play begins when four unemployed youths – Slupianek, Buescher, Braukmann and Seifert – find one of their number trying to commit suicide by hanging himself. In a last-ditch effort to fight off terminal apathy, they begin a kind of desperate game, in which – up in Braukmann's attic – they act out the story of Amundsen's successful 1911 expedition to the South Pole. In thirteen short, intensely written and often very funny scenes, the play tells the story of their journey, how they assemble the equipment they need, how they meet the threats to their solidarity posed by the depression and apathy of Buescher and by the sudden good fortune of Braukmann, who unexpectedly finds a job; of how their resolve is strengthened, at a crucial moment, by an encounter with the bourgeoisie at its most crass and charmless; of how Braukmann's down-to-earth wife Louise, pregnant, exhausted by her job in a chip shop, and concerned about the security of her child's future, nonetheless feels compelled to join them in the end; and of how they make it through the last 179 kilometres, from the point where Shackleton gave up to the point where Amundsen succeeded.

The language – cleverly translated into English by Anthony Vivis, but performed with a strong Scottish accent that brings out its toughness and ironic force – is earthy and yet theatrical, touched with a dense, modern poetic strangeness, like a cross between Brecht, Steven Berkoff, and the Anthony Burgess of *Clockwork Orange*; the play itself strikes a most delicate balance between sheer absurdity and real human struggle. But all of this – the harshness and fantasy of the tone, the underlying political anger, the wild streak in the language – seems to come absolutely naturally to Unwin and his brilliantly chosen young company of Scottish actors, who seem to know more than enough about the experience of unemployment and alienation, and who move as one around the stage, ferociously committed and unified, beautifully choreographed to a backing of wild rock music, and led by Alan Cumming (as the ringleader Slupianek) and Carol Ann Crawford (as Louise) in a pair of performances so funny, so intelligent, and so at one with Karge's language, that they had the audience bursting into exuberant little spurts of applause between scenes.

What the play amounts to, in the end, is a fierce reassertion of the right of dispossessed people to take charge of their own inner world, as a first step to regaining some control of the outer one; of their right to imagine, to dream, to create and procreate, to define their own goals, not to be browbeaten into accepting lousy jobs and lousy definitions of themselves in order to survive. It also – and this is perhaps why it makes such exhilarating theatre – reaffirms the power of the imagination, of play-acting itself, to smash through the barriers erected by harsh economic realities, to draw people into the experience of those whose misery they do not share, and to allow those who are in despair access to the strength and confidence of the powerful and fortunate. And finally, it asserts something else: that it's from those dispossessed people, those who really need the power of imagination to transform and restore their lives, that theatre draws its best strength. Without them, and without writers like Karge who care for their experience and want to draw it into the circle of human understanding, theatre itself becomes weak; drained of the guts, the significance, the passion and the real human excitement that should, if there is any justice at all, make this *Conquest of the South Pole* one of the hottest tickets of the year, at the Edinburgh Festival, and beyond.

As You Like It
Royal Lyceum, Edinburgh
The Guardian, 1 November 1988

If there were any justice – and there isn't – then Hamish Glen's new production of *As You Like It* at the Royal Lyceum in Edinburgh would be enjoying the same kind of public attention and controversy as Simon Callow's Glaswegian version of *Die Fledermaus*, and for the same good reason: because it tries so strongly, so earnestly, and with such commitment – although with some undeniable cost to the original work – to make the piece matter in the context of Scotland now. The Callow *Fledermaus* looks from a slightly metropolitan angle at the revamping of Glasgow as a smart and trendy culture city; Glen's *As You Like It* throws itself headlong into a much older and wider question of Scottish identity and politics, exploiting the basic tension of Shakespeare's plot – between the corrupt, usurping and authoritarian 'new duke' in the city, and the wise, generous 'old duke' exiled in the forest – to explore ideas and myths about a Scottish vision of Arden, the kind of once-and-future 'free Scotland' that could just still exist, beyond the shifty anglicised façade of Scottish public life today.

What Glen and his designer Peter Ling have done is to weave a pattern of powerfully contrasting images around the

73

two settings of the play, at the court of the 'new duke', and in Arden. The first forty minutes – the scenes at court – are placed deliberately on the forestage of the theatre, in front of the Royal Lyceum's rich red-plush-and-gilt curtain, with the imperial crown above the proscenium picked out in spotlight, and with the courtiers gathering in the rococo blue-plaster boxes nearest the stage to mock at young Orlando as he challenges the duke's wrestler; in other words, with great wit and justice, Glen and Ling make the Lyceum itself play the role of the anglicised, city, establishment place where all the characters – except old Adam the servant – speak in rigorous BBC English, or in ugly attempts at it.

These scenes are divided from the rest of the play by Rosalind's epilogue, given here as a prologue, as if it marked the beginning of the true action; then the curtain hurtles up on something like Macbeth's blasted heath, a wild, cold, stony, bleak, but truthful place, a kind of mythical Rob Roy country of the Scottish soul, where the music is pipes and drums and wild recorded folk-rock, where Celtic symbols of sun and moon glow over the landscape, ancient standing stones loom protectively around the stage, all the characters speak in variants of Scots, and – this is where Glen's vision meshes with Shakespeare's – these men returned to honest poverty need at last 'fear nae enemy but winter, and rough weather.' It's not Arden as we generally think of it, that twittering English greenwood inhabited by pert RADA actresses with nice accents. But I suspect it has at least as much in common with Shakespeare's forest of harsh winter winds; and although there are those who find the sound of Shakespeare spoken in Scots self-evidently absurd, in fact it's quite obvious from the easy survival of his verse-rhythms, rhymes and assonances that the sound of Shakespearean English must have been as close to traditional Scots as to modern received pronunciation.

Of course, this bold attempt to wrest Shakespeare's most lovely and joyful marriage-comedy into the world of Scottish cultural politics comes to grief in the end, for all sorts of reasons. For one, Glen has not been able to push his analysis through into the personal and erotic implications of the cultural situation he pinpoints (although these certainly exist), and therefore hasn't achieved any fresh understanding of the play's dominant theme, which is heterosexual love in its most poignant springtime freshness; as a result, the production loses energy catastrophically in the long love scenes of the second half. But mainly it fails because it asks a little too much of Glen's company, some of whom are inexperienced in large-scale theatre, and all of whom are virtually having to translate Shakespeare into Scots as they go along. They find it easy to use their native speech for the humour and gruffness and pithiness that are its stereotyped qualities, less easy to give it its full range of beauty and lyricism; and some of the verse-speaking is therefore poor, rough and throwaway, to an extent that's likely to offend some of those who cherish the sound of the words.

But despite the desperate and sometimes ruinous cultural risks it takes – Sean Scanlan playing Jaques as a kind of cross between Nicholas Fairbairn and Oscar Wilde, miles over the top and yet strangely memorable – the production throws up a whole clutch of brave, convinced and convincing performances, from Paul Samson's quite excellent Orlando, through Siobhan Redmond's blithe and intelligent Rosalind, to Sandy Neilson's cleverly spoken account of the two dukes, keystones of the contrasting linguistic and cultural dispensations. No one could call this a wholly successful *As You Like It*: it takes huge chances, it falls flat on its face, it rides roughshod over one of the most sacred combes of English literature, and perhaps only a Scot could love it. But even at its worst, it's a dauntless, passionate and creative effort to put the modern Scottish soul back in touch with a great, exuberant play about power, and love, and the whole damn thing; and I think it deserves an audience.

1989

A Man at Yir Back
Dundee Rep
The Guardian, 22 January 1989

It's a paradox about our on-yer-bike society that the only relationships it really recognises – the rigid nuclear-family ones of husband to wife and young children to parents – are becoming increasingly rare. On one hand, every social-trends survey that's published shows a growing number of single-person households and single-parent families. On the other, the economic imperatives of the day – the demand for a perfectly mobile, flexible labour force – seem to class as dispensible all the relationships that make such a single life tolerable: by and large, 'sensible' people don't turn down jobs 400 miles away, or the chance of better housing in a different area, just because their old mum likes to have them nearby, or because a beloved brother or sister or niece or friend or auntie lives in the next street. Small wonder that our society is riddled with loneliness, with people whose lives have been made emotionally barren because the emotional contacts that meant most to them had no official status, and were shattered before anyone could articulate their importance.

It's this cultural catch-22, and the personal tragedy it implies, that seems to lie behind Gordon Burnside's first stage play *A Man at Yir Back*, which opens the spring season at Dundee Rep. The title refers to the notion that life is better for a woman if she has a man behind her, a husband to support her; the play, a piece of unabashedly popular drama packed with references to local Dundee history, with old Dundee songs and old-fashioned Dundee talk, faces the melancholy fact that for generations of women in a town where the industries mainly employed female labour, a good man with a good pay packet has nonetheless been hard to find – and that now, with the old supportive communities scattered to the winds, a happy marriage is rarer and more desirable than ever.

The centrepiece of the play is an encounter between the indomitable Dolly – a poverty-stricken but feisty Dundee pensioner with a foul mouth, a wicked wit, and the proverbial heart of gold, desperately clinging to the shadow of her happy marriage to Tommy – and her social worker, a sweet middle-class girl called Dorothy who has just been given the elbow by her married lover. Both women are more frightened than they dare admit by the prospect of a lonely life ('Oh dear me, what will I do, if I die an old maid in a garret?' keens a passing neighbour, from a famous Dundee folk song), and yet neither seems able to recognise and defend the other aspects of her life that would compensate for the absence of a man. Dolly's only daughter – herself a single parent – is about to take up a job in Bristol, a fact which Dolly accepts without protest; her widowed neighbour Mina, her only regular visitor apart from the postman, is about to move into sheltered housing several miles away, apparently unaware – like Dolly herself – of the pain the separation will involve.

Burnside's play is not a complex, highly wrought piece of drama, and it often seems to come across these big themes by accident, rather than thinking them through, and building itself around them. The style is naturalistic and observational, decorated only by the occasional over-elaborate fugue of Dundee history and patter. Given this oblique, gentle approach to the play's central concerns, it's perhaps not surprising that its structure is a shade problematic, with the second act drifting too quietly towards an abrupt crisis, or that the character of Dolly is seriously underwritten; Burnside clearly prefers creating pithy patter for Dolly and Mina, and he indulges that preference too much.

But a writer who observes clearly, strongly and passionately enough to touch such a deep nerve of pain in our common experience with so little artifice clearly has a tremendous dramatic gift, and one worth developing. For my taste, *A Man at Yir Back* is a little too long and a little too couthy, its Dundee character sometimes laid on superficially with a trowel, rather than allowed to speak for itself, in the way that reaches universal truths through unadorned local ones. But with the help of Irene Sunters' magnificent bravura performance as Dolly – brave as a lion in the face of the old familiar horrors of life, but frightened in the face of new ones she can hardly name – and of Monika Nisbet's acutely observed domestic set, not comfortless but somehow bleak, the play emerges as a moving and quietly disturbing experience; a love story, a tribute to an old working-class city that no longer quite exists, but also a sad reflection on a money-grubbing, emotionally illiterate society, that has barely begun to understand the subtle damage it inflicts on itself, and whose fundamental heartlessness the battered mechanisms of the welfare state can hardly conceal.

The Guid Sisters
Tron, Glasgow
The Guardian, 3 May 1989

It's one of the myths of our civilisation that, whereas middle-class culture is international and universal, working-class culture is somehow local and parochial, a matter of 'Cockney slang' or 'Glasgow humour'. It's a comforting idea, in that it reduces the common experience of the millions of human beings who were drawn into the cities in the industrial age – their courage, their humour, their resilience in the face of unrelenting poverty and drastic overcrowding – to a matter of 'local character'; it makes a private civic joke of an experience that was, in fact, central to the development of industrial capitalism everywhere from Chicago to Kraków.

One of Mayfest's most striking achievements, as a festival dedicated to presenting the best of Scottish 'popular' theatre alongside similar work from Europe and overseas, has been the consistency with which it has blasted that myth that the Glasgow experience is somehow unique, idiosyncratic. And now, in that tradition, the Tron Theatre's Mayfest production of Michel Tremblay's *Les Belles-sœurs* – a play born in the turbulent Québec of the 1960s, and now translated into a pithy, fierce, foul-mouthed urban Scots by Bill Findlay and Martin Bowman – offers us a portrait of a bunch of worn-out housewives in a Montréal tenement that matches the experience of generations of Glasgow women in almost uncanny detail.

The play is a merciless black comedy, set in 1965, about a woman called Germaine Lauzon, who has just won in a competition no less than a million Green Shield stamps, all of which have to be stuck into books before she can cash them in for lorryloads of consumer goods. The theme – likewise familiar from previous Mayfest hits like Tony Roper's *The Steamie* – is the great tide of materialism and prosperity that began to sweep through working-class communities in the 1950s and '60s, eroding the automatic solidarity that came with intense poverty, driving wedges of ambition and greed between neighbours who were once 'all in the same boat'; the plot is beautifully structured around the slow, explosive build-up of envy and spleen among the neighbours, friends and family – fourteen in all – that Germaine invites to her stamp-sticking party.

Just as the Tremblay dialogue – written in the once-despised *joual* dialect of Québec – translates into urban Scots as though the two languages were long-lost twins, so the lives the women describe could hardly be more familiar to Glasgow audiences. There's the humour, the stoicism, the astonishing lung-power and verbal forcefulness of mothers who were always yelling to their weans out of fourth-storey windows; there are the strong ethnic loyalties and religious pieties, the snobbery about language and education, the sexual repressiveness that goes with fear, ignorance and endless childbearing, the joyless distrust of fun and pleasure that is as strong in Jansenist Catholicism as it is in Scottish Presbyterianism.

But although the Tron's director Michael Boyd has assembled a dazzlingly talented company of fifteen Scottish actresses for this production – led by the inimitable Una McLean as Germaine – it seems to me that the cast hasn't quite, yet, got the measure of Tremblay's intense social realism, of the extent to which his tragicomedy is rooted in the everyday experience of real women who might be the cast's own mothers, aunties and grannies. Tremblay's theatrical style in this play is complex, starting from a sympathetic bedrock of naturalistic observation, and then working up – through sheer intensity of feeling – into a series of stylised monologues and choral outbursts; the problem with Boyd's production, as it stands, is that it seems to approach the play the other way round, throwing a battery of fancy and alienating theatrical devices at the text – grotesque costumes and gestures for the actresses, exaggerated spotlighting for the monologues, melodramatic background music, complex choreography – and then leaving the cast to fight their way back towards the sense of recognisable character that should underpin the theatrical effects.

Some have already found their way; I particularly liked Ann Louise Ross's understated, deeply felt performance as the elder sister Gabrielle, and Gaylie Runciman as Yvette, a vague and washed-out little housewife whose rambling guest list for a family party won the biggest laugh of the night. But the rest of the cast look tense, nervy, a shade unreal and overemphatic, as if they were too busy getting into the right place at the right time, and sustaining their exotic 'style', to relax into Tremblay's magnificent dialogue, and to give their full attention to the story the characters are trying to tell. The production has the strengths to match its weaknesses: it's bold, harsh, ugly, theatrically exciting, in no danger of sliding into the lazy naturalism and rose-coloured nostalgia that too often infects plays about old working-class communities. But now that that unsentimental stance is established, I think it's time to lower the pitch, to relax the texture of the production a little. If the audience is to sense the full depth of the play, and the significance, for Scotland now, of what Tremblay is doing in using the public reassertion of a despised language as the key to a recovery of self-knowledge and power amongst people almost ground down by poverty and hard work, then they must feel the real human tragedy that underlies the farce.

Macbeth
Inchcolm Island, Firth of Forth
The Guardian, 15 August 1989

Richard Demarco, Edinburgh gallery owner and arts entre-preneur extraordinary, is one of those people who attracts high melodrama whatever he does; and his grand venture for the Edinburgh Festival of 1989 has run absolutely true to form. First there was the brilliant idea, hatched up last year between Demarco and the Sicilian theatre company Zattera di Babele, to stage *Macbeth* on the island of Inch-colm, a tiny, dramatic remnant of medieval Scotland – rocks, rough heathland, a ruined abbey, melancholy beaches, wheeling seabirds – in the middle of the Firth of Forth, in clear sight of the city of Edinburgh to the south, and the green fields of Fife to the north. Frank Dunlop bought the idea for his official Edinburgh Festival programme, and everything seemed set fair.

Then there was the disaster when, with barely two weeks to spare, the Sicilians disappeared into a *casa di cura* and can-celled their production. Demarco, determined not to fail, started pulling together a scratch company of Scottish actors under John Bett to create a substitute production. But the Edinburgh Festival withdrew its blessing, its tickets, and – most importantly – the box-office income it had already taken for the event, leaving Demarco (so he felt) with no alternative but to start selling his own tickets for the new production fast; 'otherwise we would have had NO INCOME for the show, do you understand?' he explains, at the pitch of his small but powerful lungs.

Then there was the inevitable cock-up, when at least thirty ticket-holders for the original Edinburgh Festival event – most of them from overseas, and blissfully unaware of the cancellation – turned up at Hawes Pier in South Queens-ferry (home of the *Maid of the Forth*, which plies to and from Inchcolm) to find their bookings no longer valid, and the *Maid* about to set sail without them; some occupied the gangplank, and two placid Queensferry policemen had to intervene. Finally, there were the elements, the lowering deep-grey sky over the firth, the driving rain, the wind that whipped Demarco's standard-issue grey-wool blankets (essential for theatregoing in the Firth of Forth) around the bodies of the audience on the decks, and into which, as we finally drew away from the quay, the abandoned thirty shouted transatlantic and Sicilian curses at Demarco's small retreating form.

And then, of course, there was the small miracle by which, as soon as we set sail towards the island, none of this seemed to matter. The rain drove, the wind blustered, the witches heaved up from the bowels of the ship as if they had risen from the water itself, to screech and whirl across the decks with their knowledge of evil and doom in the offing; never in my life will I forget the sound of the words 'Though his bark shall not be lost | Yet it shall be tempest-toss'd!' snatched from the mouth of the chief witch by the wind and echoing away across the steel-grey waves. The production we saw, when we finally reached the island, was a rough-and-ready affair, particularly in the fine detail of the performance; and savagely cut back (no banquet scene, no second visit to the witches) to compensate for the time we lost haggling on the quay.

But as a piece of staging it is a triumph, a succession of completely memorable images: dark figures drawn up in battle lines under a banner on the island's skyline as the boat approached; two warriors battling and stumbling in the sand; the actors standing out like statues, symbols, 'walking shadows' against the ruins of the abbey, as we walked towards them across the deep natural amphitheatre of the island. Then the deep rumble of Gaelic laments, delivered by the black-robed figure of poet Aonghas MacNeacail, that seem to merge into this little shred of Scottish landscape as though they had been carved from the same stuff; the dank abbey courtyard where the knocking at the gate echoes like the clap of doom; and the lamp-lit peace of the upper room – hard won from the elements in a thick vault of stone – in which Lady Macbeth walks behind her flickering candle, and Lady Macduff is murdered. And always, the sound of wind, the feel of rough, damp wool against the body.

There were some fine performances, particularly from the women in the cast: Ann Louise Ross, Grace Glover and Kate Gartside as the witches, Gerda Stevenson's Lady Macbeth, Sarah Collier's exquisite Lady Macduff. But what mattered was the sense of closeness to the idea, the landscape, of medieval Scotland that fired Shakespeare's imagination, and gave us this most wild and chilling of verse dramas. See *Macbeth* on Inchcolm – the wind whipping, the gulls screeching, the old capital across the stormy firth climbing grey and smoky towards its skyline – and you'll never want to see it anywhere else; as for Richard Demarco, *bandito* of the arts, he's a man who gives us immeasurably more than he takes.

The Crucible
Assembly Rooms, Edinburgh
The Guardian, 31 August 1989

The Moscow Art Theatre School's production of *The Crucible* thundered into the Assembly Rooms this week on a wave of erotic energy powerful enough to shatter a few comfortable assumptions, both about the play itself, and about the way we use – or fail to use – sex in the theatre. The British actor Brian Cox, who directed the show as part of a cultural exchange between Britain and Russia, had hoped that the production might illuminate some spiritual parallels between Soviet oppression under Stalinism, and the American experience of McCarthyite anti-communism, which inspired Arthur Miller to write the play; but in the end nothing so cerebral emerges from this young, passionate reading of it.

What we get instead, in Vladimir Mashkov's extraordinary performance as John Proctor, is a portrait of a sensual man trapped among the buttoned-up Puritans of seventeenth-century Salem, a man more relaxed in his body and in touch with himself than either his neighbours, or his virtuous wife Elizabeth, played with great dignity and feeling by Marina Kolesnichenko. His sensuality betrays him in his relationship with the cold-eyed Abigail, portrayed here by Irina Apeksimova as a smouldering teenage nymphet with a torrent of dark hair; there's a clear hint that his sexy, flirtatious manner towards Abigail and her friends may have contributed to their hysteria. But as the action unfolds it becomes clear that Proctor's sensuality, his earthiness, his unwillingness to suppress his physicality, is somehow linked to his inability, when the crunch comes, to deny what he knows to be true, and to compromise his sense of wholeness and identity by putting his name to the false confession that would save his life.

In many ways, Cox's production – briskly staged against a simple, shifting set of panels that suggest the plain wooden buildings and cabins of New England – is a rough affair: it dispenses with many of the spiritual and political subtleties of the play, the age range of the Salem community is cruelly compressed to match the youth of the actors, and some of the body language and mannerisms are blatantly anachronistic. But it is brilliantly clear in its grasp of the basic conflict between those characters who have somehow remained in touch with themselves – Proctor, Giles Corey, the sensuous motherly figure of Rebecca Nurse, and, in the end, Elizabeth Proctor – and those who have learned, in repressing vital aspects of their own personality, how to deny and ignore other truths that are staring them in the face. In Mashkov's magnificent bringing-together of the upfront, heroic, sensual tradition of Russian acting, and the inward, probing, reflective style of the classic English stage, Proctor's sexuality finally becomes not a 'fault' to be expiated by a last virtuous gesture, but a vital aspect of the kind of personality that can remain complete, and true to itself, in the face of authoritarian pressure; and for this white-hot illumination of the link between sexual and political honesty, so often half-articulated in Miller's work, we can only be grateful.

Volpone
Royal Lyceum, Edinburgh
The Guardian, 9 September 1989

I can't say that I approached the opening production of the Royal Lyceum's autumn season with any great sense of excitement. Three and a quarter hours, I thought, of a comedy gone dusty with age; the last time I read Ben Jonson's *Volpone*, in the late 1970s, it seemed to me a difficult and distant piece, too fierce and relentless in its satire on greed to be entirely dramatic, and – for all the brilliance of the writing – cluttered with commercial period detail of the most obscure kind.

Which only goes to show that a fine company of actors, thinking on their feet and feeling their way into a text, can always tell us more about a great play than we thought we knew. Because ten years on, after a decade of officially sanctioned greed in which looking after number one has been elevated to an article of economic faith, Jonson's great satire emerges from Hugh Hodgart's gorgeous and powerful production as a perfect play for today, its fierce sketches of blind money-lust and desperate enterprise drawn fresh from life, its endless 'tricks' and 'devices' and money-making projects a perfect mirror image of the scams and schemes that feature so heavily in the drama of the late 1980s. In a powerful programme note, Stephanie Dimond points out that Jonson was concerned, primarily, with 'amorality and the thrust of capitalism', and so he was: like the gruntings of a 1980s academic writing irascible letters to the *New Statesman* about the lost world of the 1960s, his poems are full of laments at London's recent big-bang development into a teeming commercial capital in which cash is the only currency of human exchange, and of nostalgia for the old paternalistic social structure of the well-run country estate.

But what is striking, in this production, is how quickly the play's theoretical relevance to contemporary Britain pays off, in practical, theatrical terms. From the first moment of the action, when Dudley Sutton as the avaricious old fox Volpone sits up in bed demanding to begin the day with a greeting to his 'saint', and a tattered red backcloth falls away to reveal a wall glittering, shrine-like, with encrusted gold plate and ornaments (which later doubles most effectively, in a different light, for a whole series of elaborate Venetian frontages), the audience seems to grasp the play's central point, its satirical stance, perfectly and completely. And from that moment on, despite the essentially static nature of Jonson's characterisation, and his heavy dependence on sheer wit and poetry to sustain the interest of the piece, they follow the twists and turns of his plot – the teasing and milking of the three hopeful inheritors by Volpone and his parasite Mosca, the outbreak of lust over the fair Celia, and the ludicrous subplot involving the moneymaking schemes of the English twit Sir Politic Would-Be – with a kind of rapt attention, as though Jonson was offering them some new, subversive and hugely entertaining insight into the way we live now.

And what's doubly impressive about this powerful sense of communication and of relevance is that it's achieved not by any obvious directorial manipulation – the play is set firmly, as Jonson demanded, in seventeenth-century Venice, and Gregory Smith's sets, while gorgeous and witty in their faded plush-and-gold evocations of opulent parsimony, are stereo-typically Venetian, in a Losey's-Don-Giovanni-gone-overripe kind of way – but rather by the actors themselves, approach-ing the text with a kind of brilliant enjoyment, a sharpness of understanding, and a creative freedom and energy in rein-terpreting Jonson's dialogue, that makes every word of the text stand out like a jewel, sparkling with meaning and wit. Paul Spence's Mosca, in particular, is a simply dazzling achievement, holding the frenetic action together on a steely thread of intelligence, athleticism, comic invention, audience rapport and sheer wicked wit; Dudley Sutton's Volpone is likewise tremendously impressive and enjoyable, vigorous, clever, savagely humorous at others' expense, and yet lyrical and beautiful of voice, perfectly capturing the sensual streak in *Volpone*'s character and in Jonson's rich poetry.

But in the end, this *Volpone* could not work so well, achieve such a sense of substance and richness, if their empathy with the text was not shared by the whole of Hugh Hodgart's fifteen-strong company, almost all of whom turn in extraordinarily strong and well-focused performances. For Jonson in this play shares not only our disgust at the rank materialism and gold-lust he portrays, but also our horrified fascination with it; like some of the satirists of the 1980s – David Hare and Howard Brenton, say, in *Pravda* – he is half-seduced by the savage logic of the marketplace, half in love with the glamorous evil and amoral ingenuity of his characters. Like those of us who oppose Thatcherism now, he hates the commercial jungle that has grown up before his eyes, and within which his animal characters – carrion birds and parasites – operate; and yet, like us, he finds it hard to resist its logic, or to envisage an alternative.

Ben Jonson is a playwright who has endured a long exile from the affection of British audiences, even when we are compelled to admire his skill and his brilliance. But we live in strange, alienating times; and with this lush, intelligent, brutal, and not-quite-English production we seem to be entering at last into the kind of intellectual and moral comradeship with Jonson's big, dissident mind that his plays always craved. So perhaps, after centuries of cold respect and odious comparisons, the time has come when we can begin to love him as he deserves, for his toughness, his courage in dissent, and his fine, surly, humorous disgust at the spectacle of what men and women can become, when the flow of cash and capital is the only measure of worth they recognise, and the fragile social fabric of duty and mutual obligation finally breaks down.

Othello
Royal Lyceum, Edinburgh
The Guardian, 30 October 1989

Of all Shakespeare's plays, *Othello* is the one that seems to have escaped the kind of modern reinterpretation that angers Shakespeare purists. There have been Freudian *Hamlets*, Marxist *Twelfth Nights* and feminist *Tempests*; but *Othello* seems to stand apart, a story of love and death so timelessly simple – man meets woman, man weds woman, evil genius plants suspicion in man's mind, man slays woman in jealous rage – that radical rethinking seems unnecessary. As long as the play is acted out competently, and with reasonable sensitivity to the language, the force of Shakespeare's storytelling will ensure that the audience responds on a soap-operatic level; so that the sheer technical mastery with which it spins its tragic yarn often becomes a theatrical smokescreen, behind which actors and directors can conceal a terrible vagueness about why the play still matters, and whether it does anything more than restate, like a rather classy episode of *Dallas*, the banal thought that jealousy is a terrible thing.

Ian Wooldridge's new *Othello* at the Royal Lyceum in Edinburgh is a production of exactly this kind. It is handsome, tasteful, well-paced and competently acted; it keeps a reasonable grip on the audience's attention by telling a strong story clearly and without fuss. Gregory Smith has designed a commendably restrained and uncluttered set, in which Venice is represented by a heavy thicket of black drapes lit by smoky flames from a hanging brass brazier, and Cyprus by a huge white-stone fortification, gleaming in sunny light, and topped (symbolically) by the shattered head of some great classical statue.

And within the space he creates, bright young actors come and go, each one apparently locked in a lonely effort to make something of his or her part. Gerda Stevenson's Desdemona is sweet, determined, intelligent, dignified and eloquent; Paul Spence – as the loyal and wronged lieutenant Cassio – lays bare the meaning and poetry of his lines with a wonderful clarity; and in the absence of the kind of dramatic context that might begin to explain the sheer force of evil in Iago's personality, Bill Leadbitter works away powerfully on his obvious vices of envy and racial hatred. But all of them, in the end, come up against the handsome blank that is Burt Caesar's Othello – holding the character's great love and great agony firmly at arm's length, as though it was all too messy to take seriously – and against the sheer artistic deadness of a production that, like so many *Othello*s, seems to have no motive beyond getting through the story in a dignified and professional manner.

Which is a pity; because the more I look at *Othello*, the more it seems like one of the most profound plays about sexual politics ever written, a play in which the glorious and ful-filling life force represented by Othello and Desdemona's sexual love is destroyed, inch by inch, by those deathly macho forces in Judaeo-Christian culture – much better understood now than a generation ago – that depend for their survival on the failure of sexual happiness, on frustra-tion, anger, and the perversion of creativity. Iago is one of those sick military misogynists – significantly estranged from his own wife Emilia – who is happiest among gangs of other men, drinking, putting the boot in, insulting women and using them without love; what enrages him is Othello's defection from those values, and he cannot rest until he has destroyed his life-affirming love and dragged it down. It's because this titanic battle between love and death is the true centre of the play that the final scene, in which Emilia finally abandons her embittered allegiance to Iago to roar out her knowledge of Othello and Desdemona's true love, is always enthralling; and why the actress who plays Emilia – in this case the gentle Ann Louise Ross, in superb form – so often emerges as the true heroine of the play.

At times, in Edinburgh, the audience almost seem to be tak-ing up this powerful contemporary theme of their own accord, pushing the production towards it; when they see Iago deliberately taunting Cassio into drunkenness, for example, they recognise his evil kind of machismo as some-thing absolutely alive in their world. But this fragmented *Othello* has no means of building on their response; and although individual performers do what they can, a produc-tion that so lacks a central drive – call it heart, guts, intellectual passion or what you will – inevitably amounts to less than the sum of its parts.

And so it was just a few weeks after the fall of the Berlin Wall, and the epoch-making changes it signalled, that Glasgow began its year as European City of Culture. There was a huge pulse of international connection in the year's theatre work, both in Glasgow and elsewhere. The major theme of the year, though – international in its reach, but drawn straight from the heart of Glasgow's recent history – was the story of the death of heavy industry, and of the struggle of a great industrial city to find a new and viable identity; and the new performance spaces opened up by Glasgow 1990 – The Arches under Central Station, Tramway, the Harland and Wolff engine shed at Govan where Bill Bryden staged his huge spectacle The Ship, *and the St Rollox Railway Works in Springburn – spoke volumes about that history, and the scars it had left behind. 1990 brought many other significant events in Scottish theatre, of course. It was, for example, the year that saw the first appearance, in a cluster of tents in Inverleith Park, of Edinburgh's Scottish International Children's Festival, which went on – under the inspired leadership of Tony Reekie – to become one of the world's leading children's theatre festivals, eventually changing its name to Imaginate, and helping to inspire a generation of fine new Scottish work in theatre for children, from companies like Catherine Wheels and Wee Stories. Yet it was the dramatic story of Glasgow, its history and rebirth, that caught imaginations far beyond Scotland, in 1990; and overall, this was a year when it was a true privilege to be a theatre critic and arts journalist, watching a great city, and a nation, wrestle with its own story, find its international resonances, form new friendships and alliances, and begin to move forward, into a different kind of future.*

1990

Jock Tamson's Bairns
Tramway, Glasgow
The Guardian, 28 January 1990

Is it easy to be Scottish, at the moment? Not particularly; not with the unacceptable face of nationalism bursting into prominence all over the decaying Soviet Empire, and posing the most sharp and uncomfortable questions about the precise nature of the movement towards national self-determination and self-confidence that has been preoccupying Scottish artists, in one way and another, these last fifteen years.

Communicado's *Jock Tamson's Bairns* – created by the award-winning team of writer Liz Lochhead and director Gerry Mulgrew, and presented at the Tramway Theatre as the theatrical opening shot of Glasgow's 1990 celebrations – was committed from the outset to an exploration of Scotland and the Scottish psyche. Its title comes from an old Scottish saying – 'We're all Jock Tamson's Bairns' (i.e. 'whatever our pretensions, we were all conceived in the same inelegant way') – which is meant to exemplify the sturdy egalitarianism of the Scottish temperament. It opened on Burns Night, the birthday of Robert Burns, the nearest thing Scotland has to a popular national feast; and it was designed, from the start, to take the celebratory form of a Burns Supper.

Under the circumstances, it was hard not to fear that the show would fall victim to the temptations either of nationalist schmaltz or – more likely, given Lochhead and Mulgrew's track-record as iconoclasts – a kind of ugly, reductive self-flagellation. That it succeeds in avoiding both pitfalls, and emerges as a tough, clever, funny, fast-moving and completely absorbing two-hour journey through the lower depths of Scottish culture, is a tremendous tribute not only to the skills of the brilliant thirty-strong company Mulgrew has assembled, but also to something deeper, a kind of clear, hard-won personal understanding of what can and can't be said about their fractious homeland, that seems to shape and strengthen the work of every artist involved.

It has to be said, of course, that the picture the show presents of Scotland is far from pretty. It begins with a burial, acted out on a rough, rain-drenched pile of boulders in the Tramway's barn-like outer hall; as the coffin is laid in the earth, the cast sing, with utter seriousness, the great *Flyting* (dispute) of life and death by the contemporary poet Hamish Henderson, as if to emphasise the underlying intensity of the struggle between destructive and positive forces in the nation's life.

The dead man – a hopeless drunk, played with a wonderful, baffled, slack-limbed lyricism by the dancer Frank McConnell – descends into hell, and the audience moves into the main auditorium; and there we encounter the Bairns, a hollow-eyed, scrappily dressed, but completely undaunted underworld rabble of tattered Scottish types – the bleating old granny full of fatalistic sayings, the whining wean, the overpowering mammy stuffing food and patent medicines into the protesting child, the coalminer granddad muttering about how 'Burns was the first communist, and don't you let them tell you any different, son.' Basted, piped in, orated over and then slashed open like the archetypal haggis, the poor drunk sees his lurid tartan entrails pulled out, mulled over and used as the raw materials for a nightmare rerun of his unattractive life, featuring grunting alienation in the parental home, regimentation at school, loveless teenage sex. There's a brief flirtation with 'A Man's a Man for A' That' nationalism – brilliantly metamorphosed, in a brilliant one-minute sequence, into an abject vulnerability to the fortunes of the Scottish football team – and then a great deal of drink.

Finally, through a strangely interrupted retelling of the narrative poem *Tam o'Shanter*, the show almost collapses under the weight of the questions it has raised, and moves into a searing but perhaps slightly overstated criticism of the failure of open, fulfilling contact between male and female that Lochhead feels is at the heart of the Scottish malaise; at the end, the cast gather and pass round a bowl in a grim parody of the Last Supper, like a bunch of exhausted disciples hardly daring to hope for redemption.

So much for the ugliness of the story the show tells; but the process of telling is shot through with so much humour and brilliance that the effect is anything but depressing. Communicado is dedicated to the idea of collaboration among all the theatrical art forms, and in this show – which runs for two hours with hardly a weakness in the pace and fluidity of the staging – Mulgrew has excelled himself, over a ten-week rehearsal period, in forcing what could have been a shapeless collage of dance, music, song, text and visual imagery into a powerful impressionistic coherence.

Liz Lochhead's text – deliberately spare and fragmented, designed to complement and enrich the action rather than shape it – is central to the mood of the piece; on the one hand, its ironic and self-critical tone is relentless, shattering what's left of Scots language into parodic fragments, mercilessly sending up the clichés and cant of traditional Scottish speech; on the other, it takes these fragments and blends them into a mosaic of such wit and colour that it affirms the possibilities of the language, and the people who speak it, more positively than any reverent reconstruction. Then there's the music by Karen Wimhurst, which takes a few traditional Scottish cadences, and drives them through a strange instrumental ensemble – saxophone, piano, cello, violin – to create a truly superb score which propels the action relentlessly forward. And Wimhurst's original music is counterpointed, always and everywhere, by the sheer limpid beauty of Burns' own songs, as sung by Rod Paterson and Christine Kydd; even at the heart of this cheeky nightmare vision, there's no attempt to gainsay the sheer miracle that produced this pure strand of erotic freedom and lyrical loveliness from the hard, rocky soil of Ayrshire.

But in the end, the strength of *Jock Tamson's Bairns* lies in the performances: the company contains the very best young Scottish actors of the under-forty generation, and they throw every scrap of their individual experience and wisdom and cultural integrity into creating a choric presence of extraordinary vividness, detail, clarity and strength. What the Bairns say to us is yes, the Scottish psyche is a mess, in this, this and this specific way; but so long as we have the guts to look the mess straight in the eye, to tell it like it is with humour and elegance and skill and panache, then there's every reason for hope, and no excuse for despair. The detail of this show is undeniably for Scots, and perhaps – interestingly, given its status in the 1990 programme – more for Scots than for Glaswegians, who have their own special cultural history. But its mood, its tone, its exhilarating mixture of powerful theatrical confidence and merciless self-criticism, pushes it to the centre of the debate about small-nation politics in the 1990s, and about the role the arts can play in enriching and humanising those politics. I hope it finds the audience it deserves, both in Glasgow, and across Europe.

The Sailmaker
Tron, Glasgow
The Guardian, 7 February 1990

Alan Spence's *The Sailmaker* began, ten years ago, as a lyrical, perfect short story about a bright working-class boy growing up in the tenement streets of Govan in the 1960s. Its mood is gentle and elegiac; and when it was first made into a play, at the Traverse in 1982, I remember being irritated both by the self-consciously poetical quality of the writing, which seemed desperately untheatrical, and, more importantly, by the self-righteous and self-pitying quality of performance it seemed to provoke in its all-male Scottish cast. In essence, *The Sailmaker* is about the death of an era of skilled manual labour on the Clyde. But true to its short-story origins, it approaches the theme not head-on and dramatically, but by a slow, exquisite build-up of detail, the purpose of which only emerges clearly in the last half-hour of a ninety-minute show. Eight years ago, I remember an impression of four actors groping their way through a mass of material which they knew had a powerful and sad significance, without a clear sense of where they were going; and the result was more sentimental or nostalgic than tragic.

But in those eight years, while Spence's story has remained like a still, clear point of remembered experience, the city itself has moved round to a completely different vantage-point. These have been the years of Mayfest and Glasgow's Miles Better, of the born-again civic image and massive post-industrial art works like George Wyllie's *Straw Locomotive* and *Paper Boat*. The city's consciousness of itself, and of the significance of its industrial history, has undergone a radical transformation, so that the cast of Alan Lyddiard's new TAG production of *The Sailmaker* – now playing at the Tron Theatre before going on tour – are able to approach the text with a much stronger sense of its meaning beyond the personal and pathetic, and therefore with an artistic maturity and discipline that makes sentimentality impossible.

The story – which begins with the death of the wife/mother who held the home together – revolves around the relationship between Alec and his father Davie. Once a skilled sailmaker, Davie still keeps his handmade canvas toolbag and all his tools in the house. But when we first meet him, he's working as a door-to-door collector for a hire-purchase company; and by the end, he has become one of the long-term unemployed. Meanwhile Alec climbs the ladder of success at school, passing his 11-plus, drifting away from his scuffling, football-kicking friends in the street, moving into a world of academic information that seems absolutely divorced from the real experience of his father's life in Govan. On the brink of university, he becomes plagued by a feeling that he's 'lost something', and begins to make links between some of the 'facts' he's learned ('Glasgow made the Clyde, and the Clyde made Glasgow') and the meaning of his father's life; but by then, Davie's loss of identity and self-respect has become so complete that he and Alec see nothing wrong, one cold night, in burning every 'spare' piece of wood in the house, including his wife's favourite chair, his sailmaking tools, and an old toy yacht of great symbolic significance.

The Sailmaker is not a perfect play. Its development is still dangerously slow, and it still allows audiences to slide too often into a cosy, nostalgic response to its period detail, particularly its affectionate, soft-centred recreation of Protestant bigotry in the back streets. But in Alan Lyddiard's vigorously paced but emotionally spacious production – lifted and energised by a beautiful, unobtrusive musical score from Gordon Dougall, who also plays Alec's cheerfully bigoted Uncle Billy – the detailed sensitivity and strength of Spence's writing compensates for any structural weakness. Paul Hickey and Andrew Barr play beautifully together as Alec and Davie, Hickey in particular turning in a memorably intelligent and disciplined performance; and although Spence has no solution to offer to the tragedy of the Clydeside worker – to the fate of a whole class, born in the industrial revolution, that has lost its work, its *raison d'être*, its outlet for creativity, its pride – his play burns in the mind like a bright, true gem made from that experience, sad but beautiful, and making beauty out of the sadness.

Brus
Tron, Glasgow
The Guardian, 1 March 1990

In the week when the Nicaraguan people decided that the struggle for independence from the US sphere of influence was no longer worth the candle, George Byatt's *Brus* – playing at the Tron Theatre in Glasgow for a short season – could hardly be more relevant. In essence, it's a long dramatic poem about Scotland's successful war of independence against the English in the late thirteenth and early fourteenth century; and it debates the key questions about such a struggle – whether the working-up of hatred along national lines can be right, however just the cause, and whether the natural yearning for dignity and self-determination can ever be worth such terrible bloodshed – in a formidable, impressive, and occasionally electrifying text, which mixes Scots and English, verse and prose, to powerful effect. As many people died on the field of Bannockburn on one day – 23 June 1314 – as in the whole Nicaraguan-Contra war; Byatt makes you feel the pride and horror of such a victory in your guts.

Byatt's company – known as Theatre PKF, or Peace Keeping Force – also specialises in a kind of simple, Brechtian, workshop-style theatre of which we don't see enough. The actors wear modern clothes, the set consists of a few simple wooden poles, there's no attempt at naturalistic casting: Brus is played here by a strange young girl with straight blonde hair, a flying jacket, a pronounced lisp, and a curiously commanding stare. Most importantly, the atmosphere is easygoing and discursive, without that heavy pall of politeness, reverence and sheer social pretension that hangs between stage and audience in most British theatres. PKF are a company with something important and topical to say, and a challenging way of saying it; and for the first five minutes of their opening performance at the Tron, I felt we might be on the threshold of one of those brilliant theatrical occasions when performers literally startle an audience into a real intellectual and emotional engagement with what's happening on stage.

But having created that chance for themselves, it has to be said that PKF largely blow it, through a combination of sloppy casting, under-rehearsed performance, and sheer indulgence in the face of Byatt's powerful but overwritten script. For the point about this kind of 'poor theatre' is that it demands more, not less, of performers. In particular, the absence of naturalistic movement and strong visual images places a tremendous emphasis on the strength, colour, expressiveness and control of the actors' voices, on which they have to depend to create character, to set scenes, to reflect the subtle political alternations of Scots and English in the script, and to generate clear variations of pace and dynamism, between battle scenes and laments, naturalistic sequences and highly stylised soliloquies. The harsh truth about Byatt's company – which includes the well-known Scottish blues singer and actress Terry Neason, as well as two or three complete unknowns – is that exactly four of them have that kind of vocal skill and capacity, and three of them do not. The performance is therefore dogged with recurrent problems of inaudibility, sagging pace, and sheer narrative confusion; and the result is a three-hour-and-ten-minute endurance test – not counting the post-performance discussion – which only rarely achieves the kind of intensity, pace and precision this script needs.

There are two good things to be said about all this. The first is that this production is bound to improve in the course of the run, as the actors become more confident in performance, and better able to take the script by the scruff of the neck. The second is that even in the middle of such terrible, inconsiderate, bum-aching boredom, the power and relevance of the theme and the writing keep cutting through indifference and hostility, picking up echo after echo of modern self-determination struggles from South Africa to the Baltic. It's therefore exasperating beyond words to see Theatre PKF make such heavy weather of material with such potential. For showing us the best of radical theatre – conviction, courage, a willingness to stand unadorned before an audience and tell the story like it is – they deserve support and love; for their lack of discipline in achieving an effective standard of performance, and their plain indulgence towards a fine but unwieldy script, they deserve – if they'll excuse such a belligerent thought – a belt round the ear.

Look Back in Anger
Royal Lyceum, Edinburgh
The Guardian, 12 March 1990

It was Kenneth Tynan who boldly wrote, after the first night of *Look Back in Anger* in 1956, that John Osborne's explosion of rage against the stifling social atmosphere of the time was 'the best young play of its decade'. History has tended to raise an eyebrow at Tynan for rushing to judgement when the fifties still had four years to run. But I doubt whether any other work from that strange decade of jazz, repression and rampant domesticity could storm on to the stage at the Royal Lyceum and hold it, for three hours, with the kind of energy and authority that radiates from Osborne's text in this compelling production by Ian Wooldridge. *Look Back in Anger* never was a likeable play, but the years have done nothing to diminish its dramatic force, or the classical strength of its three-act structure; and Wooldridge's production – built around an electrifying performance from Phil Smeeton as Jimmy Porter, Osborne's working-class graduate anti-hero – offers some absorbing insights into why the play has worn so well.

Of course *Look Back in Anger* is to some extent a period piece, locked into the peculiar social structure of post-war Britain. Osborne seems, for example, to attach considerable importance to the Church, as a symbol of reactionary and repressive attitudes. Today that imagery has lost much of its force; and so have most of Jimmy's detailed jibes against the manners and attitudes of Alison's upper-middle-class family, which belongs to a tradition of *noblesse oblige* and colonial service now entirely defunct.

But if Osborne's social politics are tied to their period, the play's savage undercurrent of sexual politics is not. Seen from the vantage point of 1990, the play looks increasingly like a frank, brilliant and romantic study of rogue male energy sloshing around in a society becalmed by stagnation and peace. Robbed (or so he feels) of 'good, brave causes' to fight for, Jimmy declares that he and his pal Cliff have no real option but to 'be butchered by the women', and instinctively turns the battering ram of his energy on to the politics of his personal life. In his rage against an establishment world view propped up by sexual prudery and polite lies, he demands Alison's complete rejection of her background, and complete loyalty to him. As she explains to Helena, 'It's a matter of allegiances'; and although Jimmy's behaviour towards both women shows a level of rage, fear, misogyny and aggression that is quite pathological, there's also something desperately human and familiar about it. It's as if there's a recognisable shred of Jimmy lurking in most male psyches; and in the world of the play, there's never any real doubt that Alison is right to prefer her husband's blood-and-guts realism, and the true erotic bond between them which is itself a touchstone of reality, to the sanitised and euphemistic world of her parents.

All of which makes the play a fascinating and challenging one for a generation brought up on the new perspectives of feminism. What it says is that men and women should be loyal to the sexual bond between them, not only because men run mad when they feel rejected by their womenfolk, but because erotic passion is a force which can break though barriers of wealth and class, create something new and positive out of something old and atrophied; the implication is that women must put up with a hell of a lot from men who really need them, because that's the only way to keep the human pageant on the road.

Of course, it's a reactionary thesis by modern standards. But at a time when relations between the sexes seem to have reached such a petulant, mistrustful stand-off, it's fascinating to see this traditionalist view of marriage argued with such force, and performed with such conviction. For Phil Smeeton, as Jimmy, not only imitates but absolutely embodies the kind of fierce, virile nervous energy that drives the character; and although Rosaleen Pelan's Alison is as slight as she is quiet, there's a sense that her stubborn strength of will is at least equal to his frightening bluster. Stuart McQuarrie's Cliff is a perfectly judged little cameo of the loving, sexually neutral friend who helps mediate their taut relationship; and the strength of the ensemble playing between these three indicates that however unpalatable

Osborne's sexual politics may be to the post-feminist consciousness, his sexy old images of male aggression absorbed and redeemed by a stubborn, unfailing female love have a good deal of life in them yet.

Hardie and Baird
Traverse, Edinburgh
The Guardian, 1 July 1990

A couple of months ago, at a conference in Glasgow, I heard the playwright Iain Heggie quote the idea of theatre as a kind of public dreaming: the job of a playwright, he suggested, is to articulate the dream his audience needs at a given moment. For all its faults, James Kelman's *Hardie and Baird: The Last Days* – the first full-length production of the 1990 Traverse season – is a play that has that quality of hitting the right theme at the right time. First commissioned for radio twelve years ago, and now thoroughly reworked for the stage, the play is set in the prison cells of Edinburgh and Stirling castles in the year 1820, and explores the state of mind of the radical weavers John Baird and Andrew Hardie during the weeks before their execution for treason as leaders of the Scottish popular rebellion of that year. Like Hector MacMillan's *The Rising*, *Hardie and Baird* is written partly out of rage that that rebellion – for universal suffrage, annual parliaments and Scottish independence – has been so largely hidden from official history, and is barely taught in Scottish schools; but those who are expecting a rousing anti-government polemic full of obvious contemporary parallels are in for a disappointment.

For Kelman's concern is not so much with the arrogance and judicial gerrymandering of the British state (although that forms the essential background of the story) as with Hardie and Baird's tremendous battle for spiritual composure, as they live through their long days of solitary confinement in Edinburgh and Stirling, knowing that their chances of reprieve and survival are slim. The play emerges, finally, as a kind of long dramatic tribute to the tremendous spiritual strength of Andrew Hardie, whose radical Christian faith – undisturbed by the hideous establishment cant of some of the clergy sent to 'comfort' him – transforms his imprisonment into a profound experience of self-discovery, a journey into his own heart and into his faith which leaves him calm, and at times almost exalted. Baird, by contrast, cannot let go of the simple rights and wrongs of the earthly battle in which they have been engaged. He rages against the injustice of the situation, lapses into hostile silence and near-madness, torments himself with regrets about the circumstances of their betrayal and arrest; he cannot help knowing that Hardie, though much younger, is the 'better', stronger man in this final ordeal.

The problem with the play – although it's directed with exquisite sensitivity by Ian Brown, and played with tremendous concentration and feeling by Simon Donald as Hardie and Tam Dean Burn as Baird – is that the fundamental balance between the two characters never shifts. Their individual moods change, as they tussle with their mental and physical demons, and Simon Donald's Hardie, in particular, often seeks to convey through body language an agitation hardly expressed in the text. The canting clergy come and go; the men are moved from solitary confinement into a shared cell. But Hardie begins with his faith well-developed, sophisticated and intact, and goes into death in the same condition; Baird finds the Christian message of acceptance and forgiveness harder from the start, and is still fighting the inevitable at the end. And what this means, in a play well over two hours in length, is a great deal of repetition, a steady, dense restatement of spiritual and emotional positions that never moves, never develops, never has any dramatic dynamism.

But given that limitation, *Hardie and Baird* is a remarkably absorbing piece of work. It reflects what I think is a growing radical interest in spiritual and moral strength, as the only real weapons poor people have against the might of money and the state, and the only weapons any of us have against the inevitability of suffering and death. It features two compelling and heroic performances; it's presented with some style and great feeling, on a dark Traverse stage filled with the strong, deliberately anachronistic rhythms of a new score by Richard Heacock. But in the end, it lacks the nerve actually to dramatise its theme; and Kelman's profound and moving understanding of the right relationship between political morality here on earth, and faith in something better beyond it, will therefore have less impact than it deserves.

Les Liaisons Dangereuses
Mitchell, Glasgow
The Guardian 12 July 1990

Coming innocent and wide-eyed to the Royal Shakespeare Company's *Les Liaisons Dangereuses* – that grand theatrical phenomenon of the 1980s, now arrived at last in Scotland for a three-month run at the Mitchell Theatre – is a strange and disturbing experience, if only because it so precisely reflects the atmosphere of the decade just gone. Somewhere within it, after all, there is a play of steel, a hard, bleak thing about the collapse of idealism and morality in personal relationships. The story of the dangerous alliance between the Marquise de Merteuil and her former lover Valmont, of the cold, competitive ethic of sexual exploitation on which it is based, and of the way in which that code destroys the possibility of love between Mme de Tourvel and Valmont – must strike a powerful and terrible chord with anyone who fully experienced the emotional wastelands of the 1980s, the collapse of expectations about fidelity, trust, and long-term commitment, the wholesale junking of marriages. De Merteuil's retreat from her love for Valmont into an impregnable fortress of self-reliance and power-plays is something I recognise; Valmont's inability to resist Merteuil's demands – embodied in the hideous scene where he deliberately smashes the relationship with de Tourvel that has brought him the greatest joy of his life – is even more interesting, as a study of the wanton emotional destructiveness to which many men feel compelled whenever real closeness threatens their self-sufficiency.

Yet *Les Liaisons* – in this elegant, restrained reworking by David Leveaux of the original RSC production – reflects the ethos of the 1980s in another, and even more disturbing way. For as a piece of theatre, it crucially lacks the courage of its own bleakness. Here and there – in the strained, powdered face of Emma Piper's Merteuil, or in the vocal harshness of Valmont's final ultimatum to her – you catch a glimpse of the ugliness and violence implicit in a plot which revolves around the deliberate seduction and moral destruction of innocents. But by and large, the spectacle is suffocatingly pretty, played out on a set of pale, slatted boudoir screens that lusciously pick up the sequence of soft pastel colour tones – pink, gold, white, grey-green, powder blue – imposed on them by the lighting. The costumes – just one for each character – are quite beautiful representations of the fashion of those other '80s, the 1780s, in which the action is set. Even worse, the terrible story is played with far too frequent and forced a recourse to humour. It's right that the Countess's cynical bons mots about sex and marriage should rouse the occasional uneasy laugh; it is absolutely wrong that Valmont's casual seduction of the fifteen-year-old convent girl Cécile should be written and played for easy comedy, perpetuating – and inviting the audience to laugh along with – the sexist lie that when women say no to sex, they usually mean yes.

I was deeply impressed, in the end, by the playing of Emma Piper's soft-voiced Countess and, particularly, by Pip Miller's Valmont, a man surprised by the residual power of moral beauty and love; the bleakness of the play's closing moments is perfect and spine-chilling, and the quality of the supporting performances never falters, despite the dangerously slow pace at which the production is played. But overall, I was left with the impression of a piece of theatre in which the comfortable, elegant packaging somehow defies the content. For the Glasgow audience – the biggest I've seen at a Culture City performance for some time – the messages conveyed by such an event have more to do with the effortless confidence and technical superiority of top-class English theatre than with the emotional devastation actually referred to in the plot; and that cannot be what was intended, either by Laclos, who wrote the novel, or Christopher Hampton, who wrote the play.

Brothers and Sisters
Theatre Royal, Glasgow
The Guardian, 29 July 1990

The Maly Theatre of Leningrad's *Brothers and Sisters* has slipped quietly into Britain: playing in Glasgow only, for a short five-day run in front of thin midsummer audiences, this latest contribution to Glasgow's World Theatre Season has attracted far less attention than it deserves. But those who came to the Theatre Royal on Saturday to see the complete, all-day performance of this two-part, six-hour epic will know that they have experienced the strongest, most comprehensive and most eloquent response to post-war Soviet experience ever seen on a British stage; and their understanding of the situation in the Soviet Union will be permanently changed and enriched by it.

Adapted from a four-part novel by Fyodor Abramov, *Brothers and Sisters* takes its title from the opening words of Stalin's famous 1941 address to the Soviet people, in which he asked his 'brothers and sisters' in the struggle against fascism to give everything they had – their lives, their wealth, their last ounce of physical strength – to the Great Patriotic War against Hitler's Germany. The novel and the play tell the story, based on Abramov's own background, of the immediate post-war experience of a village in northern Russia that took Stalin's injunction to heart. As the play opens, the war is ending, and the women who worked themselves into the ground during the struggle, ploughing and sowing the land, logging in the forests, running the commune, raising the children – 'and not one of them died' – are looking forward to the return of their men from the army. All through the war, their brave little village chairman Anfisa (a wonderful, pivotal performance from Tatyana Shestakova) has been telling them, 'Patience, women, after the war we will begin to live'; the basic theme of *Brothers and Sisters* – seen through the eyes of a boy-on-the-verge-of-manhood called Mikhail (or 'Mishka') who lived and worked through the war with the women – has to do with Stalinism's absolute betrayal of that hope, and with the decline of the people into a terrible and bitter poverty – sometimes near-starvation – no longer made bearable by idealism, comradeship, and faith in the future.

Brothers and Sisters is not, in itself, an outstanding piece of theatrical writing. The Maly Company produces its adaptations by a long-drawn-out collaborative process of experiment, rehearsal and selection, and this process remains obvious in the episodic, sometimes jerky structure of the piece; sometimes I missed the sense of context that a more unified 'concept' production can give. In the first half, for instance, I found it difficult to conjure up, from a script which naturally highlights key moments of change and celebration, a sense of the unrelenting physical work which dominated the villagers' lives. And I was troubled throughout by the problem of perspective created by Mishka's special position. On the page, he might be able to act as a conduit for a narrative about the experience and heroism of Russia's much-neglected women; in the theatre, Pyotr Semak's handsome Mishka emerges as a hero in his own right, constantly drawing the focus away from the women to whom the text pays so much lip service.

But the Maly are evidently a company more interested in the content of their work than in a burnished perfection of form; and their emphasis on a story that has deep personal meaning for them, combined with an intense Stanislavskian naturalism in creating character, produces a depth and intensity of acting that sweeps away minor imperfections of structure like a river in spate. In detail, the show is exquisitely staged around a simple log platform, which shifts and tilts with the changing scenes. The lighting is perfect, now harvest-warm, now glinting whitely through drifting snowflakes, and against this background Lev Dodin's thirty-six-strong company give a heart-stopping ensemble performance, living with the characters, moving and dancing with them; the village celebrations, for instance, have a half-hearted, broken quality that is utterly credible, as if the little joyful shreds of folk song and dance were slowly fading from the memory along with the moral universe that produced them. As Dodin points out, the great strength of Abramov's story lies in its refusal to accept the simple 'good people/bad system' stereotypes of dissident Soviet literature. It lets us see not only the hard work and heroism of the villagers, but also their sexual repressiveness and their casual cruelty towards outsiders; it lets us see the million threads that link the quality of political life to the quality of personal life, and how the creeping individualism of the post-war world undermined the communist system, just as the system failed the people.

Above all, though, *Brothers and Sisters* reminds us of the almost unimaginable scale of the struggles the Soviet people have waged in this century. It's a show big enough to contain an utterly damning indictment of Stalinism, while at the same time allowing a glimpse of the astonishing achievement of the Soviet system at its height, of the way in which a potent mix of socialist ideals and traditional Christian morality once mobilised a poor, largely peasant people to fight, to endure, to give themselves up to the collective, and abandon personal ambition, on a scale unimaginable in the modern West. It's from the contrast between this intense idealism on one hand, and the shabby moral chaos of modern Russia on the other, that *Brothers and Sisters* draws its heart-rending tragic energy; but the very completeness of its vision reminds us that the death of communism will not mean the end of the great, dangerous human impulse to try to build a heaven on earth.

The Second Coming
St Rollox Works, Glasgow
The Guardian, 13 September 1990

Test Department's *The Second Coming* – staged in the vast semi-derelict acres of the old Caley Railway Engine Works at Springburn – is one of the most compelling and tantalising events of Glasgow 1990 so far. Compelling, because it hurls itself in a bold, thrilling, formally inventive style at some questions about the 'heritage industry' that desperately need to be asked; tantalising because it's too light on dramatic and structural development to make its point clearly, and because, in the end, it attacks the wrong target. Staged by Angus Farquhar with a cast of sixty, including only eighteen professional actors and musicians, the show is a stunning visual and aural spectacle, which uses the great vistas of the space – its groves of metal pillars, its low shed roof, its great, gliding engine-repair platform, its discarded iron wheels and old, rusty flatcars running on ancient rails – to sketch the story of a dreadful, fateful turning point in the near future of the British working class.

Structured as a seventy-five-minute rock oratorio in three parts, with libretto by Neal Ascherson, the show opens with three guides – smart young women in brightly coloured parodies of public-school uniform – explaining that the once-mighty industrial 'workforce', finding itself redundant after centuries of hard labour, is being given a final chance of work as actors in a living heritage museum, commemorating their industrial past. The workforce take up their positions, and the opening recitative modulates into a long, impassioned fugue for voice and percussion – the emotional heart of the show – in which the company invoke, at an ever-increasing pitch of intensity, the deafening sounds, the physical movement, the frenzied atmosphere of the engine shed at the height of production. Welding sparks fly in the dark recesses of the shed; light plays dramatically through the vast spaces on human forms locked into a great, rhythmic pattern of effort and labour as the cast beat furiously on drums and wheelbases, do Japanese-style company exercises on the moving repair platform, heave old flatcars along the rails. At the height of the frenzy, great white sails unfurl in the far depths of the space, and on to them are projected huge images of steam engines, gathering speed, thundering into action; I can't remember seeing a piece of theatre which more powerfully captures the essence of heavy industrial labour, the brutal weight of the materials, the noise, the back-breaking effort, the sense of danger, the almost fearful pride at the Promethean power of the great engines created by these nineteenth-century industrial processes.

It's at this point, though, that the structure of the piece begins to falter. The guides begin to quote from an absurd speech – given several years ago by Enoch Powell to the Royal Society of St George – about the true nature of England, its history and destiny. When the workforce fail to react, the guides attack them with a snarling, authoritarian ferocity, accusing them of envy, greed, insubordination, and a want of patriotism. As their voices fade into cacophony the show enters its final phase, in which the workforce are driven around the recesses of the space by terrible searchlight beams, like groups of holocaust victims in the shunting yards of hell; finally, through great open doors at the far end of the shed, they heave into action a dark giant machine – terrifying and aggressive in its shape and markings – that forms the final image of the piece.

There are two problems with this. The first is that the failure to give the workforce any character or words – we see them only as matchstick figures in a huge interior landscape – makes it difficult to attach real emotional weight to their suffering, or to understand why the guides should turn on them with such fury. The second is that the extreme fascist-romantic English triumphalism expressed by the guides (and by Powell) rings no bells at all in Glasgow: in Culture City, the experience of right-wing Tory government has more to do with sharp-suited PR men and crude market forces than with dreams of feudal order and island destiny, and the temptation to nostalgia comes mainly in the familiar cloth-capped form of sentimental artefacts about Glasgow's glorious working-class past.

If Ascherson, the writer, and Farquhar, the director, had spent more time in Glasgow this last half-decade, they might have understood more about the precise forms of ancestor-worship that go on in the west of Scotland, and might have been able to address the burning question of when a legitimate hunger to tell, retell and understand the city's traumatic working-class history (well illustrated, in an

entrance-hall exhibition, by pictures of the physical devastation of Springburn in the last four decades) becomes a
reactionary habit of nostalgia, inertia and political defeatism.
But despite the show's imperfections, the world's press,
descending on Glasgow this weekend for Bill Bryden's prestigious *The Ship* project, would be well advised to take a dose
of *The Second Coming* as an antidote; if only because it
reminds us that remembering and honouring the past is no
simple business, and that in cities like Glasgow – with so
much past, and so little obvious future – it can become a
dangerous obsession.

Glasgow All Lit Up
George Square and Glasgow Green
The Guardian, 7 October 1990

It was a rough day in central Scotland. By late morning, the
rain in Glasgow had reached monsoon strength, and it
stayed that way throughout the afternoon. Saturday shop-
pers gave up in disgust, low-lying bits of the city
disappeared under water, the trains between Glasgow and
Edinburgh were delayed by flooding. But Welfare State
International, along with 250 schools and organisations
throughout Strathclyde, had been planning for over a year
to get Glasgow 'all lit up' on the evening of 6 October 1990:
over 8000 lanterns – ranging from tiny solo efforts to huge
float-sized light sculptures on the backs of lorries – were
being glued and painted and given their finishing touches,
from Argyll down to the depths of Ayrshire. The event was
to be the centrepiece of the community programme of Glasgow's year as European City of Culture, the final answer to
those who said that 1990 was all posh and Pavarotti. Welfare
State had been into every school and community hall in the
region, encouraging the creative urge, advising on techniques and materials; nothing was going to stop them now.

And nothing did. At six o'clock, as dusk gathered over the city, the rain obligingly drizzled to a halt. A big, noisy community choir assembled in a temporary bandstand at George Square – flanked by big, white lantern models of Glasgow Cathedral and the People's Palace – and began belting out popular rabble-rousers like 'Fame! I Want to Live Forever'. A crowd gathered, mums and dads and kids in little fluorescent green haloes, handed out by the stewards. And at half-past seven, almost like magic, the first of four huge processions – from the west, south, north and east of the city – suddenly materialised in the square, bobbing, dancing, gleaming against the dark trees. There were the big floats of course: a gorgeous white reindeer, a giant image of the Prime Minister shoving a gunboat out to sea, a big Rabbie Burns contemplating a huge haggis with a knife still wobbling in its entrails. St Columbkille's Primary School in Rutherglen excelled itself with a beautiful white *Swan Lake* float; and my personal favourite – a comment on the whole 'city of culture' idea – was a huge light sculpture of a reclining nude resting heavily on an arcaded couch, beneath which the labouring, straining forms of workers struggled to keep the structure in place.

But in a sense, the big set pieces were beside the point; because what was lovely, what was breathtaking, what reduced one or two cynical old observers to tears, was the children, thousand upon thousand of them pouring down West George Street and up Queen Street and down North Hanover Street, every one of them clutching a little lantern – not more than a couple of feet across, often less – skipping, running, singing, hanging on to teachers and mums and dads, sedulously keeping their little jam-jar candles alight. Say 'Eight thousand primary-school kids with their own handmade lanterns' quickly, and it doesn't sound like much; see it, and you realise that it represents an almost overwhelming outpouring of small, stubborn creative impulses.

There were beautifully made lanterns, and wee, battered, messy ones. There were boats and spaceships and churches and Mutant Hero Ninja Turtles, and lots of simple triangular lanterns with nothing but gorgeous, blobby abstract patterns on. In recognition of Glasgow's strange crest – the tree, the bird, the bell, the fish – there were hundreds of brightly coloured fish, from huge sharks to tiny tiddlers; Lochgilphead Primary School brought a whole shoal, thirty-strong. There was a Noah's Ark, with little matching pairs of lantern-bearers behind, each with an animal cut out and silhouetted against the surface of a simple white lamp; there were the kids from Milton Primary spelling out M-I-L-T-O-N in big glowing letters. There were rock groups and pipe bands and brass bands and steel bands and an extraordinary group of punk pipers, who writhed like Mick Jagger in their kilts. As the columns of light snaked out of George Square and along towards the High Street, toothless, well-oiled old punters emerged from a sawdust-and-spit pub called The Right Half, and cheered and danced on the pavement, to the kids' delight. The city beamed from ear to ear, and one visitor, watching near me, muttered, 'Croydon, eat your heart out; we could never get a feeling like this in a million years.'

Later, down at Glasgow Green, the ground was very squelchy and things went on a bit too long, as these events do. There were gorgeous forty-foot towers of lanterns, ice-cream vans, hot-dog stalls, and a big firework display; and Welfare State produced a kind of visual fantasia on the tree, bird, bell and fish theme, which ended with the tree burning down, and a gleaming white bird rising – rather limp-wristedly, on account of the rain – from the ashes. 'Why's that tree burning and falling to bits, Dad?' asked a tot in the crowd. 'Because it symbolises Glasgow, hen,' answered the Dad, with feeling. But everybody laughed, because we knew there would be a phoenix later.

The Tempest
Tramway, Glasgow
The Guardian, 1 November 1990

It is a fact universally acknowledged that Peter Brook's theatrical work has a strong 'international' quality. His casting is multinational, with actors drawn from Europe, Africa and Asia. His base at the Bouffes du Nord in Paris bears the name 'Centre International de Créations Théâtrales'; during his first two visits to Glasgow, with *The Mahabharata* and then with *Carmen*, I even felt that this intense cosmopolitanism was perhaps a weakness in an age when global homogenisation is commonplace, and a strong sense of local habitation, history and place harder to get.

But three productions in to Brook's relationship with the Tramway – which he delighted his first-night audience by describing as 'our dear new home', when he appeared briefly on his own raked-sand stage to announce a small casting change – I'm beginning to see that Brook is much too great a director to let his work drift too far away from the specific, the concrete of human experience. His magnificent *Tempest* – for my money the strongest, clearest and most challenging production he has brought to Glasgow – seems to me to be rooted deeply in the experience of francophone Africa, and of its profound and subtle confrontation with European culture; also, therefore, rooted in the flavour of life in urban France today, where – in suburbs and *arrondissements* not five miles from Brook's theatre – men and women from the Maghreb struggle to maintain their cultural identity and to come to terms with the power and sophistication of French metropolitan culture.

It's as if Brook has discovered, in this tension, a potent reflection of the tension in Shakespeare's play between modern and medieval cultures, the rational and the magical; as he acknowledges in a programme note, his African actors –

particularly Sotigui Kouyaté, his commanding Prospero, and Bakary Sangaré's big, light-footed, unforgettable Ariel – certainly bring a kind of ease, as well as a powerful vocal tradition of chants and songs, to the play's invocations of magical and spiritual powers. There is of course nothing simplistic about the production, and its treatment of the play's colonial theme. The island's colonists, Prospero and Miranda, are black, as is the childlike Ariel; whereas the low-life characters Trinculo, Stephano and Caliban (a remarkable performance by David Bennent) career round the stage like a bunch of European skinheads petulantly determined to 'get their own back'. But the sense of human dignity salvaged against the odds, and of African and European actors meeting as equals on the common ground of a great Western text that could have been used (as English generally was used) as a weapon of control and humiliation, gives a terrific richness and potency to the production's exploration of the theme of freedom, which Brook sees as central to the play.

Because, of course, with a play of this stature, strong roots in a particular human situation or atmosphere are only the basis for something which soars out to touch every kind of life; and in the end – after a slow, reserved build-up under steady bright light on an almost aggressively empty stage – Brook brings his production to a magnificent understanding that real freedom, the freedom of the spirit, goes beyond not only the drunken licence of Caliban's crew, and the brutal power-grabbing of Neapolitan politicians, but also beyond the terrific magical power Prospero has won by study and intellectual effort. In the end, in Kouyaté's superb performance, this man with so much evident reason for pride stands before us a humble, almost naked petitioner, asking for the loving prayers of his fellow human beings, which alone can really free him. It is a magnificent theatrical moment in the simple, storytelling sense Brook loves to emphasise. But to me, it also seemed to say something important and timely about Europe and its culture at this moment of fine talk about European integration and the eastward extension of the European Community: that whatever else this continent does, it cannot afford to turn its back on the south, on the dignity of its people, the richness of its culture, and the profound economic and human links that bind their destiny to ours.

Part Two

1991–2003: The Building of a New Scottish Repertoire

*A*fter the huge success of 1990, the early years of the new decade inevitably felt quieter, and more reflective. The Tramway remained, though, as a new centre for international arts and performance in Glasgow: in 1991 its director, Neil Wallace, staged a remarkable event called Theatres and Nations, which invited the four nations of these islands – England, Scotland, Ireland and Wales – to reflect on their national identity. The programme included Howard Barker's Victory, Ed Thomas's East from the Gantry, *Tom Murphy's* The Patriot Game, *and a new version of Robin Jenkins' great Scottish novel* The Cone Gatherers, *staged by Gerry Mulgrew's Communicado; and in the programme note for the event, I laid out my thinking on theatre, nations and identity, in the aftermath of 1990.*

In November 1990, meanwhile, Margaret Thatcher had fallen from power and was replaced by John Major; but the direction of UK politics barely changed and, somewhere in the psyche of the nation, a real anger began to simmer. The new generation of women playwrights who had come to prominence in the 1980s began to be eclipsed, year by year, by a new chorus of male voices, furious, nihilistic, brutalised or prostituted by the materialistic world in which they had been raised. The critic Aleks Sierz called this the 'In-Yer-Face' generation of playwrights;

in Scotland, the same mood was echoed in Raindog's angry Macbeth *of 1992, in Simon Donald's* The Life of Stuff *at the Traverse that same year, and – later – in Harry Gibson's sensational stage version of Irvine Welsh's* Trainspotting, *first seen at the Citizens' Stalls Studio during Mayfest 1994, in a superb production by Ian Brown.*

If the 'In-Yer-Face' movement had its impact in Scotland, though – not least through the work of Scottish-born but London-based playwright Anthony Neilson, raised as a child among the 1970s generation of Scottish radical writers and actors – it's striking that the leading voices of Scottish playwriting which began to emerge during the 1990s, helping build and develop a repertoire with a huge international reputation, were much gentler and more nuanced in tone, almost meditative. Sue Glover's Bondagers *opened at the Traverse in 1991, bringing a rich new female voice to the Scottish stage; and the early 1990s also saw the launch of Scotland's woman-led theatre company Stellar Quines, run at first by a group of artists including Gerda Stevenson and Irene Macdougall, and then by the actor and director Muriel Romanes, who became Stellar Quines' artistic director in 1996, and led the company for twenty years with impressive creative flair and determination. In 1992, the Traverse moved to its new home in Cambridge Street, with twin auditoria, and an end to its old club status. And in 1993, I wrote my first-ever review – a rather grudging one – of the work of a young twenty-four-year-old playwright called David Greig, who reflected intensely, humorously, thoughtfully on the recent changes in Europe: his first play was called* Stalinland.

1991

Man and Superman
Citizens', Glasgow

Bondagers
Tramway, Glasgow
The Guardian, 5 May 1991

It's been a rich, disturbing first weekend of Mayfest for those of us who think that relations between men and women have come to a bit of a stalemate, bogged down in a morass of virgin births, slasher movies, and mutual disappointment. At the Citizens' Theatre, there's a strong, exuberant production by Helena Kaut-Howson – only the second woman to direct at the Citz since 1970 – of *Man and Superman*, the long, vibrant, unsettling play in which George Bernard Shaw, stern believer in the equal rights and intelligence of women, nonetheless confronts the Don Juan myth, and tries to examine the polarity, the 'life force', that draws men and women together; and at the Tramway, the opening of a beautiful, resonant Traverse production of Sue Glover's *Bondagers*, a play about six women labourers on a Borders farm in the nineteenth century which, eloquently, contains no men at all.

What is most disturbing about *Man and Superman* is that it is, as its title betrays, an incipiently reactionary play about the power of women over men. In it, a glorious girl called Anne, beautiful, clever and cunning, lures her rich guardian Jack Tanner – a fiercely independent bachelor of strong radical opinions – into the marriage she has always wanted. The message is that once a woman is inspired by the 'life force' – once she sees the man she wants as the father of her children – then all he can do, after a respectable struggle, is to give in gracefully, and dwindle into a 'mere breadwinner'.

And anyone can see how dangerous this particular male fantasy is: once men begin to believe that women are 'deadlier than the male', then the floodgates are open to every kind of repressive measure designed to keep their power in check. It's also interesting that Shaw can only achieve his sexy, well-matched ending by creating a thoroughly unlikely hero, a man who is strong without being cold, sexy without being exploitative, generous to women without idealising them – in effect, a Don Juan with a soul; and by assuming the continued financial dependence of women with children on their husbands, 'otherwise, they'd eat us after mating, and walk off, like spiders'.

But at least the play represents the kind of dynamic, thought-provoking, lusty and cheerful male response to the changing status of women which has been so lamentably lacking these last twenty years; which is perhaps why Kaut-Howson's production seems to revel so gloriously in the wit, passion and contemporary relevance of it all. Julian McGowan's surrealist set is an outright triumph, a symphony of neoclassical library architecture cut and skewed with Dalì-esque images of broken mirrors and frozen clocks: a mixture of decadent classicism and fierce modernism Shaw would have adored, and which seems to encourage the cast – particularly Paul Mooney's superb Tanner, backed by Robert David MacDonald's wicked old Ramsden and Gerard Horan, quite brilliant as the intellectual chauffeur Henry Straker – in striking exactly the right note of sexy, combative debate, in a landscape with few stable reference points. Of course, there's a lot of stagey talking, and I could have done with rather less of the deadpan, china-doll, Donna Anna stuff from Hermione Norris's Anne. But even if the company don't always seem clear how the intellectual arguments fit with the underlying thrust of the love story, they enjoy them just as much as if they did, even giving us deftly cut glimpses of the intellectual brigands in the Spanish mountains, and the rarely performed Don Juan in Hell dream sequence.

There's a Don Juan figure, too, in the background of Sue Glover's *Bondagers* at the Tramway, but this time drawn with a clear-eyed, pitiless naturalism: a handsome, dark-eyed ploughman who performs dazzling tricks on horseback and drives women wild, but who ends up dead at the jealous hands of poor, half-daft Tottie, whom he once seduced after the 'kirn', the harvest home. To emphasise this one dramatic incident, though, is to falsify the nature of Glover's remarkable play, which traces a year in the life of six women 'bondagers', or farm labourers, in a way which makes it clear that the dominant force in their lives is not love but work: the weather, the land, the crops, the care of the bairns, the relationship each bondager manages to strike up with the wife of the 'hind', or male farm labourer, who subcontracts her to work with him and live with his family. Heaven knows how Glover's minimal, strongly paced, simple-sounding script will play in the confined spaces of the Traverse; but in the big barn of the Tramway, Ian Brown has made it the centre of a gorgeous, filmic, lyrical production, in which scenes of dialogue and monologue are swept across the earthen stage by the spacious, contemplative rhythms of Pete Livingstone's music, and by the choric songs and movement of the women themselves, sowing, reaping, hoeing, shading from work into dance.

The work of the six actresses – Eve Keepax, Anne Lacey, Hilary MacLean, Rosaleen Pelan, Ann Louise Ross, and Myra McFadyen as poor Tottie – is beyond praise, somehow managing to evoke the rich, earthbound energy and occasional beauty of their life on the land without one jot of sentimentality, one evasion of the filth and brutality of it; they spit out the magnificent Scots language of the text with a conviction that lifts the simplest line to the stature of poetry, and takes us back to a time when words were few, precious, and well weighed. Do men matter to these women? Yes, but mainly as holders of economic power, or begetters of bairns; the texture of their lives lies in each other, the shared work, the shared 'crack'. In other words, once these powerful women break free from their economic bondage to hinds and husbands, they will be capable of anything, with or without lovers and Don Juans. If only GBS were here, with a few brilliant suggestions as to what we should make of that.

A Defence of the Fringe
The Guardian, 19 August 1991

Well, so that's that then. One week into a three-week event, the story on this year's Fringe was already set in stone, or at least in print. According to one distinguished Sunday paper, it can be summed up as 'thin, wispy and grey': standards are low, talent is rare, there's too much comedy, audiences are sparse, the weather's dreadful, the whole Festival's on the slide, fings ain't wot they used to be, let's all stay in the bar. It's not a new story; indeed it's been written dozens of times in the last five years. But there's something about the Festival and Fringe that seems to invite knocking copy, as if the very size and beauty of the annual Edinburgh bubble make unhappy people itch to prick it.

The problem with the story, though, is that it isn't true. I doubt whether this will emerge as a vintage Fringe – given the depth of the recession, it would be surprising if ticket sales did not suffer, particularly at the expensive mega-venues, and even more startling if the work itself retained all its mid–eighties exuberance. But to dismiss the whole event as thin and third-rate on a swift sampling of one week's work is to administer a lazy, gratuitous insult not only to the 9000 performers who are currently pouring out their hearts in Edinburgh for little financial return, but also to their remarkable audience, who continue to hand over ticket money for shows which carry no quality guarantee, with a patience, loyalty, stamina and enthusiasm that has to be seen to be believed.

Since the *Guardian*'s impromptu debate on the future of the Fringe last Thursday afternoon, I have seen eight Fringe productions, of which two were complete turkeys, one was a small masterpiece of contemporary European theatre, and five were enjoyable without hitting the heights; that is a staggeringly high strike-rate for a completely open festival. I've seen an audience of fifteen sit patiently through a dreadful little play (called, appropriately, *Dog*) at the little backstage theatre in the Gilded Balloon, and a capacity audience of more than 100 cram into the Netherbow for George Rosie's *Carluccio*, a fierce, obscene, self-indulgent portrait of Bonnie Prince Charlie in his festering old age. I've seen one of England's leading actors, Alan Howard, briefly spellbind an audience of 100 in the exotic Dream Tent on the Meadows with stories from Christopher Logue's new *Iliad*, competing cheerfully with the shrieks of children and the grind of generators from the funfair outside; I've watched another 120 people, including a coach party from the Workers Educational Association, gather in the handsome atrium of the TSB in George Street to watch an imaginative staging of a dead-duck script about modern corporate psychology. You can call these experiences many things – sometimes dull, sometimes silly, often promising more than they can deliver. But from where I sit among the Fringe-goers, the sense of cumulative richness, of being warmed by a tremendous multi-sourced outpouring of energy and effort, is as powerful as it is moving.

And then, of course, there are the productions that make it all decisively worthwhile. Imagine, if you will, a beautiful

Georgian house in India Street, glowing with late-night lamplight: a lovely room with memorable portraits and rich red walls, the doorbell ringing, impresario extraordinary Richard Demarco circling the room kissing people and making wild statements about the importance of the event, as only Demarco can. On the floor, in the middle of the room, sits a handsome old radio, big enough to sit on; to one side, a little stove with coffee cups; and moving among us, handing out buttons to the baffled audience, three strange, wild women in faded cotton dresses, introducing themselves in broken English as Gaia, Fosca and Demetra. This is Teatro Settimo from Turin, a group of experienced Italian actors who decided, a while ago, to go 'looking for theatre' in the homes of their audience. The material for their piece, called *Stabat Mater*, is drawn from the work of South American 'magic realist' writers like Marquez and Isabel Allende; in a fragmented narrative, the three tell the story of their mother and her explosive marriage to 'the Colonel', and of their seventeen siblings named in strict alphabetical order.

But what is stunning about the production is the sheer, risk-taking nerve with which it finds theatrical equivalents for the formal pyrotechnics of magic realism. There's the dazzling swiftness with which the three actresses slip from 'our' world into 'their' world into the world of the story; the deliberate, brave blurring of distinction between their personalities and those of the sisters; the quality of stillness, extreme naturalism, yet heightened emotion in their acting, the almost animal sense of family and blood kinship they generate. The skill of these women – Laura Curino, Mariella Fabbris, and Lucilla Giagnoni, under the direction of Roberto Tarasco – is formidable, and their approach explores the relationship between being and acting in brave and original ways. I have never seen anything like it; and I saw it on the Fringe.

Theatre and Nationhood
for Tramway, Glasgow
25 August 1991

It seems strange to be writing about theatre and nationhood on a weekend when one of the two greatest nations on earth is disappearing before our eyes. Nations are like Tinkerbell in Barrie's *Peter Pan*: they only exist so long as we believe in them. For reasons too complex to explore here, people have been withdrawing their belief from the idea of the Soviet Union for decades now; and this weekend, that unbelief reached a critical mass. In that sense, nations are fictions, man-made communities conjured up and defined, on the shifting human surface of the earth, within the minds of men and women. If we feel Scottish, then Scotland is, despite 284 years of union; if people no longer feel like Soviet citizens, then the combined power of the party, the KGB and the army command cannot keep the USSR together. And it's because nationhood is this kind of thing – an intangible sense of community, subject to change and flux – that theatre often plays such a vital part in expressing and defining it. Theatre is, at its best, a forum where people come together to discover, through their live response to the same event, the feelings and experiences they share with other people; and a sense of national identity is a shared feeling, or it is nothing.

But just as there are good and bad pieces of fiction, so it seems to me that there are good and bad senses of nationhood. Bad fiction, on the whole, is cheap, simplistic, two-dimensional, easy and mendacious, whereas good fiction is rich, subtle, complex, demanding and truthful; and much the same is true of national imagery. In the case of large and powerful nations, cheap national imagery is one of the most dangerous forces on earth. Portray England as, essentially, a polite, quiet, rural sort of place, full of thatched cottages, vicarage teas, stately homes and bobbies on bicycles – as so much television drama still does – and you sanction attitudes that marginalise the north, the industrial base, black Britons, Liverpudlians, the real sources of England's wealth, and everything that has happened to the country in the last two centuries. Revert under stress – as the American right always does – to the idea that the 'normal' American family is white, cute, prosperous, Christian, descended from the Pilgrim Fathers, and sitting around a groaning Thanksgiving dinner in frilly dresses and short haircuts, and you reinforce the frightening alienation and disaffection of huge sections of the US population. The consequences of Hitler's kitsch national imagery – the blond hair, the *Lederhosen*, the 'racial purity', the compulsory virility, the rejection of blacks and Jews and jazz and urban culture and homosexuality and the gypsy tradition and every shadow of difference and complexity – are almost too horrible to comprehend; yet every nation still has its own ethnic or linguistic purists, talking the same language about immigration and dilution and erosion and pollution of the 'indigenous' culture (or language, or ethnic population), as if those factors had somehow been fixed, static and perfect until the arrival of the most recent wave of incomers.

And in the case of small, stateless, or otherwise colonised nations, this problem of idealised national imagery becomes even more complex. It's an observable fact that 'national kitsch' images usually involve a strong streak of nostalgia, of harking back to a golden, prelapsarian age before the Serbs came to southern Croatia, or the Russians took up residence in Latvia, or the Irish arrived in the west of Scotland, or New Commonwealth immigration changed England's inner cities. In the case of big dominant cultures, this streak of nostalgia is usually based on a crass, if potent, distortion of history, designed to twist the natural human sense of loss at the changes wrought by time into a vicious and ill-founded conviction that change is being deliberately imposed by hostile outsiders. But what about nations which have suffered genuine oppression, where children have been beaten for speaking their own language or telling the story of their own people, where populations have been forcibly driven out, where the use of distinctive national languages has declined under direct or indirect pressure, where the experience of whole classes of people has been edited out of history, and attempts have been made to suppress or deny national consciousness altogether? In this situation, the sense of loss and erosion – the sense that your nation and culture has been deliberately weakened, and may face extinction if it doesn't defend itself – is based partly on hard historical fact. In that sense, nostalgia, grief, anger and yearning for the past are an inevitable by-product of any attempt to look squarely at Scotland's history, and to piece together lost or suppressed parts of the nation's story. They remain dangerous emotions, carrying the seeds of hostility to change, to newcomers, to the untidy present; they carry the risk that Scots will come to see Scottishness as a thing of the past, something which once existed but has now been destroyed. But in countries with a real history of cultural repression, they have to be accommodated and allowed for.

It's through this minefield of national feeling – sometimes strong and proud, sometimes ugly and vengeful, sometimes tinged with self-contempt, sometimes downright mawkish – that Scottish theatre has to pick its way, in providing a forum in which the nation can first recognise itself, then talk to itself, and finally talk to others; and the temptation to nostalgia is only the strongest of many. A half-colonised nation like Scotland is a strange beast, full of bizarre psychosexual tropes. The men become wounded and pugnacious, the women flirt with the dominant tribe, high-flying individuals of both sexes 'marry out'; if there is one thing I was sure of, as a child growing up in the 1950s when the only explicit manifestations of Scottish culture I came across were the White Heather Club, some old Harry Lauder songs, and the odd bowdlerised Burns Supper, it was that Scottishness was an infantile business, out of which you had to grow in order to be sexy. Then again, there is the strange conviction of many Scots that Scotland is 'only wee', when in fact it is large in resources, middling in land mass, and midway between Ireland and Denmark in population. And there is the persistent stereotype – still reflected in the voices of most Scottish actors when they try to speak Scots – that ours is somehow a particularly rugged and graceless language, well adapted to flyting, fighting, and exhibitions of machismo, but unsuited to lyricism, lovemaking and philosophy. The merest glance at the poetry of Scotland's Golden Age – at Henryson and Dunbar, or *Ane Satyre of the Thrie Estaitis* – shows us that this is tosh; but we do not live in Scotland's Golden Age, and all of us over thirty carry in our brains and voices the traces of that frightful era when Scots was heard in public only in comic interludes, pawky songs, and TV versions of the *Para Handy Tales*.

And Scottish theatre still tends to reflect, in its unthinking moments, all these casual, familiar untruths about Scotland, which are part of the baggage of cultural colonisation. Productions like the Scottish Theatre Company's *Mr Gillie* of the mid-1980s, or Bill Bryden's rapturously received *The Ship* in 1990, peddle from two different cultural traditions the idea that Scottishness was something that existed, all warm and authentic, not so long ago, but is now well on the way to being smashed by forces beyond our control. Productions like the dreadful version of *Let Wives Tak Tent* that launched the Scottish Theatre Company's career still occasionally rear their sexless heads, playing comedies about lust and romance with as much erotic charge as a back number of the *Sunday Post*. The wail of 'it wisnae me, it wisnae my fault' that ended *The Ship* still echoes through our theatres, the whinge of the nation too 'wee' to take control of its own fate; there are still too many stereotyped, rough-edged, street-fighting working-class heroes on the *No Mean City* model. There are still audiences, particularly in Edinburgh, that fidget, sneer or titter when they hear Scots accents used in a classic (I remember the storm of ridicule that broke over an interesting Royal Lyceum production of *As You Like It*, where the exiled court spoke honest Scots, and the usurping court plum-in-the-mouth English), and who cannot accept Scots as a lingua franca for the translation of texts like Tremblay's *The Guid Sisters* or Alexander Gelman's *The Bench*; there are actors who use Scots so self-consciously and deprecatingly that it can only possibly work in a comedy with a Scottish setting. And there are still companies which never think of doing classics, even those with an obvious regional setting, in anything other than English 'Received Pronunciation' – except, of course, for the servants, who can be as comically Scottish as they like.

But to set against all that, there has been a tremendous effort in Scottish theatre, over the last fifteen years or so, to challenge these easy stereotypes of Scottishness with images which are more complex, and more true. For me, there have been three or four breathtaking moments, during that time, when theatre utterly transformed my image of Scottishness, and my sense of myself as a Scot; not by giving me something completely new, but by making me see something that had always been there. The first moment was the opening of John Byrne's *The Slab Boys*, at the Traverse in 1978; for that play let me see, for the first time in my life, the truth that it was possible to be both absolutely Scottish and absolutely modern; and with it, my sense of Scottishness as an old-fashioned, dying thing left me for good. Here was a play shot through with the tacky American youth culture of the 1950s, with the religious imagery of Irish Catholicism, with the consumer-boom ethos of Britain in the Macmillan era; yet it was Scottish to its fingertips, walking proof that Scotland could accommodate all the assaults of modern culture and still live on, rich, bastardised, polyglot, but there. From that moment, I was never frightened again by the 'national extinction' myth; I knew that extinction would happen only if we made our definition of Scottishness so narrow and mean and foosty that newcomers would feel excluded from it, irrelevant to it, unable to influence and enrich it.

The second moment came when I saw the work of Charles Nowosielski, the Scots-Polish director of Theatre Alba and the Brunton Company, on some of the great myths and legends of the Borders. In his serious and romantic treatment of those great stories about the full-sized, seductive faery-folk, the 'other people' of Scots legend, their powerful sexuality, their mystery, their oneness with nature, he seemed to me to be reinstating a whole neglected area of Scottish culture, more ancient, more adult, more sensual and rounded than the thin patriarchal strand which survived the Reformation. The third came with the magical STC production of *Ane Satyre of the Thrie Estaitis* that went to Warsaw in 1985. In that disciplined, outward-looking final version, the production gave me an image of the full intellectual and emotional sweep of Scottish culture in its pre-Reformation heyday, its lyricism, its sensuality, its vigour, its wit, its sophistication, its high urbanity and confidence; and I vowed that I would never again succumb to any small, ungenerous reductive generalisations about the national character and capacities, or about what our language is good for. And the fourth was connected with Liz Lochhead's version of *Tartuffe*, and her play for Communicado *Mary Queen of Scots Got Her Head Chopped Off*, in the late 1980s, because there I saw, not only Scots being used quite beautifully in lyrical, feminine and erotic contexts, but the language itself being reborn as a plastic, modern vehicle for a whole range of Scottish thought; and that made me see that a distinctive Scots

136

language – not the language of Sir David Lyndsay or even MacDiarmid, but still a recognisable Scots tongue – could still emerge from the debris of the time, given the right political circumstances. So yet another nail thudded into the coffin of the extinction myth: for if 'the' Scots language is dying, Scots language in general is not.

But there is one last point I would like to make, and that is that nations define themselves most fully, most accurately and most impressively not when they are directly examining their own nationhood, but when they are using the stuff of their own language and culture to tackle the substantial issues of their time. *The Thrie Estaitis* provides, in the passing, a marvellous sense of how Scotland must have been in 1540; but it is not about Scottishness. It is a great satire about corruption in the state, which can play and be understood across Europe; similarly *The Slab Boys* is about the emptiness of the never-had-it-so-good moment of the 1950s, and Lochhead's *Tartuffe* is first and foremost a brilliant rendering of a classic comedy about religious hypocrisy. The work of the Wildcat company in Scotland, and of 7:84 in their heyday, rarely deals with the national question directly: it gets on with the business of analysing the miners' strike, or the Clearances, or civil liberties, or the debt crisis in Scottish housing schemes. Yet it provides a solid backbone of Scottish theatre that never wavers in its task of talking to modern Scottish audiences in a modern Scottish voice. It salvages neglected bits of Scottish history (as in *The Cheviot, the Stag and the Black, Black Oil* or *The Steamie*) and lets people have their moment of nostalgia; but it always tries to set that moment in a tough contemporary context of music and politics.

So what I think I have learned, through watching Scotland talk to itself in the theatre, is that nations and cultures cannot defend themselves by being defensive. They survive, not by preserving themselves as they were fifty years ago and trying to protect that nostalgic self-definition with prohibitions and expulsions and exclusions; but by the energy and self-confidence with which they go to meet the future, and by the wit, intelligence and sex appeal with which they address themselves to the big issues of the hour. Ultimately, self-absorption, suspicion and chronic nostalgia are as unattractive in nations as they are in individuals: they alienate the young, drive away the lively, lead straight into the provincial backwaters of human affairs.

In the last decade and a half, Scottish theatre has done an intermittently brilliant job – under difficult psychological and practical circumstances – of demonstrating that Scotland has things to say to the world, about AIDS and imperialism, nationalism and feminism, socialism and consumerism, love and death and art. But to keep that power, the nation has to learn the knack of standing every day on the brink of multicultural oblivion, open to all the winds that blow across the planet, talking about the things that need to be talked about, and trusting that the Scottish voice with which we began in the morning will still be recognisably Scottish, although changed by everything it has seen and known, at nightfall. Of course that confidence requires an intimate, loving and respectful knowledge of our own cultural past, and a sophisticated understanding of the pressures which militate against smaller nations and their cultures everywhere. But to know the past is not the same as to hanker for it, yearn for it, brood on ways back to it; and in the end, paradoxically, our survival as a nation will depend on our understanding that cultural change, which can seem so threatening to a dwindling, embattled people with a history of loss, is in fact the very stuff of life, and the thing which gives us a future.

The Cone Gatherers
Tramway, Glasgow
The Guardian, 5 September 1991

The Tramway's Theatres and Nations season – designed to reopen in style, as a permanent venue, the big, tatty, glamorous and demanding space that clinched the success of Glasgow 1990 – could hardly have been launched at a moment when its theme seemed more important or more urgent. In the Soviet Union and Yugoslavia, multinational states are flying apart before our eyes; and in these islands, too, the true composition of the place – three 'stateless nations', an unhappy province, and a republic barely seventy years old – is beginning to surface again after centuries of centralised government, and deliberate attempts at homogenisation to a 'standard English' norm. The Tramway's director Neil Wallace believes that it's time for a 'kind of awakening' to the fact that England, Scotland, Wales and Ireland have tangibly different traditions in theatre as elsewhere, and for a recognition – essential to the peaceful future of Europe as a whole – that such cultural differences are to be celebrated and cherished, not feared and suppressed. 'And in any case,' he adds, 'the most exciting work in British theatre at the moment is not coming out of the standard English tradition. There's a great confidence and energy in Scotland, Ireland and Wales just now, and the best of it has an anger that is to do with not being heard for so long. Theatrically, it's as challenging as any of the European work I see on my travels...'

So Wallace has put together a four-week theatre season – with concerts, exhibitions and a two-day conference – featuring distinctive work from all four nations of Britain: interestingly, England is represented by The Wrestling School with *Victory*, Howard Barker's play about the English Revolution, which Wallace sees as an 'important point of departure' for many tensions which persist in the British state today. The Abbey Theatre, Dublin, will give five performances of *The Patriot Game*, Tom Murphy's controversial play about Easter 1916; Brith Gof take over the Harland and Wolff engine shed with their immense eco-spectacle *Pax*; and the brilliant young Y Cwmni Company, a sensation on the 1989 Edinburgh Fringe, are premiering a new play by their director Ed Thomas which deals not only with 'sex, lies, love and power', but, according to Thomas, with the question of whether art, in the conventional sense, can help defend something as dynamic and amorphous as modern Welsh culture.

It's the Scottish Communicado Company, though, who open the season this week with a new adaptation of Robin Jenkins's novel *The Cone Gatherers*; and their intense, ambitious production – dazzlingly set (by Gordon Davidson) in a towering, blue-lit pine forest created in the Tramway's foyer space, with the audience crouched on logs among the trees – offers a fascinating insight into Scottish theatre now. Set on a Highland estate during the Second World War, *The Cone Gatherers* is a strong, schematic but very beautiful novel about the problem of evil, and the routes by which the demons of hatred, vengeance and fascistic cruelty enter the human heart. The story centres on a holy fool called Calum, a gentle, kindly creature with a twisted body and the face of an angel, who works with his loving brother Neil gathering pine cones on the estate; and on his destruction, first at the hands of the gamekeeper Duror, a man driven half-mad with rage and sexual frustration by twenty-five years of marriage to a bedridden wife, and also – in a less direct sense – at the hands of Lady Runcie-Campbell, the mistress of the estate, whose attempts to live a decent Christian life are distorted into uselessness by the class arrogance and instinctive snobbery that affect her every decision.

The main weakness of Gerry Mulgrew's production is that it tends – despite a fine performance from Tam Dean Burn as the crazed gamekeeper – to emphasise the evil generated by the class structure at the expense of the central evil surrounding Duror's immense sexual and emotional frustration. The character of Lady Runcie-Campbell – rather uneasily played by Anne Lacey – is both overwritten and caricatured, whereas the central narrative of Duror's slide into madness is under-explored. In other words, Scottish theatre – as usual – would rather take cheap populist shots at the anglicised ruling classes than look into the life-denying heart of its own sexual darkness.

But despite the temptation to reduce a big, difficult novel about evil to a slight, easy piece about class, the sheer size and grandeur of the story keeps surging to the surface, through the pure magic of the set, the dark subtlety and strained organ notes of Iain McGregor's sound, the fearless stylised choreography of the deer hunt and of Duror's terrible dreams, and the immaculate and moving performances of Tam Dean Burn, of Laurie Ventry as the careworn Neil, and, above all, of Kenneth Glenaan as Calum, the boy with 'a smile for every limping dog'. Politically sharp but self-pitying, theatrically brave and inventive, well clear of the straitjacket of naturalism, but still, in its macho way, inclined to evade the deepest water of sex and emotion; it's not a bad summation of Scottish theatre in 1991, and a powerful start to a season which will be as much about uncomfortable truths as about glorious, unexpected strengths.

Accounts
Wauchope Hall, Yetholm
The Guardian, 20 October 1991

It was a wild night in the Borders when the Northumberland Theatre Company opened its new production of Michael Wilcox's *Accounts* at Yetholm: a great blustering gale blowing a smell of winter down the village street, early playgoers warming themselves with whisky around the pub fire, deep drifts of fallen leaves forming underfoot, a brilliant silver half-moon riding high above the dark Cheviots that mark the border. But Yetholm is the village where Wilcox's fine play, written ten years ago, is set; so the little hall was packed with people come to see the latest version of a story that draws its energy from their soil, and their way of life.

And they were not disappointed. Gillian Hambleton's intelligent, craftsmanlike and unpretentious production is almost the perfect village-hall show, combining simple production values and a strong, credible storyline with acting that is always competent, and sometimes achieves the kind of excellence that has an overwhelming impact in a small space. *Accounts* is an interesting play, in that it approaches one of the hottest topics of the 1980s – homosexuality, and society's attitude to it – not by putting it centre-stage, but by placing it as just another natural feature in an overwhelming natural landscape. The story concerns a widow, Mary Mawson, and her two teenage sons Andy and Donald, who, following the death of their father, give up their rented farm in Northumberland and buy their own property on the Scottish side of the Border; the play records their financial struggle through the first year of farm ownership, the intense physical labour of the two young men out on the fells with their sheep, the mother struggling with the 'accounts' in the kitchen, the nights out at the 'rural' and the young farmers, the gradual transfer of Donald's rugby-playing loyalties from his old Allendale team – and its posh, repressed-homosexual coach James – to his new Kelso side. Young Donald becomes more certain of his gay identity; young Andy has an affair with a married woman; there is a hint of sexual experimentation between the boys. But as Andy puts it, in the midst of such an epic struggle for economic survival, 'there's no need for rules, eh?'; and strangely, even the more white-haired members of the audience seem to agree.

In other words, the play succeeds by the sheer force of its humane naturalism, and the accuracy of its observation, in compelling the audience to accept Donald's sexuality without comment. The fact that Wilcox does not focus tightly on his theme, but gives equal weight to the other elements that make up the family's life, gives *Accounts* some of the episodic, contingent quality of a hill-farming soap opera, albeit a superbly truthful one; but the technique works so well that it's impossible to object. In the NTC's production, the two 'outside' performances – from John Middleton as James and Paul Sneddon as the whisky-swigging Kelso rugby coach – are a little uneasy, too thinly caricatured for comfort; and Elspeth Charlton, as Mary, weakens her sensitive performance by using a tiny, diffident voice more suitable to film than live theatre. But Joe Caffrey and Peter Peverley are quite superb – and often very funny – as the brothers, bound together in physical affection, in work, in fear for the future of their farm, in love for their mother and their lost father, in brotherly punch-ups, and finally in the mutual tolerance of two boys growing into very different men; and it's truly satisfying that the Borders Festival and the NTC have been able to find such a pure nugget of dramatic excellence, so close to home.

Bobby Sands
Tramway, Glasgow
The Guardian, 15 December 1991

If you want an eloquent and frightening testimony to the way in which evil begets evil, you need look no further than Tam Dean Burn's ferocious personal interpretation of Bobby Sands's trilogy of poems, which played for three nights at the Tramway last week. It's ten years since Bobby Sands died on hunger strike in Belfast; his trilogy was written during his 'dirty protest' in the Maze Prison, scrawled on scraps of toilet paper and hidden inside his own body, and Tam Dean Burn's performance imaginatively uses three outlying spaces of the sprawling Tramway building – a cobbled tunnel behind the stage, the claustrophobic, black-walled bar, and a damp, freezing shed in the back yard – to convey both the physical misery of Sands's experience, and the shifts of location reflected in the three parts of the poem, which take place in the Castlereagh detention centre, in a Diplock court, and in Sands's cell at the Maze. The Diplock sequence contains a certain amount of grim comic relief at the expense of fat judges and oily informers; the final scene, with Dean Burn shivering in a blanket on a pile of cold, filthy sand, conveys the horror, despair and flickering defiance of men facing a lifetime in the Maze.

But there is no doubt that the meat of the poem – at least in this version – lies in its terrifying opening sequence, in which Sands faces interrogation and torture at Castlereagh; this section, which runs for an exhausting fifty minutes, is more intense, better-written, more haunting and more politically eloquent than the others, and already contains the full range of Sands's emotions and ideas. There is profound terror; there is outraged anger; there is hatred, sometimes hot and furious, sometimes cold and calculating; and if these are the dominant emotions in the text, they dominate even more in Dean Burn's raging, anger-driven performance, which is both unforgettable and very frightening.

Sands writes in a traditional, rhythmic ballad form full of similes, analogies and internal rhymes, and it's impossible not to admire the tremendous effort of will and human spirit that must have gone into producing the work. The verse gives Sands a sense of the 'freedom of the mind' which keeps him sane; it enables him to get some perspective – even a humorous one – on the spectacle of his own terror, on the hypocrisy of the judicial system, and on the weight of suffering around him.

But what the poetry does not do is to distance Sands from his entrenched hatred for the men who capture, guard and torture him. Just as they 'know' with absolute certainty that he is IRA scum who deserves nothing but torture and death, so he 'knows', with the same kind of certainty, that they are subhuman brutes, pigs, devils and lackeys who also deserve to die. So centuries of injustice beget republican violence; republican violence begets increasing savagery and bias in the judicial system; and savagery and bias beget stone-hearted young revolutionaries who think that people's salvation grows from the heart of a 2000-pound bomb. Dean Burn's performance is a ferocious indictment both of state brutality in Northern Ireland, and of a public culture which so ignores the uncomfortable questions raised by this war that men like Sands are left to write their own stories. As he says of the artistic community, 'They never sketch the quaking wretch | That lies in Castlereagh.' But in its darkness and hate, it also represents a powerful inverse argument for the path of forgiveness which Sands is not able to find; and in that sense, it is the most important Christmas show I have seen.

1992

Niagara
Citizens', Glasgow
The Guardian, 20 February 1992

It's impossible for anyone who cares about live theatre – as opposed to the dead kind once dissected by Peter Brook – to contemplate what's going on at the Citizens' without breaking into great, beaming smiles of delight. Three years ago, building redevelopments around the Gorbals gave the theatre a spacious new double-decker foyer, glass-fronted, white-painted, plenty of space for corporate entertainment; nice enough for those who like that sort of thing, but not really the Citizens' style. So what have they done with it? They've filled it with theatres. When you enter the Citz in its latest incarnation, there's the main 650-seat auditorium ahead of you, a tiny 60-seat box to the right of the main door in the old stalls bar, and a 120-seat studio directly above it, in what were the wide-open spaces of the circle foyer. The theatres are briskly titled First, Second and Third, like the screens in a multiplex, and the effect is dazzling: a 15% grant increase from the Arts Council, support from Glasgow Development Agency and private donors for the building, and hey presto – three audiences criss-crossing in the foyer like a festival crowd, and nine productions for the price of three in this spring season alone, from the most exciting artistic directorate in Britain. It's the kind of conjuring trick that takes a special nerve, sangfroid, imagination; the Citizens' directors have it, and too many of the rest have not.

Which is why it's difficult not to read Robert David MacDonald's production of *Niagara* – which launched the season in the tiny Third Theatre on Wednesday – as a statement of intent, almost of artistic rededication, comparable to his magnificent *Chinchilla*, a dozen years ago. Written by the Chilean playwright/director Alonso Alegría in 1969, the play imagines a midlife crisis in the career of the legendary acrobat and tightrope-walker Charles Blondin (played by MacDonald himself), who, in his middle years, was famous for crossing the Niagara Falls on a two-inch wire. In his hotel room near the falls – somewhere between his fourteenth and fifteenth crossing – Blondin is approached by a strange boy called Carlo, who detects a boredom, a cheapening of Blondin's art, a weakening of discipline in his increasing dependence on showbiz stunts, and a tendency to get away with doing less than he promises his audience. He venerates Blondin's skill and courage; he believes that if Blondin remains true to his art, he could one day leave the tiny wire, and learn to walk through the shimmering air itself; and somehow they conceive the idea of crossing Niagara together, Carlo on Blondin's shoulders, creating a third creature called Icaron after the legendary figure with the wax wings – which is the two of them welded into one flesh, one single rope-dancer.

It's hard to know whether acting is the word for what Robert David MacDonald does in the role of Blondin. In the tiny, intimate space it looks more like an act of personal dedication to the high-risk process of self-examination and self-exposure, glittering white tights and all, which his and Blondin's art demands. Beautifully supported by Daniel Illsley's perfectly conceived, bookish little Carlo – around whom he moves with restless movements which are afraid and tender, fatherly and erotic, full of the sad wisdom which knows how those impulses can coexist – his performance is about the dazzling process of finding the courage to let yourself be changed, in midlife, by another human being. It's a little camp, immensely brave, immensely moving; and it leaves us in no doubt that the men at the Citz intend to keep on walking the wire, in ever more dazzling combinations, for as long as they have the strength.

Macbeth
Raindog
The Guardian, 27 May 1992

There's no doubt about what drives the group of actors, technicians and administrators that make up Glasgow's Raindog company: it is quite simply the angriest theatre group I have ever come across. Its productions shake with rage and resentment; its members – many of them senior Scottish actors unable to find enough satisfying work elsewhere, and determined not to move south – spoil and itch for battle. In his programme note to their successful Mayfest production of *Macbeth*, now transferred to the Citizens' Theatre for a three-week run, director Robert Carlyle points out that after sixteen months of existence, marked by 'widespread critical acclaim and box-office success,' Raindog has yet to receive one penny in funding. He calls the company's rejection by Mayfest, which refused to fund the current production, a 'disgrace', and concludes with the furious peroration that 'this is not a few people getting together to make a few bob. This is a struggle for identity within Scottish theatre.' Raindog's financial plight is not unique: there are half-a-dozen promising companies in Scotland in similar situations. But this company's anger has an uncommonly sharp edge; and its productions therefore have a rare crackle of life about them, a powerful emotional charge.

The trouble with anger, though, is that it can only take you so far into a play like *Macbeth*, with its dense poetic texture and rich layers of feeling. Carlyle's fierce, short, Scots-language production is striking in appearance, with a rich burnished-metal set by Andy Harris, conventional costuming, spectacular lighting by Billy Russel in shades of amber and turquoise, and an imposing, intelligent Macbeth in Alexander Morton, whose powerful, practical, physical presence dominates the stage; and the supernatural elements of the story are potently woven into the texture of the piece, the three witches looking like night creatures in the shadows of Macbeth's castle, haunting the mind of his increasingly demented wife.

But emotionally, psychologically and vocally, the production is all over the place. Some major speeches are savagely cut, and most of the cast yell or garble them in an aggressive style that strangles poetry at birth. All the characters seem in a permanent, scowling fury, although it is not clear – except in Billy Riddoch's lucid and moving Macduff – what the source or object of the anger is, and the production has all the emotional and vocal range of a raw chunk of heavy-metal music. The only tonal relief comes with Caroline Paterson's sensual Lady Macbeth, a woman agonisingly poised between competing instincts of nurture and murder; and even here, her high-pitched, strained voice does no justice to the emotional range of her performance. But in its best moments, this fascinating *Macbeth* represents an electrifying reinterpretation of a towering classic; and even at its worst, its strength and weaknesses speak so eloquently about the way Scottish actors see themselves, and their language, that it looks like a key starting point for debate about the next steps in Scottish theatre.

The Life of Stuff
Traverse, Edinburgh
The Guardian, 2 August 1992

It's not until you come across a piece like Simon Donald's *The Life of Stuff*, the second of this year's Edinburgh Festival productions at the Traverse, that you realise that most of the 'new work for theatre' we see in Britain is really nothing of the sort. It's new, all right; but it partakes of theatre in a timid and apologetic fashion, as if constantly begging pardon for not being somewhere else, on radio, on TV, on film. *The Life of Stuff* is not like that. There's something faintly filmic about it, certainly, in the sense that film dominates the genre in which Donald is working. The play is essentially a gangster story set in the nightclub headquarters – maybe in Edinburgh, maybe in Glasgow – maybe of a fast-talking, sharp-suited junior drug baron called Willie Dobie; and there are plenty of short scenes, split between the roof of the premises (where Willie can see the kingdoms of the world spread out below him, 'every dot a customer'), the nightclub floor in the middle of the building, and a basement where a nice guy called Fraser, having been drawn inadvertently into the murky scams of Dobie and his assistant, Davie Arbogast, is trying to shave off his hair to avoid the attentions of the law. Shunting between floors in a fast lift are three 'dolls', the luscious, foul-mouthed Janice, a willing sex-slave called Holly, and wee Evelyn, who only wants to get her hands, for once in her life, on some decent chemicals; and the unfortunate Leonard, a trainee thug with eczema who loves Janice with a hopeless passion.

But echoes of Philip Marlowe and *The Long Good Friday* notwithstanding, Donald's play is thunderously theatrical, with characters making spectacular, bloodstained entrances through the lift doors, soliloquising, joke-telling, shouting the odds at one another in highly wrought obscenities from opposite ends of the stage. Basically, the play represents a brutal, frighteningly nihilistic vision of the contemporary city: a bunch of youngish people living slap on the edge of oblivion and violent death, uncushioned by anything in the way of morality, poetry, politics or hope, incapable of articulating a desire for anything but money, cheap sex, drugs and loud music, so misdirected by the thin, go-for-it rhetoric of the 1980s that they can't even understand their own powerlessness.

Yet there's something in Donald's language – a clear-eyed, foul-mouthed, intimate urban Scots, tolerating no inflation – that skips and sings to a much more human and sociable rhythm. Even in the teeth of Davie Arbogast's nasty sawn-off shotgun, these kids are picking their eczema, fretting about their personal style, and telling each other terrible jokes, throwing up, falling in love and bursting into tears; the effect is at once intensely comic (*The Life of Stuff* is a very funny play indeed) and – given the underlying tightness and seriousness of the situation, well sustained by Kern Falconer as Arbogast – full of pathos. Most of the acting, particularly from Louise Beattie as Janice, Stuart McQuarrie as the scabby Leonard, and Duncan Duff as Willie Dobie, is on the smashing side of good, already full of rhythm and bite. A little tightening-up here and there, a brisk run-in, and the gorgeous new Traverse will have a real Festival hit on its hands.

The Grassmarket Project
The Guardian, 18 August 1992

Every year, it becomes more apparent that strange things have been happening to theatre audiences, since we entered the television age. They've become more sceptical and giggly, harder to convince; their suspension of disbelief has gone. Increasingly, the characters in *Brookside* or *EastEnders* strike them as 'real', whereas stage actors in heavy make-up do not. Most theatre companies have reacted to this changing consciousness by abandoning the attempt to produce illusions of reality on stage. Look, they say, we are actors up here, telling a story; you don't have to pretend otherwise. But others are going to ever more extreme lengths to restore the tang of 'reality' theatre seems to have lost, abandoning theatre buildings for disused factories, abandoning scripted drama for documentary material; and finally abandoning professional actors for 'real' people, telling their own stories.

Jeremy Weller's Grassmarket Project, founded in Edinburgh two years ago 'to explore, through theatre, the lives of the dispossessed in our society', takes the latter approach with a vengeance. Weller is a young yuppie director whose career could have taken – may yet take – a much more orthodox turn. But he believes that theatre is dying through lack of contact with reality; his remedy is to bring 'the dispossessed' themselves on to the stage, and so far his strategy has been a blazing success. First, in 1990, there was *Glad*, in which a group of homeless people from Edinburgh presented a play based on their own lives, in an abandoned Grassmarket lodging house; last year there was *Bad*, presented by a group of desperate young offenders in a school gym; this year there is *Mad*, in which Weller directs a group of nine women with personal experience of mental illness, and also *The Big Tease*, scripted and directed by his partner Jean Findlay, which deals with the lives of six women who have worked in the 'sex industry', as exotic dancers or strippers. The main charge levelled against Weller, from the outset, has been that of 'exploitation', of using wretched people's pain to enhance his own reputation as a director; and certainly anyone seeing *Mad* is bound to be moved and shocked by the generosity with which these women lay out their souls in front of a paying audience. Likewise, most people seeing *The Big Tease* will be faintly nauseated by the sleazebag nightclub atmosphere the piece relentlessly recreates, and by the long, detailed demonstrations of just how the dancers go about stimulating their grubby-looking audiences of bug-eyed men. There is a touch of voyeurism in this which is not present in theatre presented by actors: we watch Donahue and Kilroy to see real people spill their guts in public, and we flock to Weller's plays for the same reason.

But in the end, only those taking part in Weller's projects are fully qualified to answer the 'exploitation' question; and if the quality of response to the work represents a vindication of his methods, then he has it. For from the beginning, the reaction of audiences and the media alike has been electric: packed houses, rave reviews, tours to London and Berlin, acres of coverage. This year, one young journalist from *The Scotsman* went to write a preview of *Mad*, and stayed to become part of the show, declaring that, in Weller's hands, theatre becomes more than 'just art'; when *Glad* opened in Berlin, one critic remarked that 'at the end, one is inclined to ask oneself whether one should ever go and see anything made-up again.'

And there's the rub: because it seems to me that the real reservation about Weller's kind of drama lies in the way it trades on the idea of its own 'artlessness', on this notion that it operates at a superior level of reality to other forms of theatre. Of course, this kind of work has a particularly close relationship with the material on which it's based, and by bringing the people who are the source of the material on stage, it often achieves performances of an intensity that puts professional actors to shame; this year *Mad*, in particular, includes some electrifying performances. But when it comes to the editing and transforming of real life for stage presentation, all theatre productions are a matter of artifice, of selecting and reshaping the raw material of experience in a way that gets at truths that run deeper than mere facts. If Jeremy Weller is a good director, it is because he possesses some traditional dramatic skills – notably a strong sense of structure – and works sensitively with actors who are wholly committed to the project; the difference between *Mad* and *The Big Tease* demonstrates that it's not the technique itself that produces excellent results, but the artistry and integrity with which Weller shapes and manipulates the material, honing it into a dramatic statement which can be repeated over dozens of performances.

But what is alarming about the Grassmarket Project is the extent to which its success with the public seems to depend on the denial of that artistry; on the idea that this is real, and that 'made-up' forms of theatre are artificial, untruthful and obsolete by comparison. In that sense, the assumptions which are coming to surround the Grassmarket Project represent a root-and-branch attack on the idea that imaginative writing and performance can be a vehicle for truth; a resurgence of the old Puritan libel that fiction and acting equal untruth and lying. And what should worry the theatre profession, as it meets in Edinburgh for its annual jamboree, is that the punk-materialism of our age on one hand, and the weakness and self-indulgence of our imaginative theatre on the other, has provided such fertile ground for the revival of that old and dangerous lie.

Demarco in Blackfriars Street
The Guardian, 2 September 1992

The main theatre at the Demarco Gallery in Blackfriars Street is a big, beautiful, dilapidated attic studio, the top half of an old religious meeting house, full of light and shade created by the soaring, sawn-off tops of gothic arches. The grey-white paintwork peels and flakes, the plaster crumbles, the whole structure groans in windy weather like a ship under sail. It's a space that seems in permanent transition between decay and rebirth, and in the five years since Richard Demarco began to mount his astonishing wing-and-a-prayer Festival programmes there, it has become a Fringe legend; but now it seems it's time to take a last, lingering look at it, and move on. It's a brave journalist who would write the final obituary, of course. Richard Demarco is probably the most remarkable and unpredictable arts promoter in the world, 80% infuriating, 20% pure genius, chronically short of cash; he therefore shakes the dust of Edinburgh from his feet, goes into exile, loses buildings and finds them again, as often as Frank Sinatra used to give farewell concerts. But this time the Edinburgh Italian

Institute – which bailed Demarco out of a financial crisis two years ago by announcing that they would buy the building for their new headquarters – have declared their firm intention of taking possession later this month; and however the building emerges from the Institute's 'restoration' plans, it will no longer be Demarco's place.

So it was in fine elegiac mood that I arrived, on Monday lunchtime, to sample the complete new programme of work which Demarco, bold to the last, is presenting in this final week of the Festival; and found myself taking part in a typical five-act Demarco melodrama. Act the first – into which I was plunged as soon as I turned the corner of Blackfriars Street, and saw a huge, roaring machine heaving up the giant cobbles with which the old street is paved, and flinging them ear-splittingly into the back of a lorry – involved the persuading of Lothian Region to call off its Highways Department immediately, a feat accomplished with much arm-waving and telephoning of the media on Demarco's part; followed by thirty-five minutes in the upstairs theatre watching a suitably angry, if definitely under-rehearsed, student company called POW shouting their way through a vividly staged polemic about human rights.

Act the second involved watching Punchbag Theatre of Galway perform their second Festival show *Fine Day for a Hunt*, and being bowled over by the production's resident band, Gan Ainm, if slightly disappointed by the young company's handling of Tom MacIntyre's complex text; followed by last year's Guardian Student Drama Award winners Talking Tongues in one of their creepy, funny, highly accomplished two-handers about non-communication and incipient violence in modern relationships. Act the third took place in the pub down the street, where Gan Ainm were giving it hell on the bodhrán, guitar and fiddle, and I shamelessly spent two hours drinking, roaring and foot-tapping instead of watching something by Beckett. Act the fourth took me back to the little dark tunnel of Demarco's downstairs studio for a sublimely wry, funny, tragic and human fifty minutes from the Polish Teatr Provisorium, in which two superb actors – Jan Kłoczowski and the wonderful Jacek Brzeziński – performed fragments in English, German, Hebrew and Polish, from *Faust*, *Job*, *The Brothers Karamazov*, while travelling across the spiritual wasteland of Europe like a pair of male Mother Courages, on a battered black bike with a big costume-box in front.

And act the fifth – well, this was a magnificent unexpected epilogue, in the true Demarco style. I came back to the upstairs theatre for the last time, to look at the Polish Teatr Tańca Balet from Poznań in four short dance pieces under the title *The Loneliness of the Faun*; and found myself watching one of the most thrilling dance performances I've ever seen, a big company of gutsy, muscular, young dancers filling the Demarco space to bursting point, negotiating the cramped stage with angry elegance, thundering through superb, memorable short ballets about sexual politics, love, death and hell. Demarco was there as usual, infuriating the audience by stage-whispering loud ecstatic comments, snapping away with his little camera; as usual, come the foot-stamping ovation at the end, we forgave him. Out in the street, afterwards, Demarco said, 'I'm going to have to come back and watch every night this week, I can feel it'; and for a moment, at sixty-two, he looked sad and a little old, in the grip of something that won't let him rest. But then he was talking about his plans for next year, to use this Edinburgh space or that, to mount a new production on the island of Inchcolm, to try a completely new approach to programming. The Blackfriars Street Gallery was a magical place, no doubt. But Demarco is a master of the 'found space', the doing of theatre where no one else ever thought of it; and as surely as night follows day, and deficit follows bold inspiration, he will find another.

1993

Prostitution on the Fringe
The Guardian, 25 August 1993

At the end of *Desire to Become Indians* – a strange, overlong but powerful piece from Budapest playing in Richard Demarco's magical new venue at York Lane – the cast, a handsome, harassed-looking group of twelve young Hungarians known as RS9, begin to 'run' towards the audience. In terms of the story, which is about East European immigrants in Depression America, they are running to catch a train to Oklahoma, where a sinister 'boss' in a fancy waistcoat has offered them a job in the theatre. But as they run on – for three, five, six minutes, sweating and panting in the tiny theatre space – they become like some terrifying universal image of twentieth-century humanity, fleeing, chasing, struggling to get away or not be left behind, stumbling and falling, kept moving by some kindly friend or relative; and for this company, the bitter competition for a job in free-market America – 'just a job, any job' – is as good a trigger for that image of sweat and desperation as any other. And as I watched, I realised that I had seen that desperate running movement before, just the previous day, in the final moments of Steven Berkoff's monologue *Actor*; again, the frantic search for work, the sense that 'If I don't work soon, I don't exist.'

For if there is one image that has dominated the Fringe so far, it is this image of people on the edge of extinction, selling themselves to live. The East Europeans – in the middle of their short, sharp, shock introduction to the market ethos – question and grieve over this ruthless buying and selling of human horseflesh in a typically articulate stream of theatrical imagery. The Hungarians at Demarco's, the Polish Wierszalin group at Theatre Workshop with their folktale of a little boy sold for hard cash, the Theatre 77 group from Warsaw with their haunting production of Tankred Dorst's *Ja, Feuerbach*: here, in Polish and fractured English – and in a fascinating contrast with Berkoff's treatment of the same theme – an actor long banished from the stage through insanity, politics or drink, unforgettably played by Piotr Krukowski, desperately tries to sell his talent again, at an audition, to the shadowy figures of director, technician, designer, who surround him.

And the theme appears too, in less developed form, in work by young British companies on this year's Fringe. Perhaps its fullest home-grown expression comes in the Grassmarket Project's latest show *Risk*, at the Calton Studios, a brave and surprisingly shapely piece, devised during rehearsal, directed by John Mitchell, and performed with an impressive integrity and intensity, which features a combined company of professional actors, and young people who have themselves been 'at risk' on the streets of Edinburgh. But this sense of a generation with no community to fall back on, paralysed by fear of having nothing marketable to sell – except, perhaps, their bodies – also pervades shows like Anthony Neilson's brutal *Penetrator*, at the Traverse, in which two young men allow their lives to dribble away in drink, porn and indolence, and a third, selling himself to the army as a squaddie, pays a price so obscene that the play becomes almost unbearable to watch. It can be heard in quiet moments during otherwise daft style-victim productions like fecund theatre's druggie extravaganza *The Pleasure Dome*; and the whole idea of escaping from prostitution, of the mind, body or spirit, is an underlying theme of the John Clifford/Craig Armstrong opera *Anna*.

Which makes it all the more regrettable that the one Fringe production which deals directly with the subject of prostitution, *Call Me Susan* at the Traverse, makes such a miserable hash of it. Written and produced by, and starring, Jean Findlay, the piece is a kind of Socratic dialogue between an old whore and a young whore, interspersed with real-life recorded testimony from prostitutes working in Edinburgh and Glasgow, Paris, Kraków and Rome. But with that not-bad idea, the good things about this show come to an abrupt end; in fact I can't recall, in all my years of Fringe-going, a more excruciating combination of bad clothes, bad shoes, bad hair, bad pace, wretched acting, and a script so full of undigested theoretical hobby horses – about life, art, feminism – that it frequently chokes on its own half-cooked ideas, as well as on its agonising attempts to be raunchy and frank; even the real-life testimony is unforgivably mauled, voiced-over by a male actor with a lisp. But if the show is a lemon, the theme marches on: as I stood at the Traverse Bar, queuing for a restorative drink, someone came up and told me that I must go and see the Russian Circus on Ice, at the Meadows Big Top, since it was the sexiest show on the Fringe. 'What's so sexy about it?' said I. 'Well you see, it's all these brilliant skaters, all these world-class athletes like highly strung racehorses; and now they're having to do this crazy commercial show, having to sell themselves. There's something sexy about that, isn't there?' So fear twists the sexual imagination, as well as eating the soul. Where prostitution is the ultimate turn-on, what hope for a world based on anything else?

Romeo and Juliet
Citizens', Glasgow
The Guardian, 10 October 1993

It's impossible not to suspect, watching Giles Havergal's strange, hectic new *Romeo and Juliet* on the Citizens' main stage, that the whole affair has been driven by designer Kenny Miller's impulse to roll out the red plush and black bombazine, and stage something – anything – in the style of a Victorian melodrama. Here's old Capulet (Graham McTavish) as a north-country Gradgrind trying to fix an aristocratic marriage for his daughter, and the Nurse (Anne Myatt, in severe difficulties) trying to combine the vocabulary of a Renaissance bawd with the appearance of a well-padded Miss Prism; here are overstuffed chairs, swordsticks and opera cloaks, lashings of black-painted interior, and big swathes of Verdi ballet music. It doesn't work, of course; the only theme that survives intact is the dark reflection on family politics, the heavy patriarchy of Juliet's father, the conditionality and hypocrisy of his love, and the acquiescence in those values of Lady Capulet and the Nurse. For the rest, the setting is nonsensical. Whatever else Victorian industrialists did, they didn't wander round the streets indulging in sword fights with other eminent families; the bawdy sensuality of the language clashes with the setting at every turn, and even the architecture looks wrong. Nor does Havergal succeed in keeping control of the melodramatic tone; on the contrary, the staging is full of extraordinary lurches into a kind of mocking Edwardian camp that is wholly irrelevant to the play (Benvolio as a lisping gay Jeeves, forsooth), and a great deal of the acting and verse-speaking is poor-to-embarrassing.

Which makes it all the more surprising that Shakespeare's game old story somehow fights its way through to exert a firm grip on the audience. *Brookside* matinée idol Robert

Beck may not be everyone's idea of a Romeo, but he speaks his lines loud, clearly and intelligently, and he certainly knows how to play to the gallery. Shirley Henderson is a half-crazed little Juliet, shrieking her way through the part at an unsustainable voice-pitch, but her sincerity and youth somehow make the characterisation stick; and Derwent Watson plays a commendably straight bat as a genuinely well-meaning Friar Laurence. It says a good deal for these three performances that they even survive the camping-up of the Capulets' tomb, in the final scene, with three towering memorial crosses outlined in fairy lights; if actors enter into a real alliance with Shakespeare's words, it's amazing what, together, they can face down and overwhelm, even four hundred years on.

Stalinland
Citizens', Glasgow
The Guardian, 18 October 1993

What do you get when a gifted young Scottish playwright – twenty-three on his last birthday – tries to write a play about the whole meaning of the collapse of communism in eastern Europe, a subject on which he seems to know about as much as any averagely attentive *Newsnight* watcher? The answer, if David Greig's *Stalinland* in the Citizens' Stalls Studio is anything to go by, is that you get a tough, well-made dramatic structure – built to offer maximum possibilities for conflict, dialogue, reflection, pacy resolution – stuffed with every cliché in the book about relations between east and west since the collapse of the Berlin Wall. The play is set in 1991, with flashbacks to a key – but irritatingly unspecified – moment in the communist past; and what it has going for it is its bold dramatic scheme, which ruthlessly makes each of its five characters stand for a clear position in the ideo-logical debate. There's Josef, the old communist sculptor, moping in the streets over a rescued fragment of his smashed-up socialist sculpture 'The Spirit of the People'. There's the posh wife who 'never thought socialism applied to her', and left him for the west decades ago. There's the dissident daughter she left behind, lurching from hope to angry despair as the real face of the west becomes clearer to her; her worker-turned-government-minister boyfriend, falling like a ton of bricks for the smart suits and the study-trips to Paris; and the second daughter born in the west, a caricature of an insensitive and self-absorbed New Age businesswoman.

The difficulty is, though, that with the exception of the elder daughter Lydia, electrifyingly played by Mairead Carty, these characters never lift off the page for a minute; perhaps because the play contains not a single idea or observation about capitalism, socialism, and the whole damn thing, not already canvassed by dozens of western journalists and pundits. 'Write what you know' is boring advice for dramatists, and not to be taken in any literal sense. But in this play, Greig's formidable technique – which certainly suggests a brilliant career ahead – cannot conceal a fatal deadness in the language. For whatever reason, the real physical shock, slap and tang of first-hand experience is not there; and although Glasgow audiences may well lap up a play that tends neatly to confirm their low opinion of capitalism, its very neatness, in the face of a political change so complex and unfathomable, suggests to me something hearteningly well made, but finally synthetic.

The Master Builder
Royal Lyceum, Edinburgh
The Guardian, 23 November 1993

One of the key exchanges in Ibsen's *The Master Builder* comes early in the play, when the hero, Solness, is complaining to his friend the doctor about his fear of youth, and how it will one day come banging on the door, forcing him to make way. 'Well, what of it?' says the doctor. 'Then that will be the end of Master Builder Solness!' the answer roars back, all outrage and disbelief. For Ibsen's hero is a man in full rebellion against his own mortality and looming old age; and despite the occasional irony in what is often seen as a self-portrait of the artist as an ageing man, there can be no doubt that Ibsen saw his story as a tragic one. Everything about Solness – his childlessness, his sense of professional unfulfilment, the unhappiness of his marriage – cries out against the idea that this is where life must begin to end; and when the young girl Hilde Wangel strolls into his office like a streak of sunshine, seeming to offer him a new source of youth and energy, and a fresh start, he is utterly seduced, and lured on to a foolish death.

And what is strange about Brian Cox's *Master Builder* at the Royal Lyceum – co-directed by Cox himself and John Crowley – is that it captures every dimension of the play except the truly tragic one. Perhaps the mere fact of appearing in this most revealing of plays about male middle age, playing opposite his own much younger girlfriend Siri Neal, has simply used up Cox's capacity for self-exposure; at any rate, the Solness he gives us is rather held up for examination as a faintly comic, ridiculous figure – vain, egotistical, a lovable rogue in a too-youthful suit – than entered into as a human being full of immense pain, as well as frustrated energy and anger. The result is a surprisingly brisk, pacy, amusing production, which makes fine comic play of the obvious affinity between the guilt-ridden Presbyterian cultures of Scotland and Norway, but rarely touches the wellsprings of pity and terror beneath the surface. The long exchanges between Solness and Hilde zip along at a fine pace, but seem simply to state and restate the chemistry between the characters, rather than explore what they actually say; and the effect of Cox's curious distancing from Solness's inner drama is to throw too much emphasis on the character of Hilde, who, for all the insolent charm and intelligence of Siri Neal's performance, is really little more than a catalyst to Solness's crisis. Morag Hood does her best, under slightly adverse conditions, to invoke real sorrow and pain in her performance as Solness's grief-stricken wife. But the overall impression is too flippant and defensive by half: as if the pain of unhappy old men was something our feminist-influenced culture could no longer take seriously; or as if Cox had succumbed to the old exile's temptation of using his Scottish self as vehicle for satire and reductive humour, and leaving the exploration of the full, terrifying range of human emotion to more complete cultures, elsewhere.

By 1994 there was a sense of gathering pace, again, in the Scottish cultural scene. Early in the year, I left The Guardian *to become a theatre critic and political columnist for* Scotland on Sunday, The Scotsman's *new Sunday sister paper, and for me, the major theatre event of the year – apart from the first performance of* Trainspotting *at the Citizens' – was a decisive encounter, in Edinburgh in August, with Robert Lepage's great postmodern epic* The Seven Streams of the River Ota; *Lepage had been a regular visitor to Scotland ever since he first came to Glasgow in 1990. The Citizens' Theatre – which had boldly gone multiplex in 1991, opening two tiny studios in its foyer spaces – also produced some vintage shows around this time, not least a famous production of* The Milk Train Doesn't Stop Here Anymore, *starring Rupert Everett as Flora Goforth.*

Under the surface of Scottish theatre, though, a powerful new generation of writers was stirring. In 1993 Philip Howard had arrived at the Traverse as a young associate director, working alongside Ian Brown; his quiet determination to carve a distinctive role for the Traverse as an international new-writing theatre developing the work of playwrights based in Scotland was to play a key role in the development of Scottish theatre over the next decade, laying the creative foundations for the National Theatre of Scotland which finally emerged in 2006. It was also in 1993 that Kenny Ireland – a veteran of the Scottish radical theatre movement of the 1970s – became artistic director of the Royal Lyceum in Edinburgh, working hard over the next decade to reconnect the theatre with the mainstream of Scottish work. In the summer of 1995, at the Traverse, Howard directed the world premiere of Knives in Hens, *a first play by young writer David Harrower that went on to be produced in almost every country in Europe. The Edinburgh Festival received a memorable visit from the great Patrice Chéreau; and I wrote my first-ever review of a show by Suspect Culture, the collaborative company created by David Greig and director Graham Eatough – with a group of other artists – whose cool, reflective internationalism, and powerful insights into a fragmenting and individualistic world, were to help define the cutting edge of Scottish theatre in the late 1990s.*

1994

Dumbstruck
Tron, Glasgow

Trainspotting
Citizens', Glasgow
Scotland on Sunday, 5 May 1994

New young Scottish work at Mayfest: and after a long dry season in Scottish theatre, some definite, exuberant signs of life. Exhibit One is David Kane's black farce *Dumbstruck*, at the Tron, a bravura display of cultural satire and knockabout from a top Scottish cast in terrific form. Set in 1965, in a dingy theatrical boardinghouse in Glasgow, the play is subtitled 'From the Moment They Met It Was Murder', and that just about says it all: it describes the mayhem that results when an ambitious young crooner (Jimmy Chisholm, outrageous throughout) meets a repressed illusionist with a nifty sideline in putting the terminally ill out of their misery (Forbes Masson, not so much outrageous as preposterous), and their neuroses click together like two halves of a lethal weapon.

Kane's greatest admirer could not describe the show as profound; the best that can be said of it, theme-wise, is that it takes equal swipes at suburban satanism, holy-rolling Christianity, and the euthanasia lobby. But it hangs together without a hitch, it has the best crop of Scottish one-liners I've heard in years (how the audience roars when the illusionist confides that his father left Germany for Scotland because he 'didn't want to live in a defeated country'), and the whole piece is like a kick-start, a much-needed reaffirmation of Scottish theatre's ability to have a damned good laugh. Add a crop of unstoppable supporting performances – Eileen McCallum as the randy landlady, Jenny McCrindle and Maureen Carr in astonishing form as a female singing duo, and a brilliant Ronnie Letham as a hard-boiled agent in a plaid blazer – and you have a perfect 'good night out' for Mayfest; Michael Boyd directs in fine style, and Deirdre Davis, as a bitchy chorus girl, executes the single best stage death I have ever seen, a kind of aggravated death-by-cornflake.

Exhibit Two is Ian Brown's fierce, finely crafted production in the Citizens' Stalls Studio of *Trainspotting*, a new adaptation by Harry Gibson of the cult novel by Edinburgh writer Irvine Welsh. In a welter of furiously filthy language and seething frustrated energy, Welsh describes a world in which all moral bets about drug addiction are off; for his wrecked Edinburgh kids, the whole idea of life as meaningful and purposeful is a joke, and the tightly focused rollercoaster of a junkie's existence – moving single-mindedly from hit to hit – is as reasonable a way of filling in the space between birth and death as any.

In a way, the sheer vibrancy of Welsh's own work belies his vision: this is a blazing piece of theatre – superbly played by Ewen Bremner, James Cunningham, Susan Vidler and Malcolm Shields – which revels in the fact of Edinburgh as a city with its own working-class culture, explodes with life, embodies the creative energy that his characters cannot express. But there's also an overwhelming sense of grief and futility. 'I'll help you, son,' says a junkie's mother at one point, 'I'll help you beat this disease.' But Welsh's point is that this is not a 'disease'; it's simply rational despair at the fag-end of a civilisation that has lost all sense of purpose, and offers increasing numbers of its young no reason for living worth the name.

Macbeth

King's, Edinburgh
Scotland on Sunday, 12 June 1994

In the 1970s, Derek Jacobi created a Hamlet seen at the time as a revelation. It was all yearning sensitivity conveyed through soft nuances of the light tenor voice, and gentle complicity with the audience thrillingly played against a deep, enigmatic reserve; moving, human, unforgettable. But if you missed it first time round, never fear: for now you can see Jacobi doing it again, in Edinburgh and Glasgow, in his current tour with the Royal Shakespeare Company.

The play, of course, is not *Hamlet* but *Macbeth*, a fact which sets a few obstacles in the way of the performance. But Jacobi, nothing daunted by his character's history as a battle-hardened general and leader of men, continues to produce exactly the same repertoire of quavering sensitivities, swooping vocal mannerisms, and slightly veiled psychological vulnerabilities; this Macbeth is a strange, fragile, late twentieth-century construction, a Hamlet who forces himself to kill Claudius, and then goes mad at the sight of the blood. And the difficulty is that although *Hamlet* – with its ironic, questioning texture and much looser poetic structure – can tolerate this kind of modern naturalism or pseudo-naturalism, the great, taut crag of dramatic poetry that is *Macbeth* simply makes it look ridiculous. Shakespeare created a towering poetic image of warrior virtues turned dark and self-devouring by a single act of vicious ambition; what Jacobi often seems to give us – particularly in a bizarre playing of the dagger scene – is a bachelor accountant from Pinner reduced to a quivering wreck because he's killed someone in a car accident.

Nor, in Adrian Noble's strikingly vacant and ill-judged production, is he the only culprit: if Jacobi's Macbeth is disappointing, Cheryl Campbell's Lady Macbeth simply defies belief, a kind of Joan-Collins-as-Alexis-Carrington performance, sometimes frankly played for comedy. The costumes are standard medieval kitsch, the music an embarrassing string of martial clichés; and although there are some stout supporting performances – I particularly liked Christopher Ravenscroft's open-faced Banquo – on the whole the polite little southern-English voices of the cast slide blandly over the surface of Shakespeare's rugged Jacobean language, leaving its texture unexplored.

Jacobi remains, of course, a charismatic and compelling actor, and his Macbeth is better than negligible. In the early scenes, he touches on the boyish soldiering camaraderie of a man who can kill without thought on the battlefield, but falls to pieces when he has to take responsibility for a personal act of violence; there is a brief flash of brilliance around Banquo's murder, when he shows how a man dedicated to evil is driven to identify others as the source of his terror, rage and insecurity. But what he cannot do, physically or vocally, is to be the warrior-icon Shakespeare demands, both in the opening and closing of the play. He lacks the bass notes; and if this is a *Macbeth* for our time, it shows us the weakness of late twentieth-century thinking about masculinity, not its strength.

The Seven Streams of the River Ota
Meadowbank Sports Centre, Edinburgh
Scotland on Sunday, 21 August 1994

When Robert Lepage and his Québecois company first went to Hiroshima, they were struck not by the desolation of the city, but by its beauty. Like many Westerners, they expected a place of dust and ashes. But what they found was a sense of harmony and loveliness painstakingly reconstructed out of unimaginable ruin; and it's on the mystery of this link between creation and destruction, life and death, that Lepage has chosen to build his latest production, *The Seven Streams of the River Ota*, given its world premiere in Edinburgh last week.

In concept, *The Seven Streams* is a hugely ambitious work – named for the river that runs through Hiroshima – which will eventually try, in seven one-hour scenes, to get to grips with the defining horrors of our century, and to sing the resilience of one human spirit, that of a Czech-Jewish woman called Jana, born in Prague in 1930, who has survived the worst the century could throw at her, and settled, at last, in Hiroshima, the city of survivors. So far, the company has completed three of the seven scenes: and the result is a single long evening of theatre, inconclusive, tantalising, but completely compelling, full of emotional and imaginative richness, and a deep, mysterious feeling for the very pulse of twentieth-century living.

In the first scene, called 'Threshold', Jana welcomes a young French-Canadian artist, Pierre, into the peace and order of her Hiroshima house; and in a ravishingly beautiful one-hour sequence, punctuated with the gleam and splash of water falling like a blessing on Jana's roof and through her garden, Pierre gradually becomes absorbed into the delicate, unfamiliar rhythm of Japanese life, penetrating first Jana's home, then her body, then at last her mind, with its dark storehouse of memories. In the second scene, some of those memories come to life: Jana is an eleven-year-old girl in the Nazi camp of Theresienstadt, then a drug-dazed refugee from reality in 1960s New York. And in the third scene – about interactions among Canadians living in Japan – the company seek to remind us of the manners and style, the power and emptiness, of the thrusting, wisecracking, macho Western/global culture most of us spring from; this is more difficult territory, closer to home, and less successful.

But even to describe these scenes is to hint at the immensity of the themes the show is beginning to tackle: tensions between East and West, masculine and feminine, nations, races and languages in conflict. For a male Western director, Lepage is a tremendous romantic, a terrific explorer of the feminine, and of the truly erotic. His work is heavily influenced not only by modernist techniques of distancing and fragmented narrative, but also by the gossipy simplicity and emotional directness of postmodern 'women's' genres like soap opera, magic realism, the romantic family saga; and it's this open emotionalism and romanticism, as much as his willingness to leave questions unanswered and ends untied, that breaks the unspoken rules of Western high culture, and generates hostility from those in the audience who have difficulty in kicking off their psychological shoes, and letting an unfamiliar rhythm wash over them. But for those willing to go with the flow, this is an entrancing and transforming piece of theatre born of the moment we live in, strange and familiar, funny and sad, absurd and true like life itself; and it returns to Glasgow's Tramway in October – although of course, this developing work will have flowed on a little by then.

The Big Picnic
Harland and Wolff, Glasgow
Scotland on Sunday, 25 September 1994

In a sense, reviews of Bill Bryden's *The Big Picnic* – which opened at the Harland and Wolff engine shed in Govan last weekend – are beside the point: its massive physical scale and cost, the power of its sponsors, and the blaze of publicity surrounding its opening, have already guaranteed its place in history as the most remarkable Scottish theatre event of the year. Nor is the production's eminence purely a matter of hype. Something about Bryden's attitude – the language he uses, the subjects he chooses – is uniquely successful in convincing ordinary working-class Scotsmen that theatre has something to do with them; love him or hate him, Bryden reaches parts of the Scottish public other theatre directors cannot touch, and that achievement demands recognition.

But since reviewing is my job, I have to say that I find the powerful public response to Bryden's work more depressing than encouraging; for his *The Big Picnic* – the tale of a group of Govan 'pals' who enlist for the First World War – strikes me as one of the most shallow and inadequate accounts of that conflict I have ever seen. On the positive side, it boasts the astonishing Harland and Wolff performance space, transformed by the designer Bill Dudley into a long smoky stretch of No Man's Land, and a series of impressive performances from the fifteen men of Bryden's company, with Stuart Bowman and Iain McColl outstanding as, respectively, an educated socialist from Barra who stoutly resists promotion as 'officer material', and a gruff daredevil of an illiterate Govan sergeant.

But when it comes to the production's weaknesses, it's hard to know where to begin. For a start, this story of the western front sits less easily among the clanking metal gantries at Harland and Wolff than did the engineering history of *The Ship*. On the ground, this war soon became a matter of mud, blood, shit, birdsong and shattered human flesh, and Bill Dudley's attempts to make the production machinery stand as a metaphor for the 1914 'war machine' seem forced and unconvincing. Then there is the show's strange detachment from its live audience: despite half-hearted attempts at creating a 'promenade' atmosphere, the amplified sound, episodic scenes, helpless dependence on spectacle, and peculiar insistence on shifting the audience's viewpoint (Bryden shunts the seated section of the crowd up and down the shed as if it were a giant camera moving around a sound-stage), gives it the feeling of a theatre event desperately aspiring to the condition of an epic movie. The use of women in this show – mainly as silent nurses, and wan wives waving from quaysides – is embarrassingly perfunctory; the sloppy, self-righteous banality of the '70s folk-rock music is agonising; the story, which never gets beyond the obvious into deeper themes, is inexplicably feeble, pulling together a clichéd collection of war anecdotes – the Christmas football game in No Man's Land, the Angel of Mons, the rent strike in Glasgow – every one of which has been better told elsewhere.

This would all be forgivable if *The Big Picnic* succeeded in its central task of evoking the sheer horror of the 'war to end all wars', and it's here that its failure is most baffling, and most dangerous. Perhaps Bill Dudley imagined that his landscape of nice, dry, sandy earth heaped into trenches and gullies would be sufficient, under powerful lighting, to convey the mud-drenched hell of the battlefield. But in fact, it prettifies the conditions at the front to the point of falsification; and the unlikelihood of men surviving the trenches in the dry-footed, unscathed condition depicted here is compounded by a plot in which scarcely one of our heroes is killed until the last moments of the play, when they all fall neatly in battle, and then get up again to sing a rousing final chorus. We see no mud, no blood, no dismemberment, no men drowning in the stuff of their own gassed lungs; in fact the only death we see involves a jaw-droppingly vulgar exhibition of theatrical kitsch, in which the Angel of Mons – played by a dangling trapeze-artist in grubby white leather boots – arrives on a crane to hook up the dead soldier and carry him off to heaven, to a round of audience applause. Before his own death in France, Wilfred Owen produced the definitive poem giving the lie to the old '*dulce et decorum est*', the idea that 'it is sweet and fitting' to die for your country. But now, in his eagerness to make the men of Govan into heroes on a war memorial, and his weakness for spectacular *schmalz*, Bill Bryden has come perilously close to giving that

lie new life. As a trajectory for Bryden's own work – preoccupied as it is with restoring the wounded male pride of his
tribe – this flirtation with the romance of war was perhaps
inevitable. But as a sign of the times, it chills the blood. So if
you have young sons, send them elsewhere. Sit them down
with Wilfred Owen, or Vera Brittain, or Lewis Grassic Gib-
bon, or any writer who knew that terrible slaughter at first
hand. And pray they will learn that war is a much uglier thing
than Bryden conjures up here, more serious, more profound,
more filthy, more terrible, and far, far more wrong.

The Milk Train Doesn't Stop Here Anymore
Citizens', Glasgow
Scotland on Sunday, 6 November 1994

The thing about camp, at its highest, is that it's not only a
style, but a whole philosophy of life. Just as camp style tends
to freeze human gesture or style in a particular, mannered
moment, so a high camp personality – like Liberace's, say –
defies time and mortality by refusing to fade away; its pride
is to remain rigidly, unfailingly the same – same clothes,
same make-up, same manner, same act – until the moment
when the whole structure suddenly fails.

Flora Goforth, the dying film-star heroine of Tennessee
Williams's late play *The Milk Train Doesn't Stop Here Anymore*, is a monster of camp in precisely this style. Perched
high in her villa on the Amalfi coast, surrounded not by loved
ones but by staff who loathe or exploit her, succumbing to a
fatal illness whose gravity she flatly refuses to acknowledge,
she has lived the life of a cultural artefact rather than of flesh
and blood; and it's perhaps because this ageing diva is so
much more of an 'it' than a 'she' that it is so easy to accept
Rupert Everett's astonishing performance as Miss Goforth
in Philip Prowse's new production at the Citizens'.

In the world outside the theatre it is, of course, enraging to see one of the few powerful leading roles available to middle-aged actresses swallowed up by a young actor in the prime of his career. But within the world of the play – grasped and twisted, in Prowse's vision, into a strange, surreal place between life and death – there's no doubt that this brazen piece of gender-bending fully justifies itself.

Played for naturalism, *The Milk Train* can look like a bad, anachronistic joke, a fragment of elegant thirties style wrestling awkwardly with the new language and social realities of the 1960s. But played like this, on some high, bright promontory at the end of life, part villa, part hospital, part feverish dream landscape, with the dying Goforth like a great craggy sculpture standing out against a fierce blue sky, white rocks, relentless sun, the play takes on a far deeper and poetic colouring, strange, emotional, unsettling.

When the 'angel of death' appears, in the shape of the poet Christopher Flanders, superbly played by Greg Hicks, we waste little time worrying about his 'real' motives. He is clearly a figure – hungry, bleeding, young – from a wiser world of flesh and humanity, come to help Goforth face the physical transformation she has held at bay for so long. The imagery surrounding his presence – bloody wounds, brilliant white robes – is plainly Christ-like; their exchanges are superbly played, passionate, precise, charged with emotion and meaning.

All of which is not to say that the production is not funny, and often at least as silly as the play itself; Everett milks every last (canned) laugh out of Flora's camp laughter, Georgina Hale enjoys herself immensely as the lady-who-lunches neighbour, and Derwent Watson adds another caricature to his scene-stealing repertoire of fat female servants. But the cool, uncompromising surrealism of the set and production makes it clear from the start that there is more than cosy campery here. There is also death, and the fear of death; and in rising to meet the challenge of that most difficult subject, this production transforms an uneven play into a fascinating and powerful piece of theatre.

The Crucible
The Arches, Glasgow
Scotland on Sunday, 13 November 1994

'I have sensed, all across this country, the negativism, the harshness, the divisiveness, the willingness to pit people one against another; my great hope is that this state will put aside the divisions, between communities, between colours, between sexes, and that we will remember what the proper direction is for us as a people.' No, not a character in *The Crucible*, Arthur Miller's great 1953 play about the Salem witch-hunts of the seventeenth century, but ex-Governor Mario Cuomo of New York State, one of the last great liberals in American politics, signing off on Tuesday night after his defeat in the gubernatorial election. Times change, of course, and means of communication with them. But the psycho-politics of hate, hysteria and scapegoating does not change; and Miller's magnificent drama – as revived at The Arches, Glasgow, in a rough, ready, passionate and superbly timely production by Andy Arnold – links the reactionary politics of our time with the anti-communist hysteria of the 1950s, and the old madness in Massachusetts, in a single, catastrophic indictment of what men and women may do when a culture of superstition, judgementalism and legitimised cruelty is allowed to drive out common humanity and common sense.

It's difficult to say, indeed, exactly what it is that makes Arnold's simple, shoestring production so compelling. Many of the cast members are young and inexperienced, and the quality of the acting varies wildly. But some of the leading players – Marion Sangster as Abigail, the twisted girl whose sexual hysteria in a repressed community triggers the whole tragedy, and Lewis Howden, giving the gruff and heart-rending performance of his life as the reluctant farmer hero John Proctor – bring a degree of emotional intelligence, understanding and precision to their roles that could hardly be bettered.

The simple setting – in one of the dank stone tunnels to the rear of The Arches, with candles guttering in sconces on the walls and hard church pews to sit on – might have been built to contain and emphasise the stark, simple lines of the tragedy; and the eighteen-strong cast (an impossible dream in a fully professional production) throws itself into the mood of the play with such feeling and accuracy that every strand of its complex meaning, from its subtle examination of nervous patriarchy to its hatred of ignorant superstition masquerading as science, emerges with overwhelming clarity. Of course, Scots do not find it difficult to recognise the conflict played out in *The Crucible* between two faces of Presbyterianism, the one pragmatic, democratic, enlight-ened and humane, the other hysterical, censorious, dogmatic, divisive, and seething with sexual neuroses. But Andy Arnold's young company bring something deeper to the play even than that cultural understanding. They act like people who know what it is to live in a world gone mad, where common decency is subordinated to dogma, where lies become truth, and honest doubt in the face of the pre-vailing belief becomes a hanging offence; and if we do not want to find ourselves witnessing, in our society, the kind of horrible and bloody catharsis that came to the people of Salem, we had better start asking ourselves why.

1995

Mystery Bruises
Traverse, Edinburgh
Scotland on Sunday, 22 January 1995

When the satirist Peter Cook died earlier this month, one of his friends remarked that in later life he had developed a kind of distaste for the business of being funny for a living, making jokes for cash; he would, he said, rather just 'do it for nothing, for a group of friends round a dinner table.' And it's easy enough to see what Cook meant: there's something strange about a society in which so many elements of ordinary human conversation – political opinions, witty remarks, wild speculations, comical anecdotes, the kind of banter people used to indulge in after work, in pubs and on park benches – have become marketable commodities, the precious stuff of column-writing and stand-up comedy, to be dispensed only when paid for.

But it's also true that Cookie might, had he tried his hand, have found himself more at home in the world of modern live performance than he imagined; for once the money is paid and the performer on stage, many 'stand-up' shows are, in fact, pretty much like dinner-party or pub conversations, a strange substitute for social life in which one witty talker takes the floor, and sets the world to rights for an hour or two. Ken Campbell's latest extravaganza *Mystery Bruises*, at the Traverse, is a powerful case in point, a show devised – as the anarchic old stager of happenings cheerfully admits – to get round the fact that he hates learning lines these days, and therefore prefers to talk off the cuff. In essence, the whole experience is like going into a bar and being buttonholed by an energetic, likeable, witty and inquiring old geezer in a striped T-shirt who wants to tell you about everything, from his career as a 'legitimate' actor (short but lively) to his dabblings in New Age philosophy, mysticism and weird experimentation (with short excursions into Cathar theology), and the mind-bending experience of making a programme for Channel 4 about the new frontiers of science, featuring quantum physics and the concept of multiple universes.

The show is not at all slick: there's plenty of umming and erring and fluffing and pausing, and this effect is redoubled in the fragment of a new work – called *Mystic Geography* – that Campbell presents as an optional coda to *Mystery Bruises*, a half-formed meditation on the strange New Age art of 'affirmation', in which he introduces a Vietnamese-born violin-player with a funny-pretty face and a voice like an angel whom he mysteriously 'affirmed' into his life a few months ago. But what is strange is how little audiences seem to object to the elements of vagueness and self-indulgence in shows like *Mystery Bruises*, and how deeply successful they are in breaking down the barriers to real human contact that plague our hard-edged culture. In purely comic and theatrical terms, the show is probably at its best in Campbell's mad and hilarious anecdotes about his acting career, particularly his show-stopping textual analysis of the role of Angus, an attendant lord in *Macbeth* whom Campbell proves to his own satisfaction to have been a dwarf.

But, at a deeper level, this show is far more than a series of disconnected thoughts and old stories. What it shows is Campbell as a kind of Everyman – a little lonely, a little puzzled, a little disillusioned, a little hopeful, slightly unemployed, occasionally broke, always down to earth and sceptical, yet boundlessly curious – perched on the verge of a new century that may bring unimaginable changes in our perceptions of reality and our relations to it. In its tender and careful development of this character and theme,

Mystery Bruises is, in its crazy way, a fine example of the art that conceals art. And the directness and poignancy of the link Campbell builds with the audience, as we all struggle together to make sense of the strange time we live in, is something many smarter shows cannot begin to match.

Oleanna
Royal Lyceum, Edinburgh

Easy
Citizens', Glasgow
Scotland on Sunday, 21 May 1995

When David Mamet's 1992 play *Oleanna* opened in New York and London, critics shrieked about how the play represented 'a warning to the whole politically correct movement', whatever that may be; devoted couples allegedly came to blows in the stalls, men in the audience cheered the play's brutal conclusion, and women attacked the men who cheered.

The play deals, you see, with the story of a man – a liberal lecturer in an American university – whose life and career is ruined by an allegation of sexual harassment from a girl student; and its much-hyped reputation as a piece of heavy artillery ranged on the male side in the gender war now precedes it wherever it goes.

So what is striking about Kenny Ireland's fine Scottish premiere of the piece at the Royal Lyceum in Edinburgh is how firmly it precludes that kind of simplistic reaction. From the outset, this a production that listens intently to the real rhythms of Mamet's complex text, rather than reacting to public preconceptions of his meaning, and what emerges is a true American tragedy – the name Oleanna, we're told, refers to a 'failed nineteenth-century utopian experiment' – about an academic world which is supposed to be dedicated to the pursuit of truth, but is in fact completely corrupted by the politics of power.

John, the lecturer – superbly played here by Tom Mannion, with a rare, brave, vanity-free willingness to expose his character's ugliest weaknesses – imagines that he is a free-wheeling sixties radical, encouraging his students in an open-ended enquiry about the nature of society. But from the first lines of the opening scene, Mamet and Mannion make it crystal clear that his character's preoccupied, pre-emptive responses to his struggling working-class student Carol, and to her desperate anxieties about passing her course, represent a rank failure to 'hear' her, and a real abuse of the immense power university teachers have acquired in the modern academic marketplace; an abuse against which Carol (played with equal power and intelligence by Fiona Bell) has every right to react.

The tragedy lies, though, in the way modern American culture completely disables both John and Carol from understanding the nature of the alienation between them, which is fundamentally about social and economic power. Since John, as a good old-fashioned radical, will not recognise that he holds that kind of power, he cannot even begin to exercise it responsibly, or to see how it allows him to define concepts like knowledge, meaning and intelligence to suit himself.

And Carol, for her part, becomes seduced by an alternative world view which analyses the whole problem as having to do with patriarchy and 'rape', rather than with a complex interaction between sexual politics, and those aspects of John's power – his house purchase, his income, his 'tenure' – that have more to do with economics than gender; so that all she has learned, by the end of the play, is how to treat his reality with as much disrespect and brutality as he once accorded hers.

What Mamet has written, for my money, is a very clever and perceptive neo-Marxist play about a society made stupid and inhumane by false consciousness about the reality of power, on both sides of the gender debate and beyond it; and it speaks volumes for this calmly paced, elegant and sorrowful production that it allows so much breathing space for a world view – neither militantly feminist nor militantly anti-feminist, but humanistic, and full of a tragic sense of lost human potential – so unfashionable that most of *Oleanna*'s audiences seem to have missed it altogether.

And that powerful *Oleanna* sets a pattern for much of this week's theatre in Scotland, in which writers set out to tackle issues raised by feminism, but were often sidetracked by a sense of social oppression difficult to fit on to a purely feminist template. The Glasgow-based Lookout Company's *Easy*, at the Citizens' Circle Studio as part of Mayfest, is a case in point.

Written and directed by Nicola McCartney, *Easy* is a vigorous, lethally well-observed new play about the issue of 'acquaintance rape', which just can't help spreading its net to become a kind of deadly serious *Abigail's Party* for our times, a play about materialism and emptiness, about our miserable commercialised images of sex and 'sexiness', about lovelessness, the absence of real desire, and the massive implicit violence of a cash-driven society shot through with mindless competitiveness, casual cruelty, and endless jockeying for status.

If the play had wanted to do full justice to its declared subject, I suppose it should have dwelt more on the aftermath of the rape, and on the abject failure of the guilty man to understand and accept the truth of what happened; less on the long build-up to the rape, a hugely repetitive party scene in which all four characters become ever more drunk, obnoxious and embarrassing.

But the play follows its own path with immense conviction, and the action is spectacularly well played out, in strong naturalistic style, by Lucy McLellan as Rachel (a cabaret singer on the rebound), Astrid Azurdia as her friend Elaine, Grant Gillespie as Elaine's husband Martin (a hideously recognisable materialistic nerd obsessed with consumer hardware), and Timothy Webster as Martin's boss Paul, 'nice guy', blind date, and, as it turns out, rapist.

Knives in Hens
Traverse, Edinburgh
Scotland on Sunday, 11 June 1995

There was once a theory which suggested that language came in two kinds: 'restricted code', often used in traditional societies of fairly limited geographical and social scope; and 'elaborated code', the kind of fancy, generalised, multi-purpose language used by modern cultural elites and governing classes across the globe. It's a theory largely discredited nowadays. But many people in this country will still recognise the grain of truth in it: the way in which communities – in workplaces, villages, families – often deliberately restrict the language and vocabulary they use amongst themselves as a kind of gesture of solidarity; and the way in which breaking that solidarity by introducing new words and new ways of speaking can sometimes seem almost like an act of aggression, a deliberate shattering of the carefully limited world view that holds the community together.

It's around this fascinating theme – the intrusion of ever more elaborate language into our understanding of reality, the pressure of what the nameless heroine calls words thrusting into things like knives into hens – that the young Scottish writer David Harrower builds his new play *Knives in Hens*, premiered last week at the Traverse. In a sense, the setting of the play is a familiar one in Scottish literature, a kind of archetypal *Sunset Song* rural community in which an old, stable language, culture and tradition of life is gradually being disrupted by new words, new kinds of analysis, the onrush of modernity and urbanised culture.

But Harrower deals with it in a fascinatingly stylised and tightly focused way, centring his short eighty-minute drama on a brief, intense interaction between Pony William, a traditional ploughman, his increasingly restless young wife (known only as Young Woman), and the local miller, a disruptive and hated outsider in the village community, a widower who spends his time mysteriously writing down the thoughts inside his head. Slicing language into awkward, vivid, tongue-tied chunks often bereft of pronouns and conjunctions, Harrower traces the young woman's gradual evolution from placid acceptance of her village life and ways to an arousal that is as much intellectual as sexual, to rebellion, articulacy, and a growing sense of individuality.

Towards the end of the piece – meticulously directed by Philip Howard, with exquisite lighting by Bevis Evans-Teush – I felt that the story began to drift and sensationalise a little, losing its tight, archetypal quality. But Lewis Howden, Pauline Knowles and Michael Nardone turn in such a taut and compelling triangle of performances that the drama never relaxes its grip; and although it is rooted in a profoundly Scottish voice and sensibility, *Knives in Hens* has a deep, shuddering resonance to do with that transition from peasant to urban culture, from a world driven by muscle power and simple implements to one driven by language and technology, which has been one of the universal human stories of the modern age, and one to which many of us in Scotland are still far closer than we think.

One Way Street
Traverse, Edinburgh

Hill
Cathkin Braes, Castlemilk
Scotland on Sunday, 25 June 1995

'I was sitting inside the cafe where I was waiting, I forget for whom. Suddenly, and with compelling force, I was struck by the idea of drawing a map of my life.' This is the strange, resonant quote from Walter Benjamin's *Berlin Chronicle* that acts as the starting point for David Greig's *One Way Street*, a continuing theatre project (written and directed by one of Scotland's most talented young writers, and performed by actor Graham Eatough) that sets out to explore the life of its central character – a forthright, slightly chippy young writer called John Flannery, born and brought up in Burnley, Lancashire – through a kind of map-drawing project, a series of 'ten walks through the former East.'

In full flight from his family and from England, Flannery has arrived in Berlin, met a young anarchist called Greta, fallen in love, lost his love again, been commissioned to write up his 'ten walks' for a guidebook; and as he plods through the haunting, grim, darkly glamorous landscape of East Berlin, what emerges is a strange and original attempt – like a tentative English first step on the road towards Europe already trodden by Irish writers like Dermot Bolger – to explore the interface between the new post-Cold-War Europe, and a certain kind of post-1980s Englishness, baffled, inarticulate, with no strong sense of the future, angry, yet somehow apolitical.

All of this is expressed in rivers of strong, evocative writing by Greig, full of little gems of metaphor and insight, poetic but rarely over-elaborate. There are fascinating hints of a real darkness in Flannery's banal, uncommunicative family background; and the show is illustrated, oddly and thought-provokingly, with slides not of Berlin but of what looks like Glasgow, a device which, so far from narrowing the distance between the two cityscapes, only emphasises the mysterious unlikelihood of anything like Berlin's history happening in the damp, soft-edged light of the west of Scotland.

As a piece of theatre, *One Way Street* has, I think, two problems. One lies in the excessive neatness with which it tries to tie up the loose ends of Flannery's life in a brief seventy-five minutes. As the play moves into its second half, it modulates from a complex scenario, full of strange and disturbing possibilities, into a disappointingly conventional semi-comic account of how Flannery, shocked into a bout of self-examination by a surprise visit from his brother, romantically pursues Greta through the city, and settles down – in a very late-1980s kind of way – to a life of salvation through fatherhood.

Then, the play seems curiously uncomfortable with its one-man format. It lacks the clear dramatic relationship between the characters and the audience that shapes the best one-man drama; it tends to look, alternately, like a particularly good short story unaccountably flung on to a stage, or like a potentially interesting play that has lost most of its cast. Still, the quality of the writing, and of Eatough's performance as Flannery himself, makes these structural problems forgivable. *One Way Street* is a power-packed, memorable little piece, full of romance, imagination and promise.

In the business of etching a map of character on the streetscape of a European city, though, all other writers must yield to the master, James Joyce; and over the past three years the Scottish actor Tam Dean Burn, and a group called Process Ten-28, have been trying to piece together a theatrical response to Joyce's enigmatic late work *Finnegan's Wake*, with some surprisingly successful results. So it was with a light heart and high hopes that I set off for Cathkin Braes near Castlemilk, one glorious evening last week, to see the latest performance in the series, an event accompanied by a sculptural installation and called simply *Hill*.

Well, I arrived in Castlemilk. I asked many residents, walking their dogs around the warm streets, if they had ever heard of the 'Big Wood' where the performance was due to take place. None had. I demanded to be dropped in Cathkin Road, near the point marked with an 'x' on Process Ten-28's map; and, armed only with a bottle of mineral water and an overheated cagoule, walked for miles uphill through the slowly fading light, looking for any wood that might be classed as 'big'. I saw cows with calves lowing in high meadows. I saw wild flowers. I heard the soft wind rustle through hawthorn hedges, and saw the late sunlight touch the leaves with gold.

Enormous vistas of lowland Scotland spread about me under a pearly blue sky, from Dumbuck Hill in the northwest to what looked like the Pentlands in the east; Glasgow crouched below under a faint bank of cloud, like some city of sadness out of *Pilgrim's Progress*. But of Tam Dean Burn – an actor not known for his smallness of voice – I heard not a sound; and of the performance, and the installation, and the donkey and small boy supposed to co-star in it, I saw neither hide nor hair. Still, it was an experience, and of a strangely Joycean sort. 'You were nearly at East Kilbride, you know,' said the taxi driver taking me back to the station for the last train. 'And that's the Big Wood, just up there.'

Dans la solitude des champs de coton
Drill Hall, Edinburgh
Scotland on Sunday, 3 Sep 1995

Prowling along behind Peter Zadek's mighty Festival production of *The Merchant of Venice* like a dark shadow – a deeper, more searching and even more disturbing exploration of closely related themes – comes Patrice Chéreau's momentous and thrilling production, at the old Drill Hall in Forrest Road, of *Dans la solitude des champs de coton*, an enigmatic 1987 text by the late young French writer Bernard-Marie Koltès. At some dangerous hour of dusk, Koltès' two characters – called simply the 'Dealer' and the 'Client' – encounter one another in a bleak place haunted by distant sounds, the clashing of steel girders, the boom of foghorns, an occasional fierce burst of rock music or shattering glass; and for eighty minutes they circle, withdraw, argue the terms of their encounter. Dense, beautiful, fiercely poetic in its evocation of the interwoven impulses of need, lust, greed, or emptiness that drive us into 'dealing' with others, Koltès' text seems to draw its force from three areas: from the 1980s' sense of social atomisation, and the 'commodification' of relationships, that also informs Zadek's *Merchant*; from the special tension between commercial transaction and emotional need that haunts the relationship between prostitutes and clients, money and sex; and from the sense of fate, of a chance encounter with death itself, that filters through the fear-laden sexual culture of the 1990s into a wider questioning about mortality and its meaning.

But what absolutely distinguishes *Dans la solitude des champs de coton* is the impassioned brilliance of Chéreau's production, a handling of the basic elements of theatre – two figures, their words, the raw space they occupy – that literally takes the breath away with its sense of pace and space, of modernity, rigour, and purposeful energy. As for the mind-blowing performances of Chéreau himself as the Dealer and Pascal Greggory as the Client, there is something about their absolute, contained, perfectly realised individuality that seems to lift the business of acting on to a plane of reality and seriousness I have literally never experienced before; as if the combined genius of Koltès and Chéreau had somehow succeeded in creating a new place – somewhere between fiction and reality, acting and living, symbol and cold fact – that is finally where the theatre of the late 1990s needs to be.

1996

The Architect
Traverse, Edinburgh
Scotland on Sunday, 3 March 1996

Perhaps all civilisations are based on acts of oppression or exclusion; order seems to demand it. But it's also true that it's these same injustices that eventually begin to corrode the foundations on which the structure rests. *The Architect*, premiered at the Traverse last week, is a third major drama by David Greig, probably the most gifted of the new Scottish playwrights of the 1990s; and it emerges, from Philip Howard's thoughtful and well-made studio production, as a formidable contribution to our understanding of the strange impasse to which our own culture has now come, particularly in the area of gender and the family, where we can no longer live with our prejudices, and yet do not seem to know how to live without them.

The play is set firmly in contemporary Edinburgh, and, like Stanley Eveling's *The Albright Fellow*, seen in the city last year, it draws shamelessly on the inspiration and imagery of

Ibsen's great tragedy *The Master Builder*. Like Ibsen's play, *The Architect* revolves around a man whose whole sense of himself and his masculinity depends on his power to build, to make a clear and enduring physical impact on the world at any cost to that world. The play's hero Leo Black, powerfully played by Alexander Morton, is a successful Edinburgh architect who dwells with some pride on his record of building modern tower blocks for a modern city, and on the 'nice' suburban family life – pleasant house, pretty wife, grown-up son and daughter – his success has brought him.

But whereas Ibsen's (and Eveling's) heroes are driven to self-destruction by a nagging sense of personal emptiness, which leaves the structures around them still standing, in Greig's play the whole malaise has become much more overt, much more real. Leo Black's world, and the power-relationships that underpin it – between men and women, father and children, architects and tenants – is literally falling apart around him. Led by a feisty and excellent Una McLean as a tenants' leader, the residents in what was once Leo's showpiece housing development are demanding its demolition. His children hate him; and his wife Paulina – played by Morag Hood in one of the most compelling, funny and tragic studies of middle-class Scottish womanhood I have seen – is in such a state of frozen rebellion against him, and his habit of seeing her as something that fills 'a wife-shaped space', that she can hardly bear to hear him use her name.

I'm not sure that Greig doesn't overextend himself, and his play, in trying to provide equally full and rounded accounts of the lives of the Blacks' two disturbed children, their abused daughter Dorothy (Ashley Jensen), and their gay son (Tom Smith); the boy's story, in particular, is very roughly sketched. But the whole play vibrates with such ambition and intelligence – and in some places with such a breathtaking quality of emotional courage and openness –

that the odd structural imperfection is easily forgiven. It's possible to object, of course, that the emotional and physical devastation around Leo as the play ends is out of all proportion to any evil he may have done. But that, I suppose, is the tragedy of your conventional, suit-wearing, white, professional male at this end of the twentieth century. He can barely help being part of a system of power that more and more people are coming to hate and reject. And when it falls, he can barely help being dragged down with it.

Marabou Stork Nightmares
Citizens', Glasgow
Scotland on Sunday, 10 March 1996

Because he uses the language and subject matter of working-class Scottish street life, Irvine Welsh is often discussed as if he were some kind of social realist of the modern Scottish novel, describing young people's real lives with an accuracy other writers simply can't match. But the more I look at Welsh's work – and heaven knows, it's difficult to avoid looking at it this month, with theatre productions of *Trainspotting* in Scotland and London, the *Trainspotting* film on general release, and now Welsh's second novel, *Marabou Stork Nightmares*, appearing in a powerful and disturbing stage version at the Citizens' Theatre – the more it seems to me that his power as a writer has nothing to do with a naturalistic gift for describing social phenomena that others ignore; everything to do with his ability to see underlying patterns of violence and abuse in our culture, and to conjure up imaginary worlds that embody them. In *Trainspotting*, this analytical process was obscured behind a breathtaking bravura display of obscenity and visceral body-consciousness. But in *Marabou Stork Nightmares* the intellectual works begin to show; and the audience, consequently, to shift a little more restlessly in their seats.

For this time, the story focuses tightly on the theme of masculinity and violence, or the kind of masculinity that is defined through violence. The hero is a Muirhouse football casual called Roy Strong, sunk in a two-year coma after a suicide attempt that followed his involvement in a gang rape; and the relentless cycle of violence which has shaped his life is examined through flashbacks of childhood rejection and abuse by his 'genetic disaster' of a family, and through his strange coma dream of a boy's-own-paper African safari, a quest to destroy a horrible flesh-eating bird called the marabou stork.

All of this is faithfully recreated in Harry Gibson's formidable stage version. Cheerfully narrated throughout by James Cunningham as Roy, the adaptation cuts much of the detail of the safari scenes, but retains the recurring image of the marabou hunt as counterpoint to Roy's story, as it moves from the Punch-and-Judy farce of his early family life – enlivened by an inspired comic performance from John Kazek as his 'heid-banger' of a father – through the gathering darkness of his violent teens, to the apotheosis of the rape, and a final horrific punishment and atonement. The staging is slick, inventive and brilliant, the use of schmaltzy popular music fiercely ironic; Suzanne Field's surreal set captures the dream-like atmosphere to perfection; and Gibson's cast – Cunningham, Kazek, Stuart Bowman, Christopher Delaney and the unforgettable Joanna Macleod – perform with such energy and wit, and such a powerful understanding of how each character fits the story, that when they line up for their final bow it's almost impossible to believe there are only five of them.

The difficulty, if there is a difficulty, lies in the story itself. Welsh's explicit values in this novel are entirely liberal and enlightened. He wants to explain violence, and to show that it can be explained: his analysis of his hero's hate – of its roots in family abuse, class humiliation and educational failure, in our culture's pathological embarrassment over real sexual desire and the processes of life, in our habitual resort to violence as a less embarrassing outlet for that energy, and in the sudden collapse, within a generation, of the imperial and war-making projects that allowed us to export this mess of psychosexual confusion and violence to foreign climes – is impeccable. But it's the tragedy of the times – the times that have made Welsh Scotland's most popular serious writer in decades – that even when all of that is understood, the violence itself still seems to emerge, particularly in the theatre, as something more exciting, stronger, more resonant, than anything around it, the driving force of the action and the language. And in the end it's that decadent fascination with violence, and the inability to break it, that threatens to turn a legitimate portrayal of rape into a pornographic icon for confused times.

Airport
Tramway, Glasgow

Rough Crossing
Royal Lyceum, Edinburgh
Scotland on Sunday 16 June 1996

The name says it all, in a way. When they work together, the Scottish writer David Greig and the actor Graham Eatough call their company Suspect Culture, and it's a title that perfectly captures the quality of intellectual restlessness, the preoccupation with issues of culture and identity, and the healthy mistrust of the insularity of Britain's island cultures, that marks their work.

Their latest show *Airport* – which opened at the Tramway last week before moving on to the Traverse – is a perfect case in point. A devised piece set in the endless departure lounges, transit areas, cafés and shopping malls of some huge international air terminal, *Airport* was workshopped in Glasgow and Madrid, features a Spanish-British cast and uses both languages liberally and unselfconsciously. In the course of a fluid, fast-moving ninety minutes of action, it returns again and again to themes of cross-cultural understanding and misunderstanding, the use and abuse of national stereotypes, the cowardice of the sentimental ex-pat Scot facing the reality of home, the helplessness of the monoglot English-speaker in a multilingual world; it also touches on ideas about class (executive or tourist?), about the scope for fantasy and madness in the rootless world of airport encounters, on the power of sex to break down cultural barriers, and on the ultimate journey of death.

I suppose it could be argued that in *Airport*, as in so much of his work, Greig generates about half a dozen more political ideas than he and the company can comfortably dramatise. The show certainly comes to a powerful and moving conclusion – in which we, but not the characters, glimpse the deep similarity of human need and memory beneath their superficial differences – after about sixty minutes, and then bafflingly continues for another half-hour nonetheless. But in a brilliant, episodic piece of collage-drama such as *Airport* – full of sharp fragmentary encounters and images, expressing itself as much through gesture, movement, and Nick Powell's quietly superb musical score as through language, this kind of structural difficulty is easily overcome by the sheer panache and flexibility of the genre, its ability to switch instantly from the particular to the general. *Airport* boasts a superbly stylish set by Evelyn Barbour – two luggage conveyor belts divided by a ravishingly lit hint of the real, earthy landscape of home and childhood that all habitual air travellers lose and yearn for; it also features six tremendous performances, including a real tour de force from Andres Lima as a man dying of cancer in a departure lounge. It's not a perfect piece of work, but it uses the resources of late twentieth-century theatre fluently, gracefully, and with a real sense of fun, to address some of the most important issues of the age – and you can't ask for much more than that.

Kenny Ireland's Royal Lyceum production of Tom Stoppard's *Rough Crossing*, on the other hand, is the kind of show that makes me feel vaguely ashamed of having any connection with theatre at all. Freely adapted from a Hungarian comedy by Ferenc Molnár, *Rough Crossing* is a coy little spoof on the genre of 1930s musical comedy, set on an ocean liner crossing from London to New York, and featuring all the usual clichés, from a slightly ageing diva of a leading lady to a scene-stealing drunken steward. Since the plot concerns the tribulations of a pair of musical-comedy writers trying to finish off their latest Broadway opus, the text is also stuffed with self-referring witticisms about the playwright's art, obviously fascinating to Stoppard, less so to the rest of us.

Now it has to be said that the unfortunate impression created by this show at the Lyceum is not the fault of Kenny Ireland's company or of his production team, who throw every ounce of wit and commitment they can muster at Stoppard's supremely irritating text. Briony McRoberts is particularly gallant as the glamorous leading lady Natasha, hauling scene after leaden scene back from the brink of tedium; Russell Craig's mildly art deco set is a tour de force of visual wit, tilting hilariously during the storm scene. The trouble is that Stoppard, like many who have embraced Britishness as an adopted nationality, knows only one element of British culture, namely the manners, language, and style of the English upper-middle class; and in this play, he does not even attempt to achieve the moral seriousness and philosophical depth that make that narrow social focus relatively unimportant in most of his work. The result is a sad little joke of a show that sprays messages of class and cultural exclusion around the auditorium like some kind of theatrical bird-scarer.

Mull Little Theatre
Isle of Mull
Scotland on Sunday, 11 August 1996

The first thing to understand about Mull Little Theatre is that it's not even in Tobermory. It stands a good nine miles west of the Mull metropolis, in the old stone byre of a handsome grey house on the outskirts of Dervaig – a former Free Kirk manse, so they say – where Barrie and Marianne Hesketh, two professional actors who had fallen in love with the island and resolved to make themselves a life there, founded it thirty years ago. The view from the front door, beyond the lush planting of trees around the house, is of marsh and moor and empty hillsides, stretching away toward the wild Atlantic. To say that it is not easy to sustain a professional producing theatre and a full five-month summer season here, half a mile from a tiny village in the north-west corner of an island with a total population of less than 3000 – plus a variable passing trade of tourists – is an understatement. Struck off the Scottish Arts Council's list of revenue clients ten years ago, in the confused years after Marianne Hesketh's death, Mull Little Theatre survives in the 1990s on an amazingly frugal annual budget of little more than £50,000, half of it raised at the box office, the rest pieced together from the local authority, the tourist board, the local enterprise company, and donations; the last appeal produced an unexpected cheque from West End producer Cameron Mackintosh. And although there are hopes that Lottery funding may eventually help to build a new and more accessible theatre building, in the heart of Dervaig village, the company plays on, this season, in the same tiny forty-three-seat auditorium rigged up by the Heskeths in the byre – too small, as the theatre's current director Alasdair McCrone points out, to take a whole coach party, even if it wanted to.

And yet professional theatre survives at Dervaig; is even, under McCrone's direction, beginning to look in pretty good shape. For one thing, McCrone's 1996 season of four in-house productions is a miniature masterpiece of balanced programming – the dark and the light, the Scottish, the English and the international, the crowd-pleasing and the challenging: opening in May with *Not About Heroes*, Stephen MacDonald's beautifully written two-hander about the First World War friendship between poets Siegfried Sassoon and Wilfred Owen, the repertoire has now expanded to include Paul Godfrey's hilarious BBC-radio-play-style version of *Whisky Galore*, James Smith's nineteenth-century monologue for a murderous Edinburgh wife *Nancy Sleekit*, and *Speed-the-Plow*, David Mamet's foul-mouthed and brilliant exposé of macho Hollywood huckstering and deal-making.

And for another, the standard of performance and production achieved this year by McCrone's shoestring company – two young actors, one actress, a stage manager, a drama worker, an occasional designer and a couple of trainees, all on bare-minimum rates – is remarkably high; a little raw with inexperience here and there, but uniformly thoughtful, intelligent, tightly focused on the plays and their meaning, and not on the casual vanities of performance. On a quick visit to Dervaig last weekend, I missed *Whisky Galore*, this year's sure-fire tourist crowd-puller, now sold out for most performances. But I saw Cathal Quinn, as Owen, and Kevin Brock, as Sassoon, pick their way with immense feeling, and a fine sense of period, through a meticulously polished and good-looking production of *Not About Heroes* – beautifully designed by Alicia Hendrick – that left the thirty-strong audience visibly moved. I saw Caroline Hutton, in a gorgeous late-Victorian mourning gown, make a spirited try at the wicked black comedy of the thrice-widowed Nancy Sleekit, and succeed in projecting the Scots language of the text with a confidence that made her meaning clear, even to a group of Dutch tourists. And I saw all three actors make a committed, clever, energetic job of *Speed-the-Plow*, Mamet's vicious, complex, fast-moving account of how the Hollywood machine relentlessly grinds human creativity, idealism, even spirituality, into hard dollars and cents.

And yet I left Dervaig with a feeling of unease and even anger, not about the survival of Mull Little Theatre – for I think McCrone, whose contract as director has just been confirmed until 1998, will succeed in steering it towards a more secure future – but about the way the whole enterprise depends on the goodwill of talented and idealistic people who are prepared to live in near-poverty, and to work in conditions of discomfort and crowding that might reduce them to tears, if they didn't make a joke of it.

At Dervaig, more clearly than anywhere else in Scottish theatre, the cheapskate assumptions behind the funding of the arts in this country lie exposed: the idea that gifted director-managers in their late thirties should be available for £20,000 a year and talented young actors for poverty wages; that eager trainees will work for next to nothing and live on thin air; that a community can be provided with a valuable source of cultural energy – and a major tourist attraction – involving ten professional staff and a little battalion of volunteers, for a sum that would not keep one Member of Parliament for a year. Alasdair McCrone, his company and his board are doing a fine job at Dervaig this year. But they are doing it under financial conditions – the pervasive 1990s preference for ad hoc 'project' funding over regular revenue grants, for capital expenditure over employment, for rich kids who can afford to work for nothing over those tasteless enough to need a living wage – that strike me as a kind of disgrace. The arts will survive this mean-spirited climate, no doubt. But we do ourselves no credit by holding them so cheap; or by expecting two young men to give us not only of their professional skill but of their souls, as I saw Kevin Brock and Cathal Quinn doing at Dervaig last Saturday night, for a wage that will barely even buy them an old banger of a car, for the run into Tobermory.

1997 was a momentous year for Scotland, the year of the election of the Blair Government, the year when the work of the Scottish Constitutional Convention reached its conclusion, and the year of the September referendum when the Scottish people finally voted, by a margin of three to one, for the restoration of a devolved Scottish Parliament within the UK. There was a sense, among Scottish artists and writers, of a job well done, in terms of building a new, outward-looking model of national identity for the twenty-first century; and a sense that the initiative was now passing to the politicians, setting the artists free to explore wider themes.

Before the referendum, though, there were two more outstanding plays about Scotland, in the shape of Stephen Greenhorn's Passing Places, *premiered at the Traverse in February, and David Greig's beautiful romance* Caledonia Dreaming, *set in Edinburgh on a magical summer night during that year. There were also bitter endings for some of the radical theatre initiatives of the 1970s and '80s: in the late 1990s, both Wildcat Stage Productions and Glasgow's Mayfest lost their funding, and ceased operations. In 1997 I stopped theatre reviewing for a year, to become a general arts and political columnist for* The Herald. *Then in the spring of 1998 I returned to* The Scotsman, *as theatre critic and political columnist; and, during that year's Fringe, I had my first encounter with Edinburgh's Grid*

Iron Theatre Company, and with the move towards site-specific theatre that became such a powerful feature of the British theatre scene, over the next decade.

As the century rolled to a close, in 1999, Dundee Rep launched its new ensemble company, still almost unique in Britain seventeen years on. The Rep's director, Hamish Glen, became chair of a new group set up by the Federation of Scottish Theatre to develop a model for a twenty-first-century National Theatre, that would reflect the real needs and hopes of theatre companies and artists working in Scotland. Suspect Culture powered on, producing a show called Mainstream*; for the Edinburgh International Festival of 1999, David Greig wrote* The Speculator, *about the early origins of capitalism. And at the Traverse a brilliant new young associate director, John Tiffany, directed a superb production of Stuart Paterson's great Scottish tragedy* King of the Fields. *The future was thundering towards us, that year; and it was clear – as the first Scottish Parliament for almost three hundred years was elected and sworn in – that decisive change was in the air.*

1997

Passing Places
Traverse, Edinburgh
Scotland on Sunday, 9 February 1997

Opponents of Scottish Home Rule often suggest, for the sake of argument, that Scotland is really too diverse a place to qualify as a nation. 'What does a factory worker in Motherwell know of the life of a Lewis crofter?' they ask triumphantly, as if either or both might somehow have a closer affinity with a stockbroker in Esher. All the same, there is a grain of truth in the idea that Scotland is a nation with almost as many images, or self-images, as it has citizens. From the worlds of *Trainspotting* and *Taggart* to the worlds of the Hawick Common Riding and the Gaelic Mod, there are bridges to cross, huge self-discoveries to be made.

And what's fascinating about Stephen Greenhorn's new play *Passing Places*, which provides a rousing start to the 1997 Traverse season, is the wit and perceptiveness with which it follows a couple of lads from Motherwell – the dour and sceptical Alex, ejected from his job in a no-hope sports shop by his psychopathic boss Binks, and his pal, an unemployed brainbox and computer nerd called Brian – on a desperate journey in a clapped-out Lada across one of those great divides, out of the central belt to the Highlands and the far Caithness coast, and into territory that forces us to think a little less about our scorn for the tartan-and-heather tourist image of that northern landscape, and a little more about the assumptions that many urban Scots also project on to it, assumptions about cleanness and simplicity, innocence and peace.

Now it has to be said that Greenhorn's play is not the deepest treatment of these themes one could imagine on a Scottish stage. In detail, it's often superb: there is, for example, a tiny, brilliant cameo discussion of how Alex, as a west-of-Scotland working-class boy, feels himself completely dissociated, by language and culture, from a whole range of positive concepts and emotions like 'beauty' and 'hope'. But in structure, it's perhaps a little too jaunty and picaresque for its own good, skipping on to the next scene, the next brilliant one-liner; and there's something questionable about the comic-grotesque way Greenhorn handles the theme of Binks' psychopathic violence, as if the sheer cultural familiarity of his Scottish urban hard-man act, as conjured up by the indispensable Kenny Bryans, somehow made it laughable, or even lovable.

But what really impresses about Greenhorn's play, over its two-and-three-quarter-hour length, is the shimmering energy with which it sustains its wry, brilliant, unfailingly hilarious portrait of two lost lads on the loose in postmodern and pre-millennial Scotland; and the memorable, sharply drawn vividness of the central characters, who seem almost ready to step fully fledged into a long-running TV sitcom. The Traverse's assistant director John Tiffany has given the play a notably graceful, lucid and well-paced production, although for me, Mick Slaven's powerful live music – for a single electric guitar, played by the composer in long kilt, shaved head and green simmet – could have evolved in a slightly more sensitive direction after the initial burst of road-movie energy. Neil Warmington's set is simple but stunning, an old picture-postcard of thistles and castles parting to reveal a wide blue yonder dominated by a huge arching steel wave, in tribute to the Thurso surfing scene that gives the play its physical and spiritual destination; and Paul Hickey, as the hero Alex – well supported by Colin McCredie as Brian and Veronica Leer as Mirren, the girl who comes along for the ride – turns in the kind of performance, intelligent, funny, moving, well-observed, and beautifully sustained, that should, if there is any justice, make his career.

Caledonia Dreaming
7:84 Scotland
Scotland on Sunday, 15 June 1997

The audience gathers in the big main auditorium of the Traverse Theatre – itself a great cave carved out of solid castle rock – and looks down on a stage where a tiny model Edinburgh Castle glows in silhouette against the luminous blue sky of a summer evening; a tiny ScotRail train runs soundlessly past, on its last journey home from Glasgow.

Around and behind it, the city lights twinkle into the distance; and a little toy helicopter moves dreamily over the landscape, circling the Heart of Midlothian etched – just like the one outside St Giles – in the painted cobbles of the raised playing area. Every psychologist knows that to reduce the size of a thing, to make it into a miniature, an unthreatening toy, is a prime way of invoking affection for it; and *Caledonia Dreaming* – David Greig's delightful new show for 7:84 Scotland, which opened at the Traverse last week before a long Scottish tour – is the kind of love song to a city and its people, at a complicated turning point in their history, that sometimes requires that sense of affectionate distance.

Part soap opera, part serious drama, part rowdy postmodern political cabaret about Scotland on the brink of the referendum, the show also has some of the atmosphere of one those pre-millennial 'angel' stories about city life in New York or Berlin, in which we seem to sweep down on big, kindly wings into the most intimate lives of the characters, and then back into a godlike overview of the whole place. And though any play that tackles the landscape just outside the theatre with such directness and humour is bound to score a hit with audiences, the crowd at the Traverse seemed to adore this show with a special passion, not only for its sharp perception and acute local knowledge, but also for its rare atmosphere of shimmering, magical loving-kindness.

The central theme of Greig's show is, I suppose, the human need to have a dream, and the danger of too much dreaming, and he pursues it by tracing the lives of five memorable Edinburgh characters – plus Lawrence, a depressive taxi-driver who never actually appears – through a long summer night. There's Stuart, a Labour MEP half-demented with the dream of bringing the Olympics to Edinburgh; there's our heroine Lauren, a kindly sauna-worker in the city's booming sex industry, used to explaining that no, she's not posh, she's just English; there's Eppie, a middle-class house-wife sinking into alcoholism and despair; there's Jerry, a doorman at the Caledonian Hotel; and Darren, a boy from Oxgangs who idolises Sean Connery, and dreams of escape. Connery, of course, is the figure from the back streets of Edinburgh in whom Scotland's personal and political dreams tend to meet; and as rumours that he is in the city begin to spread, the characters set off on a series of journeys – walking, running, jumping into Lawrence's taxi – towards the recognition that while dreams of love and fulfilment are the essence of life, dreams of wealth, power and political empire-building are more dangerous stuff, easily perverted into ugliness.

The action is punctuated, meanwhile, with slightly surreal political choruses on topics like 'The Yes-Yes Campaign' (a campaign for defeatist old Scotland to get used, like Mollie Bloom, to the sound of the word 'yes') and the 'West Lothian Question' ('Why is it always raining in Harthill?') that give the show an almost dizzy topical edge. The whole complex structure is brilliantly handled by director Iain Reekie, his inspired designer Evelyn Barbour, his musical director David Young, and his superb cast, led by Jill Riddiford and Anne Kidd as those terrific women Lauren and Eppie, and Billy Boyd as Darren, one of the most loveable little Sean Connery soundalikes ever to walk the boards. The play could be accused, at a stretch, of a certain dramatic slightness, and over-dependence on the mood of the moment; it's certainly hard to imagine *Caledonia Dreaming* surviving much beyond this Tony Blair summer of warm rain and high hopes. But, hell, if live theatre can't be topical, what art form can? In the twenty-first century, I guess that this kind of immediacy will be one of theatre's main 'unique selling points'; and David Greig is shaping up to be one of the leading practitioners of the art.

Backlash on the Fringe
The Herald, 26 August 1997

Saturday morning, but even at home over the coffee and toast you can't escape the Edinburgh Fringe. Ned Sherrin's *Loose Ends* show on Radio 4 is coming live from the Pleasance Theatre, and is featuring a comedy trio called The League of Gentlemen, shortly to become winners of the Perrier Award. In their *Loose Ends* extract, The League of Gentlemen are pretending to be a very politically correct theatre-in-education company who have come to perform a play about enlightened sexual attitudes at a local school, but – you've guessed it – within minutes of introducing themselves to the kids, they're snarling and swinging at each other like so many cavemen, because secretly they all hate homosexuals, and suspect all the others of trying to sleep with their own girlfriends.

And this, it seems, is mainstream comedy-drama 1997 style. First you take some of those nice liberal ideas your silly old sixties parents had: the idea, say, that it isn't very nice to kick people just because they are dwarves (a notion comprehensively sniggered at in John Herdman's odious new play *Cruising*, at the Famous Grouse House), or – oh yes, that really pathetic old dream about how men and women might be able to live together as equals, with affection and respect, instead of treating one another as possessions. Then you demonstrate, at some length, just how silly and unrealistic these ideas are; how people – or at least men, since they write most of this stuff about themselves – just can't help being racist and sizeist and violent and prejudiced and faithless and rabidly possessive. After that, you laugh like drains for several minutes, congratulating yourselves on how thoroughly you've blown all that gooey old liberal rubbish out of the water. Then you sit around wondering why you feel so empty and depressed, and desperately in need of a drink.

For this is the year when the backlash hit the Fringe with a vengeance; and unfortunately, particularly on the comedy front, the idea of reasserting 'manhood' against a feminism which has 'gone too far' often seems to involve little more than a reversion to the sexual politics of the Whitehall farce – i.e. real or imagined adultery with young ladies with big breasts, plenty of punch-ups, and a lot of sheepish lying to the wife or girlfriend.

And there is, of course, one truly serious backlash drama on this year's Fringe, in the shape of Mike Cullen's powerful *Anna Weiss* at the Traverse, a triangular drama about 'recovered memories' of child sex abuse which, despite the best efforts of the writer to make the piece even-handed, simply cannot help being emotionally driven, Strindberg-style, by the sheer force of male terror and rage at the possibility of being falsely accused of sexual abuse by a pair of women – the accusing child and her therapist – who have formed a bond with one another stronger than their loyalty to the man.

But here's the rub; for most of the female-run productions I've seen on this Fringe simply are not talking this same backlash language. They see a world still largely run by men, they do not feel that feminism has 'gone too far'; and in show after show – from the brilliant staging of Angela Carter's feminist-accented Bluebeard myth *The Bloody Chamber* in the vaults of Mary King's Close, to Beth Fitzgerald's superbly acted *Bye Bye Blackbird* at the Assembly Rooms – they continue to explore the ways in which women are oppressed by conventional ideas of marriage and possession. And sometimes, this year, it has seemed to me that the battle of sexual politics, which has been such a rich theme on the Edinburgh Fringe for so long, is approaching one of those dangerous impasses where both groups – men and women – become convinced that they are the victims, and therefore become progressively less able to find a common language, and to engage in real dialogue.

1998

The Stage We're In
The Scotsman, 14 April 1998

These are strange times in which to be taking up the role of *The Scotsman*'s theatre critic: for in this year of 1998, theatre in Scotland, and in Britain as a whole, is looking down and out, defeated and demoralised, to an extent not seen in a generation.

It's not only the relentless downward pressure on public funding that is draining the life from Scottish theatres, although that has certainly been bad enough. The Scottish Arts Council's theatre budget has now been at a standstill – which means a real-terms cut – for four consecutive years; and the botched abolition of the regional councils three years ago, followed by a series of grimly restrictive local authority spending rounds, has added to the misery. In the latest round of cuts by Edinburgh City Council, for example, Edinburgh's Royal Lyceum Theatre last week lost a cool £58,000 out of its current year's budget. In crude terms, that money represents well over a hundred weeks of full-time actor employment in Scotland, and it is a blow that has been repeated perhaps ten-fold in theatre funding, over the last three to four years.

But money is not the only problem, or perhaps is only a symptom of a deeper sickness. For in 1998, theatre is simply the most unfashionable and marginalised of all Britain's major art forms; banished from the Millennium Dome, despised even by Princess Diana, and often hated, in the nineties, for its self-righteous 'educational' image, it lacks both the 'cultural industries' street-cred of film and rock music, and the rich, influential supporters' clubs that tend to cluster round opera and the visual arts. In an age of mass production and perfectly finished screen product, it is a knobbly handmade thing, woven live in front of the audience every evening. In an age besotted with spectacle, it insists on using the debased and demanding currency of words.

Worse, in an age obsessed with individualism – with the privacy of home and the anonymous darkness of the cinema – it insists that people enter into a common space, and undergo a collective experience, something that nineties man and woman can tolerate at the level of stand-up comedy, but often find embarrassing and intrusive when it comes to tragedy, or any serious emotion. In the age of 'Cool Britannia', in other words, theatre remains seriously uncool; and for that, it pays a heavy price.

So am I downhearted? Do I believe, like so many other pundits, that theatre is finally dying a well-deserved death? Not at all; in fact, what I mainly feel is anger, that an art form so fine, so necessary, so life-enhancing and so cheap to produce compared with most of its competitors, should have been allowed to drift into such an unnecessary slough of despond. I am angry, first and foremost, because I see so many people in theatre – and in Scottish theatre in particular – working so desperately hard for so little money. To put it bluntly, the whole industry operates on a basis of poverty wages and exploitation, to the extent that many mature actors with family responsibilities can no longer afford to work in theatre at all. I am angry because I know how heavily, even in this age of film and television dominance, other art forms rely on theatre as a forcing house for new talent; from Robert Carlyle of *The Full Monty* to Daniela Nardini of *This Life*, almost all of the current generation of Cool-Britannia-style Scottish screen stars were to be seen, five or ten years ago, strutting their stuff and learning their craft on the little stages of Glasgow Arts Centre and Cumbernauld Theatre, The Arches and the Tron.

208

And I am angry, above all, because I know the part Scottish theatre played in describing, inventing and giving a voice to the modern Scotland we are celebrating now, as home rule becomes a reality at last. All through the political dog days, from 1979 to the mid-1990s, producers and directors like Michael Boyd, Gerry Mulgrew, Ian Wooldridge, Neil Wallace, and writers like John Byrne, Liz Lochhead, Chris Hannan, and now David Greig and Stephen Greenhorn – whose brilliant 1997 'road movie for the stage' *Passing Places* opens in a new production at the Traverse tonight – poured out their best blood to sustain the idea of Scotland as a modern, diverse, dynamic nation that could absorb all the currents of late twentieth-century global culture and still speak in its own distinctive voice; and there is something sickening, now, about the sight of a new political establishment turning away from people in the arts who held and burnished and reinvented the creative vision of a new Scotland, in the years when so many others in public life lacked the guts or creativity for the job.

Yet beyond the anger there is also a huge measure of hope. It's not that theatre can survive without adapting; far from it. In the twenty-first century, theatre may have to move increasingly into small rooms and raw 'found' spaces, to maximise the single great advantage – its sweaty, intimate, real-time immediacy – that sets it apart from canned entertainment; certainly, the whole art form will have to drop its current deadly image, still suicidally encouraged by many theatres, as a kind of red-plush nostalgia trip into a world of Edwardian architecture, accents, and values. And the funding system is clearly in a process of upheaval. Within a few years, for instance, the Scottish Parliament will have to decide whether it intends to pursue a European-style policy of relatively generous public support for Scottish arts and culture, or to continue the present trend towards declining public involvement, with all the risks and losses that might entail for the cultural base of a small European nation caught up in the global whirlwind of English-speaking culture.

But in the end, I cannot help feeling that theatre itself is in about as much danger of being wiped out by film, television, and the digital revolution as live sex is of being entirely replaced by internet chat rooms and video pornography; and for similar reasons. We need it because it is relatively cheap to produce, and still represents the fastest route for young artists to a real, live, reacting audience. We need it because it is relatively quick and flexible. What other medium, last summer, could have had audiences all over Scotland laughing, by mid-July, at a play like David Greig's *Caledonia Dreaming*, a delicious fantasy about hope, summertime and national identity that could only have been completed after the 1 May general election?

And we need it, above all, because it is a live, unpredictable encounter between artists and audience. In the moment of performance, the actors are free as they cannot be in any other medium, and that is why theatre always comes into its own in times of repressive or totalitarian government. Of course, the screen or electronic experience diminishes risk, spares our blushes, delivers a more reliable and predictable result; we are a generation of control freaks, and distance lends control. But on those rare occasions when the real human encounter works – when there's love and passion and beauty, and real feeling aching to communicate itself – well then, it suddenly beats the band, breaks down the barriers that pinch and narrow our lives, shows us, however briefly, that we are perhaps less alone than we think. At the end of David Hare's current London hit, *Amy's View*, there is a scene in which an old actress, played by Judi Dench, and the young man with whom she is appearing in a fringe version of a Greek tragedy, are seen preparing themselves in the seconds before the performance. With their backs to the real audience, they take jugs of water and drench one another, as the opening scene demands; then they square their shoulders and walk away from us, in an abrupt blaze of light, towards the white gauze curtain, and the roar and sudden hush of the imaginary audience beyond. And that, at its best, is what theatre is: from baptism to the dying of the light, the best metaphor we have for life itself, in all its glory and stupidity, its ridiculous brevity, its short, passionate search for truthfulness in ourselves, and real connection with others.

When Scottish theatre works that magic over the coming years, I will be there, to try to catch the moment in print, and to tell it as it was. And believe me, on the good nights and the bad ones, the privilege will be mine; to be paid to go looking for joy, and occasionally to find it.

Tales of the Tartan Army
Pavilion, Glasgow
The Scotsman, 23 April 1998

Beam me up, get me outta here, help, help, help! Book me a three-month safari to that one place on earth where they've never heard of the Beautiful Game, or the ecstasy of patriotic madness which it provokes, come World Cup time. It's not that Ian Black's *Tales of the Tartan Army* takes an unduly hopeful view of Scottish football as such; on that subject, at least, his anecdotal history of sixteen glorious years in the life of a group of dedicated Scotland supporters is suitably wry, and often very funny.

No, what makes the blood run hot and cold is Black's wildly idealised vision of Scottish society, as represented in microcosm by his nine-strong detachment of fans. For a start, Black's little division of troops is rigorously inclusive in itself. It contains supporters of Rangers, Celtic, and Aberdeen;

there's even a middle-class Jam Tarts supporter from Edinburgh and a couple of women. It fights racism on the
terraces, and poverty in the slums of Mexico; it extends the
hand of international friendship to everyone except the English (dismissed as 'difficult to like'); it is beloved everywhere
it goes. At one point, Paul Samson's narrator admits that the
Tartan Army is not perfect, but the 'imperfection' he
describes involves the nutting of a neo-Nazi for bullying an
old Jew on the streets of Milan.

What can be said is that the show is brilliantly served by its
cast and director Martin McCardie, who evoke Black's
vision of this small, ideal Scottish community with perfect
comic timing and real commitment. But I spent my childhood living in a nation that thought, in a complacent way,
that by its very nature it embodied the best virtues of
mankind: freedom, democracy, a sense of fair play. It was
called Britain, and its smugness annoyed me.

And now, it seems I'm doomed to live out my maturity in a
country just as smug, convinced of its own unique grasp of
values like decency, justice, and the brotherhood of man. It's
called Scotland, and dammit, it's beginning to annoy me too.

Gaiety Whirl

Gaiety, Ayr
The Scotsman, 20 July 1998

For as long as I can remember, the world of showbiz has
been mourning Scottish variety as a 'dying art'. Every year,
come pantomime time, the cry of doom goes up again from
the newspapers and the radio chat shows: the old tradition is
on its deathbed, its style is moth-eaten and irrelevant, and
once the great old names – the Stanley Baxters, Jimmy
Logans, and Johnny Beatties – have hung up their spangly

tights and false bosoms for the last time, the game will be up for good. As for the matching tradition of end-of-the-pier summer variety – well, that is surely long gone, swept away forever in the great holidaymaking shift of the century from the Clyde Coast to the Costa del Sol.

Except that, somehow, despite all the signs of approaching mortality, the much-predicted death never quite seems to take place. Every December, the old beast of traditional Scottish panto shakes itself vigorously, sticks a few new feathers into its tattered plumage, and begins to strut its stuff. And even summer variety, it seems, is not quite dead yet. For down the Clyde Coast, for the next seven weeks, the Ayr Gaiety Theatre is proudly presenting the sixty-seventh year of the Gaiety Whirl, a classic all-singing all-dancing summer show, complete with a seven-piece band, six high-stepping chorus girls in ostrich feathers and sequinned top hats, a vaguely risqué sketch or two, and, at the top of the bill, a well-loved local comic and sentimental crooner (Dean Park), along with a clever and successful singer-impersonator (Allan Stewart), and a break-your-heart belter of a modern chanteuse (Brenda Cochrane).

'The audience here just seems to demand a summer variety show,' says Gordon Taylor, the theatre's manager. 'Last year we tried filling the programme with one-night dates, and it just didn't work. So we're going back to the idea of a modern light-entertainment show that can run for an eight-week season, and build up an audience as it goes.'

It's not, of course, that anyone around the Gaiety thinks the business of keeping Scottish variety alive is simple. For this production, the Gaiety and its owners South Ayrshire Council – who already subsidise the theatre to the tune of £400,000 a year – have gone into partnership with the young Glasgow producer, Robert C Kelly, a pale and brusque young businessman with a faintly fanatical glint in his eye who loves the variety tradition with a passion, and seems determined to pull it back from the brink of extinction at any cost. When it comes to variety theatre, Kelly is inspired by two passionate beliefs. First, he is absolutely convinced that there is no point in trying to do variety on the cheap. He believes that the sharp decline of Scottish variety after the early 1960s – when, as stars like Una McLean can testify, the gorgeous and lavish 'Five Past Eight' shows at the Glasgow Alhambra could still fill a 2000-seat theatre every night for three months – was partly caused by a 'loss of nerve' on the part of managements, who stopped investing big bucks in the quality and appearance of the shows.

Secondly, he is not interested in variety as a nostalgic exercise, an art form that takes us back to a lost world of pre-war popular entertainment; he believes it can and does exist in a nineties form, and can go on developing into the future. He is perfectly happy to include the odd flash of the tartan and swing of the kilt, so long as it is understood as a tribute to great entertainments of the past. But for him, the essential context is modern, more Trisha Yearwood than Andy Stewart; and this year's Gaiety Whirl contains only the briefest burst of a traditional Scottish song-session from Dean Park, followed by a roof-raising Scottish-country-dance-band-style spoof on the early works of Sir Andrew Lloyd Webber.

So can Kelly make his formula work, and perhaps even sow the seeds of a wider variety revival? It has to be said that the omens remain doubtful. To begin with, finances are perilously tight. Both the theatre and Kelly are noticeably cagey about the cost of the show, regarding the figures as 'commercially sensitive information'. But even at this small-to-medium scale, with a total cast of less than twenty, it can safely be said that the cost of staging an eight-week season to the standard Kelly demands runs well into six figures; that means that the show needs, on average, to fill two-thirds of the theatre's 580 seats at every performance, if money is not to be lost. Then again, even if the Gaiety season is successful, it is important to recognise that Ayr is an unusual town, both a major seaside resort and a large county town with a good-going subsidised theatre that sustains a loyal audience. No other town in Scotland can precisely match that formula.

With the whole variety tradition at such a low ebb, Kelly concedes that the 'skills base' of experienced performers on which he has to draw is dwindling by the year. 'Perhaps we should start campaigning for Arts Council funding,' he says grimly, 'or the whole tradition could just disappear.' The dancers who appear in the Gaiety Whirl, for example, have to piece out their year's work, between ever-shorter pantomime seasons, with teaching, modelling and promotional work; and like all entertainers, they have sometimes had to follow the British holiday audience on to cruise ships and cross-Channel ferries, and into hotels and holiday camps from Bangkok to Benidorm.

'Butlin's kept us going for years, didn't it?' says Dean Park in his dressing room, reminiscing with comic actor and writer Russell Lane. 'Until they decided to scrap their variety shows for bar entertainment, they said that if people were sitting in a theatre, they couldn't be buying drinks, and they had to keep their bar takings up.'

Yet sitting in on the Gaiety Whirl's first performance last week, watching a 340-strong audience – including kids of all ages, young couples, old-age pensioners, harassed mums and dads – roar out their delighted recognition of Allan Stewart's Auntie Maisie drag act, cheer the dancers at the end of their raunchy *Chicago* sequence, and sing tearfully along with Brenda Cochrane's big closing number, I couldn't help feeling that there's something so basically enjoyable, so human, so natural about this kind of evening's entertainment that it will never truly die. Of course, it may change its appearance in ways that make us feel that it has gone. It may emerge in places where we don't expect to see it, in the lounges of cruise ships and in strange little comedy clubs. Its peculiar, old-fashioned gender politics – homophobic jokes, scantily clad girls – may begin to change. It may begin to draw on the talents of a generation of performers who know nothing about the old variety tradition. It may even, as a dynamic reflection of popular culture, change its identity in confusing ways; these days, after all, if there is a real working-class counterculture in Scotland, its inspiration lies not in bens and glens or even in shipyards and tenements, but with its emigré children, in the country-and-western world of working-class America.

But none of these changes amounts to complete extinction, and so long as live entertainment survives at all, it will still be possible, at the margins, to stage events like the 1998 Gaiety Whirl. At the interval of last Tuesday's show, I caught sight of Bill Paterson and Isla Blair lurking in the back row of the stalls: two famous Scottish actors, back in Ayrshire for some filming, popping in to catch the show.

'That thing with the Andrew Lloyd Webber numbers, that was brilliant, wasn't it?' said Paterson. 'Have we just seen the world premiere of it? Fantastic!' And his face suddenly lit up with pure pleasure, a simple, perfect, beaming happiness. Because he was having a great night out at the Gaiety Whirl; and so, at that moment, were we all.

Gargantua
Underbelly, Edinburgh
The Scotsman, 13 August 1998

At the Underbelly below George IV Bridge, a great juicy watermelon of a show has landed, and if you know what's good for you, you'll grab a slice before it disappears. Grid Iron's *Gargantua* is a rich, fruity, gorgeous, uninhibited celebration of the senses, greedily gastronomic, pungently scatological, and filthily or lusciously sexual, depending on your taste; and a worthy successor to last year's smash hit *The Bloody Chamber*.

With his fine five-strong company, Ben Harrison's show takes its cue from Rabelais' fierce French sixteenth-century bum-blast against Calvinism and every kind of puritanical hostility to the flesh. But although it preserves Rabelais' spirit intact, it transfers the action to our modern, post-puritan, work-ridden society, following its three little characters – plus a friendly chef, and a violinist in chef's clothing – through a frantic, red-nosed weekend of fleshy pleasure, before Monday morning sends them back to the living death of the office; or, if the brief bright weekend is a metaphor for life, down into death itself.

The result – exquisitely staged in a descending series of magical tunnels and caverns between Victoria Street and the Cowgate – is a show that is not only rude and exuberant, but also astonishingly beautiful; and in the end both thoughtful and moving in its sense of the brevity and vividness of life, and its questioning of the forces that make it so difficult for us simply to enjoy it.

1999

Rep It Up and Start Again
Dundee Rep
10 February 1999

At Dundee Rep, they're in the thick of rehearsals for their new production of *Puntila and Matti*, Brecht's brilliant satirical comedy about a country landowner who is a complete capitalist swine when sober, and a genuinely nice human being when drunk. In the bar-restaurant, at the end of the day's work, the theatre's director, Hamish Glen, is having a drink with his cast and the writer, Peter Arnott, who explains that he has translated the play into a 'piebald version of Scots'. It happens to be Burns Night, and everyone is in a good mood because at lunchtime the whole staff of the theatre had a terrific haggis-and-neeps blowout, cooked by a member of the technical team. Then one of the waitresses comes past and asks Glen if he wants to go dancing with the crowd from the restaurant, some night next week. 'What?' says Glen, 'I'm over forty!' 'Well, it's Seventies Night,' says the waitress, 'so we thought you'd like it.'

Hamish Glen, in other words, cuts a slightly unusual figure as a Scottish rep director, and not only because of the striking rugged-but-glamorous good looks he shares with his more famous actor brother Iain, now celebrated from London to New York for taking his clothes off with Nicole Kidman in the stage version of *The Blue Room*. For what's most unusual about Glen is that he seems pretty happy in his work; in a profession noted for misery and angst, he neither expends much energy raging against the system nor mopes about how the administrative demands of the job – management, fundraising, local politics – are cramping his creative style. Glen was born into a long line of solid Scottish farmers and professional types, and his first thought, after a sharp exit from Edinburgh Academy at the age of sixteen, was to become a lawyer. But he left the law for theatre in 1984, jobbing around for a decade as a freelance director at the Royal Lyceum and the Tron, as well as in Lithuania and Finland; and in 1992 he landed the artistic directorship at Dundee, a good-going repertory theatre with strong community links and a famously friendly and unpretentious atmosphere, which he has piloted with good grace through some tough financial times, often acting as a spokesman for the whole Scottish theatre community.

But now, the long tradition of professional theatremaking in Dundee is about to receive a tremendous boost, as Glen launches a £1 million three-year programme to form a permanent eleven-strong acting ensemble at the Rep, to commission nine brand-new works for the company from leading Scottish playwrights, and to create the kind of European-style working conditions – long rehearsal periods, with actors available to develop new shows over months and years – that British reps have never, until now, been able to imitate. The core of the money, £286,000, comes from the Scottish Arts Council's New Directions Lottery fund, designed, at long last, to shift the emphasis of lottery spending away from building projects to real artistic initiatives. And before Glen even submitted his SAC application, he had already put in place the local funding he needed to match it, an impressive £209,000 each from the cash-strapped Dundee City Council and the local Tayside Enterprise company, with more money to come from trusts and private donors.

'The idea of the ensemble was born when I began to see the work of companies such as the Maly from St Petersburg, and to understand the depth and richness of performance they could get by working together in such a sustained way,' says Glen. 'I wanted to create the kind of conditions that would enable us to build up productions of real international stature, and attract major guest directors from across Europe. And I wanted to set up a company for which writers could write in a really practical way, as Shakespeare or Molière did, to bring them back into the theatre as workers.

'But if you're going to set up a project like this, you also have to be very sensitive to the priorities of the people who are providing the funding. From the point of view of Dundee City and Tayside Enterprise, for instance, we're looking to provide a repertoire of work that will be a real asset to the city, that will be good enough to export to festivals outside Scotland and the UK, and that we can exchange easily with other major Scottish theatres.

'We also looked at the Tayside tourism strategy, and the work will be structured so that we can remount the whole repertoire every year as a summer festival season, which should help to attract visitors.'

So is the Dundee audience about to find itself overwhelmed by a wave of fiercely demanding European drama? 'Not at all,' says Glen. 'The point is that the kind of new Scottish drama we'll be commissioning is very popular indeed. We're talking about a new play by John Byrne, or Liz Lochhead working on a musical with Ricky Ross. We'll also carry on developing an authentic Dundee voice in our work – in fact that's one of the things the actors will have time to do.' Glen then reels off the names of three popular Dundee writers whose work has already been seen at the Rep, all of whom are under commission to write more. As for the actors, they won't be rich, says Glen, but on a guaranteed income of just under £20,000 a year, they'll be much better paid than most actors in Scottish theatre, as well as more secure.

And why has Dundee Rep managed to put together this dream package for itself, ahead of all the other theatres in

Scotland? Glen talks a bit about the special circumstances of the city, before admitting that it might also have something to do with his own qualities as salesman and advocate.

'And then, of course, we all just worked bloody hard on getting this right. I remember when I had to give my presentation on the project to the city council, I rehearsed it two or three times in the auditorium here, with the staff sitting around giving me notes. And the work's not over. I'm thinking already about how to avoid a terrible letdown when the three years are over, what I call the exit strategy.'

Glen talks on, and I can't remember ever meeting a theatre boss who uses management jargon so well, and with such a real sense of what it might mean in artistic terms. When he was first appointed to the Dundee job, one journalist who interviewed him reported that 'Glen talks a good game.' And he does. But unlike the courtroom advocate he might have been, Hamish Glen the theatre director has the advantage of believing, heart and soul, in the case he makes. And as Dundee audiences may be about to find out, that can make all the difference between impressive-sounding hot air and the kind of substantial new achievement that energises cities, and changes lives.

Mainstream
Macrobert, Stirling
The Scotsman, 22 February 1999

Amid all the rage and controversy that accompanied the award of the Scottish Arts Council's first batch of long-term Scottish theatre touring franchises, there was one decision that was welcomed almost everywhere in Scottish theatre: for as well as awarding four major touring concessions, SAC also gave £70,000 a year, for a guaranteed four years, to Graham

Eatough and David Greig's Suspect Culture, purveyors since 1990 of a brand of cool, stylish Scottish international modernism – beautifully finished yet somehow full of emotion – that younger Scottish audiences can't get enough of.

Now that four-year funding has produced its first fruit in Suspect Culture's latest production *Mainstream*, co-produced with the Bush Theatre in London and premiered in Stirling on Friday; and although in style the show is very much a slimmed-down, smaller-scale reflection of the company's 1997 Edinburgh Festival hit *Timeless*, it seems to me if anything a stronger piece of work, beautifully performed, fascinatingly structured, more tightly focused on a richer theme, and sometimes breathtaking in the depths of meaning it reaches with terrific economy of gesture and language.

Essentially, *Mainstream* is a deconstructed *Brief Encounter* for the late nineties, the story of two people who meet on a management course in a Scottish seaside hotel – one a Glasgow-based employee of a record company, the other an 'outside' personnel consultant – and suddenly fall, not quite into an affair, but into a moment of absolute intimacy that shocks them both. But where the lovers of *Brief Encounter* are divided by duty and convention, these two are separated by the much more insidious loneliness of the late twentieth century, the emphasis on individuality and personal 'career development' that often masks both a frightening isolation – the sense that the 'mainstream' is always somewhere else – and a deep sameness of life.

On Ian Scott's beautiful, minimal hi-tech set – small table, fragment of high cocktail bar, chair, stack of plates, all in gleaming steel on a raised platform lit from below in pools of golden light – Greig's text and Eatough's production capture this sense of fragmentation first by dividing the encounter into five basic scenes, which can be revisited again and again with infinite small shifts in the dialogue; and then by spreading the two roles among four actors, two male and two female, in a way that strips away the rococo detail of 'character', while somehow emphasising both the uniqueness of the quality each person brings to the story, and their common humanity. The work of the four actors – Callum Cuthbertson, Kate Dickie, Paul Thomas Hickey and Louise Ludgate – is magnificent in its subtlety of detail, and its sense of discipline combined with deep emotion and real humour. It is supported every step of the way by Nick Powell's powerful, melancholy score for cello and violin. The show leaves behind it an almost overwhelming, but somehow enriching, sense of the sadness of a thirty-something generation for whom personality and life history have become just another 'asset' to be packaged for interview, and for whom real emotional intimacy with another human being has become the most subversive act of all.

The Speculator
The Meeting
Royal Lyceum, Edinburgh
The Scotsman, 17 August 1999

It's twenty years since Catalonia adopted something very similar to Scotland's new devolved status, and in that time Spain's first 'autonomous region' has become a byword in Europe for the sheer postmodern vibrancy of its culture.

So it must have seemed a fine idea to the directors of the Edinburgh Festival and Barcelona's Grec Festival that the cultural relationship between Caledonia and Catalonia should be celebrated and strengthened by the cross-commissioning of two new plays from two leading young writers. The only difficulty is that the plays that have emerged are so radically different in scale, style and subject that it's damnably difficult to trace any connections at all.

David Greig's *The Speculator* is a big, romantic historical drama, set in Paris in 1720, about the great Scotsman John Law, who invented paper currency backed by American 'land futures', and was for a while the richest man in the world. The underlying theme of the play is desire, and its relationship with the unique human capacity to imagine and create what never existed before. Just as Law has the vision to imagine a new world of freedom and growth based on faith in paper currency, so the young Scottish laird Islay, visiting Paris, knows that his future lies with the barmaid he loves, and she senses that her only chance of joy and freedom lies in a completely new world, of which she sometimes catches strange visions and premonitions.

It has to be said that all this emerges with difficulty from Philip Howard's production, which takes a swirling romantic epic of Shakespearean dimensions, and shoves it into a mock-classical straitjacket of gloomy interiors, fashionably dim lighting, heavy wigs, and a nightmare clutter of constantly shifting furniture. But for those who are willing to bear with its badly structured beginning, the gloom, the fragmentation and the flying furniture, this play contains a rich feast of ideas, emotion, fine original music and formidable acting, from a tremendous Scottish cast led by David Rintoul. At heart, *The Speculator* is a great play about the relationship between capitalism, modernity, and human freedom; its perspective is stunningly original, and as challenging as it is brilliant, sexy and humane.

Lluïsa Cunillé's *The Meeting*, on the other hand, is a deft and haunting piece of modern theatrical minimalism, a series of seven short scenes in which a man (played with a fine, enigmatic depth by John Stahl) moves through a modern urban landscape, and through a series of strange encounters with other people, from an old man in a park to a woman on a late-night underground station. In a sense,

Cunillé's play is a close-up study of the kind of society of free-floating individuals and compulsive speculators that Greig's John Law imagines, and those who simply surrender themselves for ninety minutes to the quiet rhythm of her work will emerge with a set of images of our modern world that have a haunting, yearning accuracy. Oddly, the rhythm of *The Meeting* is very like the work David Greig produces for Suspect Culture in plays like *Mainstream*, which suggests that, for all their differences, Greig and Cunillé share their generation's deep preoccupation with what human connection now means, in the money-driven world that John Law first imagined, and in which we now live.

Macbeth
Royal Lyceum, Edinburgh
The Scotsman, 2 November 1999

The more a work of art is true to its own origins, so they say, the more universal it becomes. Kenny Ireland's new *Macbeth* at Edinburgh's Royal Lyceum is living proof of the power of that old truism – a brave, strange, risky, but finally thrilling re-reading of the play that takes Shakespeare's text right back to its origins in the medieval politics of this island, and in the strange dreams of union that followed James VI and I's rise to the English throne, a year before *Macbeth* was first performed.

Just to glance at the stage, though, during the uncertain opening scenes of this show is to see what a high-risk strategy Ireland has adopted. For the production essentially evades the idea of Macbeth as a great tragic hero, shifts him and his wife away from the moral centre of the action, and places centre-stage – well, Scotland itself, the 'poor country' whose journey from day to night and into daylight again dictates the overall shape of the play. The boldness of the staging lies in the way Scotland is represented not only by a range of superb performances in the often neglected roles of the country's 'good men' – the old King Duncan, Banquo, Macduff and the prince Malcolm, all played with terrific poise and feeling by Michael Mackenzie, Jimmy Chisholm, Eric Barlow and young Patrick Moy – but also by the physical presence of the production. Matthew Scott's insistent soundscape is cinematic, wrapping the whole auditorium in shuddering waves of music, birdsong, night-shrieks. And Hayden Griffin's set is stunning, a pattern of huge monumental stone walls that move and whirl through the play with an almost symphonic energy against great background sheets of clear, strong light – blood-red, brilliant white – that come and go, grow and diminish, to give a most powerful and unsettling sense of time passing, location changing, and perspective shifting.

The downside of the production, of course, lies in the way it cuts Macbeth and his lady down from their usual towering size to a pair of small, driven figures in a darkening landscape. In the first two acts, Tom McGovern and Jennifer Black are plagued by uncertainties of voice, style, and body language, as they rush and mutter their way through what are usually seen as the play's most thrilling scenes. Lady Macbeth's great invocation to the forces of darkness goes almost for nothing, and Macbeth, on the whole, looks more like Banquo's shifty teenage son than his great military commander.

But towards the end of the banquet scene, as the great engine of rebellion against tyranny that drives the play's second half shudders into life, Ireland's ensemble approach to the work begins to pay off magnificently. It not only makes tremendous political sense of the whole structure of the play from the appearance of Banquo's ghost to Macbeth's death, pointing up the huge enduring power and relevance of Shakespeare's vision of a 'humanitarian war' waged by good men to end tyranny and horror, although at some loss – not dwelt on by Shakespeare, of course – of national sovereignty. It also, unexpectedly, creates space for McGovern's Macbeth to find himself at last, curling smoothly round the dark spaces of the set that once dwarfed him, and leaping out of the dark like a true demon of the Scottish landscape, unrepentant over the horrific forces of chaos he has unleashed, and possessed of a deep, precise, driven voice that makes the poetry of his fall smoke and smoulder with an almost unbearable power. The result is a visually stunning production full of pace and coherence, that truly serves the text rather than fighting it, and which demonstrates conclusively, in bringing a serious Scottish perspective and voice to what has always been called Shakespeare's 'Scottish play', that that old, tense Anglo-Scottish relationship, bred into the bones of this text, is still capable of shedding a dazzling light on it, four hundred years on.

Is This 'National Theatre' the Answer?
The Scotsman, 3 December 1999

On my desk lies the programme for the hugely successful production of *Macbeth* that has just ended at the Royal Lyceum in Edinburgh. 'The Royal Lyceum,' it says in bold print just below the title of the play, 'is part of the Scottish national theatre community'; and the boast is not an empty one. It's twenty years now since I tapped out my first theatre reviews for *The Scotsman*, and in that time Scotland's theatre artists, and the audiences who come to see them, have given me nothing less than a complete and thrilling new education in what it means to be Scottish at the end of the twentieth century. Over the years, my life has been touched and changed by the work of dozens of Scottish theatre companies and playwrights, from John McGrath's 7:84 and Giles Havergal's Citizens' Company, to Liz Lochhead,

Gerry Mulgrew, David Harrower and David Greig, not forgetting Sir David Lyndsay of the Mount.

In the last decade alone, I've reviewed more than three hundred new Scottish plays, in every form of the Scots tongue, and in many forms of English. And since 1997, I've also seen Scottish theatre companies begin to rise to the challenge of Scotland's new political life. Just a week from today, for example, TAG Theatre Company will bring dozens of schoolchildren into the chamber of the Scottish Parliament itself, to role-play their way through a serious debate on how to improve life for Scotland's young people. I've come to know, in other words, that Scotland already has a theatre community which cares for the nation, and tries to create work for and about the nation. The question is why Scotland's theatre companies, who this week put the case for creating a National Theatre structure to the Scottish parliament's education and culture committee, have come to feel that that record of good work is no longer enough.

And the main reason is not difficult to grasp; for the blunt truth is that all the achievements of Scottish theatre over the last ten or fifteen years have been carried through in a climate of underfunding that has been relentlessly mean-spirited and often disgraceful. The Scottish Arts Council currently supports fourteen theatre companies in Scotland, including building-based companies in Glasgow, Edinburgh, Perth, Dundee, St Andrews, and Pitlochry, and six touring companies; yet, as Robert Dawson Scott pointed out here earlier this week, the total government funding for theatre in this country, at just under £4 million, is less than the annual subsidy to Scottish Opera alone.

Traditionally, one reason for this relative underfunding – beyond the normal expectation that theatre workers should survive on poverty wages – was that many of Scotland's theatres had a strong local identity, and could rely more heavily than most arts organisations on local authority funding. But the recent squeeze on local authority spending, combined with the abolition of the regional councils in 1996, effectively undermined that source of funding for many companies; so that in the year following the abolition of the regions, Scottish Equity reported a catastrophic 42% decline in the number of contracts offered to actors in Scotland; and the income of Glasgow Citizens' Theatre, one of the most inspirational civic theatres in Europe, fell £200,000 below 'standstill' level over a single year.

But it's when we come to consider the underlying reasons for this shabby treatment of theatre as an art form that the picture becomes truly infuriating. Scotland is a nation, after all, that loves to talk the talk about pluralism and diversity. We like our pattern of big, contrasting cities and fine towns; we like to say the right thing about avoiding central-belt dominance of our national life, and giving due respect to voices from elsewhere. But show us an art form that is genuinely living out this image of diversity – producing its work in Glasgow and Edinburgh and Pitlochry, out on the Fife coast and in the shadow of the Tay Bridge – and we miserably fail to walk the talk; instead, the whole art form simply sinks without trace below the horizon of national life, its achievements largely ignored, its funding a joke, its struggles for survival as silent and unremarked as they are exhausting for those involved.

We might, in a better world, have learned from the recent crises in our big national arts companies – Scottish Opera, Scottish Ballet – to appreciate the value of Scottish theatre's diffuse structure, and the relatively efficient administration it seems to promote in individual companies, none of which has a monopoly on the future of the art form in Scotland. But instead, the Federation of Scottish Theatre has come to the conclusion, probably rightly, that in order to become a major player in the competition for funding, Scottish theatre also needs an institution which will seem to carry the prestige of the nation on its shoulders; and will compete with the opera and the ballet in its claim on public attention and national pride.

Now there's no question that the scheme for a National Theatre structure drawn up by the Federation is a brilliant one, which does its best to avoid the pitfalls, inertias and political pressures often experienced by big national arts institutions. The idea is not to set up a new building or even a new producing company, but rather to create a structure which will be able to commission work from all Scotland's existing theatre companies, give that work a wider audience around the country, and promote it beyond Scotland; and if it works, attracts completely new money, and avoids backsliding towards a more monolithic model of what a 'national theatre' is or should be, it's the kind of scheme that could deliver the best of all possible worlds.

But before I give the Federation's new plan my wholehearted support, forgive me if I spend a moment or two quietly spitting nails over the lengths to which theatre people in this country have had to go to win even the possibility of the support they deserve. For here we stand on the brink of what we are told will be the century of networks, of 'flat' structures, of diffuse creativity, multi-centred management and an end to old top-down structures. Here we are in a new Scotland that has a once-in-a-millennium chance to catch that tide of change, and here we have a theatre scene that reflects many of those values.

And yet what does Scottish theatre have to do, in order to excite any public interest in its fate? It has to go digging around in the fag-end of the nineteenth century for that old phrase 'national theatre', with all its resonances of Ibsen and Strind-berg, and its images of gloomy buildings in national capitals handing down official culture to the nation. If Scotland can play a part in creating a completely new concept of a 'national theatre' for the information age, then of course we will be doing a fine thing, for ourselves and for the rest of Europe.

But that still leaves unanswered the deepest question underlying this whole debate: the question of why we find it so difficult to see, and to understand, the kind of 'national theatre' we already have; and why we still resist in practice the idea so many of us now accept in theory, that strength can exist without weight, excellence without centralisation, and importance without the kind of monumental architecture – of buildings, or of the mind – that not only devours huge amounts of money, but eventually eats the soul.

King of the Fields
Traverse, Edinburgh
The Scotsman, 9 December 1999

When Stuart Paterson was working on this radically revised version of his big family drama, first seen at the Royal Lyceum in 1986, he said he was searching for a way to lift his story from the predictability of melodrama to the inevitability of tragedy; and to judge by the absorbing power of the great, blazing piece of new Scottish theatre that unfolded at the Traverse last night, he has succeeded beyond his own highest expectations. Set in Ayrshire in 1935, *King of the Fields* is a weighty text about the conflict between an elder brother, Matthew, who has been away too long – gassed in the trenches, on the road for sixteen years, and unable either to live up to, or to shake off, the reputation as a 'big man' that he picked up in his golden youth – and his cautious younger brother, Rab, who is steadily working his way out of the family's poor farming background into a new life as a successful contractor.

Given a less passionate, beautiful and deeply intelligent production than it gets here from the Traverse's John Tiffany, the play could perhaps still look a little like the dour and bitter tale of family disaster that dragged listlessly around the Lyceum stage thirteen years ago. But at the Traverse this time around, there is no chance of that. On a great bare thrust stage floored with grey stone slabs – with superb minimal design by Neil Warmington, music by John Irvine, and lighting by Chahine Yavroyan – every strand of this magnificent production comes together to support the deep, driving tragic rhythm of Paterson's story, as Rab's young wife Catherine is gradually drawn towards the dark glamour of her ruined brother-in-law, and Matt's old girlfriend, Jean, begins to see in him what no one else wants to see, a man who has come home to die.

The acting, above all, is of a quality and mature intensity that sometimes takes the breath away. At the centre of a fine ensemble, a compelling Liam Brennan as Matt, and the fabulous Blythe Duff as Jean – tough as old leather, yet radiating a deep female power and presence we can almost smell – seem to carry on their shoulders the whole weight of a nation's talent for self-destruction, or for missing its chance of joy. What's superb about Paterson's play, though, is how far it has moved from that narrow, hunched and muttering style of drama which is only about showing the ugliness and joylessness, the missed chances and cramped ambitions, that can sometimes disfigure Scottish life. In this version, the play achieves tragedy because we also see, with great clarity, the beauty, the poetry, the passion and the glamour that those attitudes destroy, as if the drama and the language were drawing strength from the land itself.

King of the Fields has a powerful subtext about Scottish attitudes to enterprise and self-enrichment, beautifully carried by Russell Hunter and Robert Carr as Rab's two hired men.

But in the end, it's the tragedy of the lost hero that catches the mind, breaks the heart, and asks the hardest questions about Scotland's ability to confront its own demons. Between them, these two brothers might have made a man in full. But so long as they both live, like two faces of the divided self that haunts Scottish literature, it seems that neither of them can breathe freely, or move on into the future, without forever looking over his shoulder.

In the early months of 2000 there was an almost audible pause for breath in Scottish theatre, as if the creative community had decided to go on sabbatical, and leave the public arena for a while. The spring season of 2000 was one of the weakest I had ever seen; and when activity resumed – with many large millennium projects under way – it was striking how many of them involved the revisiting of classical myths and legends: this was the year of Liz Lochhead's vivid version of Medea, *starring Maureen Beattie, and of Edwin Morgan's flawed but ambitious retelling of the life of Christ, under the title* A.D.

The shows that stayed in the mind, though, were most remarkable for their huge, meditative beauty, as the world moved into a new millennium: Angus Farquhar's great piece of land art The Path, *at Glen Lyon in Perthshire, or a final magnificent Tremblay play at the Traverse, directed by Philip Howard. And it was from the Traverse, in the end – and from Hamish Glen's new ensemble company at Dundee – that the first truly exciting shows of the new millennium began to emerge. In 2001 Dundee Rep toured to Tehran with a riveting version of* The Winter's Tale; *and, at the Traverse, associate director John Tiffany pulled from the pile of unsolicited scripts a play by a man called Gregory Burke, who was working as a dish-washer in a restaurant. It was a play about post-industrial despair shading into political violence, set in a computer factory in what were once the communist heartlands of Fife; it was called* Gagarin Way, *and over the next decade – after its explosive Traverse premiere during the Edinburgh Festival of 2001 – it would be performed in dozens of countries across Europe and the world.*

Burke's success was followed by a series of brilliant Traverse premieres, over the next two years, involving playwrights like Nicola McCartney, Douglas Maxwell, David Greig and Henry Adam, whose 2003 play The People Next Door *was one of the first to tackle the new age of paranoia and 'war on terror' that followed the 9/11 attacks of 2001. In 2002 Kenny Ireland signed off as artistic director of the Royal Lyceum Theatre with a magnificent new production of Howard Barker's* Victory, *revisiting his Glasgow success of 1991. In 2003 the great triumvirate of Giles Havergal, Robert David MacDonald and Philip Prowse finally left the Citizens', after an astonishing thirty-four years. And in September 2003 – after a hundred-year campaign led in its final stages by both Kenny Ireland and Hamish Glen – the Scottish Government at Holyrood, a Labour/Liberal Democrat coalition formed in 1999 and re-elected in 2003, announced the setting up of a new National Theatre of Scotland, on the model generated, through years of consultation, by the Scottish theatre community itself: a theatre without walls, and without a permanent company, but with a new production fund of almost £4 million a year – in addition to the existing Scottish Arts Council theatre budget of around £6.5 million – to be invested in co-productions with theatre companies and artists across Scotland.*

The Angel's Share
Borderline
The Scotsman, 6 March 2000

What on earth is going on in Scottish theatre? A couple of months ago, everything was looking good: outstanding autumn season at the Citizens', new ensemble at Dundee, funding improvements in the pipeline, and a new national theatre initiative in the air. But no more.

With one or two exceptions, I've barely seen a Scottish-made show since Christmas that I would seriously recommend to a paying customer; from Dundee to Edinburgh, Glasgow to Perth, there's a sudden crisis of lacklustre writing, abysmal direction, and acting so dull and third-rate that it risks driving audiences away for good.

A case in point is Borderline's latest touring show *The Angel's Share*, a long-awaited new play by short-story writer Chris Dolan. As a text, *The Angel's Share* is modest but attractive. Set on an isolated Scottish island where life revolves around the traditional distillery and the family who owns it, the play uses a well-worn flashback format to tell the story of the summer eighteen years ago when Edward, a young consultant from the distilling company, arrives on the island on a modernising mission, and soon finds himself in love with the old boss's daughter Mhairi.

The play tries to make some thoughtful observations about modernity, and how it relates to the old impulses of seed-time and harvest, hunting and gathering, sex and death; it is poetic in rhythm, with a rich sensual feel for the earthy detail of whisky-making, and some delicate characterisation. But as soon as the dead hand of Leslie Finlay's production falls on Dolan's text, whatever minor life there is in it is crushed. The staging is unbelievably static and literal, the characters standing around exchanging philosophies like a bunch of bores at a bus stop.

As for the acting, one-dimensional is too kind a word for it. The cast act like performers trained to leave their adult complexity at the stage door, and to signal very simple character traits to an audience of idiots. As a result, almost every line of the text is garbled or wrongly emphasised, so that we miss the point or the poetry of it. Heaven knows what yardstick Borderline are using when they conclude that this kind of event makes an adequate evening's theatre. But whatever it is, it won't do. No punter in their right mind would leave a warm fireside and a decent episode of *EastEnders* for this; live theatre has to offer more, or throw in the towel.

The Path
Glen Lyon, Perthshire
The Scotsman, 22 May 2000

The first we saw of it, as we drove up Glen Lyon in the gathering dusk, was a flash and gleam of fire from a high rocky pinnacle in the hills, a couple of miles away to our left. 'That's it, we're here,' breathed someone at the back of the bus; and although it had been a long journey up from the central belt, it suddenly seemed the best of places to be on a cool, clear midsummer night.

For in the very week when Prince Charles berated us all for losing our sense of the sacred, and of the beauty and mystery of the natural world, Angus Farquhar's NVA organisation has created an event that not only touches on these issues, but grapples with them mightily. It ravishes the senses with a fantastic and beautiful night-time journey, it tests the body with a tough, rock-strewn walk in the dark; but above all, it makes us think and feel about the relationship between humankind and nature, and not always in the most obvious ways.

What *The Path* does is to take an audience of a few hundred, each night, on a four-mile contemplative walk up and round a great slope of Perthshire hillside, and as we walk, we are asked – with the help of lighting, sound, sculpture, live music, and the strand of little way-lights that mark out the route like a string of jewels – to notice, and think about, the kind of high and beautiful places that human beings have traditionally regarded as magical. There are waterfalls and rock pools softly illuminated by moving light sculpture, a magnificent riverside tree flaming with red prayer flags, great boulders straining and creaking against the movement of the earth, a high, bare hilltop crowned with a mighty prayer wheel of a Tibetan cairn, with all the twists and turns of the path spread out below it like a pilgrims' way.

Most movingly, there are musicians, artists and guides from the mountain cultures of India, Nepal, and Tibet, Ireland, Scotland and Portugal; the fabulous Tibetan singer Ani Choying Drolma giving an unforgettable lament from below the great cairn; or the majestic, healing sound of Himalayan singing bowls, soaring and drifting on the night air.

And in the end, what's most interesting is this: that although *The Path* shows us a landscape full of beauty and energy, worthy at the very least of our respect, it also shows, with touching eloquence, how humans have always sought and striven with whatever technology they could command – from the shaping of a simple brass bowl to NVA's state-of-the-art computer-sequenced lighting – to make sense of the natural world. The hills stand, and are magnificent. But the human spirit also emerges from *The Path* as a great, poignant force of nature, striving, questioning, shaping, worshipping. Prince Charles would enjoy *The Path* if he were to walk it. But he would not find it an entirely soothing experience, or an easy confirmation of all his anti-scientific views; and that, it seems to me, is just exactly as it should be.

Death in Venice
Citizens', Glasgow
The Scotsman, 6 December 2000

At the end of the twentieth century, it is sometimes difficult to remember how much the whole of north European civilisation was shaped until recently by the habit of sexual repression, a sense that the social order depended for its very survival on the rigid public denial of whole areas of sensuality.

But there are still people around – and the Citizens' artistic director Giles Havergal must be one of them – who can remember that culture vividly enough; and the great German novelist Thomas Mann, who lived from 1875 to 1955, saw both the years of its greatest power, and the beginning of its decline.

So it is hardly surprising that Havergal's solo performance of Mann's great 1911 novella *Death in Venice*, in a new adaptation by Robert David MacDonald, comes across as a tremendously rich and moving evocation of a mighty civilisation crumbling under the pressure of its own contradictions. It is easy enough for any post-sixties version of this story to show its hero – the middle-aged German writer and critic von Aschenbach, who falls in love with the image of a beautiful fourteen-year-old Polish boy while holidaying on the Venice Lido, and is eventually destroyed by his own raging passion – as a bit of an old fool, almost comically undermined by his own feelings.

But Havergal's achievement here is to show von Aschen-bach's tremendous, hard-won virtues as a man, as well as his limitations; his fundamental moral decency, his courage and diligence, and his searing perceptive intelligence about him-self and the world, as well as his shocking vulnerability to passions which he understands in theory, but cannot survive in practice. Every aspect of the production, from the haunt-ing period music to Philip Whitcomb's subtle, beautifully lit set – with long turquoise water troughs quivering and drip-ping in the light like the Venice lagoon itself – gives strong, quiet support to Havergal's fine performance; and the whole event leaves us wondering how many artistic directors would be prepared, as Havergal regularly does, to take this kind of theatrical risk, holding the stage alone for ninety minutes, and building his relationship with his theatre's audience in the most direct and dangerous way possible.

2001

The Land of Cakes
Dundee Rep
The Scotsman, 8 March 2001

It used to be the slogan of a famous Dundee bakery. But now, with a twist of postmodern irony, it's the nickname of the psychiatric ward at the local hospital; and it's there that Archie, Davie, Mary, Christopher, Michelle and Dog find themselves washed up together, six characters in search of a narrator, at the opening of Don Paterson's eloquent and disturbing debut drama for Dundee Rep.

At heart, *The Land of Cakes* is a drama with live music – specially commissioned from leading Dundee composer Gordon McPherson – that consists of one powerful metaphor wrapped in another. At the beginning, we seem to be looking at a brilliantly written but familiar example of the kind of play that uses a mental hospital as a metaphor for life. Like any gathering, the group includes the vulnerable and the violent, those seeking escape and those who have found a kind of peace; the text, written mainly in a strong Dundee vernacular, fairly seethes with dry humour and sharp local references, in a brilliantly lurid portrayal of a society that contains too much brutality and despair.

But as the story unfolds, and the group begins to toy with the idea of staging a show in which each of them will display their showbiz talents, a deeper and darker layer of metaphor begins to appear, in which the idea of the variety stage as a macabre no-man's-land between life and death takes on a terrifying power. The complexity of Paterson's dramatic idea is dazzling and haunting, the writing ranges from superb popular comedy to shimmering poetry, and McPherson's music drives the action through its deepening crises with the dark power of a lullaby gone wrong. Every one of Sandy Neilson's cast rises superbly to the challenge of this most complex and magnificent show; and once again, the Dundee Rep ensemble have truly pushed back the boundaries of Scottish theatre.

Heritage
Traverse, Edinburgh
The Scotsman, 14 March 2001

Nicola McCartney's great 1998 play *Heritage* is set among Northern Irish settlers in Saskatchewan, Canada, in the years between 1914 and 1920; but to see it again, in this magnificent Traverse production by Philip Howard, is to begin to understand why – despite its distant setting – it exerts such a terrific power over modern audiences, at the end of a post-Cold-War decade so unexpectedly scarred by the return of ethnic conflict. For the truth is that McCartney's Canada, the Canada of her hopeful young heroine Sarah McCrea, acts as a metaphor for any place – from modern Scotland to post-war Yugoslavia – that believes it has moved on and left old tribal hatreds behind; but which discovers, in a time of crisis, that buried prejudices can rise again with a savage, destructive power.

In outline, *Heritage* is a Romeo-and-Juliet story, with the added twist that, at the beginning of the drama, the two families on neighbouring farms – the Protestant McCreas, the Catholic Donaghues – seem to have buried their differences, giving the young people a real chance of happiness. But back in the homesteads, the old stories are still being told, the prejudices passed on. Grandmother Donaghue has no wish to forget the famine that drove her family to Canada seventy years ago, or the British cruelty and arrogance that compounded their suffering; she speaks Irish to her widowed son, and to her grandson Michael, and teaches the boy both the old legends of Irish Ulster, and the old rhetoric of Irish nationalism.

And in Sarah's house, both her father Hugh (Iain Macrae) and her mother Ruth (a splendid Pauline Knowles) embody a kind of old Presbyterian world view still deeply recognisable to millions in Scotland and across the English-speaking world: a credo of hard work, common sense, reverence for the Bible, respect for the minister and the dominie, and unrelenting, visceral mistrust and dislike of Catholics. At first, these differences are submerged in the excitement and hard work of a new country and new opportunities. But with the outbreak of war in Europe, Protestants rally to the Empire flag and begin to sacrifice their sons; while the Catholics are increasingly drawn, through the events of 1916, to the struggle for Irish independence. Ill-will and violence begin to tear the prairie community apart, and the future Sarah and Michael hoped for is destroyed in blood and fire.

McCartney tells this great, archetypal story through a mixture of direct drama – terrific, full-bodied dramatic scenes – and much more complex, fragmented monologues by Sarah herself; the effect is perfectly balanced, and immensely powerful; and Philip Howard's beautifully crafted, passionate production uses both fine naturalistic acting and more stylised scenes of ritual dance and movement to express the driving momentum of the story.

But in the end, it's the strength of the actors, and their perfect understanding of the meaning of this drama, that transforms this production of *Heritage* from a fine evening's theatre to a truly exceptional one. As the two matriarchs and tradition-bearers, Mary McCusker and Pauline Knowles produce an unforgettable pair of performances. Iain Macrae and Eric Barlow create fascinating contrasting portraits of the two fathers, McCrea strong, playful and likeable, big Donaghue seasoned by a lifetime's understanding that someone must finally draw a line under the past. And Ian Skewis and Julia Dalkin, as the young lovers, make it poignantly clear how young men often cannot resist the call of the tribe, even when they know that to obey it is to destroy their own future; and how, in ethnic conflict, even the most courageous and spirited young woman becomes territory to be fought over, her humanity battered, sidelined, trampled.

Heritage is not an optimistic or a comforting play. But there's something about the depth of its understanding, the respect with which it records the substance and strength of both warring cultures, and the full, rounded humanity of its characters, that is uplifting, even as it confronts the worst of which men and women are capable; and that is both a definition of great drama, and a tribute to one of the most significant new Scottish plays for years.

The Winter's Tale
Dundee Rep
The Scotsman, 11 April 2001

It's the fate of William Shakespeare's less-performed plays – including this beautiful, enigmatic late romance, *The Winter's Tale* – to be most often staged, these days, in conditions very different from those for which they were made. The companies which can afford to produce them are, in the main, big national or regional theatres working out of huge, anonymous modern cities; and under those conditions, it's almost impossible to recapture the sense of intimacy and trust between a regular audience and a familiar company of actors that enabled Shakespeare to mount the kind of daring, breathtaking experiment with narrative and magic he stages in this play.

No such problems, though, at Dundee Rep, in the second year of its ensemble company. For at the Rep, audiences arrive as Shakepeare's would have done, bustling in from a small, intimate city to see actors they have come to know and love over the past eighteen months, and on the bedrock of that confident relationship between stage and audience, director Dominic Hill is able to build a passionate, gleaming, and beautiful full-length production of this remarkable play, that makes more sense of its narrative twists and turns, and its radical changes of mood, than any I have ever seen.

The Winter's Tale is essentially a play in three parts. The first is a grim, *Othello*-like tragedy of a man destroyed by his own obsession, in which Leontes, King of Sicily, is driven mad by a sudden conviction that his pregnant wife Hermione has been unfaithful to him with his visiting friend, Polixenes of Bohemia: in a harrowing ninety minutes, he destroys not only his wife, their newborn daughter, and his own reputation as a ruler, but also the life of his young son Mamillius, who dies of a broken heart.

243

The second part, set sixteen years later, is a jolly pastoral in which the grieving king's lost daughter Perdita – abandoned to die on a wild sea coast in Polixenes' kingdom – is discovered alive and well and living as the daughter of a shepherd, although wooed by the king's son Florizel. The third begins as a conventional comic denouement in which everything is revealed, but ends in a moment of soaring, ambiguous and chilling magic, as Hermione returns to life, to claim her daughter, and face the husband who destroyed her.

And the point about Hill's production – superbly designed for the handsome Dundee stage by Gregory Smith, and driven along by an unobtrusively brilliant musical score from Steve Kettley – is that it never apologises for these changes of style, or tries to smooth them over. Instead, it lunges straight at them, translating them into a vaguely modern 1950s setting that makes their meaning absolutely clear, moving from the blue-grey court architecture of the first act to a wild, bright country-and-western hoedown in the second, and assuming – for example – that the audience will trust the actress Meg Fraser enough not to blink, when they see her as the lovely, suffering Hermione in the first act, and as a wild, cat-fighting cowgirl in the second.

The result is a wonderful human epic of a show, that gradually makes it clear that this great *Winter's Tale* is not so much a play, as a kind of grand tour of human experience in all its aspects, tragic and comic, high and low, full of meaningless pain, and then again touched by absolute and unexpected magic. In a uniformly strong cast, Alexander West finds whole new depths as an actor in his portrayal of Leontes, Ann Louise Ross is magnificent in the role of the fearless old lady-in-waiting Paulina, and Rodney Matthews leads the audience with terrific flair through the adventures of the rogue travelling salesman Autolycus.

But in the end, individual performances matter far less than the sight of a committed Scottish ensemble confronting one of Shakespeare's biggest and most mysterious texts, and using the deep theatrical resources they have built up over the past eighteen months to make of it something far finer than anyone could have hoped for. At the end – strong, beautiful, cold, shudderingly strange – I could feel those shivers running down my spine that come only with the greatest theatrical moments; not a perfect show, but a magnificent one.

Gagarin Way
Traverse, Edinburgh
The Scotsman, 6 August 2001

They call it a 'terminal moraine', the great slew of rocks and gravel left behind at the end of what used to be a glacier. Gregory Burke's *Gagarin Way* – a dazzling, fast-moving debut piece co-produced by the Traverse and the Royal National Theatre – is a play set in the terminal moraine of what we used to call politics. There are plenty of brilliant, sharp fragments of political language and thought lying about in the landscape; but the play suggests that for all their vividness, they no longer have any traction or significance.

The scene is Dunfermline in Fife, once one of the heartlands of Scottish working-class communism. In a computer-chip warehouse, three workers are contemplating the slumped form of their kidnap victim, a highly paid consultant sent by the distant head office of their transnational company to assess their 'viability'. The kidnappers are a mixed bunch. Gary is a political type who retains a shred of hope that the killing of such a high-profile corporate victim might carry some wider meaning. Tom is a nice guy, a young graduate security guard who has blundered into the situation by mistake. But Eddie – played in a powerful, controlled star performance by Michael Nardone – is a dangerous man, a lethally articulate analyst of his own economic and social situation, whose intelligence does nothing to modify his ruthless obscenity of language, or his fascination with violence for its own sake. And as the victim Frank (an excellent Maurice Roëves) regains consciousness, the dialogue among the four men swerves fast and furious around the modern economic landscape, bumping deftly from Sartrean nihilism to old-fashioned Fife communism, from the crisis in masculinity, to the hidden benefits of a fat-filled Scottish diet.

If the play has a flaw, it's that its Tarantino-style conclusion is a shade too slick, its pessimism a shade too predictable. But given a typically superb, fast, stylish production by John Tiffany, this show emerges as a near-classic four-hander, in which not only Roëves and Nardone, but also their sparring-partners Billy McElhaney and Michael Moreland, turn in memorable performances, polished almost to perfection.

2002

Helmet
Traverse, Edinburgh
The Scotsman, 2 March 2002

Zock, pow, big-screen, flashy titles, company logos, name of the play in huge go-faster letters. *Helmet* at the Traverse is one of those state-of-the-art stage shows that grabs attention and claims authority by beginning as if it were a movie. Whether this is a positive development for theatre itself is debatable, but at least Douglas Maxwell's new play for Paines Plough and the Traverse has more excuse than most.

Helmet is perhaps the first play ever written in the form of an on-screen computer game: a one-hour duel between two characters in five 'levels', played out on a box-like stage that appears in the middle of the big screen. The scene is a run-down computer-games shop on the point of closing for good. Sal, the owner, is a tragicomic failed businessman in his early thirties, facing the contempt of his otherwise suc-cessful Asian family. Roddy, the would-be customer – alias 'Helmet' – is a pallid, obsessive teenager from a miserable home who does nothing but play computer games and hang around Sal's shop pestering him for the latest releases.

What makes the show work so well as theatre is the hugely entertaining tension between the stylised format and the gritty social realism of the comic dialogue. As the two bicker and spar – Helmet idolising Sal and seeking just a few more minutes in his precious store, Sal trying to per-suade the kid to go home and get a life – the screen around them records their surging and dipping energy levels, their 'lives' lost and gained, complete with sound effects; and on stage, the actors respond, spinning and dancing like little animated figures when successful, plopping suddenly to the ground when defeated.

In a sense, all these whizz-bang effects are wrapped around a fairly simple story of a badly damaged kid slowly revealing the dark emptiness of his life; there's the childhood trauma that haunts all Maxwell's writing, along with the debate about the games boys play, and the attractions and moral haz-ards of that retreat from reality. But the format, with its jerky moments of triumph and despair, its repetitions of scenes with different choices and outcomes, represents a real effort to filter the old certainties of narrative and dramatic devel-opment through a new medium with different rhythms.

And the whole event is so stylishly presented in John Tiffany's production, and so beautifully acted by Ameet Chana and Tommy Mullins, that it's simply a joy to watch, clever, funny, vivid, poignant, endlessly ingenious. After

Edinburgh, this production tours to Liverpool, Nottingham, Norwich, Manchester, Birmingham, London and Glasgow; and if the reaction of the Traverse audience is anything to go by – schoolchildren, critics and the Edinburgh establishment all cheering the show to the echo – its success is guaranteed.

Victory
Royal Lyceum, Edinburgh
The Scotsman, 1 May 2002

1979 marked a famous turning point in English history. After more than three centuries of imperial success abroad and vague political compromise at home, the nation was told it had once again to choose, between the old competing English political traditions of mercantile pragmatism and radical idealism. The way of individualism and enterprise scored a historic election victory; and it was in the immediate aftermath of that moment that Howard Barker sat down to write this great play, set in the parallel year 1660, when England's republican revolution collapsed, its utopian ideals were binned, the guns were buried and King Charles II was restored to the throne – although with a new royal job description which involved little more, in Barker's devastating phrase, than 'tickling crowds for bankers'.

The post-war landscape Barker describes is an immensely brutal one, evoked in this fine Lyceum production by a set which recalls the tilted, jagged layers of red-brown rock we see in images of war-torn Afghanistan. There is a cult of vengeful violence, both sexual and physical.

In two-and-a-half hours of vital, energetic, sexy, intelligent and deeply humorous drama, Barker never for a moment loses sight of his great overarching aim, which is to explore the profound tension in every human society between the ruthless force of political idealism represented by the Puritan revolutionaries, and the basic animal urge to survive, to grasp, to breed, to prosper in the world as it is, that is the guiding principle of King Charles's new age.

This is the third production of *Victory* with which the Lyceum's director Kenny Ireland has been involved, as actor and director, since 1983, and it is a formidable achievement. The casting – with a fine team of Scottish actors evoking the essence of England in crisis – is nothing short of superb. The lovely Kathryn Howden gives the performance of her life as the widow Bradshaw, almost gleefully casting off the memory of her husband's bloodless idealism. Gilly Gilchrist – dangerous, powerful, sexy – might have been born to play her brutal and bewildered cavalier admirer, Ball. Bob Barrett never puts a foot wrong in the difficult role of the smiling, fornicating king, and the ensemble acting is of a terrific quality, with almost every moment perfectly paced, almost every minor role perfectly stitched into the whole.

This play is strong meat, the real Brechtian stuff of life and death, sex, history and politics, thrown on to the stage without apology or euphemism. And if you are tired of theatre that merely soothes and entertains, that treats you like a privileged child or dumbed-down box-office fodder, then *Victory* is for you: sharpen your mind, open your eyes, and prepare for a thrilling evening.

Love Freaks
Tron, Glasgow

The Don
Royal Scottish Academy of Music & Drama
The Scotsman, 12 May 2002

See a play by Iain Heggie, hear people talking dirty, because Heggie is a playwright utterly committed to busting hypocrisy through the sting and stench of the harsh language we use to describe our most basic bodily functions. His view of our society is that, despite our apparent sexual frankness, we remain hopelessly mealy-mouthed and self-deceiving about the lifelong search for bigger and better sex that, he argues, motivates almost all our actions.

Sublimation bores him, politeness enrages him and, in updating Marivaux's great six-handed farce *Double Inconstancy* from the 1720s to the twenty-first century, he simply tears off the outer layers of the drama – the fancy costumes, the language of 'love' – to reveal the inner engine, a hilarious but profoundly unromantic tale of erections in search of orifices and vice versa, with everything from blatant prostitution to routine sexual abuse in the family regarded as a predictable part of the sex-hunting landscape.

Love Freaks is set in the Ayrshire training centre of a Scottish-owned designer coffee chain called Costly Coffee, all cheap Third World coffee beans and pallid minimum-wage employees. There's no denying the almost casual brilliance with which Heggie draws his parallels between a global economic system designed to shaft the weak for the benefit of the strong, and a sexual culture that operates on roughly the same lines.

The language of the play is the kind of fantastic, hyper-heightened, state-of the-art Glasgow vernacular that Heggie has made his trademark. Both Julie Austin as the heroine Celine – an unwilling Costly Coffee employee with an anti-globalisation boyfriend – and Brian Ferguson, as the helpless rent-boy son of Ringo the training assistant, make an outstandingly brilliant job of grasping the hilarious baroque rhythm of Heggie's street-speak.

In the end, though – and despite a near-perfect structure inherited from Marivaux – *Love Freaks* seems to lose direction a little, partly because it is not quite sure what to do with its own disgust. Like some of the great satirists of history, Heggie seems almost more repelled by the sexual images he uses to expose the world's cruelties and hypocrisies than he is by cruelty and hypocrisy itself. This ambivalence is reflected in a sharp volte-face in the play's attitude to global capitalism, as the action draws to a close. For Heggie, it seems sex is not so much a positive life force disrupting patterns of power, as just another expression of the same brutal human tendency to exploit and abuse. It's a grim and slightly unsatisfying view, but one put across with terrific professionalism and energy in this fine production by Graham Eatough, with excellent mock-coffee-shop design by Evelyn Barbour.

By contrast, Heggie's new version of Molière's *Don Juan* – given a brief run at the Royal Scottish Academy of Music & Drama last week under the title *The Don* – seems a much more serious and interesting play, although it's difficult to imagine any of Scotland's leading professional companies taking the risks involved in staging it. In this radically updated version of the story, the Don gains his sexual power from his status as a fading glam-rock star on tour to Manchester and Glasgow, and he abuses that power not by serially seducing grown women but by downloading kiddie porn from the internet and seeking to get his hands on ever-younger female flesh. By the time he reaches the end of this

play – given a fine production by Heggie himself and an outstanding cast of final-year students – Heggie is staring
straight into the heart of the darkness he feels at the core of
all sexual desire. It's an immensely brave and inventive
reworking of one of the world's great texts, and one that
deserves a wider audience.

New Scottish Theatre at the Edinburgh
International Festival: *Variety*
The Scotsman, 2 October 2002

It was on a Monday night just eight weeks ago that the first-
night audience gathered at the King's Theatre in Edinburgh
for the world premiere of *Variety*; and at the time, all the
omens seemed good. The production was a flagship project
of the 2002 Edinburgh International Festival, commissioned
as part of the Festival's growing effort not only to bring the
best of international work to Edinburgh, but to promote the
creation of new world-class theatre projects.

The company involved was the ambitious young Edinburgh-
based group Grid Iron, which had won a golden reputation
on the Fringe with brilliant site-specific shows like *The
Bloody Chamber* and *Gargantua*. The writer was Douglas
Maxwell, a glamorous rising star of the Scottish theatre
scene, much praised for his memorable swing-park drama
Decky Does a Bronco – also produced by Grid Iron – and for
his clever recent play *Helmet*, based on the format of a video
game; and the subject, the slow death of the great Scottish
variety tradition, was a powerful one which had fascinated
Maxwell for years.

But within a couple of days, many of the high hopes surrounding the show had turned to dust, as *Variety* became the
victim of the kind of critical drubbing that most artists only

experience in their worst nightmares. 'Jaw-droppingly awful,' snapped the *Daily Telegraph*, on the morning after the second performance; and that was only the start, as phrases like 'hopeless', 'inept', 'lumbering', 'half-baked' and 'dismally vacuous' began to trail across the national press. Worse, in the aftermath of the production, some senior figures on the Scottish theatre scene weighed in on the side of the critics, although most of them sought to shift the blame away from the artists involved, and on to the Edinburgh Festival itself, and its director, Brian McMaster. In a *Scotsman* opinion piece, the leading playwright Liz Lochhead said that the show 'made a mockery of Scottish theatre past and present'; and the Federation of Scottish Theatre (FST), in its newsletter, suggested that the whole project was inadequately supported, that it was 'unfair' to put it in a position where it would be compared with mature international productions, and that this was 'a mistake which should not be repeated'.

Variety, in other words, has not only been written down as an artistic failure in itself, it has also raised emotive questions about the representation of Scottish work at international level, questions which can only become more urgent with the development of a national theatre project which is partly designed to showcase Scottish theatre internationally. In particular, it invites us to ask whether we have a confident and mature theatre culture which is prepared to take risks on the international stage and sometimes to be seen to fail; or whether we still have only an embryonic theatre culture, which cannot tolerate the kind of setback represented by the response to *Variety*, and which has a duty, as the FST suggests, to protect itself from this kind of experience.

It's worth looking a little more closely at the *Variety* phenomenon, if only to put its perceived failure into perspective. The first thing to note is that the initial response was actually far more mixed than some reactions would suggest. Most Scottish-based theatre critics, for example, rated the show as a three- or four-star interesting effort, rather than a failure. Audiences, too, had a mixed response, with regular Grid Iron fans often enjoying the show, and others reacting with boredom, bafflement or outright disapproval, particularly of one character who kept repeating the f-word like a mantra. So there are questions to ask, in the first place, about the continuing hypersensitivity of Scottish theatre to bad reviews in London papers. 'Why,' asks Grid Iron's producer Judith Doherty, 'should the Federation of Scottish Theatre, of all people, set so much store by what the London critics say, as opposed to reviewers in Scotland?'

Secondly, even if there is agreement that the show was a qualified failure, all the artists involved categorically reject the idea that the Edinburgh Festival was at fault for somehow offering inadequate support, or setting the project up to fail: Maxwell says simply that if the play doesn't hold water in its present form, then the buck stops with him as the writer. And Jude Doherty, along with the director Ben Harrison, echoes his attitude. 'The Festival gave us every red cent we asked for,' says Doherty. 'And more when we needed it. They could not have been more supportive, they put the whole beef of their organisation behind it. Of course, with hindsight, there are things we might have done differently. But the decision to do the piece on stage, not to graft a site-specific element on to what Douglas had conceived – all of that was ours. We're prepared to take responsibility for the artistic decisions we made on this project; and we certainly don't want anyone making excuses for us.'

Third, there's no doubt that *Variety* became caught up in debates that had nothing to do with the play itself. At one level, it became just another piece of ammunition in a long-running battle between McMaster and some of the London critics, who cordially detest his taste in theatre. At another level, the very title of the play seems to have triggered a set of expectations – for a tribute to the variety tradition, or an accurate history – which the play, as a kind of theatre-of-cruelty meditation on transience and loss, was never likely to meet.

But finally, *Variety* seems to have been a victim of a clash of expectations between an alliance of artists trying to use the resources of the Edinburgh Festival to create challenging new drama, and a Festival audience – critics, public, some Scottish theatre pundits – which expects only tried-and-tested excellence. McMaster is militant about the Festival's role as a promoter of new work, and adamant that, in that role, it has the right to fail from time to time. Grid Iron, likewise, seized the offer of Edinburgh Festival funding as a chance to make three risky quantum leaps at once, drastically raising the scale of their work, encouraging Maxwell to produce a more substantial text than ever before, and abandoning the site-specific format for a more conventional theatre space. 'And let's be clear,' says Maxwell, 'in the frame of the Edinburgh Festival, it simply didn't work. In that context, every experiment we tried just looked like a mistake. And it honestly never occurred to me that there could still be an audience out there that would be offended by a character saying "fuck", I simply had no idea.'

But Doherty argues that if the Edinburgh Festival is serious about creating new work, then sooner or later audiences and critics alike will have to adopt a more relaxed attitude to the occasional experimental failure, and stop over-interpreting shows like *Variety* – or, for that matter, this year's other new commission, *The Girl on the Sofa* – either as body-blows to the national pride of the artists involved, or as signs that the Festival itself is going to the dogs.

'Either Edinburgh Festival audiences occasionally take a chance on seeing something that is less than perfect,' says Doherty, 'or we accept that it's only on the Fringe that people are allowed to take risks. Maybe I would feel differently if I had ever thought of myself as representing Scottish theatre, which I don't. But what I do know is that the Festival gave us a chance to do something we could never otherwise have done, and that for us it was a great experience, from which we learned a huge amount. And what I'd like to know is why that has to be seen as a tragedy; when it's nothing of the sort, not a tragedy at all.'

2003

The People Next Door
Dark Earth
Traverse, Edinburgh
The Scotsman, 2 August 2003

The collapse of civil society might seem like an exceptionally grand theme, even for the two opening plays of a new Traverse Festival season. But all the same, it's the threat of the tearing of social fabric – of trust in each other and in institutions, of the bonds of common civility that enable people to live together despite differences of culture and economic interest – that echoes through these two big plays.

In Henry Adam's *The People Next Door* – a follow-up to his first full-length Traverse play, *Among Unbroken Hearts* – the handling of the theme is briskly and astonishingly comic, with a streak of pure farcical surrealism. Set in a council-flat staircase in a big English city, it charts what happens to the more-or-less friendly relations among the residents – confused half-Asian Nigel with his mental-health problems, unhappy fifteen-year-old black kid Marco, and feisty Scottish granny Mrs Mac – when their peace is invaded by a psychopathic plain-clothes cop called Phil, determined to get results in the war on terrorism. In next to no time, fragile Nigel is down at the local mosque under orders to spy on the Muslim community, and discovering that there's more to the Koran than meets the eye; Marco is worried that Nigel's new faith will turn him into a fundamentalist; and Mrs Mac is prowling the stairs with a poker, under the impression, cultivated by Phil, that Nigel is using his sheltered flat as a bomb factory.

And the result is a brilliant, shifting panorama of contemporary British life, in which terrific one-liners zip around the stage like unintentional fireworks unleashed by the pressure of the situation, and each character's psyche becomes a battleground between Phil's rampant *Daily Mail* world view on one hand, and – on the other – a dose of practical common sense, oddly boosted by the emergent liberal folk-wisdom of Britain's soap and chat-show daytime television culture. There are moments when the lightly spun plot almost threatens to collapse under the weight of tragic potential inherent in the story. But in Roxana Silbert's production – featuring inspired performances all round from Fraser Ayres as Nigel, the great Eileen McCallum as Mrs Mac, and Jimmy Akingbola and Joe Duttine as Marco and Phil – the demons are just held at bay; and with a superhuman effort, Henry Adam keeps hold of his comic muse to the end, in a final burst of frantic plotting that's all the more poignant, for the way it shows the strain of remaining hopeful in dark times.

In David Harrower's *Dark Earth*, by contrast, the mood is far more sombre, weighed down by a sense of loss and dread. Harrower's focus, in this powerful follow-up to *Knives in Hens* and *Kill the Old Torture Their Young*, is the breakdown of trust between urban and rural Britain. His plot revolves around smart but dismal Glasgow yuppie couple Euan and Valerie (John MacKay and Frances Grey) who drive out in search of the Antonine Wall, suffer a car breakdown somewhere beyond Falkirk, and find themselves in the hands of the Caldwells, a once-farming family who are undergoing a kind of nervous breakdown as they lose their land, and possibly their home.

The play's problem is that this theme seems to unleash in Harrower such a weight of feelings and associations that he has hardly been able to tame them into a single play. The Caldwells, in particular, are made to represent so many lost or dying strands in Scottish life – from the rural tradition of conviviality and hospitality to faint memories of the Jacobite rebellion – that it's difficult to know whether to see them as credible characters, mythical figures in a landscape, or just stereotypes.

And yet, despite the half-formed, tentative quality of *Dark Earth*, I can't recall ever seeing a play that made a braver attempt to get to grips with the crushing sense of sadness, bitterness and loss that seems to cling around some Scottish Lowland landscapes, or to link that sense of loss to the bitter reactionary rage, among some parts of the old white community, that is becoming such a disturbing part of British life; and, beyond that, to the pathology of rootlessness, sexlessness and alienation in twenty-first-century urban life. This is not Harrower's best play, and despite memorable performances from Jimmy Yuill and Anne Lacey as Petey and Ida Caldwell, Philip Howard's production does not flatter it. But its sheer unwieldiness seems to me a sign of Harrower's courage and ambition as a playwright; and of how essential it is that he continues exploring these themes, in the quest for a form that will carry them through to fulfilment.

The Resistible Rise of Arturo Ui
Nothing
Snow White
Citizens', Glasgow
The Scotsman 3 December 2003

So this is the way the old regime at the Citizens' finally ends, not with a whimper, but with a roar of defiance and a rush towards the future. It's been a long season of swansongs in the eighteen months since Giles Havergal announced his intention to retire from the artistic directorship: there's been Philip Prowse's luscious valedictory production of *Venice Preserv'd*, and Havergal's final appearance as Scrooge in last year's Christmas show. But of all the farewells, this final round of productions sits best with the achievement of the last thirty-three years – businesslike, brilliant, clever, intensely theatrical and designed to emphasise the role the Citizens' two small studios have played, since the late 1980s, as a forcing ground for new talent.

In the tiny Stalls Studio, for example, Prowse signs off by handing the space over to brilliant young director Phillip Breen, a winner of last year's Channel 4 director's award, for a lightweight but brilliantly staged production of Bertolt Brecht's 1941 classic, *The Resistible Rise of Arturo Ui*.

There's a wave of Brecht plays written in the 1930s sweeping Glasgow's studio theatres at the moment, and it's not difficult to see why. No writer has a sharper ironic view – for our unsettled times – of how political chaos can give birth to tyranny and how fear eats the democratic soul. In the case of *Arturo Ui* – a detailed satire on the rise of Hitler and the annexation of Austria, set in a mythical movie-style Chicago – Brecht's main theme is the link between tyranny and gangsterism, and how thuggish regimes thrive by creating and exaggerating the terror from which they pretend to protect their citizens.

The only problem with Breen's generally excellent production is that the actors seem, on average, slightly too young to carry all the political weight and menace of the text; with so many fresh-faced kids running round in gangster outfits and moustaches, the atmosphere is sometimes more *Bugsy Malone* than Kurt Weill. But at a technical level, Breen's razor-sharp staging of the play for only six actors, with set by Mark Bailey – a bare space like a working-men's meeting hall – is impossible to fault, being swift, ingenious, tightly focused and impassioned. There are brilliant performances from Stewart Porter as Ui's betrayed friend Roma, from the wonderful Vivien Parry as the grieving widow of neighbouring press magnate Dullfeet, and from Stephen Ventura as Ui himself.

Upstairs in the Circle Studio, by contrast, there's a superbly mature and stylish last hurrah from Robert David Mac-Donald, who directs a new stage version of Henry Green's bitter and brilliant 1952 novel *Nothing*, performed by a terrific cast of Citizens' regulars led by Sophie Ward and Simon Dutton. In a sense, this show takes us into familiar Citizens' territory and into the theatre's long, ambivalent love affair with the manners and style of a high bourgeoisie it loves to hate – Green's novel tells the story of two frightful London toffs and former lovers, Jane Wetherby and John Pomfret, and of Jane's brutal and manipulative reaction when she discovers that her feeble son Philip, whose paternity in any case seems slightly uncertain, has fallen in love with Pomfret's frumpy daughter Mary.

However, beyond the fabulously arrogant one-liners and bitter satirical wit, there's a strong sense of the new about this production. For one thing, there's a major new writing talent on the block in the shape of Citizens' actress Andrea Hart, who has adapted Green's novel into a dozen brilliantly slick and telling scenes. For another, there's a sad and powerful contemporary resonance about Green's portrait of a hard-working post-war generation abused, neglected and let down by a selfish breed of parents born into a more hedonistic age.

The whole show is presented with such brilliance and flair, on a gradually darkening and emptying set by Annie Curtis Jones, that it's difficult to raise a single objection. MacDonald's slick staging, complete with slouching waiter clearing up between scenes, is an object lesson in theatrical irony, perspective, and pace; and in Jane Wetherby, Sophie Ward is on the way to creating one of the great sacred monsters of theatre, a pin-thin post-war Lady Bracknell with an ego the size of The Ritz.

As for the Citizens' head of design Kenny Miller, who struts his stuff in the main auditorium with a new version of *Snow White*, well, there's no need to mourn the departure of this brilliantly off-the-wall theatrical talent, because he's already been signed up by the theatre's new artistic director Jeremy Raison to direct a show next season. *Snow White*, though, is a production that should come with a few health warnings, in the sense that as cheery, child-friendly Christmas shows go, this isn't one. Instead, it's a travesty of the traditional story in the true sense of the word, a sexed-up, tripped-out, pitch-dark retelling of the original Brothers Grimm fairytale that opens with a formidably bleak childbirth scene and combines a vaguely satanic-rock-video aesthetic, and a cool, sexy dance soundtrack, with a brief nightmare tour through the imagery of Andy Warhol and a German expressionist horror movie. As a radical deconstruction of a traditional fairytale – complete with a magnificently camp performance from Julie Austin as the wicked queen – this *Snow White* has a wild, unsettling brilliance about it. Just don't go there, though, if you're a child under eight or nine; or if you're an adult in search of that old Christmas magic, and the brief, heartwarming midwinter return to the place where childhood innocence once was.

Part Three

2004–2015: The Emergence of the National Theatre of Scotland

By 2004 there was a real sense of simmering anticipation – and some apprehension – in Scottish theatre, as the National Theatre of Scotland project began to take shape. In July, Vicky Featherstone – then artistic director of the London-based new-writing theatre company, Paines Plough, and an admirer of many of the current generation of Scottish playwrights – was appointed as the NTS's first artistic director, and began the job with literally nothing but an empty, unfurnished office in Glasgow and a mobile phone; she quickly recruited her close associate John Tiffany, who had left the Traverse to join her at Paines Plough, as the NTS's associate director for new work.

There was plenty of energy around, though, from the Traverse to the Edinburgh Festival, which saw the premiere of Anthony Neilson's The Wonderful World of Dissocia, a beautiful play which swept the board at the newly founded Critics' Awards for Theatre in Scotland, set up by Robert Dawson Scott and a group of critical colleagues in 2003. And the autumn of 2004 saw an initiative that was to prove almost as important as the coming of the NTS, as David MacLennan – formerly of the 7:84 sister company Wildcat Stage Productions, which had lost its grant in a bruising confrontation with the Scottish Arts Council half a decade earlier – set up a new lunchtime theatre venture called A Play, a Pie and

*a Pint, at the new Òran Mór pub and venue in the West End of
Glasgow. Running entirely on the proceeds of its ticket sales, on a
small amount of commercial sponsorship, and on the generous support of the venue owner, Colin Beattie, A Play, a Pie and a Pint
set off on its mission – without help or hindrance from overween-
ing funding bodies – to present a brand-new fifty-minute play
every week for two seasons a year; and it soon became a runaway
success, premiering more than thirty new plays a year, and imi-
tated in cities from Pittsburgh to Moscow. A Play, a Pie and a
Pint was to transform the opportunities for new playwriting in
Scotland, and went on to form alliances, in supporting new work,
both with the National Theatre of Scotland, and with the new
Playwrights' Studio Scotland, set up in 2001 to help support
Scottish-based theatre writers. And although its short plays were
often, in effect, works-in-progress, and rarely surfaced as groundbreaking productions in their own right, A Play, a Pie and a Pint
at Òran Mór became an important new hub for Scotland's theatre life, buzzing with energy, gossip, and ideas.*

*The years 2004–07 saw one of the richest periods ever in Scottish
theatre, as the massive new NTS funding came on stream, and
the whole scene began to respond. The Edinburgh Festival of
2005 saw another thrilling Scottish premiere, in David
Harrower's* Blackbird; *and the National Theatre of Scotland
launched, in February 2006, with a stunningly radical, non-
theatre-based, nationwide event called* Home, *followed within a
few months both by Grid Iron's amazing airport show* Roam,
*and – during the Edinburgh Festival – by the company's defining
show* Black Watch. *Seizing the movement towards verbatim
theatre that swept Britain's stages in the mid-2000s,* Black
Watch *was written by Gregory Burke, but based on a series of
real interviews with Scottish soldiers who had served in the Iraq
War in 2003–04; the staging and performances – directed by
John Tiffany – were breathtaking, and the show became a
massive global success, touring across the world for almost eight
years after its first performance.*

Other Scottish theatre companies seemed to raise their game to meet the moment. And in the vintage year of 2007 – with Alan Cumming at the Edinburgh Festival playing Dionysus in the NTS's version of The Bacchae, *theatre exploding out of its traditional spaces into the wild places of Scotland, and Dundee Rep's brilliant ensemble, under its artistic director James Brining, creating one of the greatest tribute shows ever in Stephen Greenhorn's Proclaimers musical* Sunshine on Leith *– it really seemed as though Scottish theatre had come of age, and had finally moved to take its full place – and a radical, boundary-busting, twenty-first-century place at that – in the life of the nation.*

2004

Reasons to Be Cheerful
7:84 Scotland
The Scotsman, 25 February 2004

In a living room somewhere on the edge of a British city, a group of friends who were flatmates in their twenties meet again after a long separation. One of them is celebrating his forty-third birthday, and in the course of a long evening's drinking and arguing, it emerges that some have done better than others in terms of wealth and career success, that youthful ideals have been betrayed or at least severely bent, and that a couple who were once in love are still obsessed with each other, but cannot quite find it in their hearts to start over.

Sound familiar? You bet it does; it's the plot of every piece of self-indulgent thirty-something bourgeois drama that has tracked across our television screens in the last decade. But because this version of the story is set in a tower block in Cardonald, because the ideals the characters used to share were socialist ones, because it's loosely based on the book of the same name by socialist stand-up Mark Steel, and above all, because it's presented by the 7:84 Theatre Company under new artistic direction, we're supposed to accept this flabby piece of midlife angst, badly scripted by Martin McCardie, as heralding a new beginning for Scottish radical theatre. I'm afraid it's no dice, since the resulting play is about as radical as that old bore in the corner of your pub who knows that he doesn't like New Labour, but hasn't had a new thought about the reasons why since 1994.

Stuart Davids' production opens with a video montage of the politics of the last forty years – Thatcher, Blair, Martin Luther King, the Miners' Strike – and a filmed sequence of the central character, Bobby, making his way up to his tower-block flat with a pack of beer for his birthday party. This is a reasonable way into the story, but even after the onstage screen morphs neatly into Bobby's living-room window, complete with live view of the motorway, it promises more than the script is able to deliver. The point about Bobby is that he is a socialist activist who, for political reasons, continues to live a comfortless solo existence in his council flat while spending most of his time out on demonstrations and actions; and when his old friend Michael, now a successful radical comedian, and Kate, now a New Labour politician, arrive to help him celebrate, predictable rows ensue about who betrayed whom, and in what way.

But the difficulty with all this is that it makes the elementary mistake, for any attempt at radical theatre, of talking about politics in the abstract, rather than actually showing politics in action. Apart from some vague chat about the fight to save a local community centre, we never get to know what Bobby has actually been doing in all his years of political campaigning, or whether anyone has been helped by his efforts. Worse than that, the standard of the banter among the three characters is lamentably poor, with tired old clichés about New Labour opportunism and American infamy emerging with such a clanking predictability that even the most loyal audience finds it hard to raise a spontaneous laugh.

None of this is the fault of Davids' cast, who do the best they can with the material to hand. Frank Gallagher is a feisty and poignant Bobby, Maureen Carr adds a real touch of theatrical energy and passion in the difficult role of Kate, Neil McKinven walks his way through the role of Michael with reasonable poise, although he covered this territory more powerfully half a decade ago, in Stephen Greenhorn's gloomy but prophetic *Dissent*. And no doubt there are audiences out there so starved of theatre that speaks in a Scottish popular voice, and that publicly reaffirms many of their own views about the Blair-Bush era, that any old show with those qualities will be taken to their hearts. But important though it is that 7:84 should survive as part of Scotland's theatrical map, with its mission to create radical popular theatre that finds new audiences among the voiceless and under-represented, there's no point in pretending that a show as unambitious as this does much to further that aim. *Reasons to Be Cheerful* is not radical, not funny, not original, and not even very dramatic; and 7:84's loyal audience deserves better.

Six Black Candles
Royal Lyceum, Edinburgh

Sauchiehall Street
Vanishing Point
The Scotsman, 17 March 2004

They're outsiders, the six splendid sisters at the heart of this bruisingly hilarious comedy by prize-winning novelist Des Dillon, now enjoying its premiere at the Royal Lyceum after a six-year search for a theatrical home. The sisters are women in what was until recently a man's world, they're rebels by instinct, they're west-of-Scotland Catholics still living out the legacy of the industrial revolution that swept their great-grandparents out of Ireland and into Lanarkshire; and if they also dabble in a bit of witchcraft – well, what better way to express their general dissent from the pious decencies of civic life, and from the rational Enlightenment values that Scotland once exported to the world, but which somehow never meant much on the mean streets of Coatbridge.

Dillon's play – based, he says, on a true story of his own six sisters – describes an evening when all six women, plus their mother and old Irish granny, converge on the council flat of the eldest sister, Caroline, to perform the curse of the 'six black candles' on her estranged husband's nineteen-year-old girlfriend, Stacie Gracie. It's a great dramatic situation, in which the primitive Darwinian passions of lust, rage, vengeance, and fierce family loyalty come into conflict with the everyday scepticism of the sisters' modern lives, the ferocious sibling rivalry between them, the timid pieties of respectable Catholicism as represented by the hapless local priest, and – most poignantly – with the depth of Caroline's true love for her faithless man.

This is *The Slab Boys* meets *Shameless* meets *Chewin' the Fat*, with a powerful female twist; and Dillon spins physical and verbal comedy out of his scenario with all the flair of a born playwright. The characters are drawn in tremendous, larger-than-life brushstrokes, the physical comedy is in the best tradition of pitch-black farce, and the script bristles with knock-'em-dead one-liners, which Mark Thomson's terrific company could sometimes afford to deliver with just a shade more theatrical force.

In every other respect, though, Thomson's gloriously robust production is almost impossible to fault. Rebecca Minto's white-concrete set pays hilarious tribute both to modern west-of-Scotland Catholic church architecture, and to the worst kind of municipal housing development; and in terms of casting, Thomson has hoovered up most of the finest female comedy talent around, offering a brilliant, raunchy treasure-house of a company led by Eileen McCallum as Granny and Kathryn Howden as Caroline, with Gabriel Quigley, Jennifer Black, Wendy Seager, and Julie Duncanson. In the novelised version of *Six Black Candles*, published in 2002, Dillon writes of how respectable Scotland just doesn't know about the raging, anarchic working-class counterculture that thrives in its schemes and cities. But thanks to writers like Dillon, and directors like Thomson with the guts and imagination to stage their work, Scotland is getting to know itself better every day. And in looking so deeply and sharply at ourselves, we of course learn more about those great undercurrents of twenty-first-century life that go far beyond Scotland: in this case, about a western world lurching from the long age of the first Enlightenment towards something both new and more ancient – frightening, anarchic, post-patriarchal, and bursting with its own life force.

'I think the single most important thing in comedy is the target,' wrote leading Scottish playwright Iain Heggie in last Saturday's *Scotsman*. But the bitter truth is that where *Six*

Black Candles chooses exactly the right comic target, and goes for it like a ferret out of a trap, Heggie's own latest play selects the wrong victim at the outset, and spends a dismal two-and-a-half hours paying the price of that initial mistake. Set in a moth-eaten Scottish theatrical agency at the wrong end of Glasgow's most famous thoroughfare, *Sauchiehall Street* is a leaden city comedy in seven scenes that plays like an extended piece of hate-mail directed against Scotland in general, and the idea of Scottish theatre in particular. Its central character, middle-aged agent Dorothy Darvel, is a barren monster of destructive possessiveness who spends her life sabotaging the careers of her young clients so as to prevent them from leaving for London; her would-be successor Maureen is a self-proclaimed halfwit, whose increasingly elaborate postmodern malapropisms provide the play with its few vintage moments of surreal Heggie-esque brilliance.

Almost as soon as it hits the stage, though, the play runs into three fatal difficulties. The first is that this is another of those dreary plays about theatre itself, cluttered with luvvie in-jokes that have all the thespians in the audience guffawing self-consciously, and leave everyone else bored to tears. The second is that the specific image of Scotland and Scottish theatre that Heggie chooses to mock is at least two decades out of date, a kind of pre-Glasgow-1990 cultural provincial-ism that has now been replaced with other, if often equally laughable, dreams and delusions; the result is a long damp squib of a script that sets out to attack inward-looking Scot-tish provincialism, but somehow ends up embodying it in its least attractive form. And the third is Matthew Lenton's wretched production, which for poor casting, limp pace, and chronic inability to evoke those extra layers of meaning that might lift the evening a little, has to take some kind of biscuit as the least inspired staging of the year.

Linda Duncan McLaughlin, as the addle-tongued Maureen, makes a spirited stab at the play's most interesting role. But Dorothy Darvel and her actor husband Gerard, as played by Jo Cameron Brown and Peter Kelly, are as tired and unfunny a pair of stereotypes as the Scottish stage has seen in a while. 'D'you not think you should be careful not to sound like an old fart?' young actor Barry Barr asks his mentor Gerard at one point. After this lot, it's a question many will be asking of Iain Heggie himself.

Scenes from an Execution
Dundee Rep
The Scotsman, 29 April 2004

In the hall of a barracks in sixteenth-century Vienna, a woman artist paints, on a huge 100-foot canvas, a work that will make or break her career, and perhaps her life. Her name is Galactia, her subject is the Battle of Lepanto, a recent triumph over the Muslim forces of the Ottoman Empire, and the work has been commissioned by the Venetian state in celebration of its victory.

But Galactia paints the horror of war rather than its glory, in a terrifying avalanche of sliced and splintered flesh; and the question is whether the state will punish her, or accept and co-opt the painting which she imagines, on its journey up to St Mark's, as 'a giant bomb huddled under tarpaulins', ready to shatter the state with its uncompromising truths.

This is the situation around which Howard Barker builds his superb 1985 drama *Scenes from an Execution*, perhaps the most accessible of all the works of this great contemporary poet of the English stage; and Dundee Rep could hardly have chosen a more timely play to end its spring season than this powerful study of the morality and statecraft of a

Christian republic at war with the world of Islam, and of the role of the artist – and a passionate woman artist at that – in such a state.

Dominic Hill's classic production is a shade too passive in the face of Barker's mighty story to achieve the electrifying heights of Kenny Ireland's 2002 Edinburgh production of Barker's *Victory*. For that, it would need a more radical and risky engagement with the more poetic and symbolic levels of the text, and a fiercer sense of why this matters now.

But Neil Warmington's transformation of the Dundee Rep space into a beautiful in-the-round cockpit of an arena is a stunning success in its own terms. And if the company – led by a brave, earthy and magnificent Ann Louise Ross as Galactia – never quite brings that final spark of creative danger to their performance, they carry their roles well enough to generate a beautiful, well-crafted and deeply satisfying production of one of the most significant plays of our time.

Still a Bigot
Pavilion, Glasgow
The Scotsman, 21 July 2004

Summertime, and filling theatres is anything but easy. Except, that is, at the Pavilion in Glasgow, where – without a penny of subsidy in sight and on a purely commercial basis – a thousand people every night are piling through the doors to see eight Scottish actors, on an old-fashioned living-room set, bouncing and grimacing their way through a Glasgow comedy which is about as traditional as they come.

This year marks the Pavilion's centenary as one of the city's best-loved places of entertainment; and to celebrate the occasion, the theatre's boss, Iain Gordon, has revived a series of three comedies by Glasgow writer James Barclay, all written especially for the Pavilion between the 1970s and '90s. Even Gordon has been surprised by the scale of the season's success, which has reached audiences in every age group from sixteen to ninety-six – including the notoriously hard-to-get thirty- and fortysomethings – and kept the theatre buzzing for the last two months and more. Something to do with weak summer television schedules, he speculates, or his television advertising campaign, or the relationship of trust that the Pavilion has built up with Glasgow audiences over the decades.

But it also must have a great deal to do with the content of the plays, one of which – *Paras Over the Barras* – celebrates the survival of Glasgow tenement life during the Second World War, while the other two recount the adventures of one Andra Thomson, a swaggering, middle-aged, work-shy, Rangers-supporting bigot of an anti-hero who is routinely made a fool of by all the other members of his family, and, for that matter, by history itself.

In *Still a Bigot*, the second Andra Thomson play, our hero has been moved from his old tenement to a new high-rise flat with – horror of horrors – a view of Celtic Park. His daughter has married a Jew; his son is set on becoming a priest; his new neighbours are Chinese; and his lovely wife, Annie, always a Catholic, is becoming more assertive about sticking her picture of the Pope on the wall alongside his King Billy.

On the upside, the one-liners in this play flow fast and furiously, and some of them are very funny. There's a touch of pure Molière about Barclay's image of the preposterous patriarch trying to impose his will on a household that holds him in well-deserved contempt; and Iain Gordon's brightly lit, heavily amplified production is as vivid, accessible and cartoon-clear as a grown-up comic strip. On the downside, the whole show rambles on for far too long (Molière knew

how to round things off in a crisp two hours), and it's difficult not to flinch at oor Andra's consistently racist language
– he is Glasgow's answer to Alf Garnett, with all that that
implies – or Barclay's affectionate but weird obsession with
sending up Glasgow's Jewish community, complete with
mock beards and curls.

But although there's always a question around characters
such as Andra Thomson and Alf Garnett over whether they
validate the prejudices they express every time they speak or
simply encourage us to laugh at them, it's difficult to deny
the sense that this season of plays is giving Glasgow audiences
a genuinely cathartic experience. One morning last week, I
heard a sociologist on the radio holding forth about what he
said was the sad psychological plight of London's white
working class. History, he argued, had deprived them of their
old sense of imperial pride and patriotism and required them
to live through wave after wave of ethnic and social change,
without even according them the victim status available to
every other ethnic group or giving them a chance to mourn
their losses. Although it all sounded a shade self-pitying to
me, I couldn't help remembering the roars of relieved and
delighted laughter in that Pavilion audience as they listened
to Billy Armour's powerful Andra belting out the prejudices
that had until so recently been a routine part of their lives,
and then receiving his due comeuppance. And I wondered
whether things might have felt different, in London, if the
city had held on to just one institution like Glasgow's
miraculously surviving Pavilion Theatre: a people's palace of
a theatre where locals can get together in public to
acknowledge the social history they've lived through, to laugh
and cry as if they've been to a good wake, and then, with a
little luck, to let it go and move on.

The Wonderful World of Dissocia
Royal Lyceum, Edinburgh
The Scotsman, 2 September 2004

There's nothing remotely original about the idea behind this latest play by Anthony Neilson, the most challenging and disturbing of all the current generation of playwrights from Scotland: the image of the sane, everyday world as a prison house, from which only those we call 'mad' can escape, is almost as old as the idea of madness itself.

But what makes Neilson's play – commissioned by the Edinburgh International Festival and the Drum Theatre, Plymouth, in association with Glasgow's Tron – such a beautiful and thought-provoking experience is the rare boldness of its structure; and the wild rollercoaster of experience and imagery through which it leads us on the way to its quiet final act, a thirty-five-minute coda in which, through a clinical glass panel, we watch our heroine Lisa, in her bleach-bright hospital room, undergoing all the banal indignities, casual kindnesses and painful misunderstandings of ordinary treatment for mental illness in Britain today.

It's the first ninety minutes of the play, though, that burn themselves on to the mind, and will divide audiences between the delighted and the terminally exasperated: for the play begins as Lisa snaps the guitar string of ordinary life, and sets off into the looking-glass world of Dissocia, the land of Dissociative Identity Disorder. Dissocia emerges as a wonderful, terrifying and sometimes brutal Narnia-cum-Alice's-Wonderland of a place, where Lisa tumbles over scapegoats and magic polar bears, encounters weird, satirical government officials and lost-property offices disguised as hot-dog stalls, sings amazing songs to herself, and breathes the air of a faint, subversive awareness that the 'real world' is, in its way, at least as mad as this one, and not nearly so much fun.

There are echoes not only of C.S. Lewis and Lewis Carroll, but of Kafka, fantasy fiction, and the wilder reaches of sixties psychedelia. And although the play – directed by Neilson himself, and beautifully performed by a fine cast led by the stunning Christine Entwisle as Lisa – reaches no very exciting conclusion, it offers a powerful final insight into the culture clash between sixties-style open-ended creativity on one hand, and our control-obsessed post-nineties middle-class culture on the other, that has been one of the leading themes of this year's Festival. And it also has the courage to end on a faint note of hope: the sense that love may after all be able to bridge the gap between the 'sane' and the 'mad', if only because it is a form of madness itself.

2005

Look Back in Anger
Royal Lyceum, Edinburgh
The Scotsman, 19 January 2005

What's striking about John Osborne's *Look Back in Anger*, almost half a century on from its explosive first performance in London, is how near it seems in spirit to some of the angry, 'in-your-face' British theatre of the last decade; and yet how far. On one hand, it has the same sense of young, raging male energy robbed of any kind of useful social role or purpose. In the absence of war – or any grand imperial plan – it seems Britain never knows what to do with that energy; so we tend to pathologise, marginalise and fear it, from *Look Back in Anger* in 1956, to Irvine Welsh's *Trainspotting*, forty years later.

But if Jimmy Porter's furious, destructive anger seems familiar, there's nonetheless an edge to it that makes it seem –

despite the play's wordy, conventional structure – just a couple of mighty twists more radical than anything contemporary British theatre has to offer. For in the first place, Jimmy is not apolitical: he rages against the British ruling class – represented, in his world, by his fragile-looking wife Alison – in terms that are frankly shocking to contemporary audiences, inured as we are to the idea that class politics is dead and that the expression of so much envy and spite towards the better-off will get you precisely nowhere. And in the second place, he flatly refuses the idea of redemption through fatherhood that gives so much postmodern lad-literature its mushily sentimental conclusion.

Jimmy not only treats his wife like dirt in a way that post-feminist audiences can hardly bear; when he hears that she is pregnant with his child, he also makes it clear that he doesn't give a damn, that the very idea of reproducing himself in such a world means nothing to him. If he is bound to Alison, it's because they somehow recognise one another as mates, in the jungle of a decaying society. Ideas like hope, redemption and building a future just don't come into it.

Richard Baron's richly detailed new production at the Royal Lyceum is probably just a touch too passive and conventional, in the face of this colossal play, to do full justice to its radical energy. On an overwhelmingly naturalistic set by Trevor Coe – all rusty gas-rings and grubby skylights – David Tennant and Kelly Reilly give a pair of gorgeous, impassioned, and sometimes heart-rending performances as Jimmy and Alison, without ever moving much below the surface of Osborne's glittering array of words. Beautiful actors born of the age of celebrity, they can describe the dreary collectivist Britain of the 1950s, but never quite evoke it; and it's left to Steven McNicoll's unobtrusively perfect performance as Jimmy's quiet Welsh friend Cliff to bring a real sense of time, place and history to the stage.

The result is a show that takes the whole of a long first half to gather momentum, and that makes it slightly too easy for the audience to take refuge in a lightweight twenty-first-century feminism, siding with nicely spoken Alison and dismissing Jimmy as a working-class boor with the sexual politics of a caveman. It's sometimes tantalising to imagine what could have been done with this play by a radical director more willing to stand at a rigorous Brechtian distance from his characters, and a designer less interested in the minute detail of the period, and more interested in its symbolism and style. But the sheer strength of the play, and the rich professional quality of the production, makes this a tremendously worthwhile evening, nonetheless. If the audience is likely to leave the theatre not much the wiser as to why the Lyceum wanted to present this play, it still provides a full-blooded experience of Osborne at his youthful best, which leaves plenty of room for our own response; for our own sense of how much this play still matters, forty-nine years on.

The Brother's Suit
Òran Mór, Glasgow
13 April 2005

If you want to catch a sense of how much screen culture dominates our age – not only our politics, but all our lesser art forms – then you need only glance at the huge upsurge of media and public interest that suddenly sweeps through any theatre venue where a star of the small or large screen is about to make a personal appearance.

Robbie Coltrane has been a bit of a television face since the 1980s, when he appeared in John Byrne's *Tutti Frutti*. He became a small-screen star a decade later, in the great days of *Cracker*. Lately he has reached the promised land of global big-screen fame, mainly by playing a character called Hagrid in the Harry Potter films. Yet now here he is, in a cellar bar on the Great Western Road, making six lunchtime appearances in a short half-hour play by the leading Scottish screenwriter Peter McDougall. Hence the seething crowd that packs the small downstairs space a full half-hour before the show is due to start, the queue at the door, and the row of press photographers camped on the pavement outside. It's a measure of the sheer vitality and originality of McDougall's emerging theatrical voice that, by the end of the performance, the focus of the event is beginning to shift decisively away again from the star performer, and back to the play in hand.

Like McDougall's previous piece for the Òran Mór 'A Play, a Pie and a Pint' season, *The Brother's Suit* looks deep into the bleak heart of a certain kind of Scottish working-class family life – the kind where violence against women and children was common, and the word 'love' did not feature. This time, the two characters are brothers divided by the pressures of sibling rivalry, and by their parents' predictable preference for the elder son – Tam, who left for London – over the younger son, Junior, who stayed and did his duty. Now, twenty-five years on, Junior waits at Central Station for Tam's long-delayed return while a lugubrious Greek chorus – or Grim Reaper – in the shape of a poetic newsvendor, superbly played by Stewart Porter, stands by and delivers his own commentary on family and death, and on the dark and bloody inner life of the city whose evening paper he sells.

Now, there's no point in arguing that this second theatrical effort by McDougall doesn't have its regrettable moments. Some of the detail of the two men's middle-aged lives – the divorce, the problems with women, the exile from fatherhood – are achingly predictable and self-pitying; some of the old-fashioned Glasgow repartee sounds second hand; and Coltrane's tremendous natural talent as an actor takes time to assert itself over both his visible self-consciousness at returning to the live stage, and his screen actor's unwilling-ness to project his voice.

But with powerful support from Porter and from the excel-lent William MacBain as Junior, Coltrane gradually begins to sculpt Tam into a credible and tragic figure, a charismatic and talented man facing death in the knowledge that his life has somehow failed, despite his charm. As for the play itself – well, it may have its share of rough-edged moments and sudden lapses, but at the core of David MacLennan's strong, good-looking production, it's possible to glimpse a really thrilling sense of theatre – of Glasgow's Central Station as a mythical location as potent as the banks of the Styx, or the Norwegian street where Peer Gynt meets his crossing-sweeper. There's a huge tragic energy here, a wonderful ironic humour, and a passion for the high drama and deep poetry of ordinary Glasgow lives; and if McDougall can express all that in just under thirty minutes, then there's no knowing what he might produce, given the chance to write a full-length stage play.

Blackbird
King's, Edinburgh
The Scotsman, 17 August 2005

There are plenty of shows in Edinburgh this year about the dark undercurrents of the thing we call 'love', but nowhere will you see them more chillingly exposed – and with a greater searing and healing power – than in this towering production by the great German director Peter Stein of David Harrower's new play, *Blackbird*, the finest thing he has written since his debut with *Knives in Hens* a decade ago.

Set on a King's Theatre stage opened out into a wide modern space representing a bleak canteen area in a small factory somewhere in England, the play dives straight for the least acceptable face of erotic desire and obsession by showing us, in what feels like real time, a searing two-hour confrontation between fifty-six-year-old manager Ray, and twenty-seven-year-old Una, the girl with whom he had a sexual relationship fifteen years before, when she was only twelve.

In a dialogue that falls into four parts – introduction, central memory sequence, fractured resolution and a stunningly theatrical conclusion – we see both Ray's desperate need to convince himself that the relationship was nothing to do with paedophilia, that Una was mature, that he never meant to hurt and abandon her as he did; and her damaged inability to reconcile her bitter avenging rage with undeniable memories of a sweetness and intensity that she, like him, has never been able to recapture.

The play never leaves us in any doubt that Ray's actions were criminal and wrong, but its greatness lies in the way it uses this terrible confrontation as both reality and metaphor, to show us what we all know to be true: that desire is fundamentally selfish, that it always contains within it the possibilities of exploitation and abandonment, and that an erotic relationship brutally ended always inflicts unequal damage, one walking away to start afresh, the other wounded for life.

Jodhi May and Roger Allam give performances of astonishing integrity and power as Una and Ray, with May achieving almost operatic levels of intensity during the play's long central memory sequence. Peter Stein's production is an unforgettable demonstration of what a truly great director can do with a new text full of its own living, breathing energy. Ferocious in its attention to the value of every word – and profoundly musical in its piecing-together of text, movement and sound – it builds towards a conclusion that is almost breathtaking in its visual and physical eloquence and sense of tragedy: a mighty and timeless reminder that some relationships unleash demons which – with all the care and counselling in the world – can never again be fully laid to rest.

The Synge Cycle
King's, Edinburgh
The Scotsman, 31 August 2005

The curtain rises on the dark figure of a woman, standing at a simple table against a high, rough cottage wall, poised in the timeless act of kneading dough to make bread. It's an image that speaks volumes about the Druid Theatre Company of Galway's historic production of all six of the dramas of John Millington Synge; about the willingness of director Garry Hynes and her company to embrace the archetypal images of Synge's drama as well as to play against them from time to time; about the central role and power of strong female figures throughout the cycle; and about the impressive simplicity of Francis O'Connor's single set, beautifully lit by Davy Cunningham, against which the whole cycle is played out.

As Hynes's company has learned during more than eighteen months of work on the cycle, the story of the life of J.M. Synge is short and poignant enough to make a brief drama in itself. He lived for only thirty-eight years, dying of cancer at the height of his fame in 1909. If his life was short, though, it takes just a glance at any page of his writing to demonstrate that he lived it with a sensual and emotional intensity and a driving sweetness of spirit that often takes the breath away, and, if he did not survive to father children of his own, by the time of his death he had done enough, in six short years as a playwright, to make himself one of the key founding fathers not only of Ireland's national drama, but also of the whole imaginative landscape of twentieth-century literature and theatre.

It's this colossal achievement that is celebrated in this wonderful presentation of the entire cycle of Synge's work; a success that has as much to do with director Garry Hynes's ability to stand back and let a mainly youthful company of actors forge their own living relationship with Synge, as with any dominating directorial concept. Over almost nine hours, with generous pauses, the cycle leads us through the great arc of Synge's work, from the severe and rugged early tragedy *Riders to the Sea* – in which a mother figure mourns her six sons lost by drowning – through the bounce and ripple of Synge's four muscular comedies, to a final revisiting of the tragic mood in the unfinished *Deirdre of the Sorrows*, a reworking of the ancient Celtic myth in which a young queen embraces the death and destruction that is her fate, rather than live more safely and less intensely.

And the overwhelming impression created by the cycle is of the huge tension throughout Synge's work between a passionate, often deeply erotic sense of the beauty and energy of life, and a profound awareness of death and its pervasive presence. In the two tragedies, this tension expresses itself through the passionate rebellion against death, or argument with it, through which the characters must pass before they reach the final peace that comes with absolute loss. In the comedies, by contrast, Synge soars into a bold and brilliant teasing relationship with the idea of decay and death, the coffin-boards in the corner of the stage always on the point of being pressed into service, but never quite claiming their victims. And, in all of Synge's plays, the tension is played out in his magnificent language, that leaping synthesis of Irish rhythms and English vocabulary in which every sentence, stuffed with image and metaphor, has the power to ripple from darkness to light like sunlight and cloud-shadow chasing across a hillside.

All of this is beautifully captured by Hynes's nineteen-strong acting company, whose sustained commitment to and passion for the work is a real joy to experience – and there is more besides. In these plays, we can see a powerful popular and mythic challenge to the overwhelmingly bourgeois voice of late nineteenth-century theatre that was to inspire generations of twentieth-century playwrights. We can see a willingness to place women and their experience centre-stage, as the main bearers of life through and into death, that remains exceptional even today. And we can see the creation of a whole mythic and imaginative world – a kind of Ireland beyond Ireland – through which drama could begin to soar to new twentieth-century heights of symbolism and surrealism.

Unexpectedly, Hynes's cycle is perhaps at its strongest in the two lesser-known comedies, *The Tinker's Wedding* and *The Well of the Saints*, where she detaches Synge's drama from its traditional turn-of-the-century setting – giving it a kind of crusty punk-traveller flavour in the first play, and an Ireland-in-the-1960s feel in the second – to allow our imaginations to soar around the timeless qualities and possibilities of the plays, particularly the prefiguring of Beckett in *The Well of the Saints*. The two closing productions, *The Playboy of the Western World* and the strange, grave and beautiful experiment that is *Deirdre of the Sorrows*, can seem a little passive by comparison.

But, taken as a whole, the beauty, energy and complexity of this Synge Cycle is formidable. In the work of Marie Mullen – who plays the older female figure in five of the six plays, from a magnificently lustful and winning Widow Quin in *Playboy*, to the mighty female sage Lavarcham in *Deirdre of the Sorrows* – it boasts one of the richest and most powerful evocations of the many faces of womanhood I have ever seen in theatre. And it leaves us so much enriched – in our sense of the wonder of life, its terror, sweetness, dark humour and the huge power of language and storytelling to make it bearable – that it becomes one of those mighty experiences that defines a great arts festival at its best, and engraves itself on the memory.

2006

Home
National Theatre of Scotland
The Scotsman, 27 February 2006

It's half-past six on a chill February evening in Aberdeen, and a new era in Scottish theatre begins, not with a bang, but with the familiar rattle of a small hopper bus, carrying an audience of excited theatregoers out to the edge of the city. Waiting for us in the Middlefield estate are twenty actors, young and old, professional and community; and six unoccupied flats on the same low-rise staircase, each with a nameplate on the door featuring the word 'Home'.

For 'home' was the theme chosen by the National Theatre of Scotland for its unique launch event, featuring ten site-specific shows in ten locations all over Scotland. In Aberdeen, director Alison Peebles and writer Rona Munro – together with designer Martin McNee – put together a vivid, edgy, and moving meditation, in six flats and ten parts, on what 'home' means today. To the left, as we crowded into the cold staircase, a door was labelled 'home is where the heart is'; behind it, in a room full of old photographs and nostalgic decor, an old lady was living out a life of crushing loneliness, haunted by the ghosts of her long-gone family.

In the top flat, an ageing fisherman thrown on the economic scrapheap wondered who was suffering the more painful slide towards extinction – himself, or the cod he once fished. What the Aberdeen show achieved was a bringing-together of all the strands of meaning in the word 'home', from nostalgia to the quest for new places to call our own.

Across the rest of Scotland, it was as if different aspects of the theme slid in and out of focus, although never again in a show quite so rich in texture, and so clearly and confidently theatrical. In Shetland, in a beautifully finished installation show staged aboard the Northlink Ferry by director Wils Wilson, a haunting poetic text by Jackie Kay – delivered through personal guided-tour handsets – led us through a story of deeply buried female experience, and of the perennial island tension between leaving and staying, as ghostly actors dressed in 1940s or '50s costume drifted through the lounges and saloons of the ship. There was 1940s nostalgia in Dundee too, as director Kenny Miller decked out the hallway of the McManus Gallery in the glamorous glitterball pink and black of a wartime ballroom; although here almost nothing happened in terms of live theatre, as the audience sat passively watching a history film of humorous old Dundonians remembering their wartime youth.

In this context, Anthony Neilson's short, sharp Edinburgh show – a surreal thirty-five-minute session of the Scottish Parliament, written by seven primary-school children – came as a welcome shift of tone, a show which seemed genuinely more interested in our crazy present and possible futures than in the past. The problem, though, was that for local Edinburgh audiences seeing only this show, the piece was too short, slight and daft to look like the launch of anything substantial. It was also a drastic underuse of the talents of a stellar cast, including Dawn Steele, Joe McFadden, Tam Dean Burn and Daniela Nardini.

Nor was there much nostalgia in the high flats at Cranhill in Glasgow, where director John Tiffany told the ultra-dramatic story of hero Murdo's return from London to his old high-rise home, where his seventeen-year-old brother Tam is under surveillance by the state. The brilliance of Tiffany's concept was to combine live theatre – faces in windows, dark figures abseiling down the building – with intimate screen drama, transmitted live from inside the flats via surveillance cameras held to the windows by the abseilers in black. The script was often weak, but something about Tam's quest for a reunion with his dead dad – a victim of Gulf War syndrome – touched the heart, and all six professional performers on camera, led by Billy Boyd, Blythe Duff, and Colette O'Neil, acted their hearts out.

So is it possible to draw up a tentative balance sheet for the achievement of the National Theatre's first event? On the downside, I would say – on the evidence of the five shows I saw – that it has been a shade too artistically uneven for comfort; and sometimes, too, ominously short of faith in the power of live theatre, as opposed to the screen images on which many shows depended.

On the upside, though, the new company has achieved a dazzling geographical reach, and a real sense of connection with local communities that has both enabled those communities to re-examine their own story, and given them a new voice on the national stage. It's been a start, in other words; and, taken as a whole, a brave and imaginative one, designed to smash and rearrange many hostile Scottish pre-conceptions about theatre. But there are still many miles to travel before Scotland can begin to take this long-neglected art form back into its heart, and into its sense of what home is, and what it might become.

Roam
Edinburgh International Airport
The Scotsman, 12 April 2006

The new National Theatre of Scotland is all over the place, which, given its remit, is just where it should be. Back in February, it opened with ten different site-specific performances in locations from Shetland to Dumfries. Last month in Glasgow, it launched its hugely successful mainstage children's show, *The Wolves in the Walls*. And now, it's not only appearing in towns across Scotland with a youth-and-community version of Arthur Miller's *The Crucible*, but astonishing travellers arriving at Edinburgh Airport with scenes of drama and magic never seen before in those bland and functional spaces.

'What's that?' the travellers seem to ask, as a red-coated cleaning worker with large angelic wings flits through the departure lounge. 'It's the National Theatre of Scotland,' comes the reply, along with a welcome to a nation that may not yet be 'the best small country in the world', but has had the nerve to produce a truly twenty-first-century vision of a National Theatre. In truth, though, there's a great deal more than fun, and the brief shock of the unfamiliar, to Grid Iron's airport show *Roam*, commissioned by the National Theatre from the company who have become Scotland's leading exponents of site-specific drama. At first, of course, it's the playful attention to detail that charms and seduces the audience: there's the ticket that comes in an airline-style wallet with a distinctive 'roamair' logo; the passport check as we leave the Traverse Theatre for the late-evening bus trip to the airport; the 'roamair' logo repeated on the screens of the three dedicated check-in desks that await us when we arrive there. On the bus, though, the power and energy of Philip Pinsky's troubling, world-music-influenced score has already warned us that there's serious business ahead. The screens at the check-in feature not only the 'roamair' logo, but the output of an increasingly frantic twenty-four-hour news channel reporting civil disturbances across Scotland.

And what emerges, over the next 100 minutes, is essentially a show in three strands, superbly performed by a team of eight professional actors, and a group of ten local pensioners and children, some recently arrived in Scotland from other countries. There's a lyrical, poetic, erotic and sometimes comic meditation on the fate of a group of ordinary travellers trying to get home after a day's business, and occasionally pausing to consider issues of home and identity. There's a strand of surreal dance and comedy, featuring not only the angelic, red-coated cleaning workers, but also a blonde-wigged dance troupe of 1960s-style stewardesses and pilots. And there's a nightmare drama evoking the desperate flight to the airport of a group of Edinburgh residents who suddenly find, in an unexplained civil conflict, that the airports represent their only chance of escaping alive. Bullied by a terrifyingly convincing soldier into revealing endless personal and family details in the frantic quest for a boarding pass, these people begin as ordinary Edinburgh folk, and end as the wretched of the earth we usually see only on television. The transition is terrifying, and – with its hints of nationalism or sectarianism run mad – all too credible.

There are aspects of *Roam* that occasionally disappoint. The final baggage-reclaim sequence is flabby and unnecessary, and the whole event, based on a devised script by director Ben Harrison and the company, is about ten minutes too long. But the superb quality of the performances, and of the music (performed live by Galo Ceron-Carrasco and Kerieva McCormick), goes a long way towards redeeming any flaws. And the sharpness with which this show identifies the airport as one of the key points where postmodern issues of identity, entitlement and belonging are played out – matched by Grid Iron's sheer practical genius in weaving its drama through the structures and spaces of a working airport – makes this vital and important twenty-first-century theatre, which should perhaps be re-enacted in every international airport on earth.

Macbeth
Mull Little Theatre
The Scotsman, 2 August 2006

It was a perfect July night, last Wednesday evening at Mull Little Theatre. The show was over, the volunteer staff were tidying the little foyer, people stood around chatting as the last rays of evening sun sliced through the woods around the building, and I couldn't resist a last, nostalgic look back into the tiny cowshed auditorium before I walked away for the last time. It's exactly forty years since Barrie and Marianne Hesketh, two professional actors who had fallen in love with Mull after being judges at a drama festival there, decided to open a professional theatre in the old byre beside their guesthouse at Dervaig, which was once the town manse. Incredibly – through a mixture of sheer hard work by generations of actors and directors, and dogged and passionate local support – their crazy little initiative survived and thrived, outliving Marianne Hesketh, who died in 1984, and surviving Barrie's departure from the island a year later.

Now, though, it's time for Mull Theatre Company to move on, to a fine new base in Aros Forest near the island metropolis of Tobermory; and so, some time in September, it will be curtains at last for this tiny forty-three-seat theatre space, with a stage so small that it can barely accommodate more than three actors. The company are not leaving without regrets – the Little Theatre is full of happy memories. For arcane reasons to do with Scottish Arts Council funding

strategy, and the historic stinginess of Argyll and Bute
Council towards the summer theatre season, their beautiful
new building at Druimfin is not to be described or funded
as a theatre, although it will contain a performance space.
Instead, it will be known as a 'production centre', a base for
the company's Scotland-wide touring activity, which the
Arts Council is happy to fund. It's unlikely that there will
ever again be a summer theatre season on Mull on the pattern pioneered by the Heskeths. Mull Theatre's director
Alasdair McCrone is delighted, though, that the company
will continue to be able to produce theatre on Mull, and to
perform not only across Scotland, but in venues around its
home island. He hopes the move to Tobermory will bring
the company's work, and the creative and educational buzz
it creates, even closer to the heart of island life.

It's with a distinct nod to the past, though, and to the unique
atmosphere of the Little Theatre, that Alasdair McCrone
has chosen to build his final season there around a tiny,
jewel-like production of *Macbeth*, adapted for a cast of five.
A legendary puppet version of *Macbeth* was one of the
greatest hits of the Hesketh era; and Alicia Hendrick's
remarkable design for this new stripped-down version of the
play uses the full depth of the space behind the theatre's little stage. She creates a dark, sinister double hall of mirrors,
lit by lurid flashes of golden light, that perfectly reflects the
terrible inner world of dreams, illusions and violent imag-
inings that grips Macbeth's mind from his first encounter
with the witches.

It has to be said that the effort to tell Shakespeare's great
story with only five actors, plus a couple of extras, sometimes leads McCrone to extreme measures. The porter
appears only by way of a tiny video screen; the bloody soldier who reports Macbeth's victory in the opening scene is
a shivering filmed image on a bloodstained sheet; the show's

single presiding witch, played with terrific demonic force by Fiona Colliss, can only be multiplied into three with the clever use of distorting mirrors; and the acting is a shade uneven, sometimes matching the intensity of the production, sometimes losing focus a little. In the end, though, this is a production that makes a tremendous virtue of necessity, using its limited resources, and its need to range across different media, to plunge deep into the nightmarish and delusional landscape of Macbeth's mind. The visual images are often breathtaking; Martin Low's complex, eerie music and soundscape haunt the mind. And the Mull company can be proud of a closing production that exploits the rugged, claustrophobic potential of the Little Theatre as thoroughly and imaginatively as any show I've ever seen there.

Black Watch
Drill Hall, Edinburgh
The Scotsman, 7 August 2006

When Vicky Featherstone was appointed director of the new National Theatre of Scotland two years ago, one of the first potential projects she announced was a new play by Gregory Burke based on the real-life experience of the Black Watch regiment in Iraq. Even she can hardly have dared hope, though, that the idea would finally come to birth in such a magnificent, moving and mind-blowing first night as the one that raised the roof of the old Forrest Road Drill Hall on Saturday evening. Based on dozens of interviews with present and former Black Watch soldiers, the play adopts a fairly simple flashback, flash-forward structure. On one hand, there is the tense encounter in a grubby bar somewhere in Fife or Dundee between the nervous playwright and the former Black Watch men whose experience he is about to mine and exploit for his next show. On the other hand, there is the fragmented story of the men during their time in Iraq, suffering, arguing, and in some cases dying, as they seek to replace a much larger American force in one of the most dangerous zones of a war about which many of them have doubts – and at a time when, back home, their 300-year-old regiment is facing dissolution. Woven through both stories there is the 'golden thread' of Black Watch history as it is passed on to each new recruit, represented here by a rich vein of soldiers' songs, visual imagery, and stunning, sometimes heart-rending movement sequences by the associate director, Steven Hoggett.

People will argue, of course – or should – about the precise meaning of a play that pulls no punches in describing the discomfort, disillusion and suffering of the men of the Black Watch in Iraq, but has little to say about the suffering they inflict, or about the dark strain of colonial savagery in the regiment's history. And the ending of the show is undoubtedly a shade too drawn out, too in love with its own gift for music and movement.

What's undeniable, though, is the breathtaking theatrical brilliance with which the director, John Tiffany, and his team bring the main sequence of Burke's story to life, in the great echoing space of the Drill Hall, blending sound, music, light, movement, and the occasional huge projected video image, with the tremendous live performances of a brilliantly chosen team of ten young Scottish actors, each of them apparently driven by an overwhelming sense of purpose and history, and of superbly disciplined physical energy. The technical quality of this production is flawless, soaring up to and beyond the gold standard we can expect from our National Theatre. Far more important, though, is the ground-shaking energy with which it announces the arrival of the National Theatre as a force that can reassert a strong, grassroots Scottish perspective on parts of our story which, until now, have been filtered mainly through institutions of the British state.

Burke's play does not represent the last word on the history of Scotland's most famous regiment. But it does represent a massive step forward in our understanding and recognition of a vital part of our national story, and – potentially – of the relationship between Scottish theatre and the widest possible popular audience, both at home, and far beyond our shores.

Yellow Moon
Citizens', Glasgow
The Scotsman, 4 October 2006

If live theatre survives in the twenty-first century, it will be by playing to its own strengths, rather than trying to ape the achievements of other art forms. A hydraulic helicopter on stage is never going to look as good as a real helicopter on film, and theatre can never match the gritty daylight naturalism of an episode of *EastEnders*. One of the many things theatre can do, though, is to tell big, important stories with an economy of means that actually makes the narrative more sexy and gripping, rather than less so. David Greig's new play, *Yellow Moon*, for the young people's theatre company TAG, is exactly that kind of two-planks-and-a-passion show – brisk, simple and yet so full of imaginative energy that it leaves you feeling as though you've watched a full-length road movie, with added intimacy and intensity.

Played on a bare in-the-round stage furnished with just two chairs by four actors in jeans and T-shirts, *Yellow Moon* is subtitled 'The Ballad of Leila and Lee', and draws its mood and some of its rhythm from a sombre old blues song, 'The Ballad of Stagger Lee'. It tells the story of a handsome, restless teenager from Inverkeithing, Stag Lee McAlinden, who, one dramatic night, finds himself stabbing his mum's boyfriend in the local graveyard, and heading north on the Inverness train in search of his long-gone father. With him goes Leila, the silent, self-harming celebrity-obsessed daughter of a migrant family who fled some war zone in the 1990s and settled in Fife.

The story of their journey is beautifully acted by Andrew Scott-Ramsay and Nalini Chetty as Lee and Leila, and narrated by Beth Marshall and Keith MacPherson, who also play various older characters, and it emerges as a miraculous mixture of looming tragedy, wry social comedy, magical teenage romance, and profoundly serious redemption myth. In the far north, Leila and Lee find the father figure Lee was seeking, but not remotely in the form they imagined; they also find one another, a new friend, a new relationship with the land itself, and – in the end – a faint, glimmering hope for a better future for all the damaged children of our time. All of these elements are fabulously well balanced, and then powerfully drawn out, in Greig's fine light-touch script, which involves elements of rhyme and epic adventure-narrative, as well as complex interior monologue and pure naturalistic dialogue. Nigel Dunn has contributed a beautiful blues-influenced score, with overtones of Ry Cooder and its own vein of pure lyricism. Guy Hollands' production is almost impossible to fault, drawing four superb, high-energy performances from an outstanding cast, who give a masterclass in how theatre can create whole worlds using only words, light, music and pure acting skill.

Pinocchio
Royal Lyceum, Edinburgh
The Scotsman, 6 December 2006

Christmas comes but once a year; and when it comes, it's supposed to bring good cheer. It seems, though, that that single annual visit to the land of sparkly magic, happy endings and jolly audience participation is one too many for the team at the Royal Lyceum, whose 2006 children's show *Pinocchio* seems inspired by the general assumption that all that Christmas joy and magic is a bit old-fashioned, and that it's therefore more 'interesting' to turn out a show just as dark, disturbing, un-magical, self-mocking and full of moral ambivalence as the average bog-standard piece of non-Christmas theatre. That this lazy evasion of the whole idea of feast and celebration can still pass for radicalism in British theatre speaks volumes for the trashy quality of our public intellectual life; it's dispirit-ing, but hardly surprising. And what we're left with – once the cast have dispensed, in a smug opening chorus, with the idea that we're going to see anything we might associate with Christmas – is a brisk and vaguely enjoyable low-budget show for children of primary-school age, with makeshift-looking sets that just about do the job of leading us through Pinoc-chio's story, and a deluxe cast of ten who somehow manage to seem pretty thin on the ground.

Written by director Mark Thomson himself, and closely based on Carlo Collodi's original 1883 story of the little pup-pet boy whose love for his 'father', the old carpenter Geppetto, finally gives him a beating human heart, this ver-sion prides itself on avoiding the lush sentimentalism that gave the famous Walt Disney film its moral glamour and narrative ease. Instead, it allows its charismatic star, the emerging film and stage actor James Anthony Pearson, to lead us on a close-up journey through Pinocchio's inner tus-sle between heartless pleasure-seeking and loving kindness, exposing the audience to the full, uneasy sense of moral gloom that pervades Collodi's tale, with its huge repertoire of nasty exploitative villains, and its weirdly unconvincing redemptive figures.

The show's main comic strategy is to include such a strong strand of near-adult campery and send-up that there are moments when the whole cast seems about to burst into a chorus of 'I Am What I Am'. But if this is Thomson's postmodern take on the ancient festive tradition of gender-bending and cross-dressing, then it has to be said that in the absence of the true all-embracing panto form, it undermines the narrative far more than it enriches it. There are enjoyable moments in this *Pinocchio*: the train journey to the Land of Toys is particularly well realised, with Molly Innes in unforgettably sinister form as the fat controller of the magic train; and most of the older children in the audience seemed to be having a fine time.

There was one child present, though, who wasn't happy at all. She was bored, disappointed and thoroughly depressed by the show's lack of sparkle and beauty; she was my inner child, and she went home in a sulk, feeling as if Christmas had been indefinitely postponed.

2007

The Patriot
Tron, Glasgow
The Scotsman, 1 May 2007

If boldness in tackling themes from contemporary politics was enough to create great theatre, then Grae Cleugh's new play *The Patriot* – which opens Gregory Thompson's account as artistic director at the Tron – might be one of the finest shows of the year. Set in the Edinburgh New Town home of a Scottish Executive minister called Tom Gordon, it imagines a confrontation between this pillar of the post-devolution establishment, and a young SNP activist, Paul, who is enraged by the betrayals and brutalities of recent New Labour policy, and in particular by the death in Iraq of his younger brother, a soldier in the British army; the subject, in other words, could hardly be more timely.

When it comes to transforming this brilliant idea into theatre, though, Cleugh's play and Thompson's production collapse into pretty comprehensive failure. In form, to begin with, the play is bafflingly old-fashioned, complete with posh drawing-room setting, endless visits to the drinks cabinet, and hopelessly stagey dialogue. In tone, the play is desperately unpleasant, full of a sneering presumption that Scotland is self-evidently a dump, full of weird, violent nationalists who get their sexual kicks by reciting William Wallace's battle plans, and Labour folk who live like princes and stink of corruption. Both main characters are so unattractive that it's genuinely difficult to care what happens to either of them, and the family drama into which they are drawn – triggered by Tom's too-close relationship with his adored goddaughter Claire, Paul's new fiancée – is as overpitched as it is unnecessary.

Worst of all, though, is Cleugh's extraordinary tin ear for the reality of current Scottish politics, and for the mood of the times we live in. Politically this play gets absolutely everything wrong, from the social ethos of Scottish Labour to the current mood of the SNP; it plays as if it had been written by someone observing Scotland from a continent away, through a prism of scanty and inaccurate media coverage. Perhaps a more inventive production, less bogged down in the stylistic clichés of mid-twentieth-century establishment drama, might have flattered Cleugh's script a little more. As it is, it makes a dire evening's theatre. One of the characters complains, at one point, that Scottish theatre can be 'pretty parochial'. That's not true any more – except, alas, on the main stage of the Tron, over the next couple of weeks.

Sunshine on Leith
Dundee Rep
The Scotsman, 4 May 2007

In the world of tribute shows, there are three strategies that writers and producers can traditionally embrace: one is the straightforward biography, in which the life story of the artist or artists is retold using the medium of the songs that made them famous; another is the shameless musical hoedown, with very little pretence at a plot; and the third – the hugely successful *Mamma Mia!* method – is the show built around a fictional plot that somehow expresses the essence of the music, and captures the cultural moment out of which it came.

This is the strategy adopted by Stephen Greenhorn in *Sunshine on Leith*, his much-anticipated musical based on the work of The Proclaimers, which has already – if advance sales are any guide – become one of the hottest tickets in recent Scottish theatre. After a roaring success of a first night in Dundee last weekend, it's clear that James Brining's fine Dundee Rep production is unlikely to disappoint the Reid brothers' huge army of fans as it travels on to Edinburgh and Glasgow.

If subtlety of plot and dialogue is what you seek, mind you, then *Sunshine on Leith* might not be entirely your cup of tea. It tells the story of two former squaddies, Davy and Ally, who return from service in Afghanistan to try to take up the threads of civilian life in Leith; and of their families, struggling with all the tensions and ironies of life in postmodern working-class Scotland. Davy's mum and dad have been forced into a classic post-industrial role-reversal: he no longer works, since the docks were mechanised; she brings home the bacon as a cleaner and waitress on the *Royal Yacht Britannia* at Ocean Terminal. His sister Lizzie is a nurse, enraged by the new PFI ethos of the Blairite health service, and his new girlfriend

Yvonne, one of Lizzie's colleagues, is torn by the classic family dilemma of an English girl who loves Edinburgh – despite a steady drip–drip of anti-English banter – but feels too far away from her ageing mother.

Sometimes, the plot is so blatantly contrived to accommodate the great songs that the audience can almost hear the pieces clanking into place. Lizzie is considering a move to the States ('Letter from America'); Ally just can't help loving her, even though she's not so keen ('Hate My Love for You'); Yvonne might want Davy to move back to England with her ('500 Miles'). The dramatic situations, likewise, are sometimes so obvious and clichéd as to make Greenhorn's own *River City* – which he originally wanted to set in Leith – look like *King Lear*. There's the blind date that comes good, the old infidelity revealed, the warring middle-aged couple brought back together by a sudden heart attack.

If the plot sometimes seems more than a little cheesy, though – and the anti-war, anti-PFI politics are pure old-fashioned agitprop, except when the relative subtlety of the songs intervenes – the show also has a huge raft of compensating virtues. There's the music, brilliantly belted out by every member of the cast, and a nine-piece band in electrifying form. There's Neil Warmington's slick, ingenious set, recreating almost a dozen familiar city settings – at home, in the pub, on top of Blackford Hill – with extraordinary speed and fluency, and creating a rich panorama of primary colours across the stage. There's some fine choreography (by Lizzie Gee), in which this superbly practised ensemble move as one into routines brisk, tender, or just plain exhilarating. There are a series of lovely, straightforward performances from Keith Fleming and Kevin Lennon as Davy and Ally, John Buick and Ann Louise Ross as Davy's parents, and the lovely Gail Watson and Emily Winter as their strong-minded girlfriends.

302

And, above all, there's the spirit of the show, with its terrific sense of place (it must be the first true Edinburgh musical of the postmodern age) and the passion with which it evokes the powerful link between the music of The Proclaimers – with all its sense of political and economic struggle combined with a rich gratitude for the sweetness of life – and the reality of ordinary Scottish life from the 1980s to the present day. If I were Craig and Charlie Reid, I would be thrilled by the tremendous tribute to their music implied in this heart-lifting show. And I would also be moved by the tremendous energy everyone involved has clearly drawn from their special genius for giving a voice to modern Scotland; and by the huge popular success that the show, and everyone involved with it, now seems certain to enjoy.

The Flouers o Edinburgh
Pitlochry Festival Theatre
The Scotsman, 11 May 2007

The skirl of the pipes at the door, the tumbling waters of the River Tummel below, and the May sky still bright at the nine o'clock interval. Yes, it's another new season at Pitlochry Festival Theatre and, last weekend, the theatre launched its 2007 programme with a play that might have been written for the occasion, so perfectly does it combine the picturesque costume drama Pitlochry audiences love with a sharp political awareness of the very issues of culture, identity and English-Scottish Union highlighted by the election result which emerged just two hours before curtain-up. Robert McLellan's *The Flouers o Edinburgh* is not, of course, a modern play. It was written in the late 1940s, at the height of the post-war ferment of debate about Scotland's political future which led, over the next two years, to some 2.5 million Scots signing a petition for home rule.

Yet if campaigning for home rule was vigorous at the time, voters remained unpersuaded: the British state – fresh from its victory over fascism – had probably never been stronger or more widely trusted. And it was out of this passionate but contradictory period in Scottish politics that McLellan's graceful comedy emerged, part vigorous satire on the idea of 'Britishness' as it appeared in eighteenth-century Scotland, part warm and persuasive tribute to the old Scots tongue, and part sentimental homage – in a time of domestic austerity – to the beauty and poetry of the past, not a million miles in impulse from Christopher Fry's English costume dramas of the same period.

So the curtain rises on a traditional, beautifully made Pitlochry set representing the parlour of Lady Girzie Carmichael's residence, on the top floor of a tenement in Edinburgh's Canongate, on a sunlit afternoon some time around 1760. Her servant Jock, played with something close to genius by Martyn James, is baking scones in the nearby kitchen, and giving his mistress as good as he gets in the way of cheeky backchat. Instantly, McLellan evokes the ideal of an egalitarian Scottish society, where masters and servants relate more as family or clan than as members of different social classes.

Girzie – played with terrific energy and charm by Carol Ann Crawford – is a woman of immense kindly common sense, beautifully dressed in the kind of gorgeous period costume at which Pitlochry excels, and perfectly certain that whatever fashion or politics now dictates after fifty years of Union with England, she will keep a good Scots tongue in her head. Her lovely niece Kate is of the same mind; and so both are reduced to tears of mirth when Charlie Gilchrist, the son of Girzie's old friend Lord Stanebyres, returns from London full of posh English manners and sporting a would-be English accent mangled through a hilarious mouthful of plums, along with a new ambition to enter politics as MP for a local constituency.

And so it goes, over three acts, as a fashion for English language lessons takes hold in Edinburgh, and Charlie finds his ambitions thwarted by a range of dour local bailies and wealthy nabobs returned from the Indies, as well as by his father's stubborn conservatism. Richard Baron's fine and lavish production thoroughly enjoys the joke of McLellan's play, and its rich contemporary resonances, without perhaps fully grasping the depth of McLellan's writing around the idea of economic development, and its cultural and social consequences.

As a result, the production loses energy in the second act, which revolves more around Charlie's business dealings than his affairs of the heart. The show boasts an excellent central performance, though, from Grant O'Rourke as Charlie, the man on whose strangled vowels the whole comic impact of the play depends. And, so long as Crawford and Suzanne Donaldson are on stage with their servant Jock, delivering a perfect female double act of charm, smeddum and drive as Girzie and Kate, it's difficult to resist the energy of this most high-spirited of Scots comedies; difficult, too, not to admire the way McLellan finally avoids romantic cliché by driving Kate and Charlie into a cross-cultural row so fierce that anyone can see that, together or apart, they were made for each other. Just like Scotland and England, perhaps.

Venus as a Boy
St Magnus Festival, Orkney
The Scotsman, 29 June 2007

He is a special saint, St Magnus of Orkney: a martyr not for the Christian faith in general, but for his specific belief in the possibility of peace and forgiveness after bitter conflict and injury – a belief that led to his untimely death, but that left behind an undying legend of kindly and radiant love. It's a spirit that flowed through the life of the late Orkney poet George Mackay Brown, who, with his friend Peter Maxwell Davies, conceived the idea of the St Magnus Festival back in the 1970s; it is, in a sense, the spirit of the Festival itself. And it's a measure of how far the writer Luke Sutherland is himself a son of Orkney – brought up in the islands in the 1970s and '80s, as the only black boy on South Ronaldsay – that his beautiful and controversial 2004 novella, *Venus as a Boy*, itself glows with a rich strand of mystical realism, and with a profound belief in the healing, redeeming and forgiving power of love.

The only difficulty – for some, at least – is that, for Sutherland's hero, a richly bisexual young man known as Cupid, love mainly means sex, the physical ecstasy that, at its most powerful, opens doors to richly spiritual visions of angels and apple orchards, and the opening of mighty golden gates. It also provides an escape route from a small Orkney community that Cupid often finds cruel, bigoted and repressive. And so it was a brave move for the St Magnus Festival, which generally celebrates the quality of Orkney life, to join with the National Theatre of Scotland Workshop in presenting Tam Dean Burn's new stage version of Sutherland's novel, which played in Hoy, Kirkwall and Stromness this week before starting the long journey south that mirrors the short, ecstatic life of its hero, from little boy in Orkney to dying transvestite in a Soho attic, gradually and mysteriously turning to gold.

Tam Dean Burn's ninety-minute solo version of the story –
co-directed by Christine Devaney, and with Sutherland
himself, a gifted rock guitarist and violinist, providing live
music on stage – attempts no fancy tricks with the narrative,
but does three things quite brilliantly: first, in a brief pre-
amble, it places the story as an account of a real life, told by
a real human being of an actor, in a way that disarms the
audience, and helps this remarkable story to bridge all possible gaps between the close-knit community of Orkney, and
the squalid and glittering postmodern metropolis where
Cupid meets his fate. Second, it shows a powerful political
grasp of Sutherland's story as an exploration of the fascist
impulse, both as a symptom of emotional damage, and as a
phenomenon painfully well understood by all those social
'outsiders' who tend to be its victims. And finally, with the
help of Sutherland's haunting mix of live and recorded
music, it sustains, through the whole show, that ecstatic note
of shimmering mysticism that is the special hallmark of
Sutherland's writing in *Venus as a Boy*. It's wild, extreme,
sometimes close to madness; but Tam Dean Burn's performance is a tour de force, a brilliantly pitched piece of
theatrical craftmanship that keeps all these explosive elements powerfully bent towards a higher purpose, and a
glittering challenge to every kind of bigotry.

The Bacchae
King's, Edinburgh
The Scotsman, 13 August 2007

It was perhaps the most glittering first night ever in Scottish theatre, as the blisteringly high-profile National Theatre
of Scotland/Edinburgh Festival co-production of Euripides' *The Bacchae* opened at the King's Theatre on Saturday
evening. In the programme for the show, there was a quote
and a challenge, from the company to itself: 'For centuries

people have spoken of the Greek myths as something to be rediscovered and reawakened,' says the Italian writer Roberto Calasso. 'But the truth is that the myths are still out there, waiting to awaken us...'

And whatever else is said about John Tiffany's new version of *The Bacchae*, in a contemporary translation by Ian Ruffell and David Greig, it certainly comes as a disturbing and often rude awakening to a culture that has often been lulled, over the centuries, into thinking of the great dramas of ancient Greece as dusty pieces of literature, performed – if at all – with an air of sonorous reverence. First seen in 407 BC, *The Bacchae* is, to begin with, perhaps the most strange and unsettling of all the great Greek dramas. It tells the story of the god Dionysus, the son of Zeus and of the Theban princess Semele, who has lived in exile in the countries of the East since his birth, but now returns to Thebes, with his band of wild dancing women, the Bacchae, to claim his status as a god.

At one level, the play is therefore a classic human drama about the illegitimate child returning to claim his own, and wreaking revenge when he finds only mockery and rejection. But it is also a great political parable about the terrible fate that awaits a state which cannot acknowledge, and find a balance between, all the different aspects of human nature, including the Dionysian impulse to drink, dance, play and play-act, to lose the self in rituals of sensual pleasure and transformation. And in the powerful confrontation between the show's playful, dangerous star Alan Cumming as Dionysus, and a superbly grey and controlled Tony Curran as his cousin, the Theban king Pentheus, it's possible to sense a whole rich vein of resonance for our own political culture, torn as it is between a growing binge-culture of uncontrolled excess on one hand, and, on the other, a new authoritarian obsession with law and order, and the suppression of 'anti-social' behaviour.

Now it should be said that in trying to find a full theatrical expression of that confrontation, John Tiiffany's production makes legions of errors, some of them as baffling as they are disappointing. Its visual imagery, to begin with, is more intermittently spectacular than consistently dramatic and telling. Dionysus, for example, is supposed to be a physically gorgeous shape-changer, beautiful and dazzling; here, he is confined to one little golden outfit with a messy wig, and is never allowed to look fabulous at all.

Beyond the visual, the production suffers from strange lapses of pace and vocal energy: the final long, elegiac scene between Pentheus's mother and grandfather, for example, limps along at a snail's pace, despite a superbly moving performance from Ewan Hooper as old Cadmus. And most disappointingly of all, Tim Sutton's lightweight soul-based score – for Dionysus's mighty chorus of Bacchae, played by ten terrific black female actor-singers in glittering shades of red – only rarely rises to the occasion. At the height of the narrative, it never begins to achieve the kind of volume, rhythm and power that would really express the mighty ecstasy of the Dionysian rite; and sometimes, the ear aches for a few shuddering bars of Stravinsky's *Rite of Spring*, which comes so much nearer the mark.

For all these weaknesses, though, in the end Tiffany's production carries three strands of brave, ground-breaking energy that make it infinitely worth seeing. First, it achieves some astonishing visual *coups de théâtre*, blazing exhibitions of fire and light that are as witty as they are thrilling. Secondly, in the great 7:84 tradition to which he belongs, Tiffany recognises the plain didactic simplicity of Euripides' drama – recognise all the gods, or suffer the consequences – and its place in popular culture. He uses popular forms freely throughout, from the opening pop-soul numbers in which the Bacchae become Dionysus's backing singers, to the *Queer Eye for the Straight Guy* sequence in which Dionysus seduces Pentheus into women's clothes; and in every case, the popular form fits the drama better than more solemn and archaic forms of presentation.

And above all, Alan Cumming's central performance as Dionysus – alternating with a terrifying swiftness between light-hearted, ultra-camp charm and raging, all-powerful fury – represents a real, if still uncertain, landmark in marrying the new strength of queer culture to one of the oldest stories of our civilisation. For when societies grow rigid, authoritarian and blinkered, the control of the sexuality of men who challenge and transgress traditional models of masculinity always becomes a central obsession, often expressed with a terrifying brutality. In the last generation, our Western culture has taken some steps towards a true civic recognition of those aspects of Dionysian energy that were repressed for so long. But the danger of backlash, and the advance of new kinds of control freakery, still stalks our civilisation. Euripides' warning is that we may pay a heavy price for that mood of reaction; and this strange, uneven show represents a tentative but thrilling first step towards making that warning real, for a twenty-first century audience.

Half Life
Kilmartin Glen, Argyll
The Scotsman, 7 September 2007

In the far westlands of Argyll, something is stirring. Urban types in well-zipped jackets and husky boots wander along rough forestry trails, clutching soggy maps and an enigmatic guidebook. Here and there – in a handful of hidden places, thinly spread across the vast landscape of Kilmartin Glen and Crinan Moss – they find the sites they visit subtly changed. Here, the trees leading uphill to some ancient markings in earthfast rock are singed in strange patterns, or peeled so that their bark releases a heady smell of sap. There, in a deep valley near the sea, a new chapel-like roof of arched pine branches rises over a flat stone scored with deep cups and channels; in the ruin of an old mill cottage, someone has created a living image of the old northern legend of the world ground out between two millstones of heaven and hell. In many of these chosen places, small, sculpted sounds emerge from the rock and trees: the groaning, singing, roaring and twittering of the land itself, amplified a thousand times. And at night, in a clearing at Achnabreck, light gleams and flashes through the tall pillars of the trees, as a team of five actors and two musicians strive to bind the whole event together in a one-hour outdoor performance.

This is *Half Life: Journey into the Neolithic*, the first-ever collaboration between the National Theatre of Scotland and Angus Farquhar's great landscape art company NVA, most famous for creating *The Path* at Glen Lyon in 2000, and *The Storr*, last year in Skye. The aim is partly to open up this astonishing landscape at Kilmartin to a nation still largely unaware of its presence, and of the huge historic and archaeological importance of a cluster of burial and ritual sites dating back almost five thousand years. At the same time, though, Farquhar and his company are anxious to raise questions about how we relate to the past and to the dead, using the intense neolithic burial-culture of this area to remind us of humankind's epic struggle, over countless millennia, to make sense of our own lives and deaths, and to place ourselves and our fate within some pattern that gives it shape and meaning. Hence the two-part character of *Half Life*, which combines an evening show, experienced collectively, with an opportunity to spend a day or two travelling independently around the Kilmartin area, experiencing the scattered pattern of sites and monuments at our own pace; there are likely, in other words, to be as many responses to this event as there are audience members.

What seems generally true, though, is that as a total experience, *Half Life* never quite resolves the problem of trying to deconstruct and re-examine a historical narrative that most of the audience members will never have heard in the first place. If you spend a day before *Half Life* reading Rachel Butter's beautiful standard guidebook to the glen, and the *Half Life* book itself, then you may become absorbed in NVA's conversation with the place, and begin to appreciate the carefully crafted modesty of its interventions. If not, you may well find the experience disappointingly minimal and uninformative, and the size of the organisation and crew involved completely out of proportion to the effect. Either way, you will almost certainly find the evening show a shade disappointing, despite the stunning visual impact of James Johnson's beautifully made forest performance site, a great double stage within a mighty radiating crown of felled pine logs. In the effort to find a point of contact with the burial culture of Kilmartin, writer Thomas Legendre and movement genius Mark Murphy reach for a story of a modern couple with a lost child that never fully escapes the television-drama cliché and New Age self-absorption of our modern grief-culture, despite some fine acting, and superb movement-based imagery.

Yet for all these failures, *Half Life* as a whole is an infinitely enriching experience. Angus Farquhar is the leading conceptual artist of Scottish landscape and theatre, and like all conceptual artists, he faces the criticism that his work represents a minimal jolting or reframing of reality, something that looks as though anyone could have done it; in this case, he certainly could have used a stronger writer, to provide texts with a sharper intellectual and poetic edge. But in the end, as with all great conceptual artists, his critics have to concede that although anyone might have done it, no one else did. No one else had the idea, raised the cash, put together the project, and cared enough about the mighty heritage of Kilmartin Glen to lure audiences there, and to bring them into a dialogue with a vital part of their own heritage. The results are debatable, even flawed. The impact, though, is unforgettable; and the whole event is exactly the kind of project in which Scotland's National Theatre should be investing, not in a quest for perfection, but in the search for new horizons, and for a constant shifting and deepening of Scotland's vision of itself.

Bright Water
Easdale Island Hall
The Scotsman, 21 September 2007

On the pier at Ellenabeich, on Saturday afternoon, Mull Theatre Company are halfway through unloading their van when the weather changes, and great salty swathes of West Highland rain begin to sweep in from the sea. Mull's latest show, *Bright Water*, is a reflection on the life of Gavin Maxwell, mid-twentieth-century author, conservationist, upper-class adventurer, and author of the much-loved otter book *Ring of Bright Water*. The set for the short two-handed drama is not a complicated one: apart from some basic lighting equipment, there are a couple of upholstered chairs, a lightweight blue gauze backdrop, eight pieces of plywood flooring, a carpet, a box, a tiny side table, and a fragile-looking standard lamp.

But long before a little flat-bottomed boat arrives to ferry the company and its show across the harbour to Easdale, the chairs are drenched, and the paintwork on the flooring is being tested to its limit. On the grey sea, as the boat chugs across the narrow sound, the teetering pile of furniture and people looks comically vulnerable, like an image out of an ancient 1940s movie, and by the time the whole show has been carted up the long, slate-lined slipway into Easdale Hall, wet is the hardly the word for everyone involved, from the unflappable boatman, through the three-strong stage-management team, to the company's tour manager Mick Andrew, and the actor Richard Conlon, gallantly lending a hand.

Ever since the days of 7:84 – and even before that, with companies like Glasgow Rep and Theatre Workshop – this kind of 'extreme' Highland touring has enjoyed a special place in the hearts of Scottish audiences. But no other company maintains that tradition with such passion – and on such a relatively modest funding base – as Alasdair McCrone's Mull Theatre, which will visit a record-breaking nineteen Scottish islands on this current tour; and just a few hours after that rain-drenched arrival on Easdale, I walked into the village hall to find Alicia Hendrick's set looking exactly as it had the night before on Iona, a calm, melancholy, slightly shabby evocation of Gavin Maxwell's last home at Eilean Bàn off Skye, enlivened only by a faintly audible squelch whenever the actors sat down on one of the padded chairs.

When it comes to the show itself, Jon Pope's interesting script is framed as a dialogue between Richard Addison as the older Maxwell, holed up at Eilean Bàn in the months before his death in 1969, and his much smoother and more genial younger self, played with a fine, glowing poise by Richard Conlon; the difficulty is that the play seems unclear, particularly in the early scenes, about where the main tension lies between these two figures. Sometimes, the younger man accuses the older of being a 'hippy', the first Highland dropout, fleeing the pressures of urban life on an impulse that is bound to strike a chord with many of those who choose to live in the Highlands and Islands today. At other times, though, the play seems more deeply focused on Maxwell's distinctive history as a compulsive loner, whose failure in human relationships both appalls and disappoints his younger self.

The result is a show that takes a long time to find a convincing narrative thread. But there are flashes of rare beauty and eloquence in Alasdair McCrone's production, notably in the moments – beautifully illustrated by Martin Low's music – when Maxwell's reserve breaks down in the face of his passion for the beautiful animals that became his life. And by bringing Highland and Island communities together not only for entertainment or practical business, but for a couple of hours of complex, grown-up drama on the life of this fascinating local anti-hero, this is the kind of show that plays a valuable part in developing the life of those communities, as places not only of retreat from the urban world, but also of real change, reflection, and renewal.

Peer Gynt
Dundee Rep
The Scotsman, 5 October 2007

It's in the street outside Dundee Rep, five minutes before the start of the show, that I begin to suspect we're about to see something special. One of those vast, white party limousines is nosing through the Tay Street traffic, adding to the general crush. Then suddenly it swerves into the theatre forecourt, pulls up at the door, and spills out a screaming, singing, fighting car-load of drop-dead-vulgar wedding guests, who swarm into the theatre and up to the bar, where they begin to karaoke the punters to death with a series of ear-splitting country-and-western torchsongs.

This is Dominic Hill's *Peer Gynt*, his final production at Dundee Rep as he leaves to become artistic director of the Traverse, and the Rep's first major co-production with the National Theatre of Scotland. And it's a show to shout about from the rooftops, not only the finest piece of classic theatre Scotland has produced in half a decade, but also a final, dazzling counterblast to the idea this mighty epic – written in 1867, when Ibsen was not yet forty – is somehow unstageable. The secret of Hill's success is twofold: first, there's the sheer, practised richness of his long-term relationship with the Rep's permanent ensemble of actors, which gives this show the depth and sheen of a production that has been in preparation for years, rather than weeks.

Then secondly there is his understated but absolute assumption that Ibsen's great, archetypal story about the male quest for freedom and fame, and about Peer's ambiguous relationship with the ties of true love that would bind him, is not some archaic Norwegian folktale, but a hilarious, beautiful and hard-hitting story for our own age, crazed as it is by the same dream of perfect individual freedom that drives Peer's quest. Colin Teevan's new version of the text is superb, as fresh, frank, hard-edged and occasionally obscene as if he had just picked up the story on the streets of Glasgow or Manchester. Naomi Wilkinson's inspired design clears the stage back to its walls and gantries to allow full play to the imagination, deftly evoking Peer Gynt's rural background with a cigarette-advert-style image on a city hoarding, that can turn on a sixpence to conjure up ordinary walls and houses.

In this magical space, an augmented, eighteen-strong Dundee company – led by a wonderful Keith Fleming as the young Peer, and an equally fine Gerry Mulgrew as the older one – give a series of brilliant, funny, inspired, and completely purposeful performances, moving without missing a beat from the simple escape narrative of the first half to the difficult, episodic satire on earthly wealth and power that dominates the second. And what they show us is Ibsen's masterpiece reborn as a piece of world-class popular theatre for our time: not only hilarious, earthy and true, but also as full of beauty, poetry, and sorrow as Ibsen could have hoped, when he first brought together folktale and epic to tell this magnificent story of a man's struggle to be fully himself, and finally to accept the paradox that in failing to give himself to others, he has lost his own best chance of fulfilment.

Rich times – but within a year, the 2008 economic crash brought a new sense of uncertainty to publicly funded theatres everywhere. And although Scotland's new SNP government, first elected in 2007, proved a doughty defender of the general level of arts funding in tough times, the Scottish arts world was deeply shaken, at the end of the decade, by the launch in 2010 of its new funding body, known as Creative Scotland. Many leading Scottish theatre artists became heavily involved in a campaign to change the style and leadership of Creative Scotland, which initially seemed determined to play a much more strategic and directive role in deciding what artists should do and make than the old Scottish Arts Council. And although the campaign was at least partly successful in reasserting the right of artists to determine their own 'strategies', rather than having them mapped out by a government agency that addressed them in increasingly unbearable management jargon, the drain on their energy was palpable.

So it's perhaps no accident that the twin powerhouses of Scottish theatre, in these troubled years, seemed to lie in the National Theatre of Scotland – directly funded by the Scottish Government, along with the other national companies – and in David MacLennan's A Play, a Pie and a Pint seasons, which were likewise free of any entanglement with Creative Scotland. In 2008 Philip Howard left the Traverse, after a decade of outstanding success in developing a whole generation of Scottish writers; he was replaced by Dominic Hill, who moved on in 2011 to become an inspired new director of the Citizens' Theatre, and then by Orla O'Loughlin. And over the years 2008–11, theatre continued to happen in an ever more thrilling variety of places, from the ancient backstage spaces of the Citizens' Theatre, to the dreamlike eighteenth-century salon full of immaculately dressed audience members conjured up by Stewart Laing's Untitled Projects; and the wide-open virtual spaces of the internet itself.

2008

Walden
Stills Gallery, Edinburgh
The Scotsman, 6 February 2008

In the spring of 1845, young Henry Thoreau – the son of a comfortably off Massachusetts family – went into the woods at Walden Pond, near Concord, and stayed there for more than two years. He did it, he said, 'not to live cheaply or dearly, but to live deliberately'; and in this age of rapid urbanisation and environmental stress, it feels as though we have never needed his wisdom more.

Nicholas Bone's new stage version for Magnetic North of Thoreau's great essay *Walden* is therefore a tremendously timely piece of theatre, an hour-long contemplative pool of stillness tucked into a corner of modern city life. In the cool white space of the gallery, the atmosphere created by designers Sans façon is almost too bare for comfort. There's just a simple oval performance space surrounded by a bench and coat-pegs, and a pool of white sand.

In the end, though, this bold strategy works beautifully, with nothing to distract us from a finely pitched performance by Ewan Donald that perfectly captures Thoreau's profoundly American combination of high idealism and shirt-sleeve practicality. In the end, what Thoreau learned at Walden was how a whole universe exists in each glorious drop of time and experience, and how little of our frenzied activity, from day to day, really carries us any distance at all. And it's a lesson we perhaps need to relearn, if what Thoreau called our 'soft, impressible earth' is to survive the tramp of our six billion feet.

The Wall
Tron, Glasgow
The Scotsman, 7 March 2008

It's summertime, it's Stewarton, and the kids are hanging around the wall that is – well – their favourite hangout. Tall, skinny Barry is waiting for the results from his second try at Highers. His wee sister Norma has nicked some of their dad's hash, and has had it stolen in turn by Barry's wideboy friend Rab. And lovely goth-styled Michelle has one eye on Barry, and the other on her Mum's relationship with live-in 'Auntie' Alice, about which she's beginning to realise a few things.

It's a simple set-up, in other words, for this first full-length play by emerging Scottish playwright D C Jackson. But right from the opening moments, in Gregory Thompson's immaculate production for Borderline and the Tron, *The Wall* roars out of the starting blocks on a surge of fierce comic and dramatic energy that never lets up, through two hours of solid-gold banter and perfectly structured narrative development. In terms of content, the play draws its energy from a gorgeous, continuing dissonance between the small-town parochialism of the community Jackson describes, and the growing fragmentation and New Age weirdness of the world in which it sits: this is a place where the local 'neds' (a term to which Rab takes grave exception) can be found in the health food shop, nicking some Rescue Remedy.

And in terms of style, Jackson's play combines the force and vocabulary of a post-nineties 'in-yer-face' playwright with the genial popular-comedy tone always embraced by Borderline. The result is a rite-of-passage comedy of the highest quality, beautifully delivered by one of those superb four-strong casts – Scott Hoatson, Kirstin McLean, Finn den Hertog, and a magnificent Sally Reid as wee Norma – that make the audience feel as if they've watched a whole generation pass by; and touched with the kind of deceptive lightness and simplicity that is only achieved by real masters of the playwright's craft.

Cockroach
Midsummer
Traverse, Edinburgh
The Scotsman, 31 October 2008

As any teacher will tell you, a classroom full of rampaging fifteen-year-olds is a prime arena for the study of the animal aspects of human nature, and the primitive forces of aggression, competition and lust. Almost from the first moments of Sam Holcroft's *Cockroach*, though, it becomes clear that this searing debut play – the first of four in the current Traverse/National Theatre of Scotland series – is something much more than another routine social comedy about a harassed teacher trying to impose some elements of civilisation on a roomful of roaring teenage hormones.

The play begins with a bang, as wild girl Leah locks herself into the classroom, fleeing from her boyfriend Lee, who is angry with her because she has caught him having sex with lonely, disorientated Mmoma, the only black girl in the class. Then there's Leah's pretty best friend Danielle, already exhausted at fifteen by more predatory male attention than she can bear, and her nice admirer Davey, whose passion for her takes a frighteningly possessive turn; and bringing up the rear is the teacher, Beth, permanently linked by radio to the school's referral base for out-of-control kids.

Inside the classroom, though, Beth's efforts to impose order, and encourage intellectual endeavour, are strangely contradicted by the content of her classes about Darwinian evolution, hormones and natural selection. And outside the classroom, war rages ever closer to the school gates, a war half-heartedly condoned by the teacher as part of her role as a state employee, while boys begin to disappear into the armed forces, and to die. The play builds, in other words, into a nightmare vision of the collapse of civilisation, in which the teacher, Beth, is often oddly and helplessly complicit with the process of disintegration that is devastating the lives of her pupils; and in which the all-too-familiar confrontation between the codes of conduct which the school tries to enforce, and those which are rife in the world outside, is hurtling towards crisis point.

In the end, Holcroft's play loses track of itself slightly, wandering off once too often into Mmoma's strange fantasy life – a ten-minute cut in the second half would do this demanding play no harm. But Vicky Featherstone's direction is immaculate, and the performances by a young, mainly Scottish cast stunningly clear and subtle, with Meg Fraser's inspired turn as the teacher only the best of a breathtakingly fine bunch. And in the end, it's hard to forget the terrible force of Holcroft's vision of a society gradually and unwittingly eating away at the theoretical base on which its whole peaceful existence rests; and finally flipping in an instant – as in the chilling second half of Sarah Kane's *Blasted* – from our recognisable, everyday reality, into a new world in which every kind of primitive fundamentalism and raging brutality becomes not only possible, but likely.

There are plenty of primitive forces at work, too, in David Greig and Gordon McIntyre's *Midsummer*, the first in the informal Traverse Too season of off-the-cuff studio shows; it begins, after all, with a couple propelled into bed in a Marchmont flat by naked, drunken, Friday-night lust. Here, though, the tone is one of warm-hearted, beautifully sculpted musical romantic comedy, as Greig and McIntyre (of top Edinburgh band Ballboy) shape the tale of unlikely couple Bob and Helena, a pair of tired thirty-five-year-olds on the loose in a city-centre wine bar, into a lost-weekend love story that somehow succeeds in being romantic and often moving, without losing a sharp, perceptive edge of satirical comment on the way we live now.

Like a good Ian Rankin novel, the play conducts the kind of intense, almost poetic love affair with the city of Edinburgh, its light and its fabric, that Greig hasn't indulged in since his lovely devolution drama *Caledonia Dreaming*, a decade ago. And its use of McIntyre's songs is fascinating, as both Bob and Helena – the heartbreakingly beautiful and talented Cora Bissett, and the equally lovely Matthew Pidgeon – pick up their battered guitars and sing. The music, in other words, seems like something that belongs to them, domestic, unpretentious, from the heart, rather than big 'production numbers', the music from elsewhere that once used to sweep stage-musical lovers up in its current, but is now – perhaps – being replaced by something less grandiose, more empowering, and more true.

Be Near Me
Palace, Kilmarnock

Sub Rosa
Citizens', Glasgow
The Scotsman, 23 January 2009

As we are now learning – fast, painfully and all over again – economic depressions leave scars that last for generations; and it's perhaps significant that this year's spring theatre season opens with two major plays set in the aftermath of crushing economic disaster.

It's the collapse of British heavy industry in the 1980s, for instance, which shapes the imaginary community of Dalgarnock in Ayrshire, where the hero of Andrew O'Hagan's fine novel *Be Near Me* – now adapted for the National Theatre of Scotland by the actor and writer Ian McDiarmid – works as a Catholic priest. As his parishioners are not slow to tell him, the place is an 'unemployment black spot', and many of the people have little left in their lives beyond the old, sectarian tribalism of a community thrown roughly together by a traumatic industrial revolution, and then left and high and dry by economic change.

But Father Anderton is not the man to bring healing to this damaged place. Instead, he is himself in flight, using the church as a 'beautiful refuge' from a youthful tragedy in which, forty years ago at Oxford, he lost the love of his life, a beautiful working-class hero called Conor. Posh, anglicised, and full of high-camp preciousness about fine wines and fine music, he is both helplessly tempted by the faint echo of Conor he senses in a cheeky Dalgarnock boy called Mark, and constantly vulnerable to the rumbling class and cultural resentment of the town – and so the scene is set for something of a tragedy.

McDiarmid's version of *Be Near Me* is nothing like a perfect stage version of the story. The whole cadence of the novel represents a falling-off from the brief glimpse of joy and completeness contained in Anderton's youthful relationship with Conor; yet that relationship is neither conjured up on stage, nor fully described in the script. Instead, what we see is a high-class, two-act illustrated monologue, in which McDiarmid's pinched, camp and self-mocking Anderton often stands musing centre-stage, while the other characters move around his troubled mind; and – in the background – the townsfolk sing their way through a series of republican or loyalist chants.

If there's a sense that the book is not fully developed into a play, though, there's also some terrific acting on view, not least from a superb Blythe Duff as Anderton's clever and disappointed housekeeper Mrs Poole. Director John Tiffany and his designer Peter McKintosh create some bleak and memorable stage pictures, notably in the climactic courtroom scene. And although it's difficult to see what audiences in England will gain from this show, it's the kind of work that Scotland itself urgently needs to see and debate; if only because it seeks, at last, to create some real movement and dynamism around the discussion of a wounded and damaged part of Scotland's story that many, even today, would rather ignore.

At the Citizens', meanwhile, the brilliant site-specific theatremaker David Leddy offers us a sharp, bitter and haunting reminder of a Victorian world in which human life was discarded as lightly as any other cheap commodity. Set in the Citizens' Theatre when it first opened, at the turn of the 1880s, *Sub Rosa* makes brilliant use of the building's backstage and hidden spaces – from the dusty places under the main stage to the shabby glamour of the old upper circle – to tell the story in five monologues of its unseen heroine, a music-hall singer called Flora McIvor, and her doomed bid to free the theatre's artists from the rule of their sadistic manager, Hunter.

There's a magnificent feast of Scottish acting on view here, as stars like Alison Peebles, Finlay Welsh and Louise Ludgate glitter like cracked diamonds against the dusty dark; the visual and aural effects are often stunning. And as for what it says – well, we are accustomed to the idea that human life is cheap. But it's a reality with which most of us in this country no longer have to live, from day to day. And for that at least, in the flawed Scotland of 2009, we can perhaps be grateful.

Iconic Burns
Alloway, Ayrshire
The Scotsman, 30 January 2009

It's 7.15 on the night before Burns Night, and in the garden of Burns Cottage at Alloway, a quiet crowd of a thousand local people, chosen by ballot, are milling around enjoying cups of mulled wine doled out by actors in medieval costumes. There are fairy lights and flaming torches, and a young fiddler playing his heart out. Children in cosy bobble hats pose for photographs, hugging the big Burns bust on the lawn; and in the windows of the cottage, actors from Glasgow's Mischief La-Bas street-theatre company act out a series of scenes from Burns's family life – pursuit, pregnancy, parenthood – in a style that might be called crude, if Burns himself hadn't been so fond of an earthy low-life joke.

Then somewhere up the street, there's the sound of a pipe band, and the assembled street-theatre artists of Europe –

or so it sounds, from the multilingual babble in the crew canteen across the road – emerge into the crowd, pulling the great glowing steel-wire sculpture that will be the centre-piece of the night's event, an impressive twelve-foot-high image of Tam o' Shanter on his grey mare Meg, leaping wildly over the keystone of the old bridge at Alloway to escape the pursuing witch Nannie. Nannie also features in the sculpture, arms outstretched, and little cutty sark flar-ing up behind to reveal a distinctly pert bottom. The procession moves on down through Alloway, through three floral arches bearing Homecoming 2009 messages that light up breathtakingly as the sculpture pauses beneath them, and past a funfair of vaguely Burns-related booths, also created by Mischief La-Bas.

Then, as we reach the Brig o' Doon Hotel, the First Minis-ter and his guests file out of their celebration Burns Supper, and we all stand gazing towards the old bridge, where the sculpture – looking spookily convincing against the dark-ness, like the very ghost of Tam and Meg – is set on the keystone at the stroke of nine, pipe bands play Burns songs, and fireworks light up the night with waterfalls, rockets, and a cameo of Burns himself, framed in the arch of the bridge.

So what was it, all this? It had elements of serious street theatre, no doubt, including a fine central image by designer and sculptor Graeme Gilmour, and world-class lighting by Phil Supple, which showed off the romantic good looks of the Alloway riverbank to terrific effect. It was in part a real cultural celebration: many people in the crowd were singing along with the Burns songs played by the bands, and seemed delighted to be in Alloway for the 250th anniversary of a poet truly loved in these parts. But it was also partly a product launch for the Burns Anniversary and the Homecoming Year, bought with £145,000 of public money from Events Scotland and South Ayrshire Council, and designed less to entertain the live audience on the night, than to provide a series of spectacular photo opportunities for images that will be circulated round the globe during Scotland's Homecoming Year.

A hundred years ago – in a sharp reminder that strong collective identity always has its downside – the worldwide order of Freemasons, of which Burns (like his contemporary Mozart) was a member, is said to have organised the creation by local people of huge floral arches for Burns's 150th anniversary, in a style once common across the west of Scotland, and drew 100,000 visitors to Alloway for the occasion. Last week's event was good to look at, genuinely attentive to history, commendably free of kitsch, pleasant in atmosphere, and often artistically impressive, and there are hopes that Gilmour's splendid sculpture will eventually be seen by a wider audience. At heart, though, *Iconic Burns* seemed like a top-down event driven by the needs of politics and tourism, with the audience in a walk-on role; rather than a grassroots, bottom-up popular celebration, of the kind Burns himself would have loved.

To Damascus: David Greig's *Damascus* in Syria and Lebanon
The Scotsman, 19 March 2009

It's late on Thursday night when I arrive in Damascus, the ancient city sprawling its way up the dramatic slopes of Mount Qasioun; and although their second performance in Syria is in full swing, at the municipal theatre in the middle-class suburb of Dummar, the Traverse company are still reeling from the shock of the ferociously mixed reception they received the previous evening.

As playwright David Greig and director Philip Howard are only too aware, bringing a play called *Damascus* to the city of Damascus was always going to be a high-risk enterprise. It was a play that Greig wrote reluctantly, for the Traverse's Edinburgh Festival programme of 2007, after several years of work with young playwrights across the Arab world had made him acutely aware of their need to find their own voice, rather than see themselves and their society defined through Western eyes. And it was a play written almost entirely for British audiences: the story of a Scotsman who travels to Damascus to sell English-language textbooks for schools, and encounters three characters – the beautiful career woman Muna, the disillusioned academic Wasim, and the troubled hotel desk-clerk Zakaria – from whom he learns too much about the deadness of his own life, the depth of his ignorance of other cultures, the vagueness of his politics, and his lethal inability to hear others speak across the gulf of culture and power.

To audiences in the UK, in other words, *Damascus* looks like a searing piece of self-criticism directed against the well-meaning but ineffectual westerner abroad. To audiences in the Arab world, though, it inevitably looks like a thumbnail sketch of their entire culture, summed up in three troubled characters; and no one was more surprised than Greig and Howard when, following a positive response from an Arab delegation in Edinburgh, the British Council decided to take *Damascus* on a groundbreaking tour of its Near East and North African region, opening in Damascus itself, and travelling on to Beirut, Amman, Cairo, Tunis, and Ramallah in the Palestinian West Bank.

Nothing, though, had quite prepared the company for the explosive reaction to the play on its first night in Syria. First there was the performance, received with huge warmth and responsiveness, much laughter, and even a small standing ovation. Then there was the post-show discussion, in which a series of distinguished academics, and some younger commentators, queued up to accuse Greig, in particular, of everything from crass neocolonialism and insults to Arab womanhood, to grotesque stereotyping and sheer artistic incompetence.

Controversy swirled in particular around the character of the desk clerk Zakaria, who finally kills himself when Paul fails to help him achieve his last desperate hope of becoming a writer in the west. Some young Syrians saw him as an iconic figure; other voices condemned him as a hopeless stereotype of Arab victimhood. And these divisions were repeated at a major British Council seminar on Saturday, when some speakers expressed rage that a British playwright should be able to command such significant resources to caricature their culture on an international stage, while the leading Egyptian critic Mehna Al-Badawi, of *Al-Ahram* in Cairo, argued that if she had been given the script of *Damascus* in Arabic, she could well have believed that it was the work of a young Syrian writer, so clearly did it express the situation of many who are struggling for self-expression in societies full of cultural tension and political uncertainty.

After the seminar, David Greig headed off into the Old Town of Damascus, to spend a last evening with the young Syrian playwrights whose work he has already helped to present in London. And the rest of us climbed into a small bus, and rattled off over the mountains, through mist and rain and grubby border checkpoints, on the 100-mile drive to Beirut, down by the Mediterranean. It was a journey that seemed to take us from east to west, from a place still dominated by a combination of rich Islamic culture and old-style mid-twentieth-century socialism, to a war-scarred city once known as the Paris of the Middle East, where battered concrete tower blocks pierce the Mediterranean sky, and our hotel jostles branches of The Body Shop and La Senza.

Yet this, too, is a Middle Eastern city full of contrasts, where some of the women go modestly veiled, and others present spectacular displays of big hair and bling. And here, too, although the tone of the post-show discussion was more relaxed, the same tensions emerge, between those who are irritated and insulted by this apparent western attempt to sum up the Arab world, and those who feel Greig has perceived truths that need to be spoken.

Behind these debates, of course, lie some of the most profound questions facing our twenty-first-century world. There is the debate between former colonising powers, and the countries they once used and manipulated for their own ends, a debate still full of well-justified rage and resentment. There is the debate about how far the whole western model of civilisation – with its alluring dreams of freedom and self-fulfilment – can and should be extended across the globe. And there is the eternal dialogue between power and relative powerlessness, reflected in every struggle for self-determination the world has ever seen.

Sometimes, in these dialogues, there comes a moment – like Nora's great slamming of the door in Ibsen's *A Doll's House* – when the less powerful partner has to walk away, and find his or her own voice, before dialogue can begin again. If the tour of *Damascus* to the Middle East and North Africa helps provoke young writers in the region to demand for themselves the same voice, the same resource, and the same national platform that Scottish playwriting has enjoyed, in finding its own voice, over the last generation, then it will have done much of its job. And whether it does that by arousing their fierce objection, or their passionate admiration, will finally hardly matter at all.

Interiors
Traverse, Edinburgh
The Scotsman, 9 April 2009

In these early years of the twenty-first century, most think-ing theatre artists are all too aware that their art form faces a certain troubling contradiction, a creative catch-22. On one hand, any live performance that takes place in real time, over a fixed period, needs some kind of dynamic forward movement – a narrative structure, or something very like it – to hold the audience's interest. Yet on the other hand, we live in an age when conventional narrative is often mis-trusted, as providing too neat and comforting an account of a world in crisis; and it's the effort to solve this conundrum that has produced some of the finest theatre of the post-modern age.

Matthew Lenton's new production *Interiors* – made for his Glasgow-based touring company Vanishing Point, inspired by Maurice Maeterlinck's 1895 symbolist classic *Interior*, and co-produced by the Napoli Teatro Festival Italia and the Traverse – is a strikingly fine example of this kind of work, full of the energy of conventional narrative, yet aware of its limitations in every physical detail. On a dark stage, we see the outer wall of a house, with a huge jagged hole or picture window through which we can watch the domestic action within. An elderly widower called Andrew (all the charac-ters simply take the actor's own first name) is giving a midwinter dinner party for a group of six friends, including his pretty teenage granddaughter Sarah, his middle-aged neighbour Myra, and a bright young couple, Barney and Aurora.

The world outside – evoked in the play of cold light on the outer wall, and in Alasdair Macrae's bleak Arctic soundscape – is a place so threatening that all the guests arrive carrying guns. And as the party gradually deteriorates into a tragicomic evening from hell, we become aware of the presence of a narrator, at first invisible, then present, but always outside, looking in; someone who was once part of the beautiful and ridiculous hurly-burly of life, but is now an invisible wanderer, endowed with a sad knowledge of how each character will end.

Created with a mixed company of British and Italian actors, this show is unable to use language in any conventional way: we never hear the actors speak, only see them acting out their story. Yet this necessary separation between the audience and the actors is precisely what enables the show both to use narrative, and to stand apart from it – and the result is a hugely clever, rich and entertaining piece of theatre, that shifts effortlessly between farce and tragedy, laughter and dread, domestic familiarity and abstract mystery.

There are moments when the show seems to take easy, middle-of-the-road options rather than pushing its potential to the limit. The posh-estuary narrative voice begins by inviting an ugly, facile snobbish laughter at the characters' pretensions and limitations, which is never really challenged. And given the strength and energy of the play's structure, it could perhaps aim for a more original conclusion than a final sorrowful recognition of the transience of human life and longing. But the acting is immaculate, the production technically superb, the comedy sharp and funny, and the rhythm of the show both beautiful and compelling. In *Interiors*, Lenton has created a world-class piece of international theatre, that turns the limitations of the genre into genuine strengths; and in that achievement, everyone involved can take great pride.

Mixter Maxter
St Magnus Festival, Orkney
The Scotsman, 25 June 2009

In the Pier Arts Centre in Stromness, this summer, there's a deep, dark space given over to a magnificent piece of video art called *Ascension*, by US superstar Bill Viola. Filmed underwater, from a couple of feet below a sunlit surface, it shows in slow motion – and in the deepest blue and silver – a male figure plunging feet-first through that surface, and down past our gaze, into the depths; then for ages afterwards, we watch the backwash of tiny bubbles and sparkles rising from where he fell, up towards the sunlight, a billion particles disturbed and moving and reacting, almost to infinity, because of that single action, that single leap.

The Pier exhibition is not technically part of this year's St Magnus Festival in Orkney, but all the same, the Bill Viola work seems to provide a central image for a festival built, as always, around the pull and surge of the sea that surrounds Orkney, and the mystical sense of the interrelatedness of all things – humanity, nature, the very stuff of earth and water – that forms a key part of Orkney culture. And it would have been easy for the National Theatre of Scotland, wading into the delicate balance of island life for a few months to create a Transform project with young people from Kirkwall Grammar School, to have failed to produce anything that truly reflected that special spirit of the place.

Instead, though, the *Mixter Maxter* project – directed by Davey Anderson and Liam Hurley, with a team of more than two dozen students in their early to mid-teens – has produced both a moving and memorable short show, and an outstanding installation, in an old warehouse in Bridge Street, that both complements and expands the performance to create what must be one of the finest pieces of youth project art work Scotland has ever produced.

The show is a deceptively simple-looking piece, played in a bare in-the-round setting in King Street Halls, which tells the story of a Kirkwall girl called Soley, who runs away from her own life, driven partly by the unkindness of her so-called schoolfriends, and partly by her widowed father's inability to talk to her about her mother's death, ten years ago. Played by a series of different girls identified simply by slipping on Soley's little red hoodie, she runs first to an old warehouse where she keeps a little shrine to her mother, then to the pierhead, where she leaps aboard a ferry, looks out at the pattern of islands ahead and, like the Bill Viola figure, makes a leap from the deck into the ocean, towards what she hopes will be a new or changed life.

At King Street, the story is told verbally and through movement, superbly coordinated by Simon Pittman to capture the running, darting movements, the wary walking, the intent faces and scanning eyes, of teenagers marking a way through potentially hostile streets and spaces. The show ends quietly, with a series of questions about the future, but as the young cast circle the hall, intently pressing little imaginary seeds of new life into the hands of mums and dads, old folks and tiny toddlers, the sense of empathy and almost of atonement towards a troubled generation of youngsters is overwhelming, and many in the audience are wiping away tears.

If the show is powerful, though, the installation down in the old Bridge Street rope warehouse is irresistible, a series of evocations of settings, images and ideas from Soley's story – in video, sculpture, projected text, soundscapes and audio journeys, with elements of live performance – that is stewarded with palpable pride by the young people who helped create it, and by the artists (including Kim Beveridge, Alistair Peebles and Anne Bevan) who helped them. The sense of young people reconnecting with aspects of Orkney's past as a seafaring and farming island, exploring its rich cultural heritage, and using it to make sense of their own lives today, is intense; and although the Warehouse 18 installation was dismantled on Monday, along with the rest of the project, the young people I spoke to expressed an intense hope that it could somehow live on, and be seen again.

Incident at the Border
Òran Mór, Glasgow
The Scotsman, 26 November 2009

If Scotland became independent, so we're told, the border between Scotland and England would be one of those faint Euro-frontiers where traffic never stops, and they don't even bother to glance at your passport. In this week's A Play, a Pie and a Pint lunchtime drama, though – the last of the autumn season – the brilliant young Glasgow writer Kieran Lynn offers a fierce reminder of an alternative truth: the idea that borders tend to create their own divisions and conflicts, and to provide an excuse for some of humankind's most brutal behaviour.

Young couple Olivia and Arthur are sitting in the park, you see, enjoying a bit of Sunday morning peace, when a man in uniform appears with a roll of tape, and places a border between them, right down the middle of the bench. Olivia, who tries to read the newspapers and keep up with events, has a suspicion that this may have something to do with the recently agreed 'independence deal'; Arthur couldn't care less about politics, and wishes he was a duck on the nearby pond.

No names of countries are mentioned; so that we could be anywhere from Bosnia to the Baltic, although the voices are Scottish and English. Reiver, the man with the tape, is a classic postmodern jobsworth: not exactly vicious, but neither bright nor brave enough to resist the culture of ridiculous security paranoia and knee-jerk authoritarianism in which he has been trained. And so the peaceful day in the park gradually dwindles into a militarised nightmare, with both men carrying machine-guns, Olivia an agonised and vulnerable bystander, and any idea of progressive gender politics dumped in the dustbin of history.

It's a dystopian vision, of course, with many fine touches of absurdism, particularly in Keith Fleming's masterly portrayal of Reiver as an ordinary man managed into a culture of crazed control freakery. But it comes as a sharp and timely reminder of the primitive forces that can be unleashed – particularly, Lynn suggests, in the male psyche – whenever human beings give themselves any new excuse for 'us and them' thinking. And in Selma Dimitrijević's brilliant and heartfelt production, it achieves all this in a brief and vivid thirty-five minutes, with the help of fine performances not only from Fleming, but from a pitch-perfect Ashley Smith and Laurie Brown as the two young lovers, separated for good.

2010

New Man Walking
Royal Mile, Edinburgh
2 January 2010

New Year's Day on the Royal Mile, and as dusk begins to gather over a cold, clear afternoon with just a hint of a northerly breeze, the Edinburgh's Hogmanay Ne'erday theme of *Re:formation* seems to be playing pretty well with an astonishing range of visitors, from what seems like every corner of the globe.

In John Knox's House, the actor John Shedden is proving an unsettling dead ringer for the old provocateur of

Scotland's Protestant Reformation, celebrating its 450th anniversary this year. From ground-floor chamber, to tiny second-floor study overlooking the High Street, he harangues the visitors about sin and literacy, the evils of the mighty, the suffering of the poor, and the abomination of women in power, with an intensity that acts as a sharp reminder of the complexity of the man, and of the movement he led. Down at Holyrood Palace, meanwhile, people from all over the world are happily writing New Year resolutions on a temporary wall, resolving to fall in love, cook better, care more, work for peace; and over in the park, Edinburgh Puppet Lab's famous *Big Man Walking* is stirring.

Seen all over Scotland this year, and renamed *New Man Walking* for this special day, the Big Man is a beautiful blue thirty-foot puppet figure dressed in a leather kilt, like some Scottish incarnation of the Green Man of legend. And as he emerges with aching slowness from a chrysalis-like shell, gradually flexes his great hands, blinks his eyes, shakes his gleaming red-gold hair, and begins his slow, slow walk out of the park, past the Scottish Parliament, and on up the High Street, meanings seem to gather and hover around his big, benign figure in a way that is almost unsettling. He might be a once and future king or chief, returning to claim his own. In an age of unimpressive leaders, he might meet some hidden yearning for a true 'big man' around whom to gather. He might be a spirit of the earth itself, returning to remind us of what we owe to the very landscape around us; or he might be a figure of childlike innocence, awakening our instincts for affection and care.

But whatever the reason for his appeal, the hairs on the back of the neck rise a little, at the sight of his great figure, surrounded by admiring crowds with heads all tilted back to gaze at him, moving inexorably up past the ancient

Canongate Kirk towards the Tron. Something's coming, murmur the people hurrying down the pavements or waiting in the crowd; the genius of the *Big Man Walking*, old or new, is that we can't be quite sure what.

The Secret Commonwealth
Òran Mór, Glasgow
The Scotsman, 4 February 2010

The story of Robert Kirk, the troubled minister of Aberfoyle, is not a new one in Scottish theatre. In the mid-1980s, Theatre Alba discovered and produced Netta Blair Reid's two-act play *The Shepherd Beguiled*, about the strange story of the seventeenth-century man of God so fascinated by old tales of the 'good people' – the big, powerful faery folk said to live beneath the hills of his home country – that when Kirk disappeared one night among those hills, he was thought to have been taken by them, his restless spirit doomed to roam for ever in search of a way home.

Whatever the history of this strange story, though, Catherine Czerkawska's new monologue makes a powerful job of retelling it, and marks a fine opening to this spring's A Play, a Pie and a Pint season of lunchtime plays. Using the voice of the lost minister himself – played by Liam Brennan with a terrific combination of emotional commitment and sheer technical command – Czerkawska transforms the story into a lyrical yet driven fifty-minute lament over Scotland's failure to integrate its dour Presbyterian faith and dogged Enlightenment rationalism with the wilder, more beautiful and more sensual aspects of its Gaelic heritage, represented by the eerily amplified voice of singer Deirdre Graham, crooning soft old songs.

Kirk, who was a fine scholar, might have been remembered as the first man to translate the Psalms into Gaelic. Instead, he seems to have been driven close to madness by the fierce binary oppositions – rationalism or crazy superstition, respectability or sensual fulfilment – that dogged our national culture at the height of the Reformation, and still influence our thinking today. And between them, Czerkawska and Brennan come close to making him a real hero for our times, desperately struggling for ways to move on from an arid, over-rationalised modernism, without sinking back into the darkness of mindless superstition.

Peter Pan
King's, Glasgow

Turbo Folk
Òran Mór, Glasgow
The Scotsman, 29 April 2010

If ever there was a show for which any friend of Scottish theatre would have wished a glowing, unambiguous success, it's John Tiffany's massive new National Theatre of Scotland production of *Peter Pan*, which opened at the King's Theatre in Glasgow this week after years of preparation, and a formidable investment of time and treasure. It's not only that the NTS now urgently needs a new large-scale, mainstage hit, to match the triumph four years ago of the mighty *Black Watch*; it's that the show itself, in its inspiration and substance, is freighted with so many ideas that matter, and so much powerful potential.

As writer David Greig and director John Tiffany have made clear in dozens of interviews over the last few weeks, the idea is to take J.M. Barrie's mighty story of Wendy and the lost boys, and to repatriate it to late-Victorian Scotland, the land in which Barrie grew up, and in which he lived through the formative and tragic experiences – notably the death by drowning of his adored older brother – that shaped the story of Pan, the boy who never grows up. And in creating a version of *Peter Pan* that has nothing to do with Christmas good cheer – and is not aimed at children under eight – Greig and Tiffany seek to confront the darker aspects of this haunting story, while also reflecting its magical elements.

And it's easy enough to see the traces of these ideas all over the stage, in the strange, uneasy version of the show that opened in Glasgow this week. They are present most obviously in Laura Hopkins' set, a massively cluttered, heavyweight affair featuring three diamond-shaped cantilevers of an as yet uncompleted Forth Rail Bridge; the children's father, Mr Darling, is re-imagined here as an Edinburgh engineer working on the construction of the bridge. They are present in Davey Anderson's music, a fascinating and powerful collage of Gaelic work-songs and laments, traditional lowland tunes, and working navvies' songs of the nineteenth century. And they are present in the whole mood and tone of the show, which avoids prettiness and whimsy, engages powerfully with Pan's anger and emotional coldness, and features disturbing echoes of dark and threatening ideas about the supernatural; this is a *Peter Pan* with doppelgängers and avatars, and even hints of demonic possession.

The difficulty, though, is that despite the rich range of half-developed ideas that has gone into the making of the show, what emerges on stage is a royal mess, a dingy-looking voyage around the darker reaches of the Pan story that often lacks pace, always lacks clarity, and misses out completely on the exhilarating, magical sense of freedom that Pan brings into the lives of Wendy and her brothers.

The set, for example, is a brilliant idea that doesn't work in practice, filling the stage with huge chunks of metal that constantly force the actors into the wrong dramatic positions, and often fail to reflect even the most basic elements of the story. The lighting is a pretentious disaster, often just plain inadequate to illuminate the actors' faces in a large theatre. The flying is awkwardly dependent on huge, heavy black harnesses, as ugly as they are unconvincing. The casting – well, there's a fine central performance from an impressive Kevin Guthrie as Pan, but the rest of the company are frankly forgettable, and look far less like a coherent national theatre troupe than some other companies currently playing on Scottish stages.

And beyond all that, the show is plagued by a chronic lack of simple, basic storytelling drive, perhaps because it boasts a creative team of no fewer than fourteen people, and therefore looks as if it had been designed by a committee. There's one electrifying scene in which Kirsty Mackay's attractive Wendy gathers her boys in a circle and tells them a story, provoking a confrontation with Pan; just for a moment, the positions are right, and the drama is clear. But soon, we've drifted off again into a version of Tinkerbell's 'death' that not only doesn't allow us to help save her, but doesn't even tell us whether she lives or dies. And in that, it resembles far too many other moments in a *Peter Pan* that desperately needs a longer view, a clearer focus, and a ruthless visual simplification, if the brave ideas it carries are not to be lost for ever, in a sea of theatrical confusion.

After all that, it's a blazing relief to turn to a forty-minute, three-handed show that focuses fiercely on a single aspect of Scotland's myth-making about itself, tells its story with pace and economy, and delivers a real and frightening dramatic punch. This week's A Play, a Pie and a Pint lunchtime show, written by rising star Alan Bissett, is the short and brilliant tale of a doomed visit by a touring Scottish singer-songwriter to a whisky bar in some Balkan town still riven by memories of war. In the great tradition of naive Scots abroad, the guileless Cameron – brilliantly played by Ryan Fletcher – thinks everyone abroad loves the Scots and hates the English; but to his minder Miko, and the heavyweight barman Vlad (Simon Donaldson and Steven McNicoll, both in magnificent form), he is just another Brit, blood brother of the 'peacekeeping' soldiers who recently occupied, patronised and brutalised their country.

As the evening veers from the embarrassing to the danger- ous, Vlad goads Cameron into giving up his girly love songs, belting out 'Bonnie Dundee', and unleashing his inner demons of violent machismo: 'These songs are not inno- cent.' And the games Bissett plays with language are dazzling, as Vlad and Miko converse in an impenetrable Balkan tongue that reveals itself as a reinvented form of Scots; and then the linguistic tables are turned, in a final shift of power that ends Cameron's innocence for ever.

Caledonia
King's, Edinburgh
The Scotsman, 23 August 2010

The Darien Expedition of 1696 was Scotland's first and only attempt to establish an overseas colony and trading post of its own, and the enterprise was such a comprehensive dis- aster – involving death, disease, and the outright loss of more than half of Scotland's capital wealth – that it effec- tively finished Scotland as an independent nation, and left psychological scars that remain visible today, in the strange mixture of vainglory and self-contempt with which many Scots still view their national identity.

And it's straight into this morass of unresolved patriotic feelings, as well as of roaring post-crash scepticism about the whole model of high-risk venture capitalism on which the Darien project was based, that this latest production from the National Theatre of Scotland and the Edinburgh International Festival boldly marches. Scripted by Alistair Beaton and directed by Anthony Neilson, *Caledonia* is both spectacular in staging and satirical in tone, and comes across almost as a comic-book linear narrative of the Darien disaster. Many of the characters – from Edinburgh MPs to English king – are presented as *Viz*-magazine grotesques of greed and venality; jokes about bankers abound, and while some of the show's satirical comedy is effective, some is overpitched and cack-handed.

What's increasingly clear, though, is that these uncertainties of tone reflect a deep ambivalence within the play itself about the story it tells. If it merely satirises Scotland as a backward dump with foolish delusions of grandeur, it does nothing but flatter familiar metropolitan prejudices; yet if it takes too seriously the evidence that Scotland's legitimate attempt to join in the global trading boom was directly scuppered by the machinations of the English Government, it risks looking like a piece of nationalist agitprop, an outcome which Beaton and Neilson seem anxious to avoid.

It's therefore a tribute to the skill of all those involved – including a fine cast, led by Paul Higgins as William Paterson, the visionary financier behind the project – that what *Caledonia* finally achieves, in its closing scenes, is a kind of profound elegiac lyricism about the sheer human cost of the enterprise, expressed in brilliantly theatrical terms. The play probably insists too much on making the link between crazed venture capitalism and Scottish national aspirations, a link which misrepresents the character of Scottish politics. But this new NTS show fits superbly, and revealingly, into the 'new worlds' theme of Jonathan Mills' 2010 Festival. And three centuries on, it makes an interesting, debatable, and hugely theatrical start on the long collective process of coming to terms with a decisive national disaster; a process on which Scotland has perhaps only just begun.

The Freak and the Showgirl
The Arches, Glasgow
The Scotsman, 26 November 2010

He is Mat Fraser, the multi-talented singer, dancer, and stand-up raconteur who has made cutting-edge theatre out of his life as a man with the tiny, flipper-like hands of a 1960s thalidomide child. She is Julie Atlas Muz, gorgeously witty burlesque artist and stripper, and Miss Coney Island 2006.

Which of them is the freak, though, and which the showgirl, remains a more open question than you might think, as they steer their audience through an astonishing seventy-five minutes of disruptive comedy and burlesque, punctuated by ever-more gobsmacking scenes of cultural questioning, self-mocking hilarity, and politically pointed nudity. This show, which played at The Arches as part of the DaDaFest festival of theatre inspired by deafness and disability, is not for the faint-hearted, or for those inclined to blush at the sight of a bit of wedding tackle – both male and female – boldly exposed to the winter air.

In the case of Fraser and Muz, though, there's never any doubt that this is rudeness with a purpose, as they trawl the history of ridiculous forms of oppression – from the freak-show display of people with deformities, to the ritual shaving of female body hair – in order to defy every cliché about the cosy sexlessness of the disabled (Fraser is one of the sexiest male performers around), or the passivity of women as sex objects: Miss Muz rounds off her cheekiest strip routine with a rousing political speech, delivered in the buff. 'It's satirical, postmodern, and littered with irony, so everything's all right!' yells Fraser self-mockingly, as he questions the audience's motives for ogling Miss Muz. In this case, though, it happens to be true; and if it's not all right, it's certainly thought-provoking, as well as funny, human, and truly erotic, in a way the purveyors of mass-produced plastic porn could barely begin to understand.

2011

The Strange Undoing of Prudencia Hart
Tron, Glasgow
The Scotsman, 14 February 2011

As the devil points out halfway through the evening, there is no peace for the wicked. Down you go to your local pub, and who should be there but the National Theatre of Scotland, in the shape of a touring company of five terrific actor-musicians, led by the gorgeous Madeleine Worrall and an inspired Andy Clark. They start rearranging tables, playing daft games, getting you to rip up your paper napkins to create an impromptu snowstorm; and then we're off, into the thrilling, shuddering gallop through the landscape of ancient and postmodern Scotland that is this new ballad drama by playwright David Greig, with director Wils Wilson.

The heroine of the story, Prudencia Hart, is a smart young academic at the School of Scottish Studies who specialises in the mighty, sexy, elemental tradition of the Border Ballads. Snowed in at a conference in Kelso with an annoying colleague called Colin Syme, she ends up in the local pub, where folk night morphs into a disturbing, booze-fuelled karaoke nightmare, and a strange, seductive man suddenly appears, to escort her to what turns out – literally – to be the bed and breakast from hell.

In a short review, there's no decoding all the riches of David Greig's rollicking text, and the mighty jokes and connections it spins around everything from the state of modern academic life to the music of Kylie Minogue. Let's just say that the whole story is staged with a terrific, inventive sense of fun, and that even if some sequences are too long and the verse sometimes slides towards doggerel, it is, at its best, more vibrantly, sexily alive than any piece of theatre I've seen in Scotland for years. Some people don't get it about our new National Theatre: they want it in a mausoleum, rather than down the pub. But if you want to understand in your flesh and blood what the NTS is all about, then this is the show to see; as it tours from Berwick to Ullapool, over the next few weeks.

The Age of Arousal
Royal Lyceum Theatre, Edinburgh
The Scotsman, 24 February 2011

Despite thirty years of talk about equal opportunities, the latest wave of feminism has failed to make much of a dent on the traditional gender balance in theatre; plays with all-male casts remain common, those with all-female casts vanishingly rare. So it's both exciting and fascinating, this spring, to see one of Scotland's main stages occupied by a new play by and about women, which scores a roaring success in getting straight to the historic heart of the 'woman question'. Based on George Gissing's 1893 novel *The Odd Women*, and co-produced by the Royal Lyceum and Stellar Quines, Linda Griffiths's *The Age of Arousal* is set in London in the 1880s, in and around the school of typewriting run by ex-suffragette Mary Barfoot and her young lover Rhoda Nunn.

As part of their mission to save women from powerlessness and economic dependence, the two start to give lessons to the impoverished Madden sisters, two batty old spinsters and one twenty-year-old minx; but their plans are disrupted by the entrance of the one man in the story, Mary's handsome nephew Everard. As good as his name in matters sexual, Everard seduces the young minx Monica, falls in love with Rhoda, and generally creates chaos in the hearts and minds of women who want equality and freedom, but who also want sex with men, and the babies men can give them.

All of this is tremendous fun, unleashing avalanches of witty dialogue – and even wittier private asides – about the state of gender relations, and the power of desire to upset the best-organised ideological apple cart. In terms of plot, *The Age of Arousal* is no textbook of feminist theory; in the best postmodern style, it sometimes comes close to rejecting the whole dream of equality as an unrealisable project.

In Muriel Romanes' gloriously bold and inventive production, though, it emerges as a truly radical piece of theatre, presented in short, vivid, free-flowing episodes on a sparsely furnished stage backed by a screen against which each fraught tableau of characters is silhouetted. Janet Bird's costumes represent a glorious stylisation of late-Victorian dress, with hoops and bustles bursting out of their fabric shells. And the performances, from Romanes' six-strong company, are simply immaculate: from an inspired Ann Louise Ross as Mary Barfoot, to Hannah Donaldson as the youngest of the three sisters – the one who pays the old price of womanhood by dying in childbirth, leaving the others with a member of a new generation to raise, in their own highly debatable image.

Theatre Uncut
The Arches, Glasgow
The Scotsman, 22 March 2011

In London, it all happened at Southwark Playhouse. In Bristol it was the Old Vic. In Edinburgh, the student-led Bedlam Theatre staged an all-day event featuring plays, music and debates; and wherever you were in the UK, on Saturday, someone was celebrating the event known as Theatre Uncut, the first of what I guess will be many theatrical protests against the current economic regime. The brainchild of London-based director Hannah Price, Theatre Uncut invited eight leading UK playwrights to contribute ten-minute plays on the theme of 'the cuts'; and although the event I attended – at The Arches in Glasgow – covered only five of them, the intensity of the drama signalled an arts community already gearing up for protest on a scale not seen since the 1980s.

So Dennis Kelly's three-hander *Things That Don't Make Sense* is an only-slightly-surreal reflection on the growing disconnection between high-profile policing and actual justice. Anders Lustgarten's *Fat Man* is an entertaining many-voiced rant against capitalism, in its twenty-first-century incarnation. Jack Thorne's duologue *Whiff Whaff* is a chilling riff on the theory of self-sufficiency and not encouraging 'dependency'. Clara Brennan's *Hi Vis* is a frighteningly desperate account of the life of a mother whose daughter has special needs. And David Greig's *Fragile* – the most powerful of the lot – uses Greig's technique of making the audience play one of the parts to lead us through a thundering ten-minute drama in which impotent sadness over the closure of a vital support centre for people with mental problems becomes suicidal rage, and then a roaring call for political action.

In Glasgow, director Emma Callander assembled a superb scratch cast, drawing brilliant performances from actors

348

including Anne Lacey, Garry Collins, Louise Ludgate, and Kieran Hurley, heart-stoppingly brilliant in *Fragile*. Now it's time for these plays to be taken up by one of the major Scottish theatres, and presented again, in front of a much larger audience; and again and again until the message gets through – that nothing justifies wanton damage to the lives of vulnerable people, in a society as wealthy as ours.

A Slow Air
Tron, Glasgow
The Scotsman, 19 May 2011

If you want a glimpse of sheer perfection in current Scottish playwriting, head for the Tron in Glasgow, where David Harrower – one of the leaders of the generation of Scottish playwrights who emerged in the 1990s – has directed his own production of his latest play, *A Slow Air*. The play takes the form of a ninety-minute double monologue for a middle-aged brother and sister who have been estranged for the past fourteen years. Athol lives in Houston, near Glasgow Airport, with his wife and his floor-tiling business, proud of his middle-class home and achievements; Morna has stayed in Edinburgh, and survived a wild youth to become a cleaner in the houses of the rich.

From this simple situation, Harrower spins two strands of storytelling and poetry so profound that by the end of the play, it seems as if we have seen a complete, disturbing panorama of ordinary life in Scotland's central belt today: from the universal western effort to maintain a comfortable middle-class way of life in a new age of terror, to the divisions of class and income that corrode our society, the strands of culture and music that still sometimes unite it, and the strange persistence of the seemingly fragile bonds of family. Real-life brother and sister Lewis Howden and

Kathryn Howden give superbly moving performances as
Athol and Morna; and this short, magnificent play – so profound in its local sense of place, so global in its reach and its
humanity – will leave your sense of the country we live in
subtly shaken and changed, for good.

Five Minute Theatre
National Theatre of Scotland
Online
The Scotsman, 22 June 2011

It's eight o'clock on Midsummer's Night, and I am standing in Greyfriars Churchyard, Edinburgh, under a
downpour that can only be called biblical. The National
Theatre of Scotland's twenty-four-hour online epic of 235
five-minute plays, performed in front of live audiences and
beamed from all over Scotland and beyond, is three hours
old; and on top of a tombstone at Greyfriars, the actor,
writer, musician and tour guide John Kielty is haranguing
the usual rain-soaked team of tourists, out on a ghost walk
around the city.

Tonight, though, things are different, because the NTS cameras are here, and Kielty has written a five-minute play in
which his spiel is interrupted by a pair of pallid ghosts who
loom from behind the gravestones, furious with the tour
guide for perpetuating myths about Greyfriars Bobby. Meanwhile, back at Adam House, the event's Edinburgh 'hub', the
big screens are showing an experiment steadily gathering
weight and momentum. It's not that every show is excellent.
Some are vague, some are pretentious, some are badly shot.
There are plenty of technical hitches to disrupt the experience of viewing them online; and at any given moment, there
are only about three hundred people watching.

Three or four times in each hour, though, there comes a flash of brilliance that – combined with the other shows on view, and the huge range of locations where they have been filmed – begins to contribute to a truly powerful and moving cumulative portrait of the Scotland we live in, right now. There's a magnificent short drama from Dundee Rep Ensemble, written by Douglas Maxwell, about the idea of public apology; there's an exquisite, neighbourly moment of storytelling from a house in Melvich, Sutherland, about the Portskerra fishing disaster that devastated that community in 1918; there's the actress and writer Michelle Gallagher, in the back court of the Glasgow tenement where she grew up, regaling an appreciative audience of neighbours with a hilarious five-minute story of how the Pope's visit to Glasgow in 1982, when she was five, nearly drove her to run away from home.

And as show follows tiny show, I find myself more and more moved: partly by the existence of a national theatre which has worked so hard to build the grassroots relationships across all of Scotland on which this project is built; and partly by the sight and sound of the people who live in Scotland now, finding so many different kinds of voices, glorying in their diversity, and seizing the chance to exercise their imaginations, in ways that are sad and funny, down-to-earth and surreal, and rarely less than memorable.

The Salon Project
Traverse, Edinburgh
The Scotsman, 13 October 2011

At the height of their power and pomp, civilisations often indulge in a brief age of denial about the inevitability of change and decay. Over the last thirty years, though, among thinking people, that arrogance has melted away from our once-proud Western civilisation, with its unshakeable belief in progress through reason and science; and we have begun to confront all sorts of unpalatable truths, both about the fragility of the world we have made for ourselves, and about the inevitability of our own personal extinction.

Stewart Laing's astonishing *The Salon Project*, at the Traverse, is principally concerned with decline and decay; but as one of the most complete immersive theatre experiences ever conceived, it compels us – the audience – to think about these themes from a completely new angle, by making each of us take the time and the risk involved in dressing in full period costume – gorgeous Victorian, Edwardian or 1920s ball dresses for the women, smart tailcoats or military uniforms for the men. Once we are ready – and it takes a large wardrobe team a full half-hour, including make-up and jewellery – we are escorted through high double doors into a large, fragile white drawing room with chandeliers, like a deliberately provisional version of an eighteenth-century salon: here, we drift around and sip champagne, listen to music on piano and wind-up gramophone, and hear provocative thoughts about life, dress, and the future, not bound to any period, but ranging across the centuries.

The effect of this experience is astonishingly complex and rich. At first, we only exclaim and point; then we walk differently, feel differently, marvel at the extraordinary richness of centuries when each aristocratic dress was a small work of art in itself. We feel, in the end, like the privileged guests at the Duchess of Richmond's ball on the eve of the Battle of Waterloo; or like the Russian royal family, a few months before the revolution; or like characters in an Oscar Wilde play, a shade too smart and witty, courting some unnamed disaster. Before we leave, Laing and his amazing team make us watch that disaster on screen, a wrecked twenty-first-century vision of the room we stand in. Yet *The Salon Project* invites us to consider the future before us, as well as the past we have lost, to recall how much of the history of our civilisation was really the story of a tiny, aristocratic few, dressed and tended to by unsung millions. And as the finest theatre always does, it changes us a little, for good.

In May 2012 Vicky Featherstone announced her departure from the National Theatre of Scotland, after a 'life-changing' eight years, for the Royal Court Theatre in London. Her only reservation, she said, was that despite a huge welcome from almost everyone she met and worked with in Scotland, she had on one or two occasions felt 'bullied' by people pointing out that she is not Scottish; the allegations triggered another round in Scotland's ongoing furious debate about why such a high proportion of our leading cultural institutions are run by people from outside Scotland. She was replaced, early in 2013, by Laurie Sansom, former artistic director of the Royal & Derngate in Northampton, but her brave, dynamic and radical presence at the centre of Scottish theatre, during this vital period in the nation's life, had transformed Scotland's cultural landscape for ever, and was much missed.

And in 2012 too, I began to record my first reviews from a new venue in Edinburgh called Summerhall, the old Royal Dick Veterinary College on the Meadows, a great rambling place – owned and funded by Edinburgh philanthropist Robert McDowell – that had fallen heir to the huge archive collection of Richard Demarco, one of the men who founded the Traverse Theatre in 1963; and which had emerged, not only as a Fringe venue, but as a new year-round twenty-first-century arts lab, full of magnificent exhibitions and strange, wild events. According to the old Mayan calendar, the world was supposed to end on the night of 21 December 2012. And if it had, I would have been happy to mark the moment drifting through the strange, richly layered spaces of Summerhall, another powerful new centre for theatre and performance in Scotland.

The Jean-Jacques Rousseau Show
Òran Mór, Glasgow
The Scotsman, 1 March 2012

If you want to glimpse the outlines of a possible twenty-first-century revolution, then Òran Mór is the place to be, this week. To celebrate their 250th lunchtime show since 2004, David MacLennan's astonishing A Play, a Pie and a Pint team googled '250', and came up with the fact that it is 250 years since the publication of Jean-Jacques Rousseau's *The Social Contract*, one of the founding texts of the French Revolution of 1789.

Their new *Jean-Jacques Rousseau Show* – a political cabaret co-written by a team of eleven writers, including Wildcat veterans David MacLennan and Dave Anderson, and a dazzling range of younger voices – is naturally much preoccupied with Scotland's current situation, riven by economic inequalities, and faced with a constitutional choice that may or may not be relevant to the greater cause of social justice.

Yet the show succeeds in setting that contemporary debate in a deep historic context, thanks to some razor-sharp scriptwriting, a fine eighteenth-century-style pamphleteering design by Patrick McGurn, and a few terrific songs. There are excellent, witty performances from a five-strong cast, featuring young stars Julia Taudevin, Kirstin McLean and Brian James, with Dave Anderson and George Drennan.

And there is one spine-shuddering moment when, after a hilarious spoof interview between Alex Salmond and Jeremy Paxman, Paxman's chair is suddenly occupied by the spirit of revolution herself, who asks Salmond a few chilling questions about the real meaning of independence. It's enough to make you want to sign up immediately to the little Social Contract printed on the back of your programme; and to accept its invitation to draw a picture, of the kind of Scotland you really want.

Enquirer
Pacific Quay, Glasgow

Further Than the Furthest Thing
Dundee Rep
The Scotsman, 3 May 2012

In the spring of 1990, at the height of Glasgow's year as European City of Culture, I sat with hundreds of others in a great former engine shed in Govan watching the show called *The Ship*, Bill Bryden's passionate elegy for a dying shipbuilding industry.

It wasn't the greatest show I had ever seen: it offered more emotion than deep insight, more helpless anger than real empowerment. Yet it marked a vital moment in Glasgow's coming-to-terms with the end of the industrial age; and twenty-two years on, I find myself experiencing very similar feelings, as I stand just a few hundred yards upriver from Govan, on the top floor of a vacant riverside office-block, watching the National Theatre of Scotland's twenty-first century elegy for the print-newspaper industry, now reeling under the challenge of instant electronic news.

This story is closer to home for journalists, of course, so much so that I have to declare a small interest in *Enquirer*: I was one of the forty-three journalists interviewed in the compilation of the show. And in style, this show is aeons away from the scripted high emotion of *The Ship*; *Enquirer* is another example of the twenty-first century trend towards verbatim theatre, in which documentary material is presented to the audience in relatively raw form. It's also a promenade production, staged to a small audience who perch on desks or on piles of unsold newspapers, as a brilliantly cast team of six Scottish actors lead them through the newspaper day, and through some set-piece interviews with named contributors, including former *Scottish Sun* boss Jack Irvine.

What emerges from this show, *Ship*-like, is a profound sense of loss – and of anger at the undervaluing of the loss – combined with a slightly frustrating lack of analytical firepower in teasing out the underlying strands of argument, and hinting at possible ways forward. Yet the NTS's show is so shockingly timely, in its seizing of this Leveson Inquiry moment in the history of journalism, that it can hardly fail to make a major impact. Its compiled text, pulled together by Andrew O'Hagan with directors Vicky Featherstone and John Tiffany, draws a magnificent ensemble performance from a cast who seem completely seized by the paradox of journalism, by its nobility, its grubbiness, and the extent to which it finds itself under ethical attack at its moment of greatest economic weakness. And unexpectedly, this is also a beautiful show, with subtly powerful design and a fine soundscape; and evening light pouring in over the river like a final blessing, on an industry that has helped shape our political and municipal life through most of the modern age, and may soon be with us no more.

Loss is also the theme of Zinnie Harris's great debut play *Further Than the Furthest Thing*, first seen at the Traverse in 2000, and now given a stunning new production at Dundee Rep by outgoing artistic director James Brining. Inspired by the volcanic eruption on the island of Tristan da Cunha in 1961, Harris's play takes the loss of that homeland, and the displacement of its people to Britain, as a metaphor for the whole experience of modernity, with its fierce disruption of our relationship with the land, and its replacement of organic human relationships with the machine-like culture of contract that is one of the bedrocks of capitalism.

Twelve years on from its premiere, *Further Than the Furthest Thing* still strikes me as a play that has never quite had the dramaturgical attention it deserves; its dramatic impact would be even greater if it used fewer words, and trusted more in its own action. James Brining's final Dundee production, though – staged on a chill and magnificent watery set by Neil Warmington and consultant artist Elizabeth Ogilvie – is of breathtaking quality. John Harris's shuddering high soprano soundscape is unforgettable, and, among a fine five-strong ensemble, Ann Louise Ross gives the performance of a lifetime as Zinnie Harris's great island heroine Mill, a woman never humbled into forgetting where she came from, or giving up her right to return.

Krapp's Last Tape
Footfalls
Citizens', Glasgow
The Scotsman, 7 June 2012

The box-office manager at the Citizens' smiled kindly, as she handed me my ticket. 'We've put you near the front,' she said, 'because the show is very quiet.' In truth, though, there's absolutely nothing small, or incapable of commanding the big space, about the two mighty Samuel Beckett fragments currently playing as a double bill at the Citizens' Theatre. Despite their extreme austerity and restraint, and their simple framing of a single human figure against a dense field of darkness, these plays are brave, beautiful and masterly theatrical poems about the brief pain and joy of human life, born of the high modernist age in which Sam Beckett wrote, but so perfectly sculpted that they seem timeless. And

Dominic Hill's superb Citizens' production – the last in his acclaimed first season as artistic director – shapes them into one of those rare theatrical events that will leave no one who sees it completely unchanged.

So in the great fifty-five-minute monologue *Krapp's Last Tape* (1958), a shambling yet immensely charismatic Gerard Murphy takes to the stage as Krapp, a solitary man in his late sixties who, throughout his life, has made a habit of recording a tape on his birthday. Clattering and banging painfully around the dark outer reaches of his room, Krapp gradually puts together his ancient reel-to-reel tape recorder, and the tape he wants to hear before he records this year's offering. It's the one from thirty years before, when he was a 'young fool' of thirty-nine; the year when his mother died, and when he broke – for reasons he can no longer recall – with a woman he seems to have loved.

The play is essentially a duet for two versions of the same voice. There's the younger, more arrogant, more pretentious Krapp; and the one we see before us, not far from death, often disgusted by his own youthful foolishness, but still wryly humorous enough to reduce the audience to helpless laughter with the acid wit of his self-mockery. And in Gerard Murphy, this great play finds a near-perfect voice and stage presence, full of that dark relish for language, and for the absurdity of life, that is – for all of us – part of our essential human armoury against the dying of the light.

And if this version of *Krapp's Last Tape* is an almost flawless theatrical experience, it is equalled by the shuddering power of Hill's staging of the twenty-five-minute fragment *Footfalls*: a dialogue between a woman – or the wraith of a woman – who paces to and fro along the front of the stage, and the voice of her unseen aged mother, which haunts her every step. Swathed in a sheath of silver-grey rags and in her own long hair, magnificently lit by Lizzie Powell, Kathryn

Howden creates an unforgettable figure of human pain and isolation, without end; while Kay Gallie is magnificent as the voice of the mother, who somehow seems both the absolute source of her daughter's pain, and the one person in or out of the world who cares enough to wish for its end.

Macbeth
Tramway, Glasgow
The Scotsman, 16 June 2012

For all its blood and horror, and its dark dealings with the supernatural, Shakespeare's *Macbeth* is often a tragedy that lacks a real sense of human sorrow. Its hero begins as a warrior, and ends as a monstrous tyrant; and often, only his victims truly touch the heart.

There's no chance of failing to feel overwhelmed by pity and sorrow, though, in the course of Alan Cumming's astonishing 100-minute performance of *Macbeth*, which won a standing ovation at its premiere performance in the Tramway last night. Set by directors John Tiffany and Andrew Goldberg in the bleak spaces of a psychiatric isolation unit, this *Macbeth* is performed by Cumming as a monologue, with occasional beautifully pitched interventions from Myra McFadyen and Ali Craig as two medical attendants. The shifting of this medieval story of war and rebellion into the antiseptic spaces of a twentieth-century asylum – all towering walls of bleached turquoise tiles, surveillance cameras and flickering screens – is undoubtedly disorientating: there's no sense of explanation here, and no systematic attempt to link the imagery of Macbeth's story to this new location.

Yet from the first moment of the show, when we see Cumming's small, vulnerable figure being gently stripped of his street clothes, we catch the sense that this is a study of almost intolerable human suffering; of a 'mind diseased', haunted by images or memories of terrible violence, and constantly fragmenting into different voices and perspectives, as Cumming plays witches and lords, the old king, Macbeth himself, and his lady. The action is punctuated by the surging, passionate music of Max Richter, full of sorrow and compassion, and often this Macbeth seems locked in a dialogue with different versions or images of himself, captured on the big screens that dominate Merle Hensel's memorable set.

There are moments when the intensity of Cumming's interaction with the text seems to flag a little, and the huge stage looks briefly like an arena too large for a single solo performer, however gifted. For most of the show's length, though, Cumming's grasp of the poetry is so complete, and his raw emotional immersion in it so total, that the audience remains absolutely gripped by the narrative; and unable to resist the sense of being pulled by the story towards the very brink of hell – but a hell redefined for our individualistic age as a place of infinite loneliness and sorrow, where inner demons dog and destroy us, and will not be defeated.

The Artist Man and the Mother Woman
Traverse, Edinburgh

Iron
Heart of Hawick, Hawick

Glasgow Girls
Citizens', Glasgow
The Scotsman, 8 November 2012

Motherhood and apple pie: it's the phrase we use to remind ourselves of the received wisdom about motherhood – that the mother-child bond is sacred, and that all mothers are kind and nurturing. Yet as Scotland's rare autumn season of female-dominated theatre reaches its climax, here are two terrific plays sent to remind us that in the real world, things are much more complex.

Morna Pearson's *The Artist Man and the Mother Woman* is Orla O'Loughlin's first main-stage production as artistic director of the Traverse, and if its theatrical power, cultural boldness, and dark, skewed poetry are harbingers of things to come, then we can expect exciting times at Scotland's new-play theatre. In this play, the apple pie of motherhood has decayed into something more like a rancid Forfar bridie, as timid thirty-something art teacher Geoffrey Buncher and his all-consuming mother Edie argue and bicker over their increasingly fraught domestic arrangements, in a small town somewhere in north-east Scotland.

Edie, played with showstopping power by Anne Lacey, is a strange monster of late-middle-aged sensuality and weird self-satisfaction, outwardly calm, yet demonic when thwarted; Geoffrey – an equally brilliant Garry Collins – is an innocent abroad, unacquainted with his own passions until the fateful day when he meets a pretty former pupil at the help desk in the local Sainsbury's.

What's most striking about this first full-length play by Pearson, though, is its stunning post-postmodern mix of grotesque comedy, heightened naturalism, lurid neo-Doric language, and sheer horror. It is one of the funniest plays the Traverse has staged in years, full of razor-sharp observation about a small-town world dominated by low-level domestic affluence, crime-obsessed junk media, and the battle for our allegiance between giant supermarket chains; the moment when Geoffrey returns from Lidl with random shopping that features a pair of pink earmuffs and a packet of bratwurst is a twenty-first-century comic gem.

Yet Pearson finally turns the tables on us with a savage reminder that what we are laughing at here is the stunting and destruction of human lives, in ways that can provoke a terrifying reaction – and the negotiation of this bold journey between comedy and nightmare has its rocky moments. In the end, though, O'Loughlin's production is a triumph of brave, high-risk writing, magnificent acting and luridly heightened domestic design. And as we're played out of the theatre to the strains of the late Michael Marra's 'Hermless', we have the feeling of having witnessed a vital staging post in Scotland's long journey towards greater self-knowledge, and a less sentimental view of its own inner life.

Rona Munro's acclaimed play *Iron* was first seen at the Traverse a decade ago, but here, too, the image of the mother as nurturer and saint is taken apart piece by piece, in a mighty two-hour dialogue between Fay, imprisoned for life for killing her husband in a domestic row, and her daughter Josie, now in her early twenties, who returns to visit her in prison after fifteen years of silence. Meanwhile, in the background, two prison officers, George and Sheila, patrol and reflect, bouncing back some of society's confused and disturbing attitudes to lifers like Fay.

At the heart of the play, though, is the figure of Fay herself, a passionate woman who is paying a terrible price for her crime. In this new touring production by young Borders-based company Firebrand – due at the Traverse next week – Fay is played by Blythe Duff with an intensity and depth that is simply heart-stopping. And director Richard Baron excels himself, in an austere but good-looking production that features fine music, light and sound; and immaculate supporting performances from both Irene Allan as the daughter who resembles her mother a little too much; and from Crawford Logan and Claire Dargo as the officers, as flawed and human as the woman they guard.

And meanwhile in Glasgow, seven mighty young women – mothers, if you like, of the city's emerging future – are celebrated in the explosive energy and political passion of the National Theatre of Scotland/Citizens' Theatre's new musical *Glasgow Girls*. Co-produced with a whole range of partners, the show is an exuberant piece of popular theatre, direct, unsubtle, and sometimes sentimental in its retelling of the story of seven Drumchapel schoolgirls who, half a decade ago, launched a now-legendary campaign against the brutal UK immigration regime that was dragging their asylum-seeker schoolmates from their homes in dawn raids, and taking them away to imprisonment and worse.

In its more self-indulgent moments, *Glasgow Girls* plays up shamelessly to some of Glasgow's favourite dreams about itself: battling grannies sing hymns to the city's tradition of radical resistance, and teenage asylum-seekers fall in love with its rugged beauty, as glimpsed from the balcony of a high-rise flat. Yet David Greig's script – and the score, by a team of five songwriters – also involves some moments of sharp political drama, comedy and excitement, as the girls travel to Edinburgh to lobby First Minister Jack McConnell. Natasha Gilmore's choreography takes the stuff of the story, and turns it into thrilling bursts of dance and movement. And at the core of the show stand the radiant young actors who have taken on the roles of the Glasgow Girls: each one full of the same youthful passion for the fight against injustice that inspired the girls in the first place, and is now flowing out over the footlights every night, into the hearts of new generation of Glasgow theatregoers.

The End of the World (For One Night Only)
Summerhall, Edinburgh
The Scotsman, 22 December 2012

The end of the world was going well, when I had to tiptoe away and leave it. Much longer than advertised, this one-off winter solstice event designed to celebrate the Mayan prediction of the apocalypse emerged as a startlingly rich sequence of music and theatre, played out over the whole range of spaces in the thrilling, rambling arts lab that is Summerhall. When I left, the whole audience of 150 or so was gathered in the main hall, listening to a terminal concert of three new short pieces by young classical composers Hanna Tuulikki, Colin Broom and Gareth Williams; Broom's piece 'Post-human', beautifully played by John Harris and the Red Note Ensemble, was weaving fragments of speech and surges of string music together to create a tremendously powerful meditation on the fragmentary evidence of our existence the human race may one day leave behind.

We had found our way there, though, in four or five smaller groups, each led in a different sequence through space after space, lecture theatre after library, where a cast of six actors – backed by a young ensemble of more than twenty – would each tell us a different story, set in Edinburgh on the day that the world ends. Shadowy figures fretted and moaned in corridors and courtyards, and in the rooms we heard stories of love and death, youth, old age, and mathematics, all interrupted by sudden oblivion, all written by Oliver Emanuel – from a concept by Gareth Williams – with the kind of sinewy linguistic strength that binds together all the best promenade shows. The whole event was directed by the Tron's Andy Arnold, with his usual bold, exploratory energy. And in the end, it seemed like an explosion not only of creative invention, but of beauty; never to be repeated, maybe, but full of the kind of promise that makes the end of the world seem unlikely, after all.

As 2013 dawned, though, what was happening in Scotland was not the end of the world – although some felt as if it was – but a dramatic and unexpected new chapter in the nation's story. In May 2011, the SNP government had been re-elected with an unprecedented overall majority in the proportionally elected Scottish Parliament at Holyrood, and that victory presented Scotland with an inevitable referendum on independence, a yes/no choice so stark and sudden that playwrights and other artists seemed, for a year or two, almost at a loss how to respond to it.

As the long referendum campaign rolled on, though – towards the Scottish Government's chosen date of 18 September 2014 – something strange began to happen at the grassroots of Scottish public life, first a rustle, then a roar of passionate debate about the nation's future, that drew crowds of hundreds to village halls and community centres across Scotland, and swept through social media, unleashing avalanches of comment, imagery, and argument. Not all of Scotland's artists and creators lined up on the 'Yes' side of the argument; but most of those with stated opinions did, and as the debate began to explode into much more varied and imaginative forms, and to move out of the hands of mainstream political parties, playwrights like Liz Lochhead, David Greig, Peter Arnott and Jo Clifford began to emerge as key figures in the 'Yes' campaign, taking part in the Yestival *tour of arts events that criss-crossed Scotland, and – in David Greig's case – creating a brilliant year-long series of 140-character Twitter plays in the form of an increasingly surreal dialogue between two characters, 'Yes' and 'No'.*

Major full-length plays about the referendum were thin on the ground: the upsurge of debate was so rapid that it lent itself more to instant responses, short-form cabaret and satire. But the Lyceum in Edinburgh bravely staged Tim Barrow's Union, *a play about the events surrounding the Act of Union of 1707; and the National Theatre of Scotland, under Laurie Sansom, stepped up magnificently to the referendum challenge, seizing the chance – in partnership with the Edinburgh International Festival and the National Theatre in London – to premiere Rona Munro's massive Scottish history cycle* The James Plays *at the Edinburgh Festival of 2014, and commissioning a special edition of its live-streamed Five Minute Theatre initiative,* The Great Yes, No, Don't Know Show, *co-curated by the great David MacLennan of A Play, a Pie and a Pint (from the 'No' side) and David Greig (from the 'Yes').*

David MacLennan died just a week before the Five Minute Theatre event, in June 2014, after a year-long struggle with motor neurone disease, but the short pieces he and David Greig wrote for the show, among hundreds of others from across Scotland, are among the finest theatre writing the referendum period produced. And on referendum night at the Traverse, Greig presented a script-in-hand stage version of his Yes/No Twitter plays, that had a packed audience roaring in recognition and delight.

2013

Ignition
Shetland
The Scotsman, 23 March 2013

Knitting, free-running, ballroom dancing, choral singing, songwriting – and telling your story to an enigmatic figure from Shetland legend, suddenly brought to life. These are just some of the means that have been used, over the past six months, to attract, seduce and encourage Shetlanders into involving themselves with the huge National Theatre of Scotland/Shetland Arts *Ignition* project, which reaches its climax this week, in a series of performances across the islands. And if the number of islanders cheerfully aware of the project is any guide, then it must have come close to fulfilling its aim of reaching every one of the archipelago's 23,000 inhabitants.

What's more interesting, though, is the question of what a project like *Ignition* can add, to the life of a community which already knows far more about convivial lifestyles and rich, shared cultural experience than most places in modern Britain. Originally conceived following the tragic death in a road accident of a young youth-theatre member, the project is supposed to reflect on the relationship between islanders and the car, in a place where the modern island economy is built around a huge petrol-driven oil boom. And it does feature some rich and remarkable car-related stories, an entire car body knitted by a 'mak and yak' group, and a gorgeous central character in the White Wife, exquisitely played by Manchester performance artist Lowri Evans, a legendary figure who haunts the long north-south road from Unst to Sumburgh, climbing into the passenger seats of lone male drivers, and asking searching questions.

In the end, though, what emerges from the complex and flexible project put together by director Wils Wilson and associate John Haswell is more like a rich reflection on the emotional texture of island life over the past generation, loosely structured around composer Hugh Nankivell's musical journey down 'da long road', which is itself enriched by original songs written by those he met along the way. As for the show at the end of the journey, it's impossible to make a final assessment of a strikingly diffuse and – in terms of creative synthesis – slightly hesitant and underpowered event, that takes each carload of audience members along a different route, and offers only a few glimpsed fragments from this huge project, including a gorgeous twenty-minute harbourside sequence featuring parkour around a wrecked Volvo, some beautiful, elegiac ballroom dancing across generations, and the voices of eighty- and ninety-year-old residents in an island care home, meticulously heard and recorded by choreographer Janice Parker.

Yet after we return from our night-time car journeys for the great Shetland ritual of tea in the hall, there's a moment when the youngsters and volunteers pouring the tea suddenly turn towards the band on stage, raise their voices, and form themselves into a choir, singing songs of their own composing, about Shetland, their home. It's one of those moments of transformation that makes a project like *Ignition* just slightly magical, and whose impact on the life of the islands, and on the next generation of Shetlanders, is both impossible to measure, and potentially limitless.

Ane Satyre of the Thrie Estaitis
Linlithgow Palace
The Scotsman, 8 June 2013

If there is one golden rule in the world of Scottish theatre, it is never, ever to underestimate the range, the depth, the vividness, the significance or the staying power of Sir David Lyndsay's great mid-sixteenth-century morality play, *Ane Satyre of the Thrie Estaitis*. Although it was written partly for performance at the court of King James V, by a man who was a courtier as well as a poet, its political boldness is breathtaking. It challenges the corrupt power of the church, the landlords and the burgesses who run Scotland; and it imagines a new political settlement, in which John Commonweal – the Common Man – is admitted into parliament, while the wealthy are brought back under the rule of law, and the corrupt drummed out of office.

So now, this mighty piece of early Renaissance political drama has been revived, in a new complete five-hour text put together by a team of academics working with Historic Scotland, and it is being staged, this weekend, in the stunning outdoor setting of Linlithgow Peel, with the great east wall of the palace standing against the sky as backdrop. The audience sits on the grass in a little, intimate oval arena ten yards across, with a main stage at the west end, and the frolics begin, as various cheerful vices set about tempting James Mackenzie's wide-eyed young king away from the ways of wisdom, and into the arms of Ruth Milnes' gorgeous Lady Sensualitie.

In the course of its rich, long and playfully indulgent five hours, Lyndsay's play ranges from detailed contemporary social satire – full of long litanies of complaint about sharp trading and dodgy practices – to a kind of political and religious poetry that seems almost Miltonian in reach, as Tam Dean Burn's mighty, winged Divine Correction enters the fray – flanked by Veritie, Chastitie and Gude Counsell – to win the young king back to virtue. Sometimes, Lyndsay's obsession with the burning need for religious reformation makes the play seem like a voice from another world; yet seconds later, its complaints about an arrogant elite looting the nation's wealth – superbly spoken by Keith Fleming as John Commonweal – seem as if they could have been written yesterday.

And although Gregory Thompson's production is clad in traditional medieval costume, and sometimes seems a shade under-rehearsed as the forty-strong cast busk their way through the vast text, in the end there's no denying the passion and understanding with which this all-star company of Scottish actors – including a live band, led by musical director John Kielty – seem to have taken the full political meaning of the play to their hearts, and made it their own. For in the end, in whatever form, *The Thrie Estaitis* remains what it always was: a play about good governance written in and for Scotland, but so powerful in its understanding of what good governance is, that it transcends not only the five centuries since Lyndsay was born, but also the place where it was made, to take its place in the canon of great European drama about the spirit of political reform itself – a spirit that is still with us today, wherever power is abused, and the ordinary citizen excluded from the councils of state.

Ciara
Traverse, Edinburgh
The Scotsman, 8 August 2013

Mother Glasgow, the dear green place. Yet as everyone who knows and loves the city can tell you, there's an edge to Glasgow's famous warmth, and to its chatty curiosity about strangers. For as David Harrower's heroine Ciara observes, in the brilliant new solo play that bears her name, this is still a migrant city, full of competing tribes; a place where law and civic virtue can only take you so far, where family and group loyalties often matter more, and where a certain kind of crime is woven into the fabric of the city's self-image.

So Ciara – played with magnificent passion, wit and quiet glamour by Blythe Duff, once the female star of the Glasgow cop show *Taggart* – is a gallery owner, a patron of the arts; we meet her in the space that will be her new warehouse gallery. Yet her wealth comes, as she well knows, from the lifetime of organised crime pursued first by her father, Mick – 'a great man', as drunks in pubs still tell her – and then by her husband, and she speaks to us now not because she thinks we will warm to her, after hearing her story, but because the pain and contradictions of her life have reached a point where they must be told.

So in a brief hour or so of wry humour, pure tragedy, and utterly compelling lyrical narrative – all immaculately directed by Traverse artistic director Orla O'Loughlin –

Ciara offers us a glimpse of what it is to live a life where home and family are traditionally prized, but where, in the end, there is no law but force, and money, and the striking of the deal. She has to live with the truth that, as Mick's daughter, she has been traded like a commodity all her life, just as she trades in artists' lives now; and that even her brief, sweet, flaring midlife love for the artist Torrance, the crisis that makes her speak, was in some sense set up by the powerful men around her.

There's something about gender here, and something about Glasgow – but also something about civilisation and law itself, its fragility, its myths, its endless vulnerability. In that sense, *Ciara* makes a vital companion piece to David Greig's *The Events*, also playing at the Traverse. And it's both moving and fascinating to see how these two great contemporary Scottish playwrights are taking very different routes through the civilisational endgames of our time, Greig working on a global and international canvas, Harrower delving ever deeper into the reality and everyday lies of life in Scotland now, to find the universal truths that lie buried there.

Dark Road
Royal Lyceum, Edinburgh
The Scotsman, 30 September 2013

It's Edinburgh, it's 1988, and there's been a murder. Indeed there have been four, horrible, ritualistic murders, of young girls in their teens. And ambitious young Detective Constable Isobel McArthur is on the case, determined – with her boss 'Black' Fergus McLintock, and her colleague and lover Frank Bowman – to find the killer, and put him away for life.

That's the story that forms the backdrop to *Dark Road*, the first-ever stage play by Edinburgh's renowned crime writer

Ian Rankin, co-written with – and directed by – the Royal Lyceum's artistic director, Mark Thomson, and the omens were good, as an excited audience gathered at the Lyceum for Saturday's premiere performance. The play itself is set in the present, when McArthur – twenty-five years on, once Scotland's first woman Chief Constable, and now facing retirement – finds herself beset by doubts about the conviction of the alleged murderer, Alfred Chalmers. The scene seems set for a fine, dark two-and-a-half-hours of classy genre fiction in the style pioneered by television cop shows from *Prime Suspect* to *The Killing*, featuring an impressive cast led by the wonderful Maureen Beattie as McArthur, with Robert Gwilym as Frank, and a fine Sara Vickers as McArthur's teenage daughter, Alexandra.

So how to account, then, for the slow-motion car crash of theatrical bad taste, chaotic plotting, and sheer, pointless nastiness that eventually overtakes one of Scottish theatre's most promising recent projects? The first sign of trouble comes with the set, a great concrete-look revolve – often enlivened by huge projected images of the dead girls – that jolts us from home to office to prison cell in the most literal manner, as if the play had given up early on the idea of creating a cop show for theatre, and was bent on mimicking the narrative structure of a television series, gussied up with the odd explosion of superficial 'theatricality'.

And from that moment on, problems of genre seem to dog the show, as it lurches from the noirish heightened naturalism of good twenty-first-century television into a series of risible and grotesque dream sequences in which McArthur confronts the killer in her own living room, and then – towards the end – dives into an orgy of half-baked onstage violence that seems more like black farce than anything else. The play also boasts two staggeringly silly late plot twists, one of which undermines the whole preceding narrative;

and in the last twenty minutes, it completely blows its own credentials as a potentially interesting drama, to become a sickening display of sadism for its own sake.

I suppose the final scenes of *Dark Road* might become a cult hit among those who enjoy horror in all its forms, including terrible dialogue and plenty of blood, and it can't be said too clearly that Thomson's fine cast, including Philip Whitchurch as Chalmers, do all they can with the characters around whom the story is built. In terms of narrative and style, though, this show gradually fades into a silly, sensational mess, with nothing to say, and a peculiarly graceless way of saying it. Time to lower the curtain, and move on.

In Time o' Strife
Pathhead Hall, Kirkcaldy
The Scotsman, 7 October 2013

A short quote from miner and playwright Joe Corrie, on the cover of the playtext, says what is most important about his great play *In Time o' Strife*, written in the Fife coalfield in 1926, the year of the General Strike: 'I must write about the world I know best,' he wrote, 'the world of the working man and woman, their trials, loves, hates, suspicions, generosities and loyalties. I feel that it's a contribution – I am doing what I know best, for the class that needs it now.'

The question of why Corrie's play has had only three professional productions in Scotland in almost ninety years – one in John McGrath's 7:84 *Clydebuilt* season of 1982, another soon after, and now this new National Theatre of Scotland production – remains a troubling one. Yet although he was always wary of having his work adapted, it's difficult to imagine that Corrie would not be delighted by the passion, the theatrical energy and the profound feeling for

Scotland's working-class history that informs this new music theatre version by director and designer Graham McLaren, staged in an old church hall at Pathhead in Kirkcaldy, and interwoven with many of Corrie's powerful poems, as well as music and songs by composer Michael John McCarthy and a three-piece band.

Written to raise money for strikers' soup kitchens, *In Time o' Strife* is a big, full-blooded domestic drama, strikingly similar in style to Sean O'Casey's great Dublin plays of the same period. It tells the story of middle-aged miner Jock Smith and his family, of their neighbours, and of young Jenny Smith's fiancé Wull Baxter, an ambitious young man who becomes a strike-breaker, to Jenny's despair. What's perhaps most impressive about the play, apart from its powerful narrative drive, is its stubborn complexity: there's hardly a man in the cast who does not harbour some degree of doubt about the strike and the terrible intensification of hardship it brings, often to the point of starvation.

Perhaps the only fault of McLaren's production is that there's something in its atmosphere – its references via a screen to the miners' strike of the 1980s, the Clash-like stridency of some of the music, and the decision to end with a fierce singing of 'The Red Flag' – that slightly bypasses that subtlety; the play's truthfulness about the double-edged quality of the strike weapon was courageous in 1926, and should be fully honoured now. What McLaren's production unleashes, though – in a small hall perfectly laid out and lit to recall an old living-room party or church-hall social – is a memorably angry, vivid and theatrical retelling of a vital story in Scottish history, with fiercely choreographed dance interludes by Imogen Knight, and a range of fine performances, notably from Ewan Stewart, Anita Vettesse and Hannah Donaldson as the Smiths and their oldest daughter. It's an exhilarating experience, this *In Time o'*

Strife, and not to be missed. Yet it also leaves behind a faint feeling of shame, that Scottish society once produced remarkable working-class writers like Corrie, with such a story to tell, and then allowed them to come so close to being completely forgotten.

2014

War Horse
Festival Theatre, Edinburgh
The Scotsman, 23 January 2014

If you took a deep breath, and stood a long way back from the mighty drama and spectacle of the National Theatre of Great Britain's *War Horse* – at the Festival Theatre until 15 February – then you might, for a moment or two, raise questions about its message and meaning. It's a passionate reiteration – one among thousands – of England's great, endless mourning for its lost rural past, an imagined innocence finally blown to pieces in the mud and blood of Flanders. And then there's something deeper, perhaps: a story for our time about how human and animal wellbeing are somehow bound together, and can never be fully separated.

You won't want to stand back, however, nor will you be able to. For what directors Marianne Elliott and Tom Morris have made of Michael Morpurgo's story – together with the Handspring Puppet Company, and perhaps the most powerful, subtle and beautiful stage animals ever seen – is a drama of peace and war so vast in its reach, so gripping in its dramatic structure, and so breathtaking in its physical evocation of the pure horror of the western front, that it's literally impossible to look away from the stage, through two hours and twenty minutes of heart-shaking theatre. Every element of the art form comes together in a flash of brilliance to tell the story of young Albert Narracott and his horse Joey, a beautiful hunter, sent off to the front in 1914 – from the lighting, the sound, and the mighty horses themselves, to the music, great surging English folk songs magnificently sung by the company, with Songman Bob Fox. And when one of the lead horses finally collapses in death, there's a second of utter hush, while we see the three puppeteers rise out of the body, and back away like a departing soul; in one of many moments of pure theatrical greatness, in this wholly unforgettable show.

Union
Royal Lyceum, Edinburgh
The Scotsman, 29 March 2014

The time is the winter of 1706/1707, and in Edinburgh and London, the grandees of Scotland are drinking, vomiting, whoring, arguing and swearing their way through the negotiations which will seal the Union between England and Scotland. Their costumes glow with colour, their wigs are as picturesque as they are grubby-looking, and their morals are grubbier still, as they pocket bagfuls of English gold; yet their political skill is not negligible, particularly in the case of Liam Brennan's towering Duke of Queensberry. And in Mark Thomson's visually thrilling production of Tim Barrow's new play *Union*, these flawed men are surrounded by a surging symphony of images conjuring up taverns and palaces, rainy nights and drunken days, all projected – in Andrzej Goulding's memorable design – on to whirling blank walls, and accompanied by Philip Pinsky's insistent and haunting harpsichord music, always played a notch too loud for comfort.

Yet no description of this memorably rowdy and ambitious play can even begin to convey the extraordinary mixture of brilliance and incoherence it contains, the dizzying swoops from crass caricature and stereotype to sudden lyrical beauty. Somewhere at the core of *Union*, there is a play about what happens when things that should be priceless are sold for hard cash. The play's twin stories involve the love affair between passionate young poet Allan Ramsay and a prostitute called Grace, who sells herself for the money she needs to live; and the parallel sell-off of Scotland's sovereignty, as the people starve, and Scotland's leaders strike a deal which will open up our economy to English markets, and an age of empire.

This could have been, in other words, a powerful and telling historical drama about a timeless conflict between what is right and self-respecting on one hand, and what is necessary for survival on the other. Instead, though, it emerges as a fierce giant puppet show with flashes of seriousness, and long detours into strange tales like the grotesque history of Queen Anne's childless madness. It's significant that the strongest and most interesting scenes are the ones in the Scottish Parliament itself; the weakest are those set in England, where the English negotiators are portrayed as absurd fops, and the Scots as a bunch of whisky-toping drunks with uncivilised manners. Josh Whitelaw yells his way through the role of Allan Ramsay, although he sometimes modulates to a touching lyricism; Sally Reid is subtle and heartbreaking as Grace the whore; and Liam Brennan's unforgettable Queensberry is matched by Tony Cownie's sinister Lord Stair, and Keith Fleming's chilling English spymaster, Robert Harley.

In the end, the best efforts of Mark Thomson's ten-strong cast go for less than they should have done, in a play that is a full twenty minutes too long, and contains whole tracts of material that should have been saved for another day. Yet Tim Barrow's first-ever full-length play approaches the vivid history behind the choice Scotland now faces with such vigour and boldness, and such powerful flashes of poetry and insight, that everyone in Scotland who cares about the nation's future should see it – and then argue about it, far into the night.

The Great Yes, No, Don't Know Five Minute Theatre Show
National Theatre of Scotland
Online
The Scotsman, 28 June 2014

It's five o'clock on Monday afternoon. The downstairs the-atre at Òran Mór falls silent, Neil Murray of the National Theatre of Scotland makes a live introduction, and then we're off on a twenty-four-hour rollercoaster ride around Scotland and beyond, peering into our laptops, watching 180 tiny five-minute plays live-streamed from beaches and living rooms and parks and halls all the way from Dumfries to Caithness, and also from Istanbul, Paris and East Timor, all inspired by the 'Yes, No, Don't Know' theme that cur-rently dominates Scottish life.

At 'hubs' like Òran Mór – and there are others in Aberdeen, Inverness, Dumfries and Edinburgh – audiences can watch some shows being performed live; here in Glasgow, the mood is rich with mourning for David MacLennan of A Play, a Pie and a Pint, who – before his death just over a week ago – co-curated this edition of Five Minute Theatre with David Greig, and left behind a series of powerful short plays of his own, presented here by a terrific scratch team of actors. Andy Clark's beautiful performance of David Greig's final *Letter to David* will become one of the key perform-ances of the night: a reminder of the love that can survive the differences thrown up by the referendum campaign – MacLennan was a 'No' man, Greig is a 'Yes'.

Elsewhere, though, the mood is almost dizzyingly varied, as groups of schoolchildren mourn what looks like a bitter fall-out between parents, and ordinary citizens wrestle with the 'disconnect' between the rhetoric of politicians and the struggles of everyday life. There's one quietly stunning filmed piece by Stephanie McCormack, in which a woman watches Alex Salmond's fine keynote speech to the SNP conference while feeding her dog and worrying about her bills. Some superbly witty primary-school students at Craigowl Primary offer a fine Dundee take on the question, as Oor Wullie sets out to interview all the Broons about their referendum views; back at Òran Mór, ex-MSP turned cabaret star Rosie Kane performs Jen Muir's *Proud Backward Glance from Independence Day 2024*, and the resident company raise the roof with David Greig's short indecision rock opera, *We're Not Sure*.

And are there conclusions? Maybe a few. The first is that three years on from its first edition, Five Minute Theatre needs to think harder about how it presents itself to the world. There's no point in running 'hubs' where audiences can only see 'their own' shows, and get no sense of the wider event, and since online information remains scanty, perhaps the whole event needs a live online presenter, giving a one-sentence introduction to each show, its location and origin. And it certainly isn't right for the National Theatre of Scotland to punctuate this most democratic of shows with long, flashy trailers for forthcoming productions.

In terms of content, though, *The Great Yes, No, Don't Know Show* is as variable and rich as ever. The endless circling around the 'divorce' metaphor produces some predictably dire results, as well as one brilliant essay in separation, filmed with megaphones at Carter Bar. Three things finally emerge, though, that I have heard nowhere else in our independence debate. The first is something like a genuine grassroots 'No' voice, not impressed with our current UK leaders, but intensely wary of ideological nationalism. The second – in a recurring image – is a genuine fear of a UK ruled by 'Prime Minister Farage'. And the third is the voice of deep political wisdom represented by the show's two co-curators themselves: MacLennan's farewell blast, *On Our Own* – a chorale for a young socialist Green MSP and three 'pragmatic' SNP colleagues – contains perhaps the sharpest political commentary of the night. As David Greig himself puts it, in the final lines of his *Letter to David*, 'If I vote "Yes" on 18 September, I'll be voting for a country you gave me.' And in this endlessly diverse referendum debate, that's perhaps the biggest paradox of all.

The James Plays
James I: The Key Will Keep the Lock
James II: Day of the Innocents
James III: The True Mirror
Festival Theatre, Edinburgh
The Scotsman, 12 August 2014

For the huge theatrical event that is the launch of *The James Plays* – the most ambitious project ever undertaken by the National Theatre of Scotland, and its first-ever co-production with the National Theatre in London – the auditorium at the Festival Theatre has been turned into a giant arena, with part of the packed audience sitting in tiers behind the stage. Close to centre-stage, in John Bausor's design, stands a mighty sword many metres high, its blade half-buried in the ground; and it's with a classic play about kingship, and the threat of violence that inevitably underpinned medieval kingly power, that the action begins, in Rona Munro's hugely ambitious trilogy about the reigns of James I, James II and James III.

It's not Shakespeare's *Henry IV*, with its mighty poetry, and profound political commitment to the ideal of monarchy, but *James I* is a well-crafted, fast-moving and intelligent drama about a young king who spent twenty years in prison in England, and who returns to Scotland, in his late twenties, to try to forge his country into a modern state. The story of young James's return, his marriage, and his mighty struggle to assert his authority, is told with fluency and energy, touching on differing Scottish and English attitudes to kingship, as well as on the traditional unruliness of the great Scottish families.

At the centre of the story stands a group of memorable characters, from James McArdle's powerful and moving young King – a poet compelled to take up the sword – to his English wife Joan, their servant Meg, and the terrifying matriarch of the rebellious Murdoch Stewart clan, played with flair and cruelty by the great Blythe Duff. And the play is supported from the outset by Laurie Sansom's hugely impressive and brilliantly choreographed production, in which an ensemble cast of twenty swirl across the stage, evoking banquets and battles, wedding nights and sessions of parliament, in a tense and gripping pageant of essential Scottish history.

If there are cheers at the end of *James I*, though, things take a more difficult turn in the first act of *James II*, a murky dream-play built around the recurring nightmares of the young King James II, crowned king at the age of six following his father's brutal assassination. Often played by a ghost-like child puppet, as well as by an impressive Andrew Rothney, this king seems close to madness; but he survives to marry a brave young French queen played by a sweet and witty Stephanie Hyam. *James II*, though, seems like a play that never quite finds its centre: whether it lies in James's battle with his own nightmares, in the growing rebellion of the Douglas clan, or – as the final scenes suggest – in the tragedy of James's adoring friend William Douglas, bullied son and frustrated lover, played by Mark Rowley with a text-gulping intensity that commands attention, but does not fully repay it.

And then, with a final shift of style, it's on to *James III*, a historic tragicomedy in the deliberately anachronistic style pioneered by plays like *The Lion in Winter*, and completely dominated by Sofie Gråbøl's terrific, commanding performance as Margaret of Denmark, wife to Jamie Sives's terrifyingly mercurial and unpredictable James III. This James is a bisexual joker who dislikes the labour of kingship so much that he actively wishes England would invade and take over; while his queen pores over the national accounts, and conducts the business of government. Set in a time of relative plenty, *James III* features touches of modern dress, and plenty of cheerful partying between scenes. Without the steely, witty seriousness of Gråbøl's central performance, though, its relentless anachronisms and deliberately crude language would become a shade wearying, long before this eight-hour theatrical marathon reaches its end.

So what does it all amount to, this mighty trilogy in which so much time, cash and hope has been invested? On one hand, it offers an impressive vindication of the directing skills of the National Theatre of Scotland's artistic director, Laurie Sansom. This is the first show he has staged himself, since he took on the huge task of running Scotland's national theatre-without-walls, and the fluency and intelligence with which he drives his huge cast through these three very different stories is as formidable as it is entertaining.

The plays, though, are a mixed achievement, full of interesting incidents and insights – and with a commendable emphasis on the women of the royal household – but often depressingly flat and banal in language, written in a version of crude, everyday street Scots that provokes endless easy laughs from the audience, so incongruous does it seem.

As for the politics of *The James Plays*, in the run-up to 18 September – well, they sometimes grasp the central truth that relations with England always dominate Scotland's fate; and there is a final plea for courage, in the face of an unknowable future. From the outset, though, the plays are full of the kinds of patronising cliché about Scotland that some hoped, a generation ago, never to see on Scottish stages again: all that predictable nonsense about how Scotland is cold, and barren, and very small, a place with no apple trees, swathed in smoky darkness, and, above all, uniquely rough, violent and ungovernable – this in plays set at a time when England itself was riven by murderous civil war.

And if you want to understand why Scotland is likely to vote 'No' on 18 September, then all you need do is listen to the obliging laughter with which the Festival audience responds to every one of these old chestnuts, and to Queen Margaret's amazing final assertion that Scotland is a nation with 'fuck-all except attitude'. Scotland, it seems, is a nation still willing to see itself mainly through the eyes of contemptuous others; and for all its ambition, and the sheer brilliance of its staging, the *James* trilogy never achieves the levels of vision and coherence that might begin to change all that.

The Yes/No Plays
Traverse, Edinburgh
The Scotsman, 20 September 2014

Scotland's referendum bubble is well and truly burst now, lying like a crushed balloon in the gutters of the capital. While it lasted, though, it was a shining, magical thing, full of rainbow colours. And of all the words and images that have emerged from it over the last two years, there has been nothing finer than David Greig's Twitter series of miniature *Yes/No Plays*, tiny dramatic fragments in 140 characters, gathered together, this week, for two historic performances at the Traverse, on referendum day.

What's striking about *The Yes/No Plays* – apart from the slightly surreal brilliance of the writing – is that although Greig is a high-profile 'Yes' supporter, the plays themselves say nothing unsubtle about the referendum debate. In building up a dialogue between two voices – a live-in pair called Yes and No, played brilliantly by Frances Thorburn and Richard Clements – it has its fun at the expense of both campaigns and delves much deeper into the referendum's complex undercurrents of hope, possibility, fear, and desire.

And the plays also, perhaps surprisingly, make brilliant and hilariously funny live theatre, at least when performed by a superb six-strong Traverse cast, directed by Greig himself, and deftly divided into sequences punctuated by exquisite light-touch clàrsach music. This is a sad old weekend for many in Scotland. But if I had to be anywhere, during the last few hours of our great referendum debate, then I'm delighted to have been at the Traverse, revelling in David Greig's wit, humanity, and absolute sympathy for all sides of the question.

Hamlet
Citizens', Glasgow
The Scotsman, 27 September 2014

The time seems to be the 1960s, or perhaps the early 1970s. When Brian Ferguson's nervy, furious Hamlet wants to take notes about the evil he sees around him, he uses an old-fashioned BBC-style portable tape recorder, slung over his shoulder. Around the back of the stage sit more big reel-to-reel recorders, like the equipment in a pre-internet government surveillance centre; but in Tom Piper's set and Nikola Kodjabashia's sound design, there's also a hint of an old radiophonic workshop, with musical instruments lying around to be picked up and played by cast members, occasional blasts of electronic sound, voices switching into amplification and out again.

And at one level, the references to this period in social history make perfect sense. Ever since the 1960s – as family breakdown and divorce have become more widespread across the west – directors have been casting Hamlet as a furious teenage boy appalled by his mother's new relationship; very often, these sulky teenage princes completely unbalance the staging of a play which is not only about family and psychology, but also about kingship, and the ruin of a state.

Now, though, here comes a production, from Dominic Hill and the Citizens' Theatre, that goes so boldly and directly for the family drama at the heart of Shakespeare's play – even setting many of its scenes in an improvised palace living room with sofa and standard lamp – that it has the paradoxical effect of pulling the whole drama back into focus, in thrilling and fascinating style.

The secret of the production's success is twofold. First, instead of simply assuming our sympathy for Hamlet's rage and disgust, it concentrates fiercely on him, pulling apart and examining his horror to a depth that makes us fully aware of Hamlet's weaknesses, but also increasingly, poignantly conscious of his courage, intelligence and honesty. It's an interpretation that places a huge weight on the shoulders of Brian Ferguson's frail-looking, bespectacled Hamlet, but he rises to the challenge with terrific emotional nerve, shaping Hamlet's series of mighty soliloquies into fierce, dynamic waymarks on an unforgettable inner journey.

And then secondly, by linking the action to a time when the rebellion of youth itself had huge political resonances, the production offers a powerful insight into the enduring significance of Hamlet's revolt, not only against his mother and uncle, but also – at a deeper level – against the stern instruction of his father's spirit to complete an ancient ritual of revenge. The whole nine-strong cast of Hill's production seem absolutely at one with the picture painted by the production, with Peter Guinness as a suave and tormented Claudius, and Cliff Burnett as a strange, effete and bullying Polonius, in particularly impressive form.

And when Meghan Tyler's clever, complex and beautiful Ophelia transforms her 'mad scene' by coming to the microphone and roaring out her rage, grief, agony and sexual damage like some young Janis Joplin caught between blues and death metal, this *Hamlet* reaches a level of nerve-wrenching intensity and tragedy rarely achieved in more conventionally poetic productions; an intensity well earned by Brian Ferguson's brave and groundbreaking central performance, and by a company who richly deserved their first-night standing ovation.

The Voice Thief
Summerhall, Edinburgh
The Scotsman, 10 November 2014

If you're looking for a company with the nerve to take theatre for older children into the dark places of the mind and heart, then the work of Catherine Wheels – based in Musselburgh, acclaimed on the international stage – is for you. Last year, artists Shona Reppe and Andy Manley, with Catherine Wheels, produced the memorable installation-show *Huff*, a version of *The Three Little Pigs* that also touched on the horror of war.

386

And now, in the labyrinthine basements of Summerhall, the Catherine Wheels team – led by artistic director Gill Robertson – have created a promenade show that deals with nothing less than the chill hand of oppressive patriarchal power, robbing girls and young women of their voices, their anger, their individuality. Co-created by Robertson with designer Karen Tennant and performer Ian Cameron, *The Voice Thief* is a seventy-minute experience that occasionally struggles to match the strength of its central idea, as the audience are invited by a pair of spooky twin girl retainers into MIEVH, The Mackenzie Institute for the Encouragement of Vocal Harmony.

At first, all is sweetness and light. Cameron's Dr Mackenzie is an endearing, singing Willie Wonka figure in a white coat and explosive wig, the walls lined with reassuring pictures of the celebrity speakers he has helped; and for rather too long – almost thirty-five minutes – we are led through a series of experiences that seem more like design ideas than dynamic contributions to the narrative, as we're invited to don masks, pass through a human car wash, lie down in a soothing pink tent, and finally settle in a lecture theatre for an explanation of the doctor's work.

It's at this point, though, that the story darkens, as the doctor's lovely daughter Beatrice, beautifully played by Jenny Hulse, begins to rebel against his increasingly controlling instructions, and to lead us into her own magical cave of secretly saved voices. The power of the metaphor in this final sequence is almost overwhelming, as Beatrice searches for the beautiful voice of her dead mother, and strives to make her escape. And if the slightly predictable text often seems to have been added as an afterthought to the rest of the drama, the central idea is magnificently realised both in Tennent's superb design for the laboratory at the heart of Mackenzie's darkness, and in Danny Krass's unforgettable soundscape, which captures the full horror of oppression through a sub-tle symphony of half-muffled squeals and brief soaring notes, in a show that should be irrelevant to the world of 2014, but sadly still seems both timely and necessary.

The referendum result, when it came, was a 'No', although not by the overwhelming margin for which the British mainstream parties had hoped; but oddly, instead of collapsing in defeat, the grassroots debate about the possibility of a different future seemed to roar on regardless, towards the SNP landslide in the UK general election of 2015. In theatre, it was a strange time of rich achievement, and funding still reasonably well sustained, combined with a mood of deep anxiety among creative theatremakers.

In the autumn of 2014, the National Theatre of Scotland's James Plays *took London by storm; yet a few months later, The Arches in Glasgow – one of the venues which had driven the rapid evolution of Scottish theatre over the last twenty-five years – was abruptly closed down by the police and Glasgow Licensing Board, in a move that seemed to mark the end of the city's great thirty-year age of experimentation in finding new creative uses for old industrial spaces. Dominic Hill's Citizens' Theatre went from strength to strength, in the company's seventieth year, but faced a massive fundraising challenge to save the fabric of one of Scotland's best-loved theatres. New money was made available for Scotland's Highland Touring Network, and for organisations like Comar, the new Mull-based umbrella company that embraces Mull Theatre – but key creative staff were threatened with redundancy, triggering a wave of protest on the island. And in Edinburgh, Mark Thomson's Lyceum Company began its fiftieth birthday year with one of the finest spring seasons in the company's history, featuring magnificent productions of Brian Friel's* Faith Healer, *Brecht's* The Caucasian Chalk Circle, *and Goldoni's* The Venetian Twins *– only to find itself, alongside the Traverse, facing a deep cut in its Creative Scotland* *grant; Thomson announced that he would leave the Lyceum in the summer of 2016, after fourteen years.*

Then in July 2015, it was announced that the National Theatre of Scotland's Executive Producer, Neil Murray, and its Associate Director, Graham McLaren, would move on in 2016 to become joint directors of Ireland's national theatre, the Abbey in Dublin. The appointment was both a huge accolade for Scotland's new national theatre, and also a profound challenge, given the key role Murray, in particular, had played at the NTS since its first months. And as the year in Scottish theatre unfolded – with new productions of John McGrath's The Cheviot, the Stag and the Black, Black Oil *from 1973 and Jo Clifford's* Great Expectations *from 1988, and a mighty new adaptation of Alasdair Gray's 1981 novel* Lanark *– it became clear that this was a time of relatively few new plays, but of great revivals and adaptations, of coming to terms with the recent literary and theatrical past in Scotland and beyond, and of drawing rich contemporary inspiration from it.*

2015

To Kill a Mockingbird
Theatre Royal, Glasgow
The Scotsman, 9 February 2015

Tears, cheers, and a completely spontaneous standing ovation; it's rare to see that kind of response at an ordinary Saturday matinée in Glasgow. Yet after two hours and twenty minutes of passionate theatre, in this new staging of *To Kill a Mockingbird* first seen at the Open Air Theatre, Regent's Park, there was no holding the Theatre Royal audience, as they cheered this mighty show on its way to Edinburgh this week, and Aberdeen next.

For a book first published fifty-five years ago – and set twenty-five years earlier, in the hot southern summer of 1935 – what was long thought to be Harper Lee's only novel has a remarkable way of still hitting the headlines: only this week, it was announced that HarperCollins are about to publish the only other novel ever written by Lee, now a frail eighty-eight-year-old.

Yet it only takes a few moments, in Timothy Sheader's beautiful, inventive production, for his fine sixteen-strong company – including three alternating teams of spellbindingly powerful child actors – to demonstrate exactly why this terrific story of the heroine and narrator, Scout, her brother Jem, and above all their widowed father Atticus Finch, a liberal lawyer in a racially divided southern town, occupies such a special place in the hearts and minds of readers. The adult cast enter, carrying copies of the book, and, at first, they read from it in their own British voices, Scottish or northern, posh or gritty. Then Phil King's guitar music starts up, the children appear, and the actors simply merge into the narrative, like any readers becoming caught up in the world it creates.

And from there on, the story gathers speed like a mighty steam train, until it reaches its famous climax in the day-long trial of local black man Tom Robinson, for the alleged rape of a poor white girl. Daniel Betts is quietly magnificent as Atticus, blessed with the special magic that comes to those who cannot live with themselves unless they stand for what is right. And in the end, this magnificent story of civic courage in hard times still speaks uncomfortable truths about the links between power unjustly held, by force and denial, and other kinds of abuse, economic, physical and sexual. The standing ovation was well earned. But the biggest cheer of all came when the company picked up their battered copies of the book and held them high, in a tribute to the enduring power of the right words, at the right time, to change heart and minds for good.

The Slab Boys
Citizens', Glasgow
The Scotsman, 16 February 2015

2015 is the seventieth anniversary year of the Citizens' Theatre Company, and it opened in glittering style, on Saturday night, with the premiere performance of the new Citizens' production of John Byrne's *The Slab Boys*. With a vintage rock'n'roll band playing in the foyer, both the playwright and the First Minister in attendance, and the entire theatre staff dressed up in superb fifties style, the Citizens' seemed set for a brilliant celebration of Byrne's great comedy, first seen at the Traverse in 1978, but set two decades before that, in the Slab Room of Stobo's carpet factory, Paisley, in the winter of 1957.

Yet for all its simple, classic structure and workplace setting – it covers a single day, and takes place entirely in the Slab Room, meticulously realised here in John Byrne's own magnificent set – *The Slab Boys* is a glitteringly complex piece of drama, full not only of hidden darknesses, and searing insights into the casual bigotry of post-war Scottish life, but of a language – a multilayered, hyperreal version of west of Scotland vernacular – that itself represents the human capacity for humour, irony, and self-reinvention that is the play's theme. It therefore demands to be played like Shakespeare, every word given its full meaning and rhythm, each speech offered to the audience like a tiny aria.

And the truth about David Hayman's new staging, thirty-seven years on, is that, like every other I have seen, it offers a tantalising mix of actors who understand this basic demand of Byrne's great text, and actors who think they are dealing in some kind of naturalism. This time round, the glittering stars are Jamie Quinn as slab boy Spanky, Scott Fletcher as the much-bullied Hector, and a fabulously theatrical Kathryn Howden as the tea lady Sadie; elsewhere – even in Sammy Hayman's pleasingly dangerous Phil McCann – the acting is often more introverted, the comic rhythm less secure.

In the end, this production gets away with it: the cast begin to overcome their first-half nerves, the pacing and rhythm grow more confident, the laughs come thick and fast. Frankly, though, it would be good, after nearly forty years, to see at least one revival of *The Slab Boys* that just gets this great play right first time, without excuse or apology. By the time it reaches Edinburgh next month, this may be the greatest *Slab Boys* ever seen. But at the moment, despite its occasional brilliance, it misses that mark in ways that seem unnecessary, and therefore all the more frustrating.

The Caucasian Chalk Circle
Royal Lyceum, Edinburgh
The Scotsman, 23 February 2015

Theatre. It's rough, it's often pretentious, and it's always a more risky bet than any form of screen entertainment. There are moments, though, when a play and a company come together in such an explosion of energy and passion that everyone who experiences it learns all over again, with every cell of their bodies, why people make live theatre, and always will. The new Royal Lyceum version of Brecht's *Caucasian Chalk Circle* – written in 1944, now revived in a brilliant production by artistic director Mark Thomson – marks one of those moments, and everyone with a heartbeat should strive to see it, or be poorer for missing it.

The timeliness of the story is what seizes the attention first. The play famously begins with a village debate about land ownership, which is then put on pause while the local people perform a play based on a traditional story about justice – its usual failures, and one magic moment when it works. There's plenty of onstage music, too, reminding us of the direct line of descent from Brecht's work, through the touring Theatre Workshop of Ewan MacColl and Joan Littlewood, to our own 7:84 and Wildcat companies. As the village play begins, the musician and choreographer Sarah Swire (of Belle & Sebastian's *God Help the Girl*) arrives in glamorous shades, and becomes the play's chorus, leading the cast in Claire McKenzie's bold, rock-based score with ever-increasing conviction and clarity.

And then the story begins, as the palace kitchen girl Grusha, a twenty-first-century refugee in bobble hat and backpack, flees the revolution that has killed her boss, but cannot resist taking with her the governor's baby son, left behind in the chaos. 'Terrible is the seductive temptation to do good!' glows the great neon sign on stage, in the most famous of all Brecht quotes; but Amy Manson's breathtakingly wonderful Grusha, and the little, growing puppet-baby she takes with her, already have our hearts in the palms of their hands, as they travel on through danger and deprivation, and painful compromise with the need to survive, to the decisive moment when they reach the court of the unconventional peasant judge, Azdak.

Mark Thomson's thirteen-strong ensemble – including a superb Christopher Fairbank as Azdak – perform like a company possessed by the brilliance and significance of their story: they are funny, moving, compelling, unstoppable, right to the final fade to darkness. 'Why did they kill all the governors, judges, landowners, bankers?' roars Azdak. 'Why do you think? Too much injustice, too much war.' Some things, in other words, never change; and neither do the Grushas of this world, travelling, struggling, finding a space for the next generation to thrive, in spite of everything.

Last Dream (on Earth)
Tron, Glasgow
The Scotsman, 30 March 2015

Leaving Planet Earth, seeking new worlds: as humankind circles helplessly around the issue of climate change, it's an image that recurs ever more often in the work of the current generation of artists. It was there in Grid Iron's 2013 Edinburgh Festival show *Leaving Planet Earth*; it's at the Traverse this weekend, in Curious Directive's Fringe First-winning *Pioneer*. And it's the shaping force behind this beautiful and thoughtful new show by the Glasgow-based designer and theatremaker Kai Fischer, in association with the National Theatre of Scotland, which is set to tour on from Glasgow to St Andrews, Paisley, Lerwick and Inverness.

Not so much a play as a beautifully shaped one-hour meditation in words, music and occasional visual images, *Last Dream (on Earth)* takes the form of a sound-sculpture performed live by two musicians and three actors, to an audience wearing headphones for the full, intense effect. Fischer's script – researched over many months of visits to key sites of the immigration crisis in the Mediterranean – brings together two narratives: one based on the personal stories of African migrants who risk their lives to reach an imagined new world in Europe, and the other following the cockpit recordings of the messages between ground controller Sergei Korolev and the world's first cosmonaut, Yuri Gagarin, as he became the first human being ever to see the earth from space.

Both texts are beautiful, full of an intense sense of humanity stretched to its limit, facing unimaginable extremes of danger and exhilaration in the quest for a new future. In Fischer's own production, actors Ryan Gerald, Mercy Ojelade and Adura Onashile pitch their voices perfectly to the texture of the story, while musicians Gameli Tordzro and Tyler Collins produce an extraordinary range of music and sound, on guitar and percussion, as they bring to life Matt Padden's extraordinary soundscape. And the whole show reminds us with terrific force of this truth about human history: that where we can go, some of us will always have the courage to go, particularly when crisis or oppression makes life at home intolerable – and the risk of oblivion a better option than inaction, as we head into the unknown.

Great Expectations
Dundee Rep
The Scotsman, 8 June 2015

It's perhaps the greatest of all his great novels, a vast, swirling story of love and longing, class and money, set against the backdrop of explosive economic and social change that was England in the 1850s. And now, out of the darkness of Becky Minto's towering set – all black picture frames and niches that double as grand interiors, the walls of city streets, and something beyond – comes a stage adaptation that takes the full measure of Charles Dickens's mighty 1861 novel *Great Expectations*, and does it more than justice.

First seen in a small-scale TAG production in 1988, Jo Clifford's great stage version focuses tightly on the story of Dickens's iconic young hero, Pip, brought up by his hard-handed elder sister and her kindly husband Joe at a blacksmith's forge in the Essex marshes, but destined to have his life transformed both by the intervention of the eccentric

Miss Havisham – a wealthy and reclusive local lady who wants him as playmate for her beautiful ward Estella – and, later, by a strange anonymous bequest of money that transforms him into a young London 'gentleman'.

And now, this beautifully clear and passionate version is revived in a co-production by Dundee Rep and Perth Theatre, directed by the Rep's Jemima Levick, that simply ravishes audiences, over almost three hours, with a combination of storytelling, drama, light, music and movement so powerful that the emotional effect is sometimes almost overwhelming. Both David Paul Jones's passionate and lyrical live piano score, and EJ Boyle's fine choreography, make an outstanding contribution to the story, as the score sometimes swoops from the nineteenth into the twentieth century with songs of love and longing that bring Pip's obsession with Estella frighteningly close to us, and as the movement – exquisitely delivered by a Dundee Ensemble cast of eight – echoes great recent Scottish shows like *Black Watch* and *The Salon Project*, using the ritual of clothing to trace Pip's transformations from poor boy to gentleman.

Thomas Cotran is eloquent as Pip, Ann Louise Ross haunting and magnificent as Miss Havisham, Millie Turner a chilling and heartbreaking Estella. And if, in the final scenes, the pace flags slightly, it's a minor flaw in a stunningly well-made show, that leaves the audience in no doubt about how the politics of wealth and class damages lives, distorts desire, makes a mockery of love; and ensures that traditional happy endings are hard to find, even in the world of great imaginative fiction.

Lanark
Royal Lyceum, Edinburgh
The Scotsman, 25 August 2015

In the beginning, there is water, or an image of water: light and darkness moving over the face of the deep. We see a man tumbling towards us, like some fallen angel moving through water rather than air; then we see that same man, apparently come to rest on the grubby first-floor balcony of an art-house cinema just a little like the Hillhead Salon. The balcony belongs to the cinema bar, the Elite; and our hero, or anti-hero, stands waiting for the faint glimmer of sun – just a couple of minutes a day – that occasionally lights the horizon of the city where he now dwells.

These are the opening moments of Alasdair Gray's *Lanark*, as re-imagined by writer David Greig and director Graham Eatough, for this mighty new four-hour stage version of the novel, which was first published in 1981 – although, since we are dealing here with a great postmodernist dedicated to the disruption of form, we begin not at the chronological beginning of the tale, but at the start of what the novel calls Book 3, and Greig calls Act 2, when our hero's life as a young, asthmatic and eczema-ridden would-be artist called Duncan Thaw, in the relatively familiar setting of post-war Glasgow, has reached a crisis that leads to the transition – drowning, rebirth or shift to a parallel universe – that we have just glimpsed.

It's this huge imaginative leap – from an all-too-recognisable mid-twentieth-century Glasgow of war and rationing, limited horizons and endless petty agonies and sexual humiliations, to the dystopian fantasy-vision of a future Glasgow called Unthank – that gives Alasdair Gray's great novel its huge, transformative significance in late twentieth-century Scottish literature, not least because it so clearly links the conventional twentieth-century narratives of working-class Scottish life to some of the great emerging global genres of the twenty-first century – to science fiction and fantasy, to dystopian narratives of environmental collapse driven by monstrous corporate greed, and to the idea, less well established in 1981 than today, of parallel universes which are both familiar, and profoundly, strangely different.

And it's because it embraces and explores all those genres with such confidence and flair, while never losing sight of the essential narrative of Lanark/Thaw/Gray's astonishing journey, that Greig and Eatough's new stage version – co-produced by the Edinburgh International Festival and the Citizens' Theatre – comes so close to the impossible goal of doing full justice to this magnificent novel. The linchpin of the production is Sandy Grierson's astonishing performance as Lanark himself: thoughtful, self-absorbed, sometimes childlike, yet sexually and creatively driven, and – crucially – possessed of a physical precision and athleticism that enables him to switch in an instant between naturalism, and a much more stylised, metaphorical sense of Lanark's journey.

Grierson is supported every step of the way, though, by so many other strands of Eatough's astonishing production. There's Jessica Hardwick's terrific matching performance as Rima, the Eve to Lanark's Adam, and the defining woman of his life, often given the freedom completely to contradict Lanark's version of his own narrative. There's the superb ensemble work of a company of ten actors who are also great Scottish theatremakers, many of them deeply linked to the wave of unstoppable cultural change in Scotland that began in the early 1980s: the company includes Gerry Mulgrew, George Drennan, Louise Ludgate, Paul Thomas Hickey and Andy Clark, alongside a trio of younger actors.

And there is the constant, inventive stream of shifting imagery, both visual and aural, delivered by designer Laura Hopkins, lighting designer Nigel Edwards, video artist

Simon Wainwright, and composer and sound designer Nick Powell, who created a 'supergroup' of musicians influenced by Gray's work to conjure up scenes like the unforgettable fifties-style 'Unthank Jazz' sequence, with superb choreography by EJ Boyle; there's also an inspired use of video, and of the old song 'Ca' the Yowes Tae the Knowes', to conjure up the vague remembered glimpses of Glasgow that haunt Lanark when he reaches the brave new world of The Institute, a hospital–like, pseudo–Utopian circle of hell that also features in Act 2 of the story.

Just here and there, there's perhaps a slight sense of this huge scene-by-scene ingenuity acting as a substitute for a deep analysis of Gray's themes; and then again, an understandable tendency to rely a little too heavily on Grierson's charismatic central performance, in a way that slightly diminishes Gray's intense scepticism about Thaw/Lanark's voice, and its reliability.

In the final, apocalyptic scenes, though – where Greig plays boldly and theatrically with Gray's questions about the shifting layers of fiction within the story, and even takes us, in a superb moment of graphic imagination, to visit Gray himself, before returning us to Lanark's poignant final scene at the Unthank Necropolis – this brave adaptation seems wholly at one with the bold, mysterious and infinitely searching spirit of Gray's novel. On Sunday night, after the premiere of *Lanark*, David Greig sent a Twitter message about Alasdair Gray, now eighty years old, and in intensive care in Glasgow: 'Thinking of Mr G right now. Wishing him well and wishing he could be with us. He wrote an amazing transformative book. The rest is homage.' What's certain, though, is that if Alasdair Gray could see this version of *Lanark*, centre-stage at the Edinburgh International Festival, he would know that this story alone represents a great life's work; and that its impact – not only in Scotland, but across the world of twenty-first-century imagination – has barely begun to be measured.

The Cheviot, the Stag and the Black, Black Oil
Dundee Rep
The Scotsman, 14 September 2015

It's been a mighty late-summer theatre season for Scots who care about the range and brilliance of their recent cultural inheritance, with new stage versions of Alasdair Gray's *Lanark* and Alan Warner's *The Sopranos* taking audiences by storm.

And now, at Dundee Rep, comes Joe Douglas's glorious revival of what's arguably the single most important show in the whole history of Scottish theatre: important not only because of its angry, hilarious, brilliantly researched political content, still almost frighteningly relevant today, but because its ceilidh form, and its passionate commitment to touring to communities large and small, galvanised an irreversible change in what Scotland thought theatre was, what it could do, and who its audience might be.

The task of reviving 7:84 Scotland's great 1973 masterpiece *The Cheviot, the Stag and the Black, Black Oil* is therefore a hugely complex one, charged with cultural meaning. And what Joe Douglas and his Dundee company have done is to find a powerful, joyful and hugely effective middle way between a faithful revival of the original text and songs – which they certainly deliver – and the kind of full-scale updating that this show could certainly take, and may one day get.

There are moments when the sheer scale and luxury of the production seem slightly startling, compared with the rugged original. The stage at Dundee Rep is a comfortable and spacious place, opened out, in Graham McLaren's design, into a warm, wooden-floored arena surrounded on three sides by café tables. The band – under the direction of MD Alasdair Macrae – features cello, clàrsach and double bass as well as the more traditional accordion and fiddle; the ten-strong cast is bigger, and includes a higher proportion of women.

If the staging is more lavish, though, the force of the material remains the same, as the show charts the story of the use and exploitation of Scottish land and resources from the clearances of the eighteenth century to the 1970s oil boom and beyond. The stage rings to the sound of Gaelic song, beautifully owned and sung by the women of the cast, Irene Macdougall, Jo Freer, Emily Winter and Christina Gordon. Young John Macaulay makes a superbly absurd Duke of Sutherland, Billy Mack is a fine top-hatted villain as the hated Sutherland factor Patrick Sellar.

And if the roars that greet Macaulay's fleeting appearance as David Cameron, or the odd reference to the independence referendum, suggest an appetite for updating that this memorable production doesn't quite fulfil, those responses only point the way to a great continuing future for this vital play. In the opening scene, the script points out that the story of Scotland's land and people is one with a beginning, a middle and, as yet, no end; what this fine, dynamic revival achieves is to ensure that 7:84's great play will reach out to a new generation, and continue to evolve, develop, and live, along with the story of Scotland itself.

Waiting for Godot
Royal Lyceum, Edinburgh
The Scotsman, 23 September 2015

Vladimir and Estragon, Didi and Gogo. The two old tramps who take the stage in Samuel Beckett's groundbreaking minimalist masterpiece – first seen in Paris in 1953 – are perhaps the most significant characters in the whole of twentieth-century drama, the ones who, in the words of the play's first British director, Peter Hall, 'challenged and defeated a century of literal naturalism, and returned theatre to its metaphorical roots'.

Yet in all the productions I have seen and loved, over the years, I have never experienced one that lavishes so much care and genius on the development of the characters of Didi and Gogo – their different energies, and their contrasting responses to the situation in which they find themselves – as this 50th Anniversary staging by Mark Thomson of the Lyceum, featuring the magnificent pairing of Brian Cox and Bill Paterson as Vladimir and Estragon.

That these two actors are no longer young is no secret: Cox actually appeared, aged nineteen, in the very first production of the Lyceum Theatre Company, fifty years ago this month. Yet what's extraordinary about their combined performance – as they wait and survive beside their shrivelled tree, in that empty landscape that soon comes to seem like a metaphor for human life itself – is how clearly we can see the little lads they once were, beneath the battered hats and thinning hair. Cox's Didi is mercurial, restless, funny, always performing, the very image of the lively, energetic one who can never quite believe that there is now nothing more to be done; Paterson's Gogo is much quieter and more poetic, more confused and defeated by their situation, yet also closer to a recognition of its reality.

In this infinitely rich evocation of character – absolutely Scottish, yet completely universal – the detailed quality of the acting is sometimes breathtaking: Cox's body language and facial expressiveness a tragicomic revelation, Paterson's presence more subdued, but perfectly pitched. I've seen productions that gave the two central characters more support, towards the play's long-drawn-out end; that were more sharply paced, or that made more of this double act's music-hall or fairground roots.

Yet given world-class support from John Bett as rich class-enemy Pozzo and Benny Young as his desperately ill-treated servant Lucky, and an exquisitely empty, luminous set by designer Michael Taylor and lighting man Mark Doubleday, Mark Thomson's anniversary production offers a unique, austere, yet immensely rich insight into what may be the greatest play of the last century; and gives absolute primacy to two great creative actors, not young, but – enthrallingly and obviously – still in their prime.

The Golden Anniversary production of Waiting for Godot *marked the climax of an exceptional year at the Royal Lyceum; and the excitement was all the more intense because the board had announced, early in September, that the theatre's next artistic director – from the summer of 2016 – would be David Greig, the first playwright to take on the directorship of one of Scotland's great building-based companies since James Bridie at the Citizens' in the 1940s.*

It was a great moment, for the playwrights whose sheer creative force has driven much of the recent story of Scottish theatre. Yet David Greig's appointment to such a major public role also confirmed the feeling that we might have to wait a while for their full creative response to the latest phase in our shared experience. It seems to be a truth about theatre, evident from the whole of this story, that it often runs perhaps twenty years ahead of formal politics in its recognition of cultural change, and a few years behind in its response to unpredictable events.

And so, for the time being, Scotland remains the stateless nation it was in 1982, although one utterly transformed, and infinitely more self-aware. And like every other stateless nation, it remains a rich field of dreams, where ideas about identity, belonging, past and future are always in play; a place where the drama of our shared life has found an increasingly passionate and confident voice in the drama we present on stage, and where the dreaming we share in theatre plays a subtle but profound role in shaping our future, by transforming our sense of what we have been, what we are, and what we might become.

Afterword   *Philip Howard*

On 17 September 2014, the day before Scotland's Independence Referendum, the National Theatre of
Scotland curated a twelve-hour event at the Assembly Hall,
Edinburgh, entitled *Blabbermouth* – 'a celebration of Scotland by Scotland's most celebrated people'. Filled with live
music, the day featured artists, politicians, journalists, actors
and writers reading their favourite piece of writing about
Scotland, the only proviso being that it had to have been
written by a Scot.

McMillan knew that the result of the Referendum the next
day would, most likely, leave Scotland divided roughly in
half. So she chose and read the last chapter ('Good-bye') of
Robert Louis Stevenson's *Kidnapped*, adventure story but
also fable of Scotland's binary nature – in which young
David Balfour, the rational Lowland Protestant, and Alan
Breck Stewart, romantic Catholic Jacobite outlaw, part company after their Highland adventure at the spot known as
Rest-and-be-Thankful, on Corstorphine Hill outside Edinburgh. David walks on, down into Edinburgh to the British
Linen Company to pick up his papers – there's a sense that,
having learned so much about the other half of Scotland, he
is now ready to begin his life as an adult under the Union of

Parliaments, still relatively in its infancy. Entering the city, he is stunned by the height of the buildings, the finery and the foulness, but, more than that, he thinks of Alan, up there on Corstorphine Hill, still an outlaw, and feels a cold gnawing in his heart, 'like a remorse for something wrong'.

McMillan tells me how important this piece of writing is about the 'doubleness' of Scotland, about how this is a creative thing, about the sense of walking alongside the opposing half. It strikes me how well this idea of trying always to hold the other side of the argument in your heart applies to her career as a theatre critic.

Acknowledgements

Kerry Black, librarian at *The Scotsman*
Craig Nelson, librarian at *The Scotsman*
Simon Bell, The British Library, Colindale
National Library of Scotland
Nicola McCartney
Jackie McGlone
Amanda Fitzalan Howard

And the arts editors, editors and staff of the newspapers which supported most of the work collected here: *The Scotsman*, *The Herald*, *Scotland on Sunday*, *The Guardian* and the *Sunday Standard*.

Index